HISTORY OF BENGALI LANGUAGE AND LITERATURE

HISTORY OF BENGALI LANGUAGE AND LITERATURE

A SERIES OF LECTURES DELIVERED AS READER TO THE CALCUTTA UNIVERSITY

(In Two Volumes)

(Volume 2)

DINESH CHANDRA SEN

GYAN

GYAN PUBLISHING HOUSE

NEW DELHI-110002

History of Bengali Language and Literature

Rs. 1800 (Set)

ISBN: 81-212-7835-543-4 (Set)
ISBN: 81-212-0936-6 (Vol. II)

Published in 2007 in India by
Gyan Publishing House
5, Ansari Road, Daryaganj,
New Delhi-110002
Phones: 23261060, 23282060
Fax: 91-011-23285914
E-mail: gyanbook@vsnl.com
Website: http//www.gyanbooks.com

Printed at : Salasar Imaging Systems, Delhi

CONTENTS

CHAPTER VI.

The post-Chaitanya Literature.—613-775.

CHAPTER VII.

The Modern Age, 845-1002.

VOLUME - 2

CHAPTER VI.

THE POST-CHAITANYA LITERATURE.

I. (a) The Court of Rājā Krisṇa Chandra of Nadiā.—Vitiated classical taste and word-painting.

(b) Alāol—The Mahāmedan poet who heralded the new age. His life and a review of his works.

(c) The Story of Vidyā-Sundara.

(d) Early poets of the Vidyā-Sundara-poems.

(e) Bhārata Chandra Rāi Guṅākara—the great poet of the 18th century. Prāṅarāma Chakravarti.

II (a) The Court of Rājā Ṛājavallabha of Rāja Nagara in Dacca. Its poets. Jaya Nārāyaṅa Sen—Ānanda Mayī Devī.

(b) The poets of the school of Bhārata Chandra.

III. Poetry of rural Bengal.

(a) The Kaviwalās and their songs—Ṛaghu, the Cobbler—Haru Thākur—Rāma Vasu and others. The Portugese Kaviwallā Mr. Antony.

(b) Religious Songs.

(c) Rāma Prasāda Sen and poets of his school.

IV. The Jātrās or popular theatres.

V. The three great poets with whom the age closed—Dāsarathī—Rāmanidhi Gupta—Içwara Chandra Gupta.

VI. The folk-literature of Bengal.

I. (a) The Court of Rājā Krisṇa Chandra of Nadiā.—Vitiated Classical taste and word-painting.

A new era was dawning in our literature. Society after a great movement sinks into callousness. A great idea passes away; and in the age

The Reaction and its effects.

that follows the spasmodic efforts of common men to reach the high ideal expressed in some great historic character slowly spend themselves. Lesser men arise who pose as leaders of society, scoffing at all that constitutes greatness; and custom and convention—two hoary-headed monsters—once more clasp the people in their iron grip. This is an age when craft and ingenuity find favour instead of open-hearted sincerity; when moral courage, character, manliness and strength of conviction fall into disfavour and worldly manœuvres of all sorts pass for high qualities and are praised as indicating wisdom.

In the literature of such an age, we miss that genial flow of noble ideas—that freedom of thought and freshness of natural instincts which characterise great epochs in a nation's life, and in their place we find the poets struggling to furnish long and wearisome details about a small point till it is worn thread-bare by its very ingenuity; a small idea is over-coloured and followed in frivolous niceties on the lines of a vitiated classical taste till it becomes almost grotesque or absurd.

Such an age came upon the society of Bengal and its influence is stamped on the literature of the 18th century. This was an age when Mahamedan power had just decayed. Robbers and bandits over-ran the country; and knavery of all sorts was practised in the courts of the Rājās. The school set up by Aurangeb in politics became the model for his chiefs to follow in their own courts. Conspiracies, plots and counterplots amongst brothers and relations who wanted to elbow down and kill one

The political atmosphere.

another to gain the *gadi*, were events of every-day-occurrence in the courts of Indian noblemen. Rajā Kriṣṅa Chandra of Navadwip by a stratagem which was highly praised, deprived his own uncle of his rightful ownership of the *gadi* of Kriṣṅagar. Kriṣṅa Chandra's son Çambhu Chandra played a similar dodge and tried to usurp the possessions of his father, by spreading a false report of his death. The Rajā was thus going to be paid in his own coin. His agent at Agradwip in Burdwan by an equally unscrupulous action ousted the rightful owner out of the possession of that place and gained it for his own master. In the Courts of Serajuddulāh, the Nabab, plots of a far more important character were being formed fraught with consequences which were to change the history of the whole of India.

Rājā Kriṣṅa Chandra.

It was not an age conspicuous for its appreciation of high ideas or of noble sentiments. "Rājā Kriṣṅa Chandra was hostile to the followers of Chaitanya."* He frustrated the efforts of Rajā Rājavallava who had tried to obtain sanction of the Pundits of Bengal to the remarriage of Hindu widows of tender ages. Yet Kriṣṅa Chandra was the most important man of the period in the Hindu Society of Bengal. His Court had gathered round it some of the greatest Sanskrit scholars of the country. He appreciated merit, patronised literature, and encouraged art. The far-famed clay-models of Kriṣṅagar and the fine cotton-industry of Çāntipur owe their perfection to the patronage of the Rājā. The Rājā was friendly to the English and it was he who first put the idea of overthrowing Serājuddulāh by the help

* Khitiça Vamçābali Charita P. 29.

of the English into the head of Mirzāfar and other influential men engaged in conspiracy against the Nowāb. Krişņa Chandra was himself a scholar of no mean order. He could discuss knotty problems of logic with Hari Rāma Tarka Sidhānta and in theology he was a match for the far-famed Rāmānanda Vāchaşpati. He was well-versed in the doctrines of the six schools of Hindu philosophy, and made endowment of lands to the great exponents of that learning of the period—Çiva Rāma Vāchaşpati and Vīreçwara Nyāya Panchānana. He could compose extempore verses in Sanskrit and competed personally in public with Vāneçwara Vidyālankāra—the famous Sanskrit poet of his court.

The great patron of Bengali.

Besides all these Rājā Krişņa Chandra was the great patron of Bengali literature of the 18th century.

The ove drawn similes of Sanskrit and Persian models.

Poetry under such patronage became the creation of schoolmen and courtiers. It no longer aimed at offering its tribute to God but tried to please the fancy of a Rājā; the poets found the gates of the palace open to receive them and cared not if the doors of heaven were shut. For models of Bengali court-poetry, we shall quote here a passage translated from the Naişadha Charita—a Sanskrit poem held in great admiration by the scholars of the period.

" How shall I describe, O, King, the profuse hair on Damayanti's head! They compare it to the hair of a *chamari* (a species of deer). But it is foolish to compare Damayanti's hair to what that animal hides behind him as a mark of shame. They say her eyes are as beautiful as those of the gazelle. But it is as a sign of his disappointment and defeat that the gazelle kicks the ground with his hoofs. God took the quintessence of the moon and made Damayanti's face. So a hole was made on the moon's surface and they call it a spot. The lotuses have all fled into the watery forts being struck by the beauty of Damayanti's face. Before God had created Damayanti, he exercised himself in the art of creating feminine beauty by his creation of all other women, so that he might give perfection to that single form of Damayanti; and when the ideal was reached in her, the subsequent forms were created only to establish the superiority of Damayanti over the rest."

Not only the Naiṣadha Charita, but Daçakumāra Charita, Harṣa Charita and other Sanskrit works admired in this period, abound with passages like the above, and these served as models to the Bengali writers who were under the immediate influence of the courts, and they themselves began to regale on niceties which now seem so absurd to us. The Persian poems which were favoured in this age, also contain long drawn-out similes verging on the ridiculous, and the noblemen and scholars, who prided themselves on a vain-glorious pedantry, encouraged our poets to introduce similar artificial compositions into Bengali. Here are a few short passages translated from a favourite Persian work of the period.

"Her black hair was like a net to catch the wise." "The lustre of her nails kept the hearts of all men fixed on them. They were like so many rising moons". "Her waist was slender as a single hair or rather half of it."—*Zelekhā*.

Slenderness of the waist was held to be a point of feminine beauty, hence absurdities passed for niceties and were admired as poetic skill!

The Kutnis.

The literature that sprang up under the patronage of courts was thus vitiated by their influence. Not only in the style of writing but in its subject-matter also, it showed the control of those evil stars that held sway over the literary horizon of Bengal at this time. The romantic conceptions of Persian tales are often singularly unpleasing to the Bengali mind; especially does this remark apply to those *kutnis* or serving women, who acted as agents in matters of illicit passion. Yet these women figure prominently in the literature of this period. Here is an extract, translated from Zelekhā, a Persian poem, in which a *kutni* is vaunting her powers before the heroine of the tale. The Bengali poets were trying their level best to import such characters into their poems.

"Who is it that has tampered with your heart? Tell me why it is that your face beautiful as a flower has grown pale and yellowish. Why are you waning day by day like the moon? I am afraid you have fallen in love. Tell me who is that person. If he be the very moon whose abode is in the sky, I will make him come down to the earth as a slave to your wishes. If he be a spirit of the mountains, I know such charms that he would be put into a phial and brought to you. If he be merely a man, take my word, I shall make him a bond-slave to you. He will be made to minister to your wishes in every matter and you need not care to please him by offering him your services."

The maid-servants of the Hindu classics not to be confounded with Kutnis.

These *kutnis* are numerous in Persian tales. They are not of the class of Durvalā, the maid-servant described in the Chandi Kāvyas dealt with by us in a previous chapter. The latter are knaves who repay the kindness shown to them by creating disunion amongst the members of a family to serve their own selfish ends and by robbing their masters as much as they can, when entrusted with marketing. Durvalā bears a family-likeness to Mantharā of the Rāmāyaṅa, though placed in different situations, and these women should not be confounded with the *kutnis* of the Māhomedan stories; they are not accessories to immoral purposes. The *dutis* perform a quite different function in the Vaiṣṅava poems where love is spiritualised.

Indeed the Hindu poets had hitherto taken particular care to keep scenes of illicit love out of their poems. But the *kutni* now became a very common thing in our literature, especially in the poems of Vidyā-Sundara. A very striking instance of such women as figuring in the poetry of the age is found in the character of Hirā mālinī in Bhārata Chandra's Annadā Maṇgala—the most popular Bengali poem of the day.

The depraved taste in style and in spirit.

Thus in the style of poetry as well as in its spirit, the court literature of Bengal presents a striking difference to the earlier Bengali works. The style and the spirit both became depraved—the former by a vain-glorious pedantry which made descriptions grotesque by their over-drawn niceties, the serious often passing into the burlesque—and the latter by scurrilous obscenities grosser than anything in Sterne, Smollett or Wycherley and by the introduction of characters like those of Hirā mālinī and Vidu Brāhmini—accessories to illicit love of the most revolting type. The descriptions of men and women are often marred by overcolouring like those of the beards of Hudibras described by Butler in a well known lengthy passage.

The merits of the literary epoch.

But a literary epoch cannot be wholly without its redeeming features. There must be some really meritorious points by which it can attract and make people its votaries, reconciling them even to its vices. In this age, a rigid classical taste gave a unique finish to the Bengali style and enriched it with the variety of Sanskrit metres that so powerfully appeal to the ear. Bhārata Chandra Rāy, the court poet of Rājā Kriṣṅa Chandra, stands alone in the field of our old literature as a word-painter. No poet before him contributed so much to our wealth of expression or had such success in importing elegance to our Sanskritic metres. The poet here, like a true Indian artizan, applied himself patiently to the sphere of decorative art. He hunted for and found choicest expressions and strung them into the most elegant metres and carried the whole school of Bengali poets after him maddened by the zeal to imitate his style. The heart had been feasted to satiety on the emotions contained in the Vaiṣṅava literature, the ear now wanted to be pleased. High sentiments expressed in rich poetry had abounded in the literature of the Vaiṣṅavas ; enough of such. The scholars would have a brief day of their own. They would show feats of clever expression, pedantry and wealth of words strung together with masterly skill. The people were drawn by this novelty. After the strain of a high-strung idealistic spirituality, they were glad to revel

The great poet Bhārata Chandra.

in grossly sensual ideas. They descended from heaven to have a little taste of the mundane pleasures. The Sanskrit vocabulary and Sanskrit works of rhetoric became the chief sources of poetic inspiration; yet the period, by a strange irony of fate, was ushered in by one who was not a Hindu, as it would be natural to expect, but a Māhomedan. A Māhomedan writer arose with a mastery of the Sanskrit tongue, the like of which we rarely find among Hindu poets in the Bengali literature. He was Syed Ālāol, translator of

Syed Ālāol. Padmāvata a Hindi poem written by Mir Māhammad in 1521 A.D.

(b) Ālāol—the Māhammedan poet who heralded the new age—His life and a review of his works.

Ālāol was the son of a minister of Samser Kutub, the Nawab of Jālālpur (in the district of Faridpur). When a youngman, he undertook a sea-voyage in the company of his father. The crew were attacked by Portuguese pirates, known in the country as *Hermadas* (from *Armada*). We have a line in the Chandi Kāvya by Mukunda Rāma describing the great fear in which sailors held these *Hermadas*. "Night and day the merchant plied his oars in fear of being overtaken by the *Hermadas*."* The father of Alāol was killed in a hand-to-hand

His father is killed. fight with the marauders and our poet narrowly escaped a similar fate, and fled to Arācan where Māgana Thakur, the Moslem Prime minister of the ruling Chief of the place, received him hospi-

* "রাত্রি দিন বয়ে যায় হার্ম্মাদের ডরে।"

Kavi Kaṇkana Chandi.

tably, being pleased with the great scholarship of the youngman. He resided at this place for many years and when he was verging on forty, he was ordered by Māgana Thakur to translate the Hindi poem Padmāvat into Bengali and he did so to please his patron and master. Some years passed in this high and agreeable company, and our poet seems to have tasted during this time the sweets of life after the woes that had befallen him in the early part of his career. He was again ordered by Māgana Thākur to translate a Persian work named Saiful Mulluk and Badiujjamāl into Bengali. But he had now declined 'in the vale of years' and when a few chapters of this book were written, Māgana Thākur, the poet's friend and patron, met with an unexpected death, and Alāol in great disappointment left the half-finished poem and retired into a life of rest. But it was yet reserved for him to be subjected to further vicissitudes in life; and greater sorrows than those hitherto experienced were still in store for him. Sujā, brother of Aurangzeb, had come to Arācān about this period and a fight ensued between the unfortunate prince and the Arācān Chief,—the former being completely defeated. A wicked man named Mirzā gave evidence against Ālāol, to satisfy a private grudge implicating him as a party to Sujā's action against the Chief of Arācān. Alāol was thrown into prison, where he spent a few years, subjected to all sorts of cruel treatment. He was, however, released and spent 9 years of his life in close retirement. Syed Musā, a rich nobleman of Ārācān, took some interest in the poet during these evil days and at his request he completed his translation of Saifulmulluk and

Enjoys the patronage of Māgana Thakura.

Māgana Thakura dies.

Ālāol thrown into prison

His poetry halts.

Badiujjamāl. Alāol had grown old by this time and had lost his wonted spirit—the spring of all his nöble poetry. In the last part of this translation we miss his characteristic genial flow and sweetness of expression Besides the above two works he wrote sequels to the stories of Lora Chandrāni and Sati Maina—poems written by Doulat Kāzi in Bengali. The latter works were undertaken by our poet at the command of Sola-mān, another minister of the Arācān Chief. At the request of an influential man of the court named Syed Mahamed Khan, Alāol translated the Persian poem Hastapaikār by Nizāmi Gaznavi. Besides these, Alāol wrote several poems on Rādhā and Krișña, some of which display exquisite poetic touches. Alāol was born about the year 1618; was thrown into prison in 1658; and being released lived to a good old age, till the close of the 17th century.

A list of his works.

It will be seen that Alāol the poet worked manly in the field of translation, and the chief work of his Muse on which his fame rests—the Padmāvati—is only, as we have said, the Bengali translation of a Hindi poem. But Alāol's translation is not only free but is also marked by great originality, and though conforming in the main to the tale of the Hindi bard, is an improvement upon it in many respects.

An improvement on the original.

The Padmāvati is written in a high flown Sanskritic Bengali. Alāol is the first of the poets who aimed at word-painting and at that finished Sanskritic expression which is the *forte* of the Bengali literature of the 18th century. In fact Ālāol, though, generally speaking, inferior to Bhārata Chandra, because he lacks the "elegant genius" of the latter, eclipses nearly all the other poets of Bengal in his profuse use of Sanskritic terms. For a Moslem writer to have the credit of importing the largest number of Sanskritic words into a Bengali poem and thus heralding an age of classical revival, is no small achievement, and we are bound to admit that none of the Hindu poets of the age in which he lived, was in this respect, a match for him.

The Sanskritic style and the Hindu spirit.

Alāol has given descriptions of the religious ceremonies of the Hindus, their customs and manners with an accuracy and minuteness which strike us as wonderful, coming as they do from the pen of a Mahomedan writer. He has given a classification of feminine emotions in all their subtlest forms as found in the Sanskrit books of rhetoric, in the portraiture of such characters as Vāsakasajjā, Khanditā, Kalahantaritā, and Vipralavdhā. He has represented the ten different stages of separation from a lover (বিরহের দশ দশা), closely following the rules laid down in Sāhityadarpaṇa and in Pingala's works on rhetoric. He has discoursed on medicine in a manner which would do credit to a physician versed in the Aurvedic lore. He has, besides, shown a knowledge of the movements of the planets and their influence on human fortune worthy of an expert astrologer. In his accounts of the little rituals connected with the religious ceremonies of the Hindus such as the Praçastha Vandanā, he displays a mastery of detail which could only have been expected from an experienced priest. He has, besides, described the rules of long and short vowels, the principles মগণ, রগণ etc. by which the various Sanskrit metres are governed, and quoted Sanskrit couplets like a Pandit, to serve as texts for the theological matter introduced in his book. The Moslem poet is profuse in his eulogies of Çiva the Hindu God, and all through the work writes in the spirit and strain of a devout Hindu. Curiously enough his work has been preserved in Chittagong by Mahomedan readers. The manuscripts of Padmāvati hitherto obtained, all belong to the border-lands of Ārācān in the back-woods of Chittagong, copied in Persian characters and preserved by the rural Mahomedan folk of those localities. No Hindu has ever yet cared to read them. This goes to prove how far the taste of the Mahomedans was imbued with Hindu culture. This book, that we should have thought, could be interesting only to Hindu readers, on account of its lengthy disquisitions on theology and Sanskrit rhetoric, has been strangely preserved, ever since Aurungjeb's time, by Moslems, for whom it could apparently have no attraction, nay to whom it might even seem positively repellent. From the time of Māgana Thākura the Mahomedan minister, till the time of Shaik Hāmidullā of Chittagong who published it in 1893—covering a period of nearly 250 years, this book was copied, read, and admired by the Mahomedans of Chittagong exclusively. What surprises us most is the interest taken by the rustic folk in its high-flown Sanskritic Bengali. The Province of Chittagong must have been once a nucleus of Sanskrit-learning to have disseminated so deep a liking for the classic tongue of the Hindus among the lowest strata of society, and specially amongst Mahomedans who might have been expected to have the least aptitude for this.

His work read admired and preserved by Mohamedans.

The Sanskritic culture of Chittagong people.

The poem Padmāvati deals with a well-known episode in Indian history. The Emperor Alāuddin of Delhi had heard of the wonderful beauty of Padmāvati, queen of the Rāja of Chitore, and demanded her for his harem. Bhim Sen, the Rāja, who is called Ratnasen in the Bengali poem, treated this request with the contempt which it deserved, and the result was that for twelve years the Emperor laid siege to Chitore. Bhima Sen was eventually defeated, and his queen sought death on the funeral pyre,—true to the traditions of Rajput women. This story had formed the subject of a poem by Mir Mahomed in Hindi which contains about 10,000 lines. The Bengali Padmāvati by Alāol has about 10,500 lines.

The subject of the poem.

I have said that the classic taste, which made the Bengali poets of the 18th century revel in exaggerated and high flown imageries, was indicated in the work of this Mahomedan poet, to such a considerable extent, that he may be said to have heralded the new epoch. Alāol rang the bell of the new age and the sound was caught by a host of other poets amongst whom Bhārata Chandra was the most prominent. I shall here quote some passages from Alāol's Padmāvati to show how his description owns kinship with those found in the Sanskrit and Persian poems already referred to by us, as also with the high sounding flourishes of style which characterise the Bengali poems that followed the age of Alāol.

The new age.

*" The light that beams in the face of Padmāvati puts to shame the light reflected from a golden mirror.

---

*কনক মুকুর জিনি মুখজ্যোতি সাজে—
দেখহ অপূর্ব্ব রীত বদন উপরে।

Far-fetched similes.

One curious fact with regard to the face is that two lotuses are confined in the disc of the moon (her face.) The sun who finds his friends so confined by his enemy, came to the rescue, in the shape of the vermilion mark on the forehead. The god of love, in aid of the sun, held the bow of her eye-brows, and aimed his shafts, which were the glances of her eyes. The only regret is that these friends though so near were not allowed to see each other."

The lotuses are her two eyes. The sun according to the poetic tradition of Sanskrit rhetoric (কবি-প্রসিদ্ধি) is a lover of the lotus. The moon is unfriendly towards the lotus according to a similar tradition. The lotus blooms in the day-time and fades in the evening—a circumstance which caused the acceptance of this idea by the poets.

For pages and pages one may follow descriptions on this line. The ingenuity of such compositions, greatly favoured, as they were, by the scholars of a particular epoch, show the artificial taste of the age—the absurdities that passed for intellectual feats and the grotesque and the uncouth that were accepted as beautiful.

পদ্মযুগ বন্দী হয় চন্দ্রের মাঝারে ॥
শত্রুমাঝে মিত্রবন্দী দেখি দিবাকর।
ধরিয়া সিন্দূর রূপ আইল নিয়ড় ॥
ভুরুযুগ ধনুক ধরিয়া পঞ্চবাণ।
তিলে তিলে হানে বাণ কটাক্ষ সন্ধান ॥
কমল নয়নী মাত্র মনে এই দুঃখ।
নিকটে থাকিয়া মিত্র না দেখায় মুখ ॥

Alāol's Padmāvati

But Alaol's poems often reach a high degree of excellence from the wealth of their Sanskritic expressions. It is to be regretted that the excellence of their style, and the effect produced by the jingle of classic words and associations suggested by them, are not such as can be conveyed in translation. The author frequently imitates the style of the great song-masters of Bengal with a happy effect. The following passage reminds us of some well-known lines from the Sanskrit Gita-Govinda by Jayadeva.

The untranslatable beauty of style.

*" In the spring season the bridegroom revels in the joyous company of his bride. They are like two moons, shedding, as it were, ambrosia in the lovely smiles on their softly curving lips. The flowers are in full bloom, and from the floral bowers the cuckoo cooes pleasantly in the company of its mate; the bees hum delightfully; the cool Malaya breeze charged with the scents of flowers, softly touches the bridegroom heightening the charm of the sweet words of his lady-love. The *acvatha* tree, the prince of the forest, displays its wealth of new leaves, the *tamala* stands obliquely and the mango-creepers are rich with fresh foliage and

---

*বসন্তে নাগরবর নাগরী বিলাসে
বর বালা দুই ইন্দু, স্রবে যেন সুধা বিন্দু,
মৃদুমন্দ অধরে ললিত মধু হাসে
কুসুম প্রফুল্লিত মধুব্রত ঝঙ্কৃত,
হুঙ্কৃত পরভৃত, কুঞ্জে রত রাসে
মলয় সমীর সুসৌরভ শীতল,
বিলোলিত পতি অতি-রস-ভাসে ॥

tendrils. The hearts of the youthful pair are gladsome. They are decked with the wreaths of the *rangan*, *mallika* and the *malati* flowers."

Alas, the beauty of metre and of choice Sanskrit words that characterise this passage is but ill-conveyed in the above translation.

Indebted to earlier poets.

The line "চলিল কামিনী, গজেন্দ্রগামিনী, খঞ্জন-গমন-শোভিতা" is evidently inspired by Vidyāpati's "গেলি কামিনী, গজহুঁ গামিনী, বিহসি পালটি নেহারি" and the lines beginning with "আজি কেন বিপরীত তোমার বদন" breathe the sentiments of Chandi Das in his well-known passage opened by the line "আজি কেন তোমায় এমন দেখি।"

The description of the seasons is full of delicate sentiments and calls up familiar scenes by suggestive lines. During the rains the lovers sit up at night in merry talk and *"if there be a sound of thunder she is startled, and throws herself into the arms of her lover—an unexpected surprise to him."

প্রফুল্লিত বনস্পতি কুটিল তমাল দ্রুম।
মুকুলিত চূত-লতা কোরক জালে।
যুবজন-হৃদয় আনন্দ-পরিপূরিত।
রঙ্গ-মল্লিকা-মালতি-মালে॥

Alāol's Padmāvati.

*"চমকিলে বিদ্যুৎ চমকি কণ্ঠে লাগে।
বজ্রপাতে কমলিনী ত্রাসিত হইয়া
ধরয়ে পতির গীমে অধিক আঁটিয়া॥"

Alāol's Padmāvati.

There are many pretty lines in the poem recalling scenes of domestic affection and of the delicate associations of love.

In praise of God.

The preliminary lines in praise of God are full of sincerity and devotion. *"He created life to manifest Himself in love, and death to show that He is also the terrible. Sweet scents of flowers He created to indicate heaven and evil odours to warn men of the filth of hell. As a sign of His high favour, He created sweet things, delicious to the taste, and the bitter and pungent, to indicate His wrath. He secretly hid the honey in the flowers and by creating the bees He brought it to the knowledge of the world. He created all in the twinkling of an eye, and the great firmament created by Him stands without the support of pillars. The sun and the moon He created, and also created the night and the day. The winter and the summer He created, and the heat, the rays of the sun and

*" আপন প্রচার হেতু সৃজিল জীবন।
নিজ ভয় দর্শাইতে সৃজিল মরণ॥
সুগন্ধি সৃজিল প্রভু স্বর্গ বুঝাইতে।
সৃজিলেক দুর্গন্ধ নরক জানাইতে॥
মিষ্ট রস সৃজিলেক কৃপা-অনুরোধ।
তিক্ত কটু কষা সৃজি জানাইল ক্রোধ॥
পুষ্পে জন্মাইল মধু গুপ্ত আকার।
সৃজিয়া মক্ষিকা কৈল তাহার প্রচার॥
এতেক সৃজিতে তিল না হইল বিলম্ব।
অন্তরীক্ষ গঠিয়া রাখিছে বিনিস্তম্ভ॥
সৃজিলেক দিবাকর শশি দিবা রাত্রি।
সৃজিলেক নক্ষত্র নির্ম্মল পাঁতি পাঁতি॥

the clouds which He lined with lightning. He pervades the universe—both revealed and unrevealed. The virtuous and the saintly know Him, but the vicious know Him not."

In this hymn Alāol follows more or less the Hindi original of Mir Mahomed.

The characteristic features of a Mahomedan tale.

But though in the main story Alāol follows a style on the line of the Sanskrit classics and shows a wonderfully close acquaintance with the manners, customs and religious life of the Hindus, yet reading between the lines one may discover the vein of a Mahomedan poet by the non-Hindu elements to be found in his work, though couched beneath a highly Sanskritised form of Bengali. A certain extravagance of imagination reminds us, at every stage, of the excesses of fancy which characterise Arabic and Persian tales. Raja Ratna Sen heard of the beauty of Padmāvati, and even before he saw her, fell into a fit of violent love; renounced the world as an ascetic, and wandered through the forests. And "with him 1600 princes turned ascetic."* The

---

সৃজিলেক সুশীতল গ্রীষ্ম রৌদ্র আর।
করিল মেঘের মাঝে বিদ্যুৎ সঞ্চার॥
প্রকট গুপ্ত রহে সবাকারে ব্যাপি।
ধার্ম্মিক চিহ্নয়ে তারে না চিহ্নয়ে পাপী॥

Alāol's Padmāvati.

*নৃপতি গমন শুনি হইয়া বিরাগী॥
ষোল শত রাজার কুমার হইল যোগী॥

Alāol's Padmāvati.

princess was sad, and the message of her sorrow was carried by the bird *cuka*. The poet describes the mission of the bird and the effect which his flight produced on the objects that he came in contact with.

*"The message of her sorrow was carried by the bird through the sky, and the clouds became dark, in an excess of grief. A spark of this sorrow touched the disc of the moon and created a spot on its surface. The wings of the bird drooped under his burden of sorrow and they looked like lightning. The bird passed over the sea and its waters, in their deep woe, became saline."

These excesses of fancy, which should not be confounded with the play of poetic imagination, make the passages such gibberish as children may be heard amusing themselves with in their folk-lore.

Ratna Sen's wrestling-feats.

Ratnasen's wrestling-feats and skill in riding, which have been graphically described in the poem, have many points which remind us of the feats exhibited by modern circus troupes. They give us

---

* দুঃখের সংবাদ লয়ে বিহঙ্গ উড়িল।
সেই দুঃখে জলদ শ্যামল বর্ণ ভেল॥
স্ফুলিঙ্গ পড়িল উড়ি চাঁদের উপর।
অম্বরে শ্যামল তহি ভেল শশধর॥
উড়িতে নারিল পাখা শূন্যের উপর।
উল্কাপাত হয় হেন বলে তারে নর॥
সমুদ্র উপর দিয়া করিল গমন।
জলনিধি হইল তহি পূর্ণিত লবণ॥

Ālāol's Padmāvati.

a complete idea of the manly sports and pastimes that found favour during the Māhomedan period, though the description is not altogether free from exaggeration.

The story is a failure.

Ālāol's Padmāvati has little interest as a story. The characters are not delineated with skill, and the conception of the plot does not show any great mastery of the poet over his incidents. Its main charm rests on those stray glimpses of poetic elegances and high classical refinement, with which the book abounds, and no less on the great erudition of the poet, indicated in many noble passages. We appreciate the truth of what Ālāol says of himself in the preliminary chapter of Badiujjamāl.

Poet's great scholarship.

*" At the order (of Māgana Thākur) I wrote Padmāvati; therein I showed the utmost powers that my intelligence possessed."

Another poem by Ālāol.

Though greatly inferior to Padmāvati in poetic merit, the Saifulmulluk and Badiujjamāl of this poet contains occasional passages of much beauty. The preliminary hymn to God is quite a match for that which we found in Padmāvati. †" Where would be the glory of light, if it were not

---

*" আজ্ঞা পাইয়া রচিলাম গ্রন্থ পদ্মাবতী।
যতেক আছিল মোর বুদ্ধির শকতি ॥

Ālāol's Padmāvati.

†" উজ্জ্বল মহিমা নাহি অন্ধকার বিনে।
অধম না হলে বল উত্তম কেবা চিনে ॥
লবণ কারণে চিনে মিষ্ট জল সীমা।
কৃপণ না হত কোথা দাতার মহিমা ॥

placed side by side with darkness! If the wicked were not in the world, who would know the value of a saintly life! The salt water of the sea makes us appreciate more the boon of sweet fresh water. If there were no misers, we could not give our tribute of praise to liberal minds. The true and the false represent but two sides of a picture. Don't you Ālāol, care to listen to the praise or blame of this world. The little stock that you have in your own heart, give freely to the world, without feeling ashamed of it."

In the preliminary account of Padmāvati Ālāol says that Māgana Thākur, the prime minister of the Chief of Āracān, had employed him to translate the Hindi poem into Bengali,—high-flown Sanskritic Bengali,—because the people of Āracān did not understand Hindi but understood Bengali. This leads us to the conclusion that the popular literature not only of Āssām but also of the borderlands of Āracān used to be written in Bengali, a circumstance confirmed by the other fact to which we have already drawn attention, *viz.* that it was the low class Māhomedan population of these places who have preserved these poems for about 250 years.

The faults and merits of Padmāvati are characteristic of the literary works of the period that

---

সত্য যে অসত্য দুই মতে হল যত।
ভাল মন্দ যে বলে না ক'রো কর্ণগত॥
যেই পুঁজি আছে মাত্র হৃদয় ভাণ্ডার।
লাজ ছাড়ি আলায়োল ব্যক্ত কর তার॥

Ālāol's Padmāvati.

The style and the taste.

follows. The Sanskritic style used by Ālāol was greatly improved by Bhārat Chandra. The descriptions of the school that follows abound with niceties which mystify the reader, as in the case of Padmāvati. In Bhārat Chandra, the great master of the age, we only find these niceties somewhat curtailed, and absurdities often reclaimed, by a sweet jingle of words, which please the ear, like the warblings of birds—without conveying to us any clear sense or meaning.

The moral tone became more and more vitiated; and Bhārat Chandra, had he lived in this age, when poets are not allowed to revel in the unrestrained language of sensualism and the grosser passions, could not have given us his masterpiece the *Vidya-Sundara*. The literature of Bengal in the 18th century was pitched in the key of a high-strung classic taste; yet it bore no mark of any master hand, that could shape circumstances and give them life. The works of the period are nevertheless full of sparkling passages and delicate sentiment, and they display above all a unique treasure of choice expressions which has greatly enriched our literature.

The poets had betaken themselves to the painter's art. They did not aim at inspiring life; they wanted to give finish to the form. They busied themselves with colouring, till some of the pictures they drew became blurred by their very efforts to embellish them. For it was not the natural that engaged their poetic powers, but the artificial and exaggerated, which pandered to the vitiated taste of mere scholars. From the time of Ālāol the tone gradually degenerated;—the good sense, the sound principles, and the domestic instincts that aimed at purity were lost. There was a violent return to the senses. Sensualism of the grossest kind—unrestrained and vulgar sensualism, redeemed only by fine literary touches and embellished by choice metaphors—pervades a considerable portion of the literature of this age. The poets in their strenuous attempts to depict vulgar scenes cared only to produce effects by their rhythmical pomp; and when one reads such passages he thinks more of the metre and of the niceties of expression than of the wicked and immoral spirit that they breathe. Hence the lawless tone loses much of its force and the scenes themselves appear as harmless as painted devils. Poetry sank to the level of mere painting, as I have said, and to that of a merely decorative type,—painting in which skilled and ornate designs are worked up with inexhaustible patience by gifted hands like those we find in the caves of Elephanta.

——:O:——

The Story of Vidyā Sundara.

The story of Vidyāsundara finds a prominent place in the works which are called Annadā Maṅgala or Kālikā Maṅgala. Annadā, Kāli and Chandi are all names of the same goddess though their forms are different. These poems therefore are written in honour of a deity. The religious element however, is introduced by way of apology. It was not the custom of the old Bengali poets who rose with the revival of Hinduism to write on a subject which had no touch with religion; and the religious garb of the story is thus accounted for. Grossest matter however is introduced into these works, though bearing a holy name. Those who have

Annadā Maṇgal.

seen the sculptural figures in bās relief on the walls of the Puri and Kanāraka temples will not be astonished to find a religious work associated with these scenes of vulgar sensualism which are to be found in Vidyāsundara—a poem forming part of the religious work Annadā Maṅgala.

Sundara, son of Rājā Guna Sindhu of Kānchi (Kanjivaram) hears a report of the remarkable beauty of the Princess Vidyā, daughter of Rājā Vira Siṁha of Burdwan. Vidyā was not only a peerless beauty, but her scholarship was so great that she had sent a challenge all over India offering her hand to the person who would defeat her in scholarship. The challenge was accepted by many distinguished princes who flocked to the Burdwan palace, but they were all defeated by the princess whose scholarly discourses in various branches of learning completely out-witted them.

Sundara hears a report of Vidyā's beauty.

Sundara, without taking permission of his royal father, went alone *incognito* and riding a noble horse reached the capital of Rājā Vira Siṁha. A large Bakula grove spread its shadow in the precincts of the city and the fragrance of its flower was carried on all sides by the pleasant evening breeze, when Sundara alighted from his horse, and sat in the grove, not knowing where to seek shelter for the night. At that moment a rather elderly woman whose charms were not altogether lost by years,—a courtezan and a coquette, happened to come there to gather flowers,—for Hirā was a flower-woman whose duty it was to make wreaths and garlands for the ladies of the Rājā's house at early dawn every day. She was charmed with the hand-

Comes to Burdwan and meets Hirā.

some appearance of the Prince and offered to lodge him for the night and as long as he might wish to do so, if he wanted to put up at her place. He called her aunt, and though she was not pleased with the prince for calling her so, as in her heart of hearts she entertained the hope of being flattered with a little attention from him, yet she showed him every hospitality at her house; but when she asked him who he was and what his mission was at Burdwan she could elicit no satisfactory reply. The Prince said he was a youngman who had taken a fancy to travel in various lands for the sake of pleasure.

The evening passed in pleasant conversation, and in the night the flower-woman began to wreathe her floral store into garlands; and placed them in a beautiful basket, and Sundar asked her what she would do with them. She said that the garland would be presented to Princess Vidyā at early dawn, a task which it was her duty to perform every morning by appointment from the queen. The Prince was very much delighted to find in Hirā a woman who had access to the Princess. He asked her many questions about the beauty of Vidyā and Hirā following the close lines of classical metaphor and a highly ornate style, as dictated by the Sanskrit rules of rhetoric, drew an over-coloured sketch of the Princess which had the effect of greatly heightening the desire of the Prince for an interview with the far-famed beauty. He made a request to Hirā to allow him to weave a garland of flowers for Vidyā to be presented to her next morning; of course he did not mean that it was to be offered in his name; as usual she would give it to the Princess;—the garland was to be woven by him—this was all that

Offers to present a garland.

he wanted. Hirā did not see any harm in this and Sundar, who was an expert in the art of preparing floral wreaths applied his whole heart to the work and prepared a garland with remarkable skill;—the petals of the flowers were so arranged as to form characters by which he conveyed his love to the lady in a beautiful Sanskrit sloka.

Love's message and its effects.

Hirā had to sit up till a late hour of the night, as much time was taken by Sundar in artistically preparing the garland; so she was late in arriving at the palace the next morning, and Vidyā reproved her for her delay threatening that she would bring her conduct to the notice of the King. Hirā said that it had taken her a long time to weave one special garland for her, and that the Princess should pardon her for this first fault. "Where is the beautiful garland of which you speak?" She said; and as Hirā handed the thing to her she felt the dawn of love in her heart as she read the name of the Prince, and the message conveyed to her by the exquisitely artistic arrangement of the flowers. It was as though reading an elegant poem; the garland rich in design, perfect in execution and containing the sweet message of love, charmed her heart and she importuned Hirā, asking her to tell her who it was that had made it. Hirā at first tried to maintain her position by declaring that she herself had done so; but the Princess laughed at all attempts on her part to establish this point by oaths and long speeches, and she was afterwards obliged to confess the whole truth to Vidyā who, on hearing it, could not disguise her feeling from the flower-woman and wanted to have a sight of the gifted youngman.

The inner apartments of a Rājā's house are eternally shut against all out-siders; but through the shutters of her window, Vidyā saw Sundara, who was brought by Hīrā to a convenient place that they might have a sight of each other. It should be stated here that Vidyā's learned discussion with those who courted her hand were always, following the custom of Hindus in such cases, managed behind the screen with the help of interpreters and in no case was a prince allowed to have even a peep at her.

A sight of each other.

They saw each other and fell in love. How could an interview be effected? It was impossible to attempt anything like it on the face of the guards—those eunuchs who kept a strict and vigilant watch at the palace gate. Sundara disguised himself as a Sannyasin, wore matted locks and a false beard and covered his face with ashes and saw Rājā Vīra Sinha. To the surprise of the Rājā and his courtiers he declared his desire to enter into a scholarly discussion with Vidyā, and, if he succeeded in winning the game, to take her for his wife. A strange story from the lips of an ascetic! Such a challenge would only be entitled to credence and approval if a prince were the suitor. But as Vidyā had promised that any man was welcome to accept the challenge irrespective of age and social status, the false Sādhu insisted on being ushered behind the screen to have a discourse with her in various branches of learning and win her for his bride. The maids of Vidyā humourously asked her to match her powers with his and if she should prove the weaker of the two, to court the lot of an ascetic's wife and wonder with him bare-footed,

Sundara as a sannyasin.

Vidyā puts off the date. visiting shrines like Benares, Gayā and Prayāg! But Vidyā whose mind was full of the handsome prince would not allow the Sannyāsin to approach her, and put off the date for doing so to an indefinite time on some pretext or other.

Both the prince and the princess were longing for an interview. Hīrā was taken into their confidence, but she was afraid of the guards who would tear her to pieces if they had a scent of her having a share in the business.

Equipped with a charmed rod. Prince Sundara felt that life was unbearable without an interview with Vidyā. He fasted and worshipped Kāli with true devotion, who granted him a charmed rod wherewith the prince worked out a subterranean passage from the room in which he lodged, leading through a mazy tunnel to Vidyā's room in the palace.

The meeting. The maids of Vidyā were taken into her confidence and they all promised secrecy. One night when the starry sky, with its grey linings of clouds looked beautiful, causing sweet emotions to grow in young hearts.—Vidyā felt a great longing to meet the prince. The maids attending on her suddenly saw that a deep cavity had been made inside the room, through which a turban sparkling with diamonds rose before their bewildered gaze, and shortly after there appeared a human form, the handsomest that had ever met their eyes—Sundara was smiling in triumph and looking to Vidyā assured her that it was all through the grace of Kāli that he had at last succeeded in making an underground passage leading to her apartments. The maids felt reassured at this words; but Vidyā said to them that though she could excuse the thief and the intruder, it was not possible to break her promise; unless and until he could defeat her in scholarship there was absolutely no hope for him. Sundara readily accepted the challenge and there followed a discussion in Kāvya, Nyāya, Dharmaçāstra, Philosophy and all other subjects of human knowledge. At every turn Vidyā was brought to bay by the intellectual acumen and profound scholarship of the prince and when so vanquished, she had a smile for him, which, coupled with the glances that they stole at each others face, invested her defeat on the field with a sense of conquest over the heart of her antagonist and lover. Vidyā now acknowledged that she was defeated and that she saw no objection to her being united to him in marriage, true to her promise. Among the various systems of marriage of the Hindus there is the *Gandharva vibaha* or marriage in secret which makes the vows sacred and legal by mutual election of the bridegroom and the bride. No priest or third party is required to minister to the ceremony,—the only condition required to bring this marriage to a consummation is to exchange garlands of flowers worn by each other. Vidyā in great delight took off the floral garland from her neck and offered it to Sundara and Sundara did the same to her. So the marriage was completed. The poets say that Kāmdeva or the God of love, unseen by others, discharged the priestly function in this ceremony. The marriage parties consisted of six seasons headed by the spring and tinkling sounds of the ornaments,—the *napura*, the bracelets, the *kankana*

The defeat and marriage in secret.

worn by maids, sounded the musical notes to consummate the event.

Thus Vidyā and Sundara met every night. The maids connived, and nothing was known about the marriage by the Rājā or his queen. Even in daytime they met, for Vidyā had a compartment in the palace all reserved for herself, and her parents visited her only occasionally, and when they did so they generally sent previous informations of their visit. Chapter after chapter is devoted by Bhārata Chandra to describing the manœvres of the husband and wife to give pleasure to each other by surprise-visits and by every form of play imaginable in which the young couple indulged to their heart's content. Rājā Vīra Sinha continued now and then to send information to his daughter about the ascetic till waiting as suitor for her hand, but Vidyā would not listen to it. She declared that she would lead the holy life of a nun and had despaired of marriage as no prince could yet defeat her in scholarship. The ascetic, as I have said, was no other than Sundara himself, who passed his days in the city in the garb of an ascetic, with the object of avoiding attention as he was ostensibly without any occupation. The prince and the princess in the meantime both insisted whenever they met Hirā, the flower woman, on her helping them to have an interview with each other, and the poor woman was at her wit's end to devise some plan for their doing so. She was completely ignorant of the affair that was going on *subrosa*.

The maids of Vidyā were alarmed to find that the princess was *enceinte* so that the fact of her marriage could not be longer concealed from her royal parents. In great dismay they discussed among themselves what was to be done at this crisis. It was settled that the matter should be brought to the notice of the queen; for the disclosure of the circumstances through other sources, which was inevitable, would expose them to the risk of losing their lives, as they would be implicated in a share of the guilt. They would not disclose Sundara's name but would bring the matter itself to the queen's notice—a course to which Vidyā had reluctantly to give her consent, as there was no other alternative.

Concealment no longer safe.

The queen heard of it; she visited the princess, and after vainly attempting to extort the right information from her and rebuking her as best as she could, asked the maids to disclose the name of the person who was so bold as to violate the sanctity of the royal *zenana*; but they washed their hands clean of all knowledge about any one and maintained a determined silence, in answer to all enquires on this point. In a great rage the queen approached the Rājā, who was taking his afternoon nap at the time; the maids in attendance were waiting with *chamars* and fans—standing silently like painted figures by his bed-side. The queen in a violent paroxysm of anger flew into the royal apartments and the tinkling sound of her *napura* awoke the king who was surprised to find her in such a condition.

The exasperated queen.

She related the story to the Rājā, declaring him to be quite unfit to hold the sceptre since such a thing could happen in his own palace. The police staff was worthless, if they allowed a thief to enter the royal *zenana* and perpetrate such a heinous crime under the king's nose, what safety was there for the life and property of the poor people living in his dominion ?

The Rājā convened his court immediately. The chief officer of police came trembling before the enraged chief, and Vīra Sinha after relating the story said, "You base-born fellow, there will be one grave dug into which you and your children will be thrown if you cannot detect the thief." The officer with folded palms asked for seven days to make an enquiry and find out the thief. The Rājā granted him the time saying, if on the expiry of seven days, the thief should not be brought to his presence, the officer would lose his head and his children would all be killed.

The police officer's danger.

The police officer commenced operations of a thorough inspection of the palace. Vidyā was made to leave her apartment, and the police people flocked to see through what passage a thief might enter the house inspite of such a strong body of guards. It took them no time to discover the hole—the passage made by Sundara. They entered the hole but came back feeling as if the vaults of hell were open,—there was no passage of light or air, the gloom that pervaded it over awed them and choked them. The bravest of them repeated his attempts several times and as many times came back apprehending the approach of a venomous snake or some devil. Dhumaketu, the Inspector, pronounced it to be a hole made by a serpent and Yamaketu, another officer of the staff, said that it must have been made by some black spirit. Whatever it might be, they were unanimous in their opinion that in all probability that was the passage used by the thief. They all sat round the hole and contemplated the best method of carrying on a sifting investigation as to where it could lead. They thought of excavating the whole ground covered by it, but that course would require such an extensive operation through the hard ground-floor of the palace that seven days might not suffice for finishing the work. Kālaketu, a police officer, said :—" Brethren, let us wait here in the disguise of maids; the thief may come of himself to visit the princess."

This idea was accepted by all. They brought various dresses and ornaments from the Rājā's theatrical stock. One of them who had a charming face put on the dress similar to that of Vidyā and twelve officers disguised themselves as twelve maids decorating themselves with great skill in-order to practise the deception successfully. Thirteen men belonging to the police staff had thus stationed themselves in the apartments of Vidyā. Sonā Rāya and Rup Rāya, the chief officers, sat at the main gates leading to the palace. There were 28 minor gates and as many police Inspectors guarded them with a vigilant watch. One of the old women belonging to the family of a police Inspector, who used to wear a red coloured *sadi* and a garland of *java* flowers round her neck, visited every house on some pretext or other, and employed her maidens on a similar mission, making enquiries of the women-folk of the town to get a clue to trace the thief. A thorough search was made of the incoming and outgoing boats and all arrivals and departures were subjected to a most careful search.

Vidyā could find no possible way to send information to Sundara, as her apartments were occupied by officers of the detective department. The police were trying to detect a thief, that was all that the people knew; no inkling as to a guilty connection with the royal *zenana* was obtained by any outsider, and Sundara had no thought of all this investigations having been aimed at the detection of his crime.

As usual dressed in his best attire,—scented with *atar* extracted from the rose and jessamine, with his turban and apparel sparkling with diamonds —his head full of love's reveries, Sundara entered the subterranean passage in the evening and appeared at the other end of the hole. The police officers looked at each other and smiled. Sundara could not recognise them in the dim light which the police had purposely kept in the apartments. He sat smiling by the side of one who wore Vidyā's dress and attemped the gay amours with her to which he was accustomed; but the false lady hid her face behind the veil and would not show any sign of reciprocating his warm sentiments,—at which he feared she was angry with him for some unknown cause. The prince looked helplessly around, and asked the maids to intervene in his behalf to make his lady-love as kind to him as she had ever been. The maids responded to his call and all at once seized him—his lady-love also was not slow in joining her maids in according him the reception which a thief deserved at the hands of the police.

In the meantime some of the officers groped in the darkness of the subterranean passage, attempting to discover the residence of the arch-thief whose daring and ingenuity was so great as to have outwitted the whole staff of guards. They were no longer afraid of the devil dwelling in the cell, nor of snakes, since they had seen the thief entering Vidyā's apartments through it with his fine apparel, nothing soiled by the dirt of the cell. They had to go a long way before they saw the region of the sun and the moon, and it so happened that the first light they saw, discovered to their eyes a charming *bunglow* which was familiar to them all, as forming part of the house of Hīrā the flower-woman. The faded beauty, whose face showed a strange combination of wrinkles and loveliness, was dragged out of her room and belaboured for giving shelter to a thief and helping him to dig a passage under the earth. Hīrā swore by all that was holy to her,—by her father's name—by the name of Rājā Vīra Sinha and by the head of Sonā Rāy, the chief officer of the police, that all was a mystery to her and that she knew nothing of such developments in her house and in the palace. Dhumaketu remarked :—" How could the thief have the knowledge of Vidyā's apartments, if you did not draw a map for him, you old hag ?" They bound her in chains and drove her like an animal to the palace.

The flower-woman in the trap.

Rājā Vīra Sinha sat on his throne to pronounce his judgment on the daring thief who appeared to him to be a remarkable man, and whose performance sounded like a romance. Sundara was brought before him bound in chains ; the courtiers felt the influence of the charm of his personality. He appeared perfectly indifferent to his fate, and with a stately demeanour approached the throne. He was more handsome than all the princes that had stood as suitors for the hands of the princess. Rājā Vira Sinha felt compunction at the noble sight of the young man who would be welcome as his son-in-law, if only his birth, status in life, and learning, had qualified him for the high honour, and if he had not stooped to the wicked device of a thief for winning the heart of his pretty daughter. The sword of the chief officer of police was unsheathed and it stood ready awaiting only the command of the king to sever the head of the thief from his body before all the assembled court. The Rājā asked the young man to relate his story,—who he was, what was his father's name and why he stooped to such a mean device for gaining the princess. Sundara said in a half-humourous tone, "My name is Vidyāpati (lit. husband of Vidyā), my father's name is father-in-law of Vidyā, my home is in Vidyā-nagar (village of the name of Vidyā) and I belong to the caste of Vidyā." The offended chief was angry beyond measure at the audacity of the man, and the chief officer of the police wanted permission to kill him on the spot, but the chief by a glance cast secretly at the officer forbade him to do so. The more the Rājā tried to bring the thief to a confession of his guilt as also to giving an account of himself, the more did he frustrate him by ingenious replies, and at last recited 50 *slokas* composed by himself, extempore, in which he described his love to Vidyā, but these *slokas* (in

The prevarications of Sundara before the Rājā.

Sanskrit) which are found in the Vidya Sundara of Bharata Chandra and are well known as "Chora Panchaçata" could also be interpreted as signifying praises in honour of the Goddess Kali. They have double meanings. The Raja was struck by this display of erudition and felt that he was no ordinary person, but as he persisted in his waywardness, at last gave orders to take him away from his sight and lead him to the place of execution.

Order for execution.

The handsomest young man that ever met the eyes of men in Burdwan, being cruelly bound hand and foot, was being carried to the execution-ground, and the citizens that witnessed the scene felt sorrow and sympathy for the prince, especially the women-folk who made all kinds of reflections, some of which were not in good taste, as many of them expressed in an unreserved language their envy at the good fortune of Vidya in having possessed him. These descriptions do not really represent the Hindu women whose natural shyness would scarcely allow them to overstep the limits of decency in such a gross manner. We have in our literature of to-day feminine characters like Āyeṣā and Kunda-nandinī—imitations of Rebecca and Haidee, who though they do not actually come in gowns and bodices, display the heart of European maids through the thin cover of Indian *sadi*. The feminine characters depicted in Vidya Sundara and the ideas attributed to them are similarly foreign to us. They unmistakably show the stamp of the influence which the literature of an alien people left on our own.

Saved by the Mother.

Sundara being taken to the execution ground, prays to Kali for succour. The story of Çrimanta

Sadāgara repeats itself here. Sundara prays to Kāli invoking her by names which begin with each of the 34 letters of the Bengali alphabet. He receives the never failing help of the mother; a great army of ghosts come and bind the king's army with chains.

In the court of the Rājā the bird *cuka* communicated a strange story. It told the Rājā that the thief was no other than the far-famed prince of Kānchi, Sundara, whose learning, handsome appearance and martial acquirements were the pride of Southern India. The Rājā asked *cuka* as to why he did not give an account of who he was, though he was repeatedly asked to do so. The bird said, it was not the custom with a prince to give an account of himself, the royal ambassador introduced him to Rājās of those countries which he might happen to visit. The ambassador Gangābhāta had been sent to Kānchi to proclaim the challenge of Vidyā in that city and he was called in. After making obeisence to the Rājā he said in reply to the query put to him about the prince,—"The prince of Kānchi has the title of Mahākavi or great poet, because he possesses poetical powers in an uncommon degree. I saw him at Kānchi; than him a more handsome prince does not exist in the world; when he heard of the beauty of Vidyā and of the challenge she had offered, he suddenly disappeared from the city and since then nothing is known of him. His royal parents in great distress sent messengers everywhere to make enquiries about his whereabouts. But so long as I was there he did not return. It is not unlikely that he has come to Burdwan."

The story told by Çuka confirmed by Gangā Bhāta.

Sundara identified.

The Rājā sent the ambassador to the execution-ground to identify the thief if he was really the prince. Gangābhāta came back forthwith and declared that the thief was the prince, to whom he had, while at Kānchi, delivered the letter of challenge.

The Rājā himself went to the execution-ground. There he saw his army mysteriously bound with chains and unable to speak, and the prince in an attitude of prayer looking up to heaven. He seemed so completely resigned that he looked like a beautiful statue placed there to dispel the horror of the execution-ground. The Rājā went and embraced him as his son-in-law, and by the grace of Kāli the royal army was released from the chains and was once more set free.

Marriage and public festivities.

The marriage of Vidyā and Sundara had already taken place according to the Gandharva system,—the ritual of which consisted only in the exchange of flower-garlands between the couple as a sign of their mutual selection of each other, and the public ceremony was now performed with great *eclat*. Sundara after having stayed at Burdwan for some time went to Kānchi with his wife Vidyā and lived many long years in happiness. Nor must we omit to say that during the marriage festivities Hīrā the flowerwoman was released and rewarded by Rājā Vīra Sinha.

The flower-woman rewarded.

——o——

(d) Early poets of the Vidyā Sundara-poems.

The oldest Vidyā Sundara that we have been able to secure, was written by Govinda Dās in

1595 A. D. The poet was born at Deogrām in Chittagong and belonged to the Atriya Gotra, and to the line of Naradās who was probably a Kāyastha. It appears that there had been previous poems on Vidyā Sundara from which our author drew his materials. We find in the Brahma khanda of the Bhavişya Purāṅa* the story of Vidyā Sundara described at some length in racy Sanskrit verses. It is wrong to suppose that Bhārata Chandra was the first to connect the story with the Burdwan Rāj-family and that he did so to satisfy a private grudge. In the Brahma khanda we find mention not only of Burdwan as the place of occurrence of its incidents but also of Rājā Vīra Sinha; and Rāma Prasāda whose Vidyā Sundara is earlier, as well places the scene in Burdwan. Besides these, in the Padmāvati by Ālāol we find a reference to the underground passage dug by Sundara which proves that the tradition of the story had existed in the country for a long time. The mould in which it was subsequently cast by Bhārata Chandra and other poets of his school bears the mark of Māhomedan influence. Govinda Dās's poem was free from those vulgarities which are now associated with the story, owing to the way in which Bhārata Chandra dealt with it. But Govinda Dās wrote in a highly Sanskritised style and in this respect had affinities with subsequent schools of poets. The following passage shows the sort of style which now came gradually into favour and from which it is so hard to translate, owing to the fact that its merits lie wholly in its literary art :—

The story is an old one.

Govinda Dās 1595 A. D.

---

* According to Wilson, Brahma Khanda was composed shortly after 1550 A.D. See Indian Antiquary vol. XX P 419 (1891).

*"All praise be to the Lord of gods Çiva,—the saviour of the world. Many salutations do I offer to thy lotus feet. The stream of the Ganges adorns thy locks,—the moon is thy crown;—garlands of flowers and snakes coiled into the form of wreaths adorn thy neck and soft curls of hair hang loose and touch thy ears. Thy three eyes though half shut gleam fiercely, and the lustre of thy body is like unto a silver mountain. O Thou, the destroyer of the enemies of the gods and of the god of love,—Thou Prince of ascetics, regaling thyself in the joy of Yoga, thou Lord of Gouri—thy humble votary pays his worship unto thee." **A hymn to Çiva.**

Govinda Dās was of a religious turn of mind and often his reflections are worthy of one versed in Vedānta philosophy. Here are a few lines:—

† "As one sees the reflection of himself in a mirror, so is Kāli reflected in the universe. All emanate from her and pass into her, just as the waters of the sea rising to the sky fill the streams and rivers with rain and flow back to the sea." **Vedantic ideas.**

---

* জয় দেবনাথ জগত তারণ চরণ সরোরুহে বহু মিনতি।
সুর নদীচন্দ্রিম মুকুট মাল ভূষণ ফণিমাল কুন্তল যোহেশ্রুতি॥
টলমল ত্রিনয়ন জ্বাল আধমিলন রজত ধরাধর অঙ্গদ্যুতি।
সুররিপু ত্রিপুরহরদাহন অবহেলন সীমবরণ শিবযোগপতি॥
বিলসতি যোগভোগ ভববাসন দীনশরণ জয় গৌরীপতি॥

Kalika Mangala by Govinda Dās.

† প্রতিবিম্ব দেখি যেন দরপণ তারা।
সংসারের যত দেখ সেইত শরীরা॥
সমুদ্রের জল যেন নদ নদী ভরে।
সেই জল পুনরপি মিশায় সাগরে॥

Kalika Mangala by Govinda Dās.

After Govinda Dās the next writer of Vidyā Sundara that we have been able to trace is Krisna Rāma. He was a Kāyastha by caste, born at Nimtā a village close to Belghariā, a station on the East Bengal Railway. Krisṇa Rāma's Vidyā Sundara was written in the year 1686 A. D.

Krisna Rāma 1686 A.D.

Kṣemā-nanda.

Of Kṣemānanda's Vidyā Sundara—the date of composition is quite unknown. It is evidently very old to judge from the hand-writing of the incomplete manuscript that has been obtained.

Madhu Sudana.

Vidyā Sundara by Madhu Sudan Kavīndra—The story is told very briefly in the poem. The date of composition is not known.

Vidyā Sundara by Rāma Prasāda Sen.

Rāma Prāsada.

Rāma Prasāda was that great saint and poet of the 18th century whose name is known and revered throughout Bengal. Whatever was the cause, this saintly poet conceived the whim of writing the indecent story of Vidyā Sundara. His poem was the model which inspired Bhārata Chandra to write in a similar strain. Ram Prasāda was favoured by Rājā Krisṇa Chandra as appears from the grant of 100 bighās of rent-free land which was conferred on him by the Rājā in 1785 A. D. It may have been under court-influence or due to some juvenile poetic freak that Rāma Prasāda set his hand to the task of writing a poem for which nature had not fitted him. He has been outdone by Bhārata Chandra whose poem of Vidyā Sundara far excels the one he wrote. But Rāma Prasāda in his vulgarities, his pedantry, and other faults of the age was not a whit behind his more successful rival. The details of vulgar and indecent love which are found in Bhārata Chandra's poem were all anticipated by Rāma Prasāda, and in fact the former seems in such matters to have taken his cue from him. Bhārata Chandra gave a finish to the style by a harmony of expression which Rāma Prasāda had sought for in vain. Though himself a learned scholar and Sanskritist, Rāma Prasāda scarcely shows a musical ear in this work. His efforts to introduce high sounding Sanskritic words are far from happy; they remind us of the attempts of the elephant to please Adam and Eve in the garden of Eden, as described by Milton :—

Failure of Rāma Prasāda in Sanskritic style.

> "The unweildy elephant,
> To make them mirth, used all his might, and wreathed
> His lithe proboscis."

The style of Rāma Prasāda is made cumbrous by Sanskritic expressions, such as :—

* "সহজে কলঙ্কী সে তবাস্য সম নহে"
† "জলস্থলে চান্তরীক্ষে"
"ক্ষেপ করে দশ দিক্ষু লোষ্ট্রবিবর্দ্ধনে"
‡ "পূর্ণচন্দ্র শোভা যেন পিবতি চকোর"
§ "আগত ভানু রজনী চলি যায়।
বারে বারে ডাকে রাণী, জাগৃহি, জাগৃহি
উঠ উঠ প্রাণ গৌরী. এই নিকটে গিরি,
এবমুচিতমধুনা তব নহি নহি।
সূতমাগধ বন্দী কৃতাঞ্জলি কথয়তি
নিদ্রা জহিহি জহিহি।"

---

* "The moon is spotted and so cannot bear comparison with your face."

† "In water, on land and in the sky."

‡ "As if the beauty of the full moon were drunk by the bird Chakora."

§ "The sun is rising and the night goes away. O my Umā, awaken. There stands your father. You should not behave so. The bards and singers with closed palms are singing 'arise, awake from your sleep'"

As the above is quoted to show how the poet fails to produce an effect by his high sounding words, a translation is hardly called for though I give one in the foot-note. The words 'তবাসা,' 'দিক্ষু,' 'চান্তরীক্ষে,' 'পিবন্তি,' 'জাগৃহি,' 'এবমুচিতমধুনা,' 'কথয়ন্তি' and 'জহিহি' are pure Sanskrit forms and though Bengali is now a highly Sanskritised dialect, the above forms could have no chance of being introduced into our written language.

These passages show a curious medley of Sanskrit and Bengali words and remind us of the similar style of Krişṅa Dās Kavirāja's Chaitanya Charitāmrita.

Bhārata Chandra and Rāma Prasāda—a contrast.

Bhārata Chandra destroyed the temple of fame which Rāma Prasāda had erected for himself in the poem of Vidyā Sundara, and with those materials raised one to glorify himself. He is so profusely indebted to the preceding poet that there is scarcely a line in Rāma Prasāda's poem, the ring of which is not echoed in Bhārata Chandra's work. Yet the latter produces such a singular effect by harmony of words, that Rāma Prasāda, upon whose work he draws freely for materials, must be satisfied with the wages of a day-labourer while Bhārata would claim the reward of the artist who creates a master-piece. I quote below * extracts from both

---

A description of Vidyā's beauty.

* "ডুবিল কুরঙ্গশিশু মুখেন্দুসুধায়	"কাড়ি নিল মৃগমদ নয়ন হিল্লোলে,
লুপ্তগাত্র তত্রমাত্র নেত্র দেখা যায়॥	কাঁদেরে কলঙ্কী চাঁদ মৃগলয়ে কোলে॥
নাভিপদ্ম পরিহরি মত্ত মধুপান।	নাভিপদ্মে যেতে কাম কুচশম্ভু বলে।
ক্রমে ক্রমে বাড়িল বারণ কুণ্ডস্থান॥	ধরিল কুন্তল তার রোমাবলী ছলে।

poems, and place them side by side to show to what extent the one has drawn upon the other. I shall not attempt a translation of the passages into English, as no sense could be imparted without

কিম্বা লোমাবলী ছলে বিধি-বিচক্ষণ।	কে বলে শারদ শশী সে মুখের তুলা।
যৌবন কৈশোর দ্বন্দ্ব করিল ভঞ্জন॥	পদনখে পড়ে তার আছে কতগুলা॥
কোন বা বড়াই কাম পঞ্চ শরতূণে।	কেবা করে কামশরে কটাক্ষের সম।
কত কোটি খর শর সে নয়ন কোণে॥	কটুতায় কোটি কোটি কালকূট সম॥
Rāma Prasāda.	Bhārata Chandra.

Marriage under Gandharba form.

"উত্তম ঘটক সুন্দরের গাঁথা হার	"বিবাহ নহিলে হয় কেমনে বিহার।
বরকর্ত্তা কন্যাকর্ত্তা চিত্ত দোঁহাকার॥	গন্ধর্ব্ব বিবাহ হইল মনে আঁখি ঠার॥
পুরোহিত হইলেন আপনি মদন।	কন্যাকর্ত্তা হইল কন্যা বরকর্ত্তা বর।
বিদ্যালাপছলে বুঝি পড়াল বচন॥	পুরোহিত ভট্টাচার্য্য হইল পঞ্চশর॥
উলুদিছে ঘন ঘন পিক সীমন্তিনী।	
নয়ন চকোর সুখে নাচিছে নাচনি॥	
বরযাত্র মলয় পবন বিধুবর।	কন্যাযাত্র বরযাত্র ঋতু ছয় জন।
মধুকর নিকর হইল বাদ্যকর॥	বাদ্যকরে বাদ্যকর কিঙ্কিণী কঙ্কণ॥
উভয়তঃ কুটুম্ব রসনা ওষ্ঠাধর।	নৃত্যকরে বেসরে নূপুরে গীতগায়।
পরস্পর ভুঞ্জে সুধা মুখেন্দু উপর॥	আপনি আসিয়া রতি এয়ো হল তায়॥
নূপুর কিঙ্কিণী জালে নানা শব্দ হয়।	ধিক ধিক অধিক আছিল সখি তায়।
দুই দলে দ্বন্দ্ব যেন চন্দন সময়॥	নিশ্বাস আতস বাজি উত্তাপে পলায়॥
সস্ত্রীক আইলা কাম দেখিতে কৌতুক।	নয়ন অধর কর জঘন চরণ।
দম্পতীরে পঞ্চশর দিলেক যৌতুক॥	ইঁহার কুটুম্ব সুখে করিছে ভোজন॥
Rāma Prasāda.	Bhārata Chandra.

elaborate annotations of such words as 'চন্দনসময়,' 'কুচশম্ভু,' 'মৃগমদ,' 'উলু,' etc., and even by such notes the affinity of the passages in point of language could not be fully conveyed to readers unacquainted with the niceties of our tongue.

Rāma Prasāda.

But Rāma Prasāda was a great poet, greater in many respects than Bhārata Chandra. His other works, to which we shall have to refer hereafter, have made landmarks in the history of our literary and spiritual thought. He was a seer and a saint, and though he was beaten in his juvenile attempts to compose a love poem, he shortly after achieved fame by his songs, which have immortalised him in Bengal and made him dear to the heart of every Bengali. We need not regret that he failed in his attempt to say an artificial thing, for his soul was artless. It is well that he was defeated in his effort to win precedence in a court where scurrility reigned ;—the pity is that he soiled his hands by such an attempt to pander to the vitiated taste of the age. He was a scholar, but it is only when he forgets vain-glorious erudition, that he displays himself in his best and most favourable aspects. He was a finished literature and the language he had at his command was rich and varied, though he was not happy in his attempts to mingle Sanskrit and Bengali. It is when he appears as a child and uses the child's language, singing songs that welled up

---

"রাজা বলে কাট চোরে মশানে বাধাই।	"চাহে কাটিতে কোটাল, চাহে কাটিতে কোটাল।
আঁখি ঠেরে আর বার করে নিবারণ॥"	নয়ন ঠারিয়া মানা করে মহীপাল॥"
Rāma Prasāda.	Bhārata Chandra.

in his heart out of the exuberance of his devotional feeling,—when he sees the Divine mother in nature and forgets every thing else saying—"Enough O mother! Like the bee attracted by a painted flower, have I roved amongst the vain pleasures of the world. Enough have I tasted, I desire no more. Now the evening has come. It is the dusk of the evening, O mother, take this thy child, to thyself."* —that he appeals irresistibly to the heart. Each line of his songs throbs with the deep yearning of the soul. We shall deal with them hereafter. Rāma Prasāda himself said truly in one his songs †" My poems will crumble into dust but I shall live in my songs." Even as a child plays at being a soldier in dress that passes for a soldier's uniform, and, soldier-like, brandishes his little sword, but when he becomes weary, runs to his mother all covered as he is with the dust of the play-ground, and there in his natural aspect looks most lovely, so did Rām Prasāda—sick of the false play of pedantry which had occupied him for a while but had not realy satisfied him—run at the close of the heyday of his worldly career, to seek his Divine mother's grace. He now soothed his heart, vexed with the world's turmoil with songs, which, with their deep-toned melancholy and their resignation to the divine mercy ring out even now in the

His Songs.

---

* "বৃথা আশা চিত্রের পদ্মেতে পড়ি ভ্রমর ভুলে র'ল।
যা হবার তা হ'ল এখন সন্ধ্যা হল
কোলের ছেলে মা কোলে নিয়ে চল॥"

† "গ্রন্থ যাবে গড়াগড়ি গানে হব ব্যস্ত।"

Rāma Prasāda.

villages of Bengal. There is no rustic, no old man, and no woman in Bengal who has not drawn a truly inspired consolation from them in hours when the wrongs and sorrows of the world were like to bruise the heart and make it heavy-laden.

—— o ——

(c) Bhārata Chandra Rāi Guṇakara—the great poet of the Eighteenth Century.

A short time after Rāma Prasāda's Vidyā Sundara was composed, Bhārata Chandra described the same story in his poem, called the Annadā Maṇgala, which at once rose to the highest point of fame and popularity, throwing into the shade all the earlier works on the subject.

His life. Bhārat Chandra Rāi was born in the year 1722. A. D., at Peroñ Basantapur in the district of Hughly. His father Narendra Nārāyaṇa Rāi was a Zeminder of the place and had obtained the title of Rājā from the Nawab of Mursidabad. There arose a dispute between Narendra Rāi and the Rājā of Burdwan on a boundary-question and the former is said to have given offence to the independent chief by a public mention of Viṣnu Kumari, his queen. Two Rajput soldiers named Ālam Chandra and Kṣema Chandra were sent by the angry Rājā to chastise Narendra Rāi. They were accompanied by a number of armed men who took all the lands belonging to Rājā Narendra Narāyaṇa by force and ousted him from his possessions, allowing him to retain his hold on his homestead only. Narendra Rāi was, as may be understood, reduced to great poverty after this event. His son Bhārata Chandra stayed with his maternal uncles at Noāpārā and prosecuted his studies in a Sanskrit *tol* at Tājpur. When only fourteen, he married a girl of the Keçarkuni family of Brahmins at Sārada, (a village in Pergana Maṇgalghāta) whose status in society was much inferior to his own—in the face of great opposition from his parents and brothers. They were not prepared to receive him or his bride at their house; so the young fellow came to Devānandapura in the district of Hughly and sought the favour of a wealthy Kāystha named Rāma Chandra Munsi who accorded him a warm reception, being pleased with his talents. He learned Persian at his place and on an occasion of worship of the god Satya Nārāyaṅa composed a short poem in honour of the deity, which greatly pleased the audience. This poem was composed in 1737 A. D., when Bhārata Chandra was only fifteen. At this time his parents permitted him to return home though they would not allow his wife to come with him. He came back to his family-residence and was deputed by his father to settle certain questions about their landed property with the Rāja of Burdwan. But for some reason or other Bhārata Chandra was thrown into prison by the Rāja for a few months. On being released he felt a desire to visit the Jagannātha temple of Puri. Arriving at the shrine he met with a warm treatment from some of the Pāndās who were delighted with his learning. He was greatly impressed with Vaiṣnavism at the time and is said to have taken into his head the idea of turning ascetic and leading a holy life in the Vrindā groves. With this object he marched bare-footed, but the village Khānākula lay in his way, where a relation of his wife stopped him and by persuasive arguments, the force of which he took no time in appreciating, brought the

Troubles owing to marriage.

A poem on Satya Nārāyaṅa 1737 A.D.

Thrown into prison.

young aspirant for a holy life to the village Sāradā where his wife lived. The Vrindā groves with the vision of God, that had inspired the poet, melted away like mist from his imagination, and in the village of Sāradā he found a metal more attractive where he spent some time in the company of his young wife.

In the Company of his wife

Our poet next came to Farāsdāngā where a zemindar named Indra Nārāyaṅā Chaudhari took some interest in him and introduced him to Rājā Krisṅa Chandra of Navadwipa. This Rājā, who, as already said, was a great patron of letters, discovered in the young man poetical talents of an extraordinary order and immediately appointed him as his court-poet on a pay of Rs. 40 a month.* The clouds that had gathered over his fortune, now passed away and he met with sunny days. His Annadā Mangala was composed by the command of Rājā Krisṅa Chandra. The book was completed in 1752 A. D. About this time he built a new home at Mulājore—a village which was shortly after leased by Rājā Krisṅa Chandra to one Rāma Deva Naga. This man was very exacting and our poet was sore troubled by his growing demands. He wrote 8 couplets in Sanskrit describing the oppression of Rāma Deva Naga, the naive humour of which so greatly pleased the Rājā that he granted to his favourite poet 105 *bighas* of rent-free land at Gusta in Pergana Āmalpur and 16 *bighas* more at Mulājore. Bhārata Chandra died of diabetes in 1760 A. D. three years after the English had won the battle of Plassey. He was decorated

Introduced to Krisṅa Chandra.

Annadā Mangala in 1752.

105+16 bighas of land.

Death in 1760 A.D.

* It was not at all meagre at the time, Warren Hastings' pay as a Member of Council being Rs. 300 a month in 1764.

with the title of Rāi Guṅākara by Rājā Kriṣṅa Chandra.

The popularity of Vidyā-Sundara.

Bhārata Chandra's Annadā Maṇgala was at one time so popular in Bengal, that there was scarcely a young man or young woman with any pretensions to learning who could not reproduce passages from it. The story of Vidyā Sundara was popularised by his work to such an extent that our popular theatres called *yatras* at one time rang with the songs of Vidyā and Sundara. The long poetical descriptions did not suit the *yatras*, so Gopāla Uriyā, a famous Yātrāwālā of later times took the cue from Bhārata Chandra's writings and composed short and light songs based on the text of his poem, which became very popular in the country. In these *yatras* the dance of Hīrā, the flower woman, was a point of great interest. We may quote the following song as a specimen :—

Adopted in yātrās.

*"It is so curious that a handsome man like you is in quest of lodgings. There are many lotuses to receive the bee, why should there not be many hearts to welcome thee ! Hear me, O youngman, when I pluck flowers, the bees fly around me—that is the pleasure that keeps me at Burdwan."

The prince is brought to the house of Hīrā where he constantly harps on Vidyā: the flower-

---

* "হায়রে দশা কি তামাসা বাসার জন্য ভাবছ কেনে।
হৃদকমলে দিতে বাসা আশা করে কতই জনে॥
শুন নাগর তোমায় বলি, নিত্য নিত্য কুসুম তুলি,
সঙ্গে সঙ্গে ফিরে অলি, এই সুখে থাকি বর্দ্ধমানে॥"

A song sung in Gopāla Uriyā's *yatra.*

woman again sings* "What a foolish young man! He constantly says 'aunt, give me my Vidyā.' Is she a jewel that a woman can keep tied in the end of her *sadi* and produce on demand!" These songs and hundreds of such, a attributed to Gopal Uriyā and other Yātrāwālās, were once in every man's mouth. Their inspiration came direct from Bhārata Chandra. In fact in the depraved atmosphere of towns, directly affected by court-influence on the eve of the downfall of the Mahomedan power, Vidyā-Sundara became the craze of the young dilettantes of Bengal who revelled in the literature of sensualism.

The contents of Annadā-Mangala.

The Annadā Maṇgala by Bhārata Chandra, of which Vidyā Sundara forms a part, is divided into three parts. The first part is devoted to the sacrifice performed by Dakṣa, the death of Satī, her rebirth as Umā, her marriage with Çiva and subsequent domestic scenes at Kailās. It also describes the futile attempt of the sage Vyāsa to build a second Benares, with the object of thwarting the God Çiva, and gives account of Harihoḍa and Bhabānanda Mazumdār—ancestors of Rājā Kriṣṇa Chandra. The second part describes the story of Vidyā-Sundara. The last part is devoted to a description of the wars of Rājā Pratāpāditya of Jessore with Mān Sing, the Governor of Bengal,

---

*" কোথাকার হাবা ছেলে হাসি পায় শুনে,
সদা বলে কই মাসি তুই বিদ্যা দিলিনে,
আঁচলে কি বাঁধা আছে দিব তা এনে ?"

Sung in Gopāla Uriyā's *yatra.*

the eventual defeat and death of Rājā Pratāpāditya, and further accounts of Bhabānanda Mazumdār, who helped Mān Sing in his fight with the Rājā; it also describes Bhabānanda's visit to Delhi where he is said to have held a heated controversy on religion with Jāhāngir, who in a great rage ordered him to be imprisoned. An account is also given of his release from prison and of the emoluments he received from the Emper

His other works.

Besides Annadā Maṇgala, Bhārata Chandra wrote Rasamanjurī in Bengali, in which he classifies feminine emotions and gives illustrations in imitation of Sanskrit works on Rhetoric. His incomplete drama, called the Chandināṭaka, shows a curious admixture of Sanskrit, Bengali and Persian, proving that he was a finished master of the three languages. There are many short pieces besides the above, which Bhārata Chandra wrote on various subjects.

Onomatopoetic expressions.

One of the elements which we find in profusion in Bhārata Chandra's poetry is a liking for onomatopoetic expressions. A richness of sound is sometimes lent to his lines by a harmonious assemblage of words not to be found in any vocabulary, yet nevertheless conveying sense by the imitation of natural sounds. This is made very effective to the ear by the clever manipulation of the poet. Bhārata Chandra had a store-house of such words; he revelled in them; they were often coined by him; but he is nowhere unmeaning, as he always took his cue from natural sounds. It would be impossible to translate words which do not occur in any vocabulary. I shall quote a passage here, in the translation of which I cannot help introducing the very sounds which the poet imitates, and the effect of which would be lost in a different language. The piece describes the dance of Çiva at the time of the final dissolution of the universe.

*"Çiva assumes the form of the great destroyer; the sound of his horn is terrible—*va vam bham-va vam bham*. His matted locks shake to and fro—*latapat-latapat*, and the murmuring stream of the Ganges flows—*chalacchal*, *kalakkal*, *talattal* through them. The snakes hiss—*phaniphan phaniphan* and the moon on his forehead burns like the sun : fire issues from it—*dhakadhvak-dhakadhvak* ; and from his mouth come the deep sounds *va vam bham-va vam bham*. The naked ghosts and goblins dance—*tadhia-tadhia*.''

A word in explanation of these lines :—Çiva the god of destruction is represented as having the moon on his forehead ; the Ganges flows from his locks. The popular belief of the Hindus is that

---

* " মহারুদ্র রূপে মহাদেব সাজে।
ভভম্ভম্ ভভম্ভম্ শিঙ্গা ঘোর বাজে॥
লটাপট্ জটাজুট সংঘট গঙ্গা।
ছলচ্ছল্-টলট্টল্-কলক্কল তরঙ্গা॥
ফণাফণ্ ফণাফণ্ ফণীফন্ন গাজে।
দিনেশ প্রতাপে নিশানাথ সাজে॥
ধকধ্বক্ ধকধ্বক্ জ্বলে বহ্নি ভালে।
ভভম্ভম্ ভভম্ভম্ মহাশব্দ গালে॥
ধিয়া তাধিয়া তাধিয়া ভূত নাচে।
উলঙ্গী উলঙ্গে পিশাচী পিশাচে॥"

Bhārata Chandra's Annadā Maṇgala.

the Ganges originates from the feet of the God Viṣṅu and its stream is caught by Brahmā in his *Kamandalu* (water-pot). Thence it flows down to the matted locks of Çiva and thence it comes down to the earth.

The words *chalacchal*, *kalakkal* and *talattal* in the fourth line which refer to the waves of the Ganges are singularly happy. *Chalacchal* in the colloquial dialect seems to signify a flow, *talattal* transparency, and *kalakkal* the sweet murmur of the waves. Three onomatopoetic words not to be found in the Bengali vocabulary have thus been strung together in the same line, to suggest to the ear three qualities of a stream ; a line more happy could not be conceived. The whole of this poem is written in the sublime Sanskrit metre called the Bhujangaprayāta. It is to be read with special care to place the proper accents on the vowels. The lines rhyme in measured sounds with a sweet jingle and the whole is an instance of admirable word-painting in poetry.

The tendency to onomatopœia in poetry which was taken from Bhārata Chandra, is marked in many later poems, and often the effect produced by such combinations of words is singularly happy, as in the passage given below from Jaynārāyan's Harilīlā.* We refrain from giving an English

* "সভামধ্যে রত্নসিংহাসনে নরপতি।
শিরে শ্বেতছত্র ইন্দুকুন্দ জিনি ভাতি॥
ফক্ ফক্ জ্বলে ভস্ম ত্রিপল্লব জ্বালে।
মিস্ মিস্ যজ্ঞভস্ম ক্রমধ্যে জ্বলে॥

translation of the piece as it is impossible to convey, even in a small degree, any idea of the sonorous music created by its onomatopoetic expressions.

Rhyming perfected by Bhārata Chandra.

The rules of rhyming had not hitherto been strictly followed. As poetry used to be sung, the defects in metrical form were made up for by the tune. But as the domain of poetry gradually separated itself from that of music, the art of poetical composition became gradually more finished, and perfection in rhyme was aimed at by Bhārata Chandra and the poets of his school. Hitherto it was held sufficient if the last letters of a couplet rhymed with one another; but the keener perception of the ear now required not only a fulfilment of the above condition, but also an agreement of the vowels preceding the last letters of a rhyming couplet. According to the last principle rhyming of লোক with অভিষেক, রস with বাস, বনমালা with গেলা, করে with তীরে would be faulty. Among the Vaiṣnava *Pada-karttas* Govinda Dās, whose ear was naturally the most keen to a harmony of sounds, had committed the smallest number of faults in

---

টলমল মুকুতা কুণ্ডল কাণে দোলে।
টল্ টল্ গজমতি মালা দোলে গলে॥
কস্ কস্ কসাতা সটুকা কাটিতে।
ঝল্ ঝল্ ঝকমকে স্বর্ণ ঝালরেতে॥
ডগমগ সপ্ত কন্যা চামর লইয়া।
ধীরে ধীরে দোলাইছে রহিয়া রহিয়া॥
ঝন্ ঝন্ লাগে কাণে কঙ্কণের ধ্বনি।
ঝক্মক্ চামর দণ্ডেতে জ্বলে মণি॥"

Jaynārāyan's Harilīlā.

this respect. But perusing closely the Annadā Maṇgala by Bhārata Chandra (a poem running over 13000 lines) we scarcely find one instance of disagreement of vowel-sounds in the final syllables of rhyming couplets. One or two examples of this defect are found in his short poem on Satya-nārāyaṅa which the poet composed when he was only 15 years old. In the whole range of Bengali literature, no poet has shown a finer sense of harmony of sound or a greater skill in the choice of his words than Bhārata Chandra. In our own day some poets have followed the principle in rhyming stated above; but in an earlier epoch of the history of our literature, it was Bhārata Chandra who held up the torch that lighted the path of subsequent poets, so all credit is due to him. The Sanskrit metres that Bhārata Chandra introduced into his Bengali poems are faultless. As the long and short sounds of vowels are missed in the spoken dialect of Bengal, it required a remarkable power to introduce the measured sounds of noble Sanskrit metres in our tongue, and Bhārata Chandra's poems in the Totaka and Bhujangaprayāta metres not only show perfect adherence to classical rules, but they flow so easily and with such a natural grace, that no one would doubt, after perusing them, that Bengali is a true daughter of Sanskrit, and that a poet who knows the resources of the language can give her a form which would prove her striking affinity in all respects with that of her august parent.

Though it is so difficult to convey to our readers an idea of the beauty of Bhārata Chandra's poems, depending, as this does, on a singularly happy arrangement of words, we here attempt a translation of one passage of remarkable elegance :—

The advent of the spring.

*" While the cuckoos sang and the bees hummed about the *bakula* flowers, the Goddess Annapurṅā sat in a jewelled shrine. A stream of cool and lotus-scented water over-flowed its banks and the waves danced to the melody of the air. The Spring season had arrayed himself like a prince, and, accompanied by the six modes of music had taken up his abode beneath the *acoka* tree. Here and there the bees were humming about the flowers, and the god of love had strung his bow. Laughing blossoms gemmed the wood-land bowers. Bhārata Chandra was charmed to see the advent of the Spring."

But the original passage subjoined in the footnote discovers to us that Bengali is one of the sweetest tongues of the world. The words chosen for this piece chiefly consist of the soft letters *l*, *m*, *n*,—the hissing *s* and the harsh *r* are, generally speaking, omitted from these lines. The poem, when recited with proper accentuation, charms the ear and sounds like music unsung. Many passages of Bhārata Chandra afford examples

---

*" কল কোকিল, অলিকুল বকুল ফুলে ।
বসিলা অন্নপূর্ণা মণি দেউলে ॥
কমল পরিমল, লয়ে শীতল জল, পবনে টল টল, উছলে কূলে।
বসন্তরাজা আনি, ছয় রাগিণী রাণী, করিলা রাজধানী, অশোক মূলে ॥
কুসুমে পুনঃ পুনঃ, ভ্রমরে গুনগুন, মদন দিল গুণ, ধনুক, হুলে ।
যতেক উপবন, কুসুম সুশোভন, মধু-মুদিত-মন ভারত ভুলে ॥

Bhārata Chandra's Annadā Maṇgala.

of this decorative art in composition for which Indian genius has a remarkable aptitude.

Spoiled by too much attention.

When Bhārata Chandra makes it a point to describe a beautiful woman, the metaphors gleaned from Sanskrit and Persian works cloud his poetic horizon. Niceties become absurdities and his learning stifles the natural flow of sentiment. When, however, a minor character is introduced, on which the poet does not consider it worth while to lavish classical metaphor preferring to trust to his own powers, his sparkling lines produce a far clearer impression. Vidyā's beauty as described by Bhārata Chandra is culled from all that the poet had read in books, and this again is overcoloured by his own monstrous fancy for the purpose of matching the classic poets in their own field. One can scarcely find his way through the thick array of wild and far-fetched similes, and we wonder at the taste which tolerated the unrestrained exaggerations, the wild excesses, and the puerile funs on words which they disclose. But, reserving all his learning for the description of Vidyā, the poet draws off-hand a picture of Hīrā, the flower woman.

Happier in delineating minor characters.

Hīra, the flower-women.

*" As the sun set and the night approached, there came along a flower woman, of the name of Hīrā

*" সূর্য্য যায় অস্তগিরি আসিল রজনী।
হেন কালে তথা এক আসিলা মালিনী ॥
কথায় হীরার ধার হীরা তার নাম।
দাঁত ছোলা মাজা দোলা হাস্য অবিরাম ॥
আছিল বিস্তর ঠাট প্রথম বয়সে।
এবে বুড়া তবু কিছু গুঁড়া আছে শেষে ॥"

Bhārata Chandra's Vidyā Sundara.

(lit. a diamond) whose words indeed sparkled like the diamond. Her teeth were painted ; she moved with a pleasant gait, and there was always a smile on her lips. She had been very charming in her youth, and though now grown matronly, she possessed some small traces of her better days."

The lines 'আছিল বিস্তর ঠাট প্রথম বয়সে। এবে বুড়া তবু কিছু গুঁড়া আছে শেষে॥' sparkle with humour, especially in the clever use of the words বুড়া and গুঁড়া. In another passage the line 'অস্তগেলা রোষ, উদয় রস' (with the setting of resentment, arose grace) indicates the passing away of one emotion and the rise of another, by a happy suggestion of the setting of the sun, followed by the rise of the moon in the sky. There is much beauty in the pun on the words রোষ and রস. There occur innumerable passages of the nature in which the poet skilfully polishes and sets each word, as a jeweller might polish and set a stone in a piece of gold.

We shall here attempt to translate a passage from the Annadā Mangala, in which the poet describes a flood that destroyed a considerable part of Mān Sing's army.

The flood.

†"The sky was overcast with dark clouds. The winds began to blow with redoubled force,—the thunder roared,—the lightning flashed,—the wind

---

† 'দশ দিক আঁধার করিল মেঘগণ।
দুন হয়ে বহে উনপঞ্চাশ পবন॥
ঝঞ্চনার ঝঞ্চনী, বিদ্যুৎ চকমকী।
হড়মড়ী মেঘের, ভেকের মকমকী॥
ঝড়ঝড়ি ঝড়ের, জলের ঝরঝরী।
চারিদিকে তরঙ্গ. জলের তরতরী॥

rustled and the waters splashed. Waves came rushing from all sides; the trees trembled at the sounds of thunder; darkness prevailed, and hails pattered. The outer screens of the Rājā's tents were carried away by the winds; people became terror-struck; the huts raised for the soldiers were swept away by the flood which now overtook the camp; elephants were drowned;—carriages were hopelessly wrecked in mud and the camels perished:—the soldiers threw away their guns, their turbans, their uniforms and swords, and with their shields abreast swam across the foaming stream. Thousands of men were drowned. Urdu-bazar with all its goods lay under water;—the carcasses of sheep, cocks and hens were all huddled together; the fruit-seller with his wife took to swimming. Heaps of grass went floating by, and upon one of them sat the young woman who used to sell it. She was weeping and lamenting her lot saying 'Never O Lord, was such a disaster seen. I am only 15 or 16 years of age; by divorce and death I have changed eleven husbands by this time. This present son of a slave has brought me here to die, but if I die, the matrimonial prospects of how many others will be gone!' The drummer with his drum was carried past by the flood, and the musician

---

থরথরী স্থাবর, বজ্রের কড়কড়ী।
ঘুট ঘুট আঁধার, শিলায় তড়তড়ী॥
ঝড়ে উড়ে কানাৎ, দেখিয়া উড়ে প্রাণ।
কুঁড়ে ঠাট ডুবিল, তাম্বুতে এল বাণ॥
সাঁতারিয়া ফিরে ঘোড়া, ডুবে মরে হাতী।
পাঁকে গাড়া গেল গাড়ি উট তার সাথী॥

clasped in his arms the long gourd of his lyre (*vina*) as he floated across the stream. There was panic on all sides. The very soldiers were lamenting saying 'All is lost by this journey to Bengal. All the hard earned money won by risking our lives, is lost. Oh woe to us! Woe to us!'"

The first eight lines bring before us a vivid scene of storm and flood, by means of an array of

---

ফেলিয়া বন্দুক জামা পাগ তলোয়ার।
ঢাল বুকে দিয়া দিল সিপাই সাঁতার॥
খাবি খেয়ে মরে লোক হাজারে হাজার।
তল গেল মাল মাত্তা উরুদু বাজার॥
বকরী বকরা মরে কুকড়ী কুকড়া।
কুক্কড়ানী কোলে করি ভাসিল কুক্কড়া॥
ঘাসের বোঝায় বসে ঘেসেড়ানী ভাসে।
ঘেসেড়া মরিল ডুবে তাহার হাভাসে॥
কাঁদি কহে ঘেসেড়ানী হায় রে গোসাঁই।
এমন বিপাকে আর কভু ঠেকি নাই॥
বৎসর পনর ষোল বয়স আমার।
ক্রমে ক্রমে বদলানু এগার ভাতার॥
হেদে গোলামের বেটা বিদেশে আনিয়া।
অনেকে অনাথ কৈল মোরে ডুবাইয়া॥
ডুবে মরে মৃদঙ্গী মৃদঙ্গ বুকে করি।
কালোয়াৎ ভাসিল বীণার লাউ ধরি॥
বাপ বাপ মরি মরি হায় হায়।
উভরায় কাঁদে লোক প্রাণ যায় যায়॥
কাঙ্গাল হইনু সবে বাঙ্গালায় এসে।
শির বেচে টাকা করি সেও যায় ভেসে॥"

Bhārata Chandra's Annadā Mangala.

onomatapoetic words, each of which has been chosen with singular care, the effect of the whole being such that it cannot be rendered in translation. In the remaining portion of the piece, the poet strives more for an artistic effect of language than for a realistic description of the flood. The whole thing looks like a storm painted on a scene under a mellow light. We miss the actual cries, the wringings of the heart and the death-agonies consequent on the devastating catastrophe. The descriptions of horror grow almost charming, being set, as it were, to a musical air. The lines 'ডুবে মরে মৃদঙ্গী মৃদঙ্গ বুকে করি। কালোয়াত ভাসিল বীণার লাউ ধরি॥ and 'কাঙ্গাল হইনু সবে বাঙ্গলায় এসে' show that the poet's heart did not melt into pity at the sight of a disaster which had killed thousands of men, but that he could enliven its description by a poetic touch, and was even willing to enjoy the scene, maintaining a vein of light humour in his gay couplets.

Niceties of sound.

Poetry was now reduced to an art; it delighted in niceties of sound. Bhārata Chandra's poems are untranslatable. Take away the outer garb, and the picture that he draws loses all its attraction. His delicacy of colouring is perhaps peculiarly oriental. His finest things become poor in translation. The whole may be pronounced 'words, words, words' in the language of Hamlet; but, as a Bengali critic lately said, 'Bhārata Chandra's poetry is the Taj of Agra made in Bengal,—not in marble but in words.'

There are critics who would deprecate this art in literature. In a language like Bengali which may be so easily wrought into exquisitely melodious strains, the artistic effect produced by a clever manipulation of sweet sounding words, can not be ignored. One who can raise emotions and portray pathos by metrical lines writes noble poetry no doubt, but there is a skilled labour in poetry which creates emotions not wholly definable, as do the unmeaning warblings of birds or the musical notes of a lyre. There is much poetry in mere sound—in its meaningless harmony and we must not deprecate the value of this in our mellifluous Bengali tongue.

Prāṅārāma Chakravarty.

After Bhārata Chandra, Prāṅārāma Chakravarty wrote a Vidyā Sundara in which we come across the following lines :—

* "The first Vidyā Sundara was written by Kriṣṅarāma, a native of the village Nimta ;—next we find one by Rāma Prasāda. After these two poets, Bhārata Chandra came to the field and incidentally described the story of Vidyā Sundara in his poem called the Annadā Maṅgala." He evidently did not know the names of those earlier poets who had written on the subject before Kriṣṅarāma.

---

*" বিদ্যাসুন্দরের এই প্রথম বিকাশ।
বিরচিলা কৃষ্ণরাম নিমতা যার বাস॥
তাঁহার রচিত পুঁথি আছে ঠাঁই ঠাঁই।
রামপ্রসাদের কৃত পরে দেখা পাই॥
পরেতে ভারতচন্দ্র অন্নদামঙ্গলে।
রচিলেন উপাখ্যান প্রসঙ্গের ছলে॥"

Vidyā Sundara by Prāṅārāma.

II. (a) The Court of Rājā Rājavallabha in Dacca. Its poets—Jaya Nārāyaṅa Sen—Anandamoyī Devī.

Under court influence poetry became debased; though it is true that a few exquisite poetic touches might enliven scenes of sensualism. But the vocabulary of Bengali was enriched during this period by a treasure of choice expressions imported from Sanskrit. In Western Bengal Bhārata Chandra, as far as the Bengali language was concerned, ruled supreme in the domain of letters. The court of Rājā Kriṣṅa Chandra was the nucleus from which flowed fashions and tastes which the aristocracy of Bengal loved to imitate. In Eastern Bengal Rājā Kriṣṅa Chandra's great contemporary and rival Rājavallabha tried at his capital of Vikrampur to outdo him in all matters. Rājā Rajvallabha was not as great a scholar as Kriṣṅa Chandra, but was by far the more powerful of the two, having been placed at the helm of the administration of several of the provinces of Bengal. He was besides immensely rich. Kriṣṅa Chandra founded a town called Civanivāsa, and the temples and edifices he built there show a bold attempt to combine saracenic with Hindu architecture. But the town of Rājanagara in Vikrampur, founded by Rājā Rājavallabha, far outshone the splendour of Çivanivāsa. With the unlimited resources that Rājā Rājavallabha commanded in Bengal, his new city was made a paradise, the like of which was not to be found in the country at that time outside Murshidabād. The famous Ekuça Ratna, with its twenty one spires, which in the distance looked like the crest of a diadem

Rajanagara the capital-town of Rāja-vallabha.

painted on the clouds,—the Navaratna, with nine spires, and the Sapta-ratna with seven spires, displayed great architectural beauty, and the Dolmancha with its mazy staircase and lofty cupola rose to a greater height than the Ochterlony monument of Calcutta. There were besides palaces in which the utmost sculptural skill available at the time in India was employed. All this gave to the town a look of wealth and grandeur which it would have been vain for Rājā Kriṣṅa Chandra to attempt to approach in his new town, though Çivanivāsa in its own way was certainly a beautiful place. Rājanagara was unfortunately situated on the dreaded stream of the Kirttināçā—'the destroyer of fame'; this name had been earned by the river, which was a branch of the Padmā, by destroying a rich town founded by Chānd Ray and Kedār Ray —two chiefs of Bengal, in the 16th century. But a second time—in the middle of the 19th century the stream showed again one of its furious moods and by destroying Rājanagara caused a loss to Bengal, which for the Hindus can not be repaired. This beautiful city is now in the bed of the river. It was situated six miles away from the river, when suddenly in the year 1871 A.D. there was a cataclysm. It is said that people suddenly felt the roots of grass and plants snap beneath their feet, and a crack was created, which gaping wide open like the jaws of death made the whole plain, covered by a number of villages and city of Rājanagara, slowly fall down into the river bed with a crash; this catastrophe took a whole year for being complete. The desolation began in august 1871 and was complete about the same time in 1872. The spires

The catastrophe of 1871.

of the monuments, the Ekuçaratna, the Navaratna and the Dolmancha seemed during the cataclysm to struggle for a few moments with the stream of Kirttinaça which in its fierce play dashed against the blocks of massive stone and bricks of which the town was built, till the whole scene passed from the sight like a dream, and the waves danced over the town, disclosing not a sign of its former grandeur and pomp. Rājā Rājavallabha's Rājanagara is now reduced to a dream. But the Rājā had not only built a city, far outshining in its glory the town of Çivanivāsa, but in his court there were poets of great power who were not unworthy rivals of Bhārata Chandra. In their elegance of style,—in the sweetness of choice Sanskrit expressions with which their poems are replete, Jayanārāyaṅa and his gifted niece Ānandamayī showed poetical powers of a remarkable order, and it is a pity that the Harililā and Chandī by Jayanārāyaṅa in which there occur many noble lines composed by Ānandamayī, could not have the circulation and the far-reaching fame which Bhārata Chandra's poems attained in the more favourable soil of Western Bengal. Jayanārāyaṅa as a poet was certainly a match for Bhārata Chandra, though all points considered, his poems lack the finish of his great rival's works. There are passages in the poem of the East Bengal poet which may rival the sparkling lines of Bhārata Chandra; but in common details Bhārata Chandra's hand moves more freely, and though the poems of both the poets have a family likeness in their ornate classical style, and in the depraved taste of the age, the favourite poet of Krişṅa Chandra is a more finished master of his art, as he is also more

The poets of the Court of Rāja-Vallabha.

Jaya-Nārāyaṅa compared with Bhārata.

concise, and commands a greater facility in the use of Sanskrit metres in Bengali.

Family-history of Jaya Nārāyaṅa

Jayanārāyaṅa was a cousin of Rājā Rājavallabha and was a Vaidy by caste. His ancestor Gopi Ramana Sen's name is mentioned by Mr. Beveridge in his history of Backerganj. Gopi Ramana's second son Kriṣṅa Rāma obtained the titles of Dewan and Krori (millionaire) from the Nawab of Murshidabad. From an account given in the 5th of the reports of the East India Company, we see that he was employed in collecting revenue of *Pergannah* Chāndpratāpa and other places. The family residence of Kriṣṅa Rāma was at the village Japsā near Rājanagara. Lālā Rāma Prasāda, his son was famous for his extensive charity. The Lālā had four sons. The eldest Rāma Gati was famous for his high character and learning; he wrote a well known work in Bengali called the Māyātimir Chandrikā to which we shall have occasion to refer hereafter. The youngest Jayanārāyaṅa was one of the best poets in Bengal, and it was he who conjointly with his niece Ānandamayī wrote the poem called Harilīlā which displays a wonderful command over the language and abounds in passages of intrinsic poetic merit. All the members of this gifted family of noble men, the ladies not excepted, were well versed in Sanskrit. Ānandamayī was widely known for her learning. She at one time surprised the scholarly Brāhmins assembled in the court of Rājā Rājavallabha to perform the Vedic sacrifice called the Agniṣtomayajña, by offering the solution to a knotty point in connection with the sacrificial rite, with ample quotations from

Rāmagati.

Jayanārāyaṅa and his niece.

Ānandamayī.

the Vedic texts as authority. The passages in Harilīlā composed by Ānandamayī bear evidence of her erudition ; in metre and wealth of words they closely follow classical Sanskrit, and when recited they sound more like Sanskrit than Bengali. Ānandamayī was married in 1761 to Ayodhyā Rāma Sen of Payagrāma in the district of Khulna.

We have had already occasion to quote some passages from Jayanārāyaṇa's poems on pages 360-361. His Harilīlā was composed in honour of the god Satyanārāyaṇa. As usual, in the case of poems of this class, the work which is of a considerable dimension, relates a story, the sequel of which illustrates the grace of the god towards his followers in the shape of gifts of earthly fortune. I quote another passage from Harilīlā below :—

From Harilīlā.

*"The night passed in this way. The eastern horizon was painted with the purple colours of the dawn. The stars gradually disappeared from the sky. The birds left their nests and flew in all directions. The raven was crowing from the tree and did not as yet alight on the ground. Chandrabhāna the hero) held the hands of Sunetrā (the heroine). 'Permit me to go' he said again and again to her. At the dawn of the day which was auspicious for the journey he left her, and her tearful eyes followed the course he took. She

The parting.

---

*" ঘোরতর রজনী অতীত এই মতে ।
পূর্ব্বদিক রক্ত দিনকর-কিরণেতে ॥
আকাশে নক্ষত্রগণ ভাঙ্গি যায় মেলা ।
পাখিগণ ইতি উতি নিজ বাস ছাড়ে ।
বিরলে ডাকিছে কাক ভূমে নাহি পড়ে ॥

stood and looked wistfully as far as her eyes could see him. The moon, with false promises, left the beautiful *Kumuda* flower that had been so gay and happy during the night. The flower turned pale at the approach of the sun."

Ānandamayī, as I said, is fond of displaying her erudition. In her compositions she generally adopts Sanskrit metres, the pompous sweep of which she well retains in Bengali. A passage is given below to illustrate her learned style, which thinly veils under grandiloquent language, the immodest taste that characterised her age.

A marriage Scene by Ānandamayī.

†"Look at the bevy of women assembled in myriads to the front and rear, peeping through the windows and confronting you at every point. The

---

চন্দ্রভাণ করযুগ ধরি সুনেত্রার।
'যাই' বলি বিদায় মাগিছে বার বার॥
উষাকালে যাত্রা করি যায় চন্দ্রভাণ।
সজল নয়নে ধনি পাছেতে পয়ান॥
যতদূর চলে আঁখি চাহে দাঁড়াইয়া।
সুধাকর যায় ইন্দীবর ভাঁড়াইয়া॥
নিশি ভরি কুমুদিনী কৌতুকে আছিল।
রবি অবলোকনে মুখ মলিন হইল॥"

Harilīlā by Jaynārāyana.

†" হের চৌদিকে কামিনী লক্ষে লক্ষে।
সমক্ষে, পরক্ষে, গবাক্ষে কটাক্ষে॥
কতি প্রৌঢ়ারূপা ওরূপে মজন্তি।
হসন্তি, খলন্তি, দ্রবন্তি, পতন্তি॥

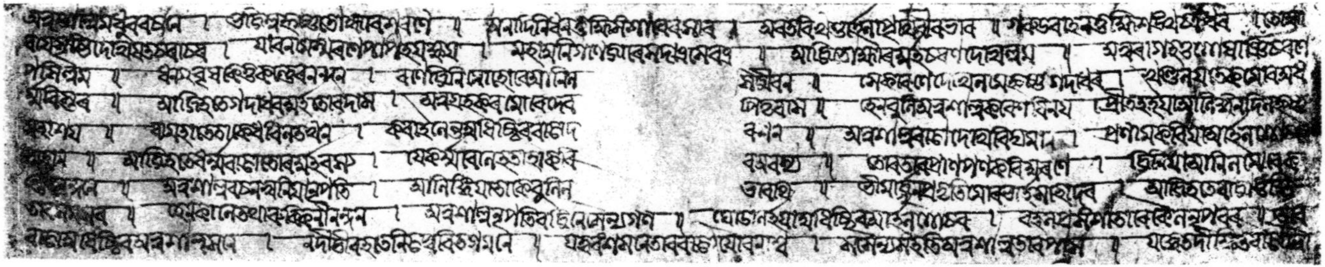

Page of old Bengali M.S. from Chittagang District Dated 1597 A.D. Note that the script coming from a remote part of Bengal shows characters which are very old, though the actual date is comparatively recent.

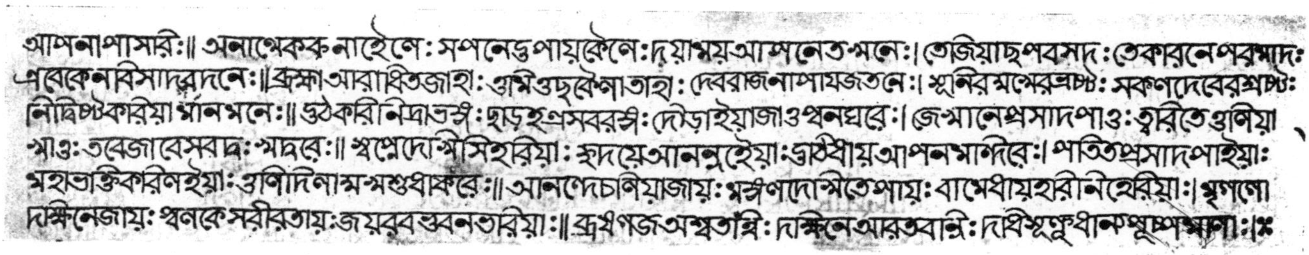

Page of Bengali M.S. of Hari Lila from Dacca District. Date late eighteenth century written by a woman, Gangamani Devi.

beauties assembled there were running about at play, fantastically tripping and breaking into charming laughter. Even the sedate matrons of the group were overpowered by the beauty of the bridegroom. Look at the array of sweet and charming faces, of aquiline noses and of flowing tresses; and behold how beautiously bedecked they stand! With what fascination they speak and smile! Behold the slenderness and coquettish manner of the worthy belle. Look at her graceful flirtations, which show how well she is versed in the ways of Cupid, and in the art of captivating her admirers. Looking at Chandrabhāna, they found themselves lost in bewilderment and in an all-absorbing delirious excitement. The impassioned matron, the gay spinster, the wedded wife and the coy maiden, all stirred about in excitement and glee. Their dazzling earrings contused the lovely neck of many a merry woman. But they all moved about in gaiety. Some bore on their lips the marks of their lover's kiss. How many a golden beauty was

---

কত চারুবক্ত্রা, সুবেশা, সুকেশা।
সুনাসা, সুহাসা, সুবাসা, সুভাষা॥
কত ক্ষীণমধ্যা, সুভঙ্গা, সুযোগ্যা।
রতিজ্ঞা, বশীজ্ঞা, মনোজ্ঞা, মদজ্ঞা॥
দেখি চন্দ্রভানে কত চিত্তহারা।
নিকারা, বিকারা, বিহারা, বিভোরা॥
করে দৌড়িদৌড়া মদমত্তা প্রৌঢ়া।
অনূঢ়া, বিমূঢ়া, নবোঢ়া, নিগূঢ়া॥
কোন কামিনী কুণ্ডলে গণ্ড-ঘৃষ্টা।
প্রহৃষ্টা, সচেষ্টা, কেহ ওষ্ঠদষ্টা॥

secretly pierced to the heart by the flowery arrows of Cupid! Many had come with dishevelled hair; many overcast with pallor; and many faint and slender. The tresses of many were in disorder and many had the *sadi* girt about the waist. The necklaces of others were loose and slipping off. The ornaments on their persons were falling and so was their wearing apparel. Many of them, smitten with the ardour of Cupid, broke into enchanting strains; and some put their arms on the shoulders of their companions and indolently stood addressing sweet and pleasing words to others. Some poured water on Sunetrā and others on Chandrabhāna, but all did so with great care, and they all poured water with their own delicate little hands, and as it fell on their persons, gurgling from the pitchers it kept time with the tingling music of their ornaments. The girl-friends of the bride

---

অনঙ্গাস্ত্রভিন্না কত স্বর্ণবর্ণা।
বিকীর্ণা, বিশীর্ণা, বিদীর্ণা, বিবর্ণা॥
কারো ব্যস্ত বেণী নাহি বাস বক্ষে।
কারো হার কূর্পাস বিত্রস্ত কক্ষে॥
গলদ্ভূষণা কেহ নাহি বাস অঙ্গে।
গলদ্রাগিণী কেউ মাতিয়া অনঙ্গে॥
কারো বাহুবল্লী কারো স্কন্ধ দেশে।
রহিয়া সাধুবাক্য বক্তে প্রকাশে॥
সুনেত্রাকে কহে, কেহ চন্দ্রভাণে।
করে সেক তোয়ে সবে সাবধানে॥
সুহস্তে ঢালিছে সর্ব্ব বারি অঙ্গে।
ঝনৎ ঝনৎ গলৎ গলৎ পড়ে নীর অঙ্গে॥

addressing Chandrabhāṅa said in jest (alluding to the match) 'A diamond necklace dangles from the neck of a crow.' The bride and the bridegroom heard the jest, and hung down their heads in modesty, and the women burst into loud laughter."

—:o:—

(b) The poets of the School of Bhārata Chandra.

A host of poets who imitated the style of Bhārata Chandra and who wrote in the latter part of the 18th century contributed works which have been suppressed by the Indian Penal Code. Stray copies of such works that came into our hands 25 years ago, are no longer available. But early in the 19th century, the stories of Chandra Kānta, of Nayantārā, and Kāminī Kumāra enjoyed great popularity with certain sections of our community. The authors of these poems were not great scholars like Bhārata Chandra, Jayanārāyaṅa or Ānandamayī, but they carried the depraved and indecent taste of the new school a step further. The moral atmosphere of young men living in towns was contaminated by their influence. Lord Byron's gallant character, Don Juan, entered the harem of a moslem monarch, disguised as a female servant and so palmed himself off

Chandra Kānta and Kāminī Kumāra; their bad taste.

সখী চন্দ্রভাণে বলে চাতুরীতে।
এ রত্নের মালা কাকের গলাতে॥
শুনি চাতুরী দম্পতী হেট মাথে।
চলাচল্ গলাগল্ সখী সর্ব্ব ভাষে॥"

A marriage-scene by Ānandamayī
from Harilīla.

upon its occupants. Chandra Kānta, the young merchant, in the poem of the same name is described as having done similar freaks in the inner apartments of a Rājā. The influence of Persian literature is stamped on many of these works; but the Bengali language in these poems, it must be admitted, made further progress towards elegance. High sounding Sanskritic words were gradually dropped in favour of small and sweet colloquial words of classical origin and the metres run in a genial flow in these. I quote the following passage from Kāmini Kumāra by Kāli Krisna Dās.

The advent of spring.

*"The reign of autumn came to an end, and Spring, the Prince of seasons came to rule with his mighty host. The southern breeze, the royal messenger, proclaimed his approach to the world. The flowers, who constituted the army of the prince, dressed themselves beautifully to give them a reception. The *ketaki* with saw in hand stood proudly smiling. The *champaka* held a spear, and hastened to the spot. The *baka* tree wore the crooked bow of its flowers like the crescent moon.

---

*"হিমান্ত হইলে পরে বসন্ত রাজন।
দলবল লইয়া আইল করিতে শাসন॥
প্রথমে সংবাদ দিতে পাঠাইলা দূত।
আজ্ঞামাত্র চলিলেক মলয়া মারুত॥
বায়ু মুখে শুনি বসন্তের আগমন।
সুসজ্জা করিল যত পুষ্প সেনাগণ॥
কেতকী করাত করে করিয়া ধারণ।
দম্ভে দাঁড়াইল হইয়া প্রফুল্ল বদন॥

The rose and the jessamine, two gallant warriors, approached in full bloom to join the fine army. The *gandharaja* wore white apparel and the *java* with red spikes stood ready. The *palaca* held a bow and the *rangana* looked like the arrow of that bow. The lotus floating in the pond looked like the shield of Cupid. When this gay army had made itself ready to receive the prince, the god of love led them as their general. He aimed his five arrows at those who lived in separation from the beloved. He ordered the cuckoo and the zephyr to spy on all who were slow in giving response to this call of love. The royal command was communicated to all. The prince wanted tribute. The cuckoo was ordered to kill the defaulters by his sweet strain. The birds seated on the bough of a tree with their melodious cooings intimated the royal command."

শূল হস্তে করি শীঘ্র সাজিল চম্পক।
অর্দ্ধচন্দ্র বাণ ধরি ধাইলেক বক॥
গোলাব সেঊতি পুষ্প সেনার প্রধান।
প্রস্ফুটিত হইয়া দোঁহে হইল আগুয়ান॥
গন্ধরাজ ধাইলেক পরি শ্বেত বস্ত্র।
ওড় জবা ধাইলেক ধরি তীক্ষ্ণ অস্ত্র॥
মল্লিকা মালতী জাতী কামিনী বকুল।
কুন্দ আদি সাজে তারা যুদ্ধেতে অতুল॥
পলাশ ধনুক হস্তে করিয়া দাঁড়ায়।
রঙ্গন তাহার বাণ হেন অভিপ্রায়॥
সরোরুহ ঢাল হয়ে ভাসিল জীবনে।
এইরূপে সজ্জা কৈল পুষ্প সেনাগণে॥

This idea is followed up till one has almost reached the bottomless pit of indecent realism.

Giridhara's translation of the Gīta-Govinda.

That stamp of ornateness for which this age in literature is famous is very marked in the translation of the Gīta Govinda by Giridhara who finished the poem in 1736 A. D.,—sixteen years before Bhārat Chandra had completed his Annadāmaṅgala. It is his finished Sanskritic style that marks his affinity with the poets of the school of Bhārata Chandra. This translation threw into the shade the earlier attempt by Rasamaya Dās who had translated the Gīta Govinda in the metre called *payar chanda*, so commonly adopted by the early Bengali poets. Giridhara's poem reproduces in Bengali as far as

---

মলয়ার মুখে শুনি রাজ আগমন।
অগ্রগণ্য সেনাপতি সাজিল মদন॥
শরাসনে সন্ধান করিয়া পঞ্চশর।
বিরহী নাশিতে বীর চলিল সত্বর॥
কোকিল ভ্রমরে ডাকি কহিল মদন।
দেখ রাজ্যে বিরহিণী আছে কোন জন॥
প্রতি ঘরে ঘরে গিয়া দেহ সমাচার।
শীঘ্রগতি কর দিতে বসন্ত রাজার॥
বিশেষ রাজার আজ্ঞা কর অবধান।
যে না দেয় কর, তার বধহ পরাণ॥
আজ্ঞা পেয়ে দুই সেনা করিল গমন।
রমণী মণ্ডলে আসি দিল দরশন॥
প্রথমে কোকিল গিয়া বসি বৃক্ষপরে।
রাজ আজ্ঞা জানাইল নিজ কুহুস্বরে॥

Kaminī Kumāra by Kāli Kriṣṇa Dās.

possible the spirit of the original in all the gay metres which we find in the Sanskrit poem, nay, he imports with an easy grace the very words of Sanskrit which admirably suit his classical Bengali. I give two passages in the foot-note which retain wonderfully the music and sweep of the stanzas of the great lyrical master of Sanskrit.*

---

* (1) "এ সখি সুন্দরী যুবতী জনে হরি, নাচত কত প্রকার।
পবনে লবঙ্গলতা, মৃদু বিচলিত, শীতল গন্ধ বহায়,
কুহু কুহু করি, কোকিলকুল কুজিত, কুঞ্জে ভ্রমরীগণ গায়॥
বকুল ফুলে, মধু পিয়ে মধুকরগণ, তাহে লম্বিত তরু ডাল।
পতি দূরে যার, তার প্রতি মনোরথ, মনমথনে হয় কাল॥
মৃগমদ গন্ধে, তমাল পল্লব, ব্যাপিত হইল সুবাস।
যুবজন-হৃদয় বিদারিতে, কামের নখ কিবা হইল পলাশ॥
মদন নৃপের ছত্র হেম নির্ম্মিত কি নাগেশ্বর ফুল।
শিলিমুখ সদৃশ বাণ নিরমাওল, পাটলী ফুল অতুল॥
দেখি বিলক্ষণ, জগত ফুল ছল, তরুণ করুণ কিয়ে হাসে।
কেতকী কর সদৃশ করি নিরমিল, বিরহী বিদারণ আশে॥
(2) যমুনাতীরে, মন্দ বহে মারুত, তাহাতে বসিয়া যুবরাজ।
কর অভিসার, করি রতিরস, মদন মনোহর বেশে।
গমনে বিলম্বন, না কর নিতম্বিনী চল চল প্রাণনাথ পাশে॥
তুয়া নিজ নাম, শ্যাম করি সঙ্কেত, বাজায় মুরলী মৃদুভাষে।
তুয়া তনু পরশি, ধূলিরেণু উড়ত, তাহে পুনঃ পুনঃ প্রশংসে॥
উড়াইতে পক্ষী, বৃক্ষদল বিচলিতে, তুয়া আগমন হেন মানে।
দ্রুতগতি শেষ করতঃ, পুনঃ চমকই, নিরখত তুয়া পথ পানে॥
শবদ অধীর, নূপুর কর দূরে, রিপুর সদৃশ রতিরঙ্গে।
অতিতমপুঞ্জ, কুঞ্জবনে সখী চল, নীল ওড়ানি নেহ অঙ্গে॥"

III. Poetry of rural Bengal.

The villages of Bengal.

Let us pass from the city to the village. The villages of Bengal, half a century ago, were the abodes of peace, of love and of devotion. The vices of the towns stamped the literature of the courts degrading it to wicked sensualism ; the vain pedantry of scholars introduced into it erudite absurdities of far-fetched imagery ; non-Hindu ideas found favour with the citizens, directly under the influence of an alien civilisation. But the quiet Hindu was not in his element in the city. His true home lay in the village ; there, under the canopy of the blue sky, on which the gay seasons of our tropical clime present in succession their ever-shifting array of scenes, the Hindu had found leisure for centuries to ponder over the deeper problems of life ; undisturbed he devoted himself to interpreting the texts of the çāstras like some Epicurean god sitting over his nectar—careless of mankind. Political squabbles rent the life of cities ; kings were dethroned, and new flags were unfurled in ancient capitals ; but a change of government did not affect the conditions of life of a Hindu village.

Long distance separates these villages of Bengal from the seething life of political centres. These homes of the people are counted sacred by reason of the noble rivers on whose banks they stand,—the rushing Ganges, the ever-white Dhaleç-wari, the foaming Padmā, the furious Dāmodara, the great Brahmaputra, the dark-watered Meghna, and many others that branch themselves into a hundred streams to flow to the sea, keeping up a never ceasing music by their murmurs. How do these villages adorn themselves with gardens, through whose green foliage peep the scarlet *java*, the white *kunda*, and the crescent-shaped yellow *atasi*,—gardens where the sacred *bel* and *nimba* trees rustle in the breeze the long summer day ! There from thick groves of mango and jack, starts suddenly spire-like to view, the tall Bengali *devadaru* rising above the majestic *asvattha*—far beyond the tiara-shaped domes of temples. Here, under the sacred *tulasi* plant, the lamp is lighted at even-fall and the brow marked with vermilion bows down to leave its scarlet traces at the root. Here the sound of the evening conch summons the villagers to the temple ; while on the edge of the meadow the cows stand quietly waiting the call of the shepherds to lead them to the shed ; and the *madhavi* creepers, rich with the treasure of the spring, diffuse their fragrance as the weary pilgrim approaches his earthly paradise, his straw-roofed mud-hovel. From these same simple Bengali homes sprang the Navya Nyāya —the logical system of modern Bengal—which some of us hold to be the greatest achievement of the pure intellect in modern times. In these villages the poems of Vālmiki and Vyāsa, of Kalidās and Bhababhuti have, for hundreds of years, cast the spell of their beauty upon the people. In them the lofty principles of Vedanta philosophy have been taught by Brahmins who realised that man was one with the universe,—a flute through which might sound the whole music of god's kingdom,—and that his greatest good lay in returning to the consciousness of his oneness with the Supreme Principle. These

Bengali villages are hallowed above all by the wonderful sacrifices of the *satis*, and their heroic death on the funeral pyres of their husbands, when, with a gentle wave of the hand from the midst of flames, they would often indicate a wish to hear the name of god recited at the last moment. Here in Bengal the renunciation of Buddha has been practised by princes from age to age, by Dīpaṅkara *Sri Jnana* of Eastern Bengal—by Gopi Chānd of the Pāl dynasty, by Narottama of Kheturi, by Raghunātha Dās of Sātgaon, and in our modern times by the saintly Lālā Babu of Pāikpārā, all of whom left their worldly glory, and went forth, beggar's bowl in hand, caring for naught but the highest truth vouchsafed to man. Here the dynasty of the ancient *risies* and seers of the Vedanta Philosophy remains unbroken to the present day in the person of Ram Kriṣṅa Paramhaṅsa, who exemplified self forgetful divine love in the eyes of men now living. These villages of Bengal should not be taken for the homes of men like Mirzāfar, Umichānd and Nanda Kumāra,—political intriguers, trained in courts to heinous vices revolting to the nature of a rural people. Fifty years ago the one great fear of Hindu parents in Bengal was lest their sons should take the vow of the Sannyasin. They would not allow them even to sit on a *kusasana*,—a seat which was generally used by Sadhus. Since the time of Buddha, renunciation in the cause of the highest truth has been no idle dream, no will-o'-the-wisp theory, amongst Hindus. It is a goal towards which the whole Indian civilisation has continued to move, even as Western civilisation moves towards patriotism, and against political serfdom.

Renunciation, the goal of Hindu-life.

The homes of Bengal have even been seed-beds of high thought. The control of the passions, the mastery over self, the training of the mind to concentration and yoga—till it can reach the state of final beatitude—are aims which have engrossed the energy of our people; and Hindus have never been afraid of privation, pain or sacrifice to reach this goal. They have sought a revelation of god within the soul,—the highest aim that can attract a mortal. A certain mystery enshrouds those who scale the greatest heights; but the Yoga Philosophy is a system which enables a man to arrive at a definite realisation, and those who would cry it down must first study the vast literature which has gathered round the subject, and understand what is really meant.

The Songs.

The home life of Bengal has been best expressed in its songs. In these, one may find out all he wants to know about the Bengali people. They are as thoroughly Indian as the *kunda* flowers of the soil; and many of them spring from sincere souls as tributes to god, even as *kunda* flowers are offered by Brahmin to Viṣṇu. From the highest truths of Yoga down to the pettiest concerns of daily life, every point that touches our aims, our ideas and our manner of life is embodied in these songs. Many of them have been composed by saints like Rāma Prasāda and Fikir Chānd, which no one who is not an adept in Yoga, can well understand. Those on Dehatattva, or the spiritual principles governing the human body, are too abstract for laymen. Their language is not difficult, but they offer points of perplexity because they illustrate an experience of which we know too little.

Grouped in four classes.

Bengali songs may be grouped in main four classes :— I. The *kirtana* songs to which we have already aluded, II. The songs of the *kaviwallas*, III. Religious songs, IV. The songs of the *yatras* or the popular drama.

(a)—Kaviwallas and their Songs.

Let us begin with the second of these groups, *viz.*, the songs of the *kaviwallas*. The *kaviwallas* were parties of minstrels who sang songs mainly descriptive of incidents in the life of Krisṅa. Their party consisted of men and women who stood and sang in chorus. They were for this reason called Dāṅḍa-kavis or the standing minstrels. Their leader generally composed songs relating to the love of Rādhā and Krisṅa or to domestic scenes in Kailās—the abode of Çiva and his consort Umā. Latterly a good deal of competition arose amongst different *kaviwallas*. Çambhu Chandra, a son of Rājā Krisṅa Chandra of Navadwipa, about the time of the battle of Plassey, began to organise professional bands of *kaviwallas*, and a new element was introduced into their songs. The chief singer of one party, as a sequel to his own songs, would begin to compose extempore verses attacking the leader of the opposite party who would next occupy the stage. The latter would not be slow to make a retort at the end of his songs, and the seething satire and gross vulgarity which came to characterise these fights of the *kaviwallas* evoked a most animated interest from city audience. But this corrupting influence was, comparatively speaking, absent from the performances of village *kaviwallas*.

Dāṅḍa Kavis.

Attacks on rival parties.

The origin of the kavi songs.

The *kavi* songs had originally constituted parts of old *yatras* or popular plays. The simple episodes in the *yatras*, especially those of the nature of light opera, were in course of time wrought into a separate class of songs, which were sung by these distinct bodies of professional bards called *kaviwalas*, whose domain was thus completely severed from that of the *yatra* parties. The *kaviwalas* used the musical instrument called the *madala* to mark time in their songs. The notes of the *madala* were lighter than those of the grave *khol* which was used by *yatras* and *kirtana*-parties.

Raghu, the cobbler.

The earliest *kaviwala* about whom information has been obtained was Raghu, a cobbler who flourished in the 17th century. The low caste of this singer shows that the institution was based upon the amusement of the rustics. Gradually the higher classes came to take an interest in it. But the chief audiences of the *kaviwalas* have always consisted mainly of illiterate rural people. Alas, these songs are heard no more in Bengal! The death-knell of this institution, once so popular, was sounded by the new Bengali drama influenced by European models; and though the *yatras* still exist, they are only like ghosts of their former selves. We miss the national tone in them. Our *Yatrawalas* now mimic the modern theatres. They can not afford the costs of making a stage or purchasing scenery, hence they generally hold their performances in temporary sheds, raised for the occasion, or oftentimes under the open sky. They have abandoned the ground that once belonged to them, and from which they once wielded so great a moral

The degeneracy of the old yātrā.

and spiritual force, and any one who can recollect the old *yatras* and has the misfortune to attend their modern carricatures, is involuntarily reminded of Hamlet's famous line, "Look here upon this picture, and on that!"

The bashful Hindu wife.

The songs of the *kaviwalas* in former times gave pictures of the domestic life of Bengal with all its gentle lights and shadows. The coy Bengali wife unable to speak out those sentiments of love with which her heart is filled, is beautifully portrayed in them. I quote below a song by Rāma Vasu, a *kaviwala*, who once enjoyed great popularity in the country. The song opens the door to a chamber into which outsiders have no access;—where the coy wife whispers her tale of grief to her maid and *confidante*. It is no free speech of love; we may well imagine the stops, the sighs and tears with which she delivers her tale, in a voice scarcely audible. Unfortunately it is impossible to convey the wailing cadence of the tune of the song. The bashful woman is longing for a sight of her husband, yet she could not speak out at the moment of farewell. Here is a picture of the Hindu wife that we miss in those poems and novels of modern Bengal which have been influenced by English literature.

Rāma Vasu.

* "I could not tell him what I felt. My heart was filled with sorrow. But it was hidden so deep! I tried to speak, when he said good-bye, but shyness

---

* "মনে রইল সই মনের বেদনা।
প্রবাসে যখন যায় গো সে, তারে বলি বলি আর বলা হ'ল না।
সরমে মরমের কথা কওয়া গেল না॥

overwhelmed me and I said nothing. You see I am a woman, so how could I beg him not to leave me? Oh! why was I made a woman? May I not be so again!

"In the dawn of my youth and in the bloom of the spring he has left me! When he smiled and said 'I am going' I wept to see him smile,—smile at the hour of parting! My heart yearned after him; I felt a longing to clasp him and detain him, but shyness came upon me, and seemed to say—'But how can you touch?' I saw his face beaming with smiles. I covered my own to hide my flowing tears. How cruel he was—he seemed to feel no pain at saying farewell! Oh! he has left me, left me without a sigh."

A high spiritual tone.

Often a high spiritual tone pervades the *kavi* songs. The love of Rādhā and Kriṣṅa is the theme which has for ages inspired the Bengali imagination with the highest emotions. Rāsu

---

যদি নারী হয়ে সাধিতাম তাকে।
নিলর্জ্জ রমণী বলে হাসিত লোকে॥
সখি ধিক্ থাক্ আমারে, ধিক্ সে বিধাতারে,
নারী জনম যেন আর করে না॥
একে আমার যৌবন কাল, তাহে কাল বসন্ত এল,
এ সময়ে প্রাণনাথ প্রবাসে গেল॥
যখন হাসি হাসি সে 'আসি' বলে।
সে হাসি দেখে ভাসি নয়ন জলে॥
তারে পারি কি ছেড়ে দিতে, মন চায় ধরিতে,
লজ্জা বলে ছি ছি ছুঁয়ো না।
তার মুখ দেখে, মুখ ঢেকে কাঁদিলাম সুজনী,
অনায়াসে প্রবাসে গেল সে গুণমণি॥"

Rāsu Narasiṇha.

Narasiṇha who lived in the middle of the 16th century sang the following and similar other songs. They indicate the high spiritual plane from which the poet gave an interpretation of love.

* "Speak to me, O my friend, of love. I am sick at heart and weary of the world. I yearn for love. O speak of love divine which heals a weary heart and opens the eyes to truth. Where may it be had? O tell me this! I yearn to visit its sacred shrine.

"I have heard from those who know, that you are an adept in the secrets of this love. Be thou sincere and soothe my wounded heart by telling me of it. Weary of life, I have come to you for this.

"Where is the fountain of that great love, for which Prahlāda, the son of Hiranyakaçipu, left the world, and courted hardships in the forest—for which the god Çiva spends day and night in Yoga in holy contemplation? Where is the fountain of that love which made Prince Bhagīratha bring down the stream of the Ganges from the celestial regions for the good of the world? What is that

* "কহ সখি কিছু প্রেমেরই কথা, ঘুচাও আমার মনের ব্যথা।
করিলে শ্রবণ, হয় দিব্যজ্ঞান, হেন প্রেমধন উপজে কোথা॥
আমি এসেছি বিরাগে, মনেরি রাগে, পিরীতি প্রয়াগে মুড়াব মাথা।
আমি রসিকের স্থানে, পেয়েছি সন্ধানে, তুমি নাকি জান প্রেম-বারতা॥
কাপট্য ত্যজিয়া, কহ বিবরিয়া, ইহার লাগিয়া এসেছি হেথা।
হায়, কোন প্রেম লাগি, প্রহ্লাদ বৈরাগী, মহাদেব যোগী কেমন প্রেমে।
কি প্রেম কারণে, ভগীরথ জনে, ভাগীরথী আনে ভারতভূমে॥

love which created the heart-rending woe of the maids of the Vrindā groves when Krisṅa left them for Mathurā, and by dint of which the *Madhavi* creepers on the banks of the Jumna had the good fortune to touch his lotus feet?"

Here is another song by Rāsu Narasiṇha which sounds very like a sermon.

* "This earthly love, O maids, is no love. Of her who yields to earthly love, suffering is the destiny.

"Forsaken by friends, slandered by the world, she is subjected to shame. Would you love, O maidens? Love so that both here in this world and in the next you may have nothing but happiness! Love Krisṅa the healer of all sore hearts. Why drink ye poison leaving nectar! Why expose yourselves to slander, which is worse than death?

"In the temple of your heart place him from whom flows the fountain of all happiness. Close your eyes and call him dearest and offer your soul unto his feet. Then partings cannot come to cause you woe, nor the slanderous tongue pursue you.

কোন প্রেমে হরি, ব'ধে ব্রজনারী, গেল মধুপুরী করে অনাথা।
কোন প্রেম-ফলে, কালিন্দীর কুলে. কৃষ্ণপদ পেলে
মাধবীলতা ॥"

* "সখি এসকল প্রেম প্রেম নয়।
ইহাতে মজিয়ে নাহি সুখের উদয় ॥
সুহৃদ ভঞ্জন, লোক গঞ্জন, কলঙ্কভাজন হতে হয়।
এমন পিরিতি করি, যাতে তরি, দুদিকে, ঐহিকে আর পারত্রিকে
শ্রীনন্দ নন্দন, দুঃখ ভঞ্জন, সদা রাখি মন তার পায় ॥
অমিয় ত্যজে, গরলে মজে, উপজে কি সুখ।
কলঙ্ক ঘোষণ, জগতে মরণ হ'তে অধিক ॥

"Let your mind be the bird *chakora*, and cry for a drop of mercy, even as the bird cries for a drop of water from the clouds. From the divine feet bearing the marks of ধ্বজ (the flag), বজ্র (the thunder), and অঙ্কুশ (the hook) flowed the Ganges, and what is that but the stream of His mercy? Bathe yourself in this, the sacred stream of divine mercy. You will be immortalised in love.

"Take refuge in the feet from which springs all light; they will dispel the darkness of the mind; that light will cause your heart to bloom, even as the sun's rays opens up the lotus. Be deep-drunk like the bee with the honey of his love.

"The creator has placed nectar and poison in the same cup, and given you eyes to discriminate between the two. Why should ye prefer poison to nectar like a blind man? He who acts like a blind man though he has eyes, misuses and loses carelessly the precious gift of love".

হৃদয় মন্দির মাঝে, রসরাজে, বসায়ে দেখিব আঁখি মুদিয়ে।
বিকায়ে সে পদে, বাঁধি হৃদে, কলঙ্ক বিচ্ছেদে নাহি ভয়ে॥
মনেরে করে চাতক পাখী রাখ্‌ব বিশেষে।
জলং দেহি জলং দেহি ডাকৃব প্রেমের প্রয়াসে॥
ধ্বজ বজ্রাঙ্কুশ যুত পদ হইতে, জাহ্নবী হলেন যাহাতে।
সে কৃপাজলে মন ডুবায়ে, করিব কালেরে পরাজয়॥
কমলজজন, সেবিতধন, অরুণচরণে।
মনের তিমির বিনাশ পায় সে কিরণে॥
হৃদে আছে শতদল, সে কমল ফুটিবে, প্রেম পিযুষ ঘটিবে।
মন মধুব্রত হয়ে যেন, রত সেই নামামৃত সুধা খায়।
অমিয় আর গরল দুই রাখিয়ে সাক্ষাতে।
নয়ন দিছেন বিধাতা দেখিয়ে ভক্ষিতে॥
ত্যজিয়ে এ সুধারস, কেন বিষ ভক্ষিবে, কলুষকূপে ডুবিবে।
থাকিতে নয়ন অন্ধ যে জন, পেয়ে প্রেমধন সে হারায়॥

The motherhood.

In the songs of Menokā and Yaçodā we find true portraits of the tenderness of Bengali mothers. In those days there was scarcely a Bengali mother who did not pass sleepless nights of longing for some girl-child of eight, sent to a stranger-family to play the housewife under a veil. These little wives were not allowed to move about or talk except in whispers to others of her own age! We all know the silent agonies of the mother's soul for her little widowed daughter living on a single meal a day, and observing fasts and vigils! This throbbing motherhood with its anxious eyes and fervent faith is called up to the mind's eyes as we hear these old songs of the village bards. We find in them the deep spirituality which has always made Bengali women bear the ills of life in a contented spirit; we see, besides, their devotion to their husbands, and notice their skill in the culinary art and their hospitality in these songs. Above all we have a glimpse of their deep piety proving them to be the true daughters of those who showed such marvellous fortitude and faith as *satis* on the funeral pyres of their husbands. These songs represent the feelings of the village people of Bengal, full of tender domestic instincts, who have lived plain lives, but have aspired to scale the loftiest heights in religion.

A list kaviwalās

We give a list of *kaviwalas* below:—

1. Raghu the cobbier was a resident of Ṣālkiā —a village on the western bank of the Ganges facing Calcutta. He lived in the middle of the 16th century.

* { 2. Rāsu Narasiṇha, resident of Gondalpārā, near Chandernagara.
3. Gozlā Gui.
4. Lālu Nandalāla. }

5. Haru Thākura (Hare Krisna Dirghāngi) born in 1738 at Simlā in Calcutta. One of his songs runs thus :—

Songs by Haru Thākur.

† "The dark night is still. Its silence is broken from time to time by thunderous clouds. The bird *chatak* and the peacock are happy to hear the sound. Tell me, O my maids, where is my Krisna now? The fragrance of the *kadamva*, the *ketaki*, the *jati*, the *champaka* and the *seuti* flowers fills the air. They remind me of Krisna, who is not with me. The fire-flies dance and the lightning flashes, and the scene is suddenly lit up as if by day-light. The bird *sadi* sits quietly with her mate and they touch each other with their bills in love. Where is my Krisna, O my maids, at this hour?"

---

* The three bards whose names are bracketted were contemporaries of Raghu.

† "সুধীর ধারে বহিছে এই ঘোরতরা রজনী ॥
এ সময়ে প্রাণ সখীরে, কোথায় গুণমণি ; ঘন গরজে ঘন শুনি ॥
ঐ ময়ূর ময়ূরী হরষিত, হেরি চাতক চাতকিনী ॥
ঐ কদম্ব কেতকী চম্পক জাতি সেউতি সেফালিকে ।
ঘ্রাণেতে প্রাণেতে মোহ জন্মায় প্রাণনাথে গৃহে না দেখে ॥
বিদ্যুত খদ্যোত দিবা জ্যোতিময় প্রকাশে দিনমণি ।
প্রিয়মুখে মুখ দিয়ে সারিশুক থাকে দিবস রজনী ॥"

In another song he says:—

* "Do not be slow to recite the name of Krişṅa, come what may. Would you give up hope, my soul, because suffering has been your lot in this world? Would you sink your boat in the water because there are waves in it?"

Haru Thākur died in 1813. Though he used to compose songs for professional parties, he himself was an amateur, and cared not to earn money by the profession of a *kaviwala*. At one time Rājā Nava Kissen of Grey Street, Calcutta, was so pleased with his songs that he offered a valuable shawl as a present to him, but he indignantly made a gift of it to a low caste drummer of the party.

Rāma Vasu and others.

6. Rāma Vasu, born at Sālkiā in 1786, died in 1828. We have already quoted one of his songs on page 698, describing the pathos of love and especially scenes of parting.
7. Nityānanda Vairāgi, resident of Chandernagar, born in 1751 and died in 1821.
8. Nīlu.
9. Rāma Prasāda.
10. Udaya Dās.
11. Parāṅa Dās.
12. Bhavānī Veniā.
13. Mohana Sarkār.
14. Thākura Sinha.

---

*"হরি নাম লইতে অলস হইও না, রসনা, যা' হবার তা' হবে।
ঐহিকেরই সু'খ হল না বলে, কি ঢেউ দেখি তরী ডুবাবে॥"

15. Nilu Hari Pātni.
16. Kāçi Nātha Pātni.
17. Bholā Mairā.
18. Chintā Mairā.
19. Valarāma Kāpāli.
20. Govinda Ārajavegi.
21. Krisña Muchi.
22. Uddhava Dās.
23. Parāña Sinha.
24. Rāmrupa Thākur of Dacca.
25. Jajnecwari, a woman.
26. Goraksa Nātha.
27. Goura Kavirāja.
28. Sātu Rāy.
29. Gadādhara Mukerjee.
30. Jaynārāyaña Mukerjee.
31. Thākura Dās Chakravarty.
32. Navāi Thākur.
33. Kāci Chandra Guha.

Not influenced by English ideas.

The names included in this list from No. 15 onward refer to contemporary *kaviwalas* or to those who were nearly contemporary to one another. They flourished in the earlier half of the 19th century. It should be said here, that though many of the *kaviwalas* lived when English rule had been established in India, their school was not at all influenced by English ideas.

The Portuguese Kaviwalā Mr. Antony.

We have not named in this list one *kaviwala* who enjoyed great popularity in Calcutta and its suburbs early in the 19th century. This was Mr. Antony of Chandernagar. He and his brother Mr. Kelly were of Portuguese parentage, and had settled in Bengal. They had accumulated immense wealth by successful trade in India. Mr. Antony, when a young man, fell in love with a remarkably handsome Brāhmin widow of Chandernagar. He did not marry her, but the pair lived as husband and wife in his garden house at Gereti near Chandernagar, where the remains of his house may still be seen. Antony did not interfere with the religious views of the Brāhmin woman, nay, he encouraged them as best as he could ; for in his house at Gereti, the religious festivals of the Hindus were performed by her with great *eclat*, and he heartily joined the festal ceremonies. The temple of Kāli known as Firingī Kāli, at 243, Bowbāzār Street, Calcutta, was erected by him at her desire.

Antony acquired Bengali so well that he gained a perfect mastery over its colloquial forms. During the religious festivals of Hindus, his house became a resort of the *kaviwalas* who showed their enthusiasm in reviling their rivals in extempore verses. Antony took so great an interest in these free competitions of the *kaviwalas*, that he himself founded a party of his own, and employed a bard named Gorakṣanātha to compose extempore verses of satire to be levelled against others. He however soon found that he was himself more than a match for many a *kaviwala*, dismissed Gorakṣa nātha, and himself appeared on the stage singing Bengali songs ; and as a sequel to them he attacked the rival parties in doggerels composed extempore by himself,—vilifying, slandering and abusing them to the height of his power. It was a curious sight to see a European leave his trousers, coat and hat, dress himself like a Bengali with a *chadar* hanging down from his shoulders, and the *kocha* of his *dhooti* neatly flowing in strict Bengali fashion, and singing songs in praise of the goddess Kāli as follows:—

* "I am a Portuguese and don't know how to worship thee. Oh Kāli, be merciful to me."

This he did for the sake of amusement; for he remained a christian all his life, though by living with his Hindu consort and in the atmosphere of Hindu ideas, he had acquired the liberal views of the Hindus on matters of religion and was quite devoid of crude bigotry. Mr. Antony's party soon acquired the fame of being invincible in their extempore satirical verses. Thākura Sing, the leader of another party of *kaviwalas*, made a charge at him in the following couplet.

† "Tell me, O Antony, for I want to know, why you have, coming to this land of ours, turned a vagabond without a coat?"

Mr. Antony was in the midst of audience consisting of common folk who would not appreciate any shrewd humour or clever stroke of wit. He was not only required to be coarse in his abuse, but to couch them in Bengali idioms of these rustic folk, and it must be admitted that he was

---

* "ভজন সাধন জানিনে মা, নিজেত ফিরিঙ্গি।
যদি দয়া করে কৃপা কর হে শিবে মাতঙ্গী॥

† "শুনহে এণ্টনি, আমি একটী কথা জানতে চাই।
এসে এদেশে, এবেশে, তোমার গায়ে কেন কুর্ত্তি নাই"

fully equal to the task. Here is the extempore doggerel with which he made his retort. There is no greater abusive word in Bengali than that of 'Çāla' (wife's brother, and Antony accosted his rival as such, although not in so many words.

*" I am happy in Bengal in the costumes of the natives, and from having been elected as son-in-law to the father of Thākura Siṇha, I have lost my taste for hat and coat."

The town and city—a contrast.

Such abuse, as I have said, stains that portion of the *kavi*-literature which had found favour in cities and large towns. In the cool recesses of the villages, the rustic folk assembled to hear tales of sacrifice, resignation, sufferings for love, and of tender domestic scenes sung by their unassuming bards. Nor do I know if anywhere else than in India the lowest stratum of society, which the *kaviwalas* mainly represented, could show so much spirituality, love, and tender pathos in their literature, chiefly contributed as this was by illiterate men of the lowest classes. The gentler classes, the dilettantes belonging to the aristocracy, favoured the *kaviwalas* in later times only to stamp this folk-lore with their depraved taste; but away from the town, the villages preserved unspoiled, the well of Hindu thought—undefiled, and fit to satisfy the spiritual thirst of those who were humble in spirit, kindly in disposition and who approached God as the Hindu wife approaches her husband.—in deep reverence and love.

---

*" এই বাঙ্গলায় বাঙ্গালীর বেশে আনন্দে আছি।
হ'য়ে ঠাকুরে সিংএর বাপের জামাই, কুর্ত্তিটুপি ছেড়েছি॥

(b) Religious Songs.

Twenty-five years ago, in the twilight on the river Khoyai in Sylhet, I saw a boatman rowing a small boat, and as he rowed he sang:

The boatman's song

* "Take back thine oar, O boatman, I can no longer ply it; all my life I have struggled to bear my boat upstream, but backwards it has gone inspite of me, and now in my old age I find my efforts gone for naught. The prow of the boat is broken, and the planks are falling away. It can no longer be kept from sinking."

This means that he had fought with his passions all his life trying to control them, and bring the mind under discipline; but he could not. And now when life's ebb-tide was setting in, the despairing boatman could only call upon the Lord to take the charge of the boat of his life for him, conscious as he was of his own incapacity to control it, at the last moment.

This song, which I heard at Habiganj in Sylhet, may be heard sung by the rustic folk at Mymensing and Dacca and even here in Calcutta.

Spirituality in rustic life.

This clear idea of self-control as the supreme good, is not confined in the country to the literate and higher classes. Through long years of the spread of Buddhism and the Vedanta Philosophy, it has filtered down to the lowest stratum of society, and illiterate villagers realise the deepest meaning of this spiritual truth, no less than men of rank and learning.

---

*"মন মাঝি তোর বৈঠা নেরে, আমি আর বাইতে পারি না।
জনম ভরে বাইলাম তরী রে, তরী ভাইটায় গোয়ায় উজায় না॥
নায়ের গুড়া ভাঙ্গা, ছাপর নড়া রে, আমি আর বাইতে পারি না॥"

There are hundreds of songs describing the transitoriness of life and the vanity of human wishes ; and there is hardly a rustic in a Bengal-village who does not sing to himself some favourite tune having for its burden the mutability of fortune, as, after his weary day of labour, he lays down his tools to retire to rest. Here is another song of the same class : —

*"Tell me who are you, carried on a bamboo bier to the funeral ground ? Some of your fellows bear you on their shoulders, and while others follow with faggots for the pyre. Your little child is calling for his father. Why so unkind that you have no word for him to-day. Did you not, with the sweat of your brow, earn gold mohurs and rupees, wandering from Delhi to Lahore and thence to Dacca, for the purpose ? You strove to heap up wealth. You would not spend for your own comfort a four anna-bit or even a pice. Tell me, brother, how much of this hard-earned money are you carrying with you now ?"

These wailing songs are sung by the villagers in chorus. The melody is high-pitched, and the air resounds on all sides with the chant.

---

*" বাঁশের দোলাতে উঠে, কেহে বটে, শ্মশান ঘাটে যাচ্ছ চলে,
সঙ্গে সব কাঠের ভরা, লাটবহরা, আতবেহারার কাঁধে চড়ে
..............................ছেলে কাঁদে বাবা বলে
ও তুমি কওনা কথা, নাইক ব্যথা, কিসের জন্য এমন হলে ?
ঘুরে যে দিল্লি লাহোর, ঢাকার সহর, টাকা মোহর এনেছিলে,
খেলে না পয়সা সিকি, কওনা দেখি, তার কি কিছু সঙ্গে নিলে "

A popular song by Kangal Harinatha.

If life is a truth, death is no less so. If one realises this, and turns his back upon the sweets of life, saying that they are not worth caring for, since they are so transitory and because they are held in the same cup with poison, what can a materialistic civilisation offer to such a soul?

The mind turns naturally from the horror of death to God. The soul, that has the power to revel in the permanent delights of god-realisation, becomes the all engrossing matter of attention. Though confined in its temporary shed, it may free itself from its "fleshy vesture of decay" and by the process of Yoga reach a state of permanent bliss. This is realised by the Indian aspirant of a spiritual life, and all the religious songs of Bengal have this burden.

(c) Rāma Prasāda Sen and poets of his school.

Life of Rāma Prasāda Sen.

Amongst those who have composed religious songs, there is no higher name than that of Rāma Prasāda Sen. Born in the quiet village of Kumārahatta, near a station on the East Bengal Railway, in 1718, he was at first influenced by the depraved taste of the court of Rājā Krisṅa Chandra of Navadwipa. It may have been owing to satisfy the Rājā or his own youthful poetic vanity, that he wrote the indecent poem of Vidyā Sundara which was very soon after its composition, outdone by the more brilliant Vidyā Sundara by Bhārata Chandra. Soon after this Rāma Prasāda retired to his native village, where the Panchamundi or seat on which he sat day and night to practise Yoga, is still to be seen.

Rāma Prasāda was the son of Rāma Rāma Sen, a Vaidya by caste. By the machinations of his relations, the father had been deprived of his inheritance, and the poet passed his early life in poverty. While yet in his teens he was admitted as an apprentice in the revenue office of a Zemindar and was entrusted with the work of keeping the accounts. One day his master was taken by surprise to find some remarkably beautiful songs scribbled over the pages of the account-book, evidently in the hand-writing of the young apprentice. When he came to know that Rāma Prasāda was their author, he was so highly pleased with the poetic talents of the young man, that he conferred a pension of Rs. 30 on him, and allowed him to retire to his village and devote himself to the composition of songs. Rāma Prasāda also obtained a pension from Rājā Kriṣṅa Chandra, besides a gift of 100 *bighas* of rent-free land in 1758. After his retirement his fame spread all over Bengal, and his songs composed in the soul-captivating *Ragini* called the *Malacri*, wrought a revolution in the spiritual world.

These songs came spontaneously from the soul. The motherhood of God is a definite realisation in them. Like a child, the poet prattles in them of his griefs and sorrows to the Divine Mother Kālī.

Kalī, the mother.

Rāmā Prasāda was a devout worshipper of Kālī,—Kālī with her fierce destructive look, with a complexion dark as the darkest cloud, and with four hands, one holding the decapitated head of a sinner, another a sword, the third offering benediction and the last assurance to those who would not swerve from virtue's path. When we call God all merciful, kind, and benign, there is one element which we try to white-wash to please our fancy. Surely the

Creator is also the Destroyer. In vain do we discourse sweetly on the tender aspects of the Deity; there is no playing fast and loose, no shilly-shallying with another feature of the Divinity, the awe-inspiring, the dark and the terrible, the fierceness of which confronts us at every step. The Çāktas have proclaimed the worship of Kāli to be only possible in a higher stage of spiritual development. A sweet and complete resignation of one's self to the Divine power knowing it to be terrible, makes the devotee, according to them, grapple better with the problems of life, from a spiritual point of view. Some Çākta-interpreters have explained the dark colour of Kālī as signifying the mystery that enshrouds the primary cause of the universe. The worshippers of Kāli hold her to be at once destructive and protective. Rāma Prāsada especially speaks of her as the mother who beats the child, while the child clings to her only the closer, crying "Mother! Oh Mother!" Here is his song:—

The Çākta interpreters.

"Though the mother beat him, the child cries Mother! Oh Mother!' and clings still tighter to her garment. True I cannot see thee, yet am I not a lost child. I still cry 'Mother! Mother!'"*

Through the fierce and the terrible he sees the sweet moonlight of grace that suddenly breaks forth, and Kāli is no more than a symbol to him,—a symbol of divine punishment, of divine grace, and of divine motherhood. She is as much a symbol as the word God. If the symbol of a word is admitted into the vocabulary, why object to the symbol of a figure in the temple? One appeals

The terrible, and the beautiful.

* See Kali the Mother, by Sister Nevedita p. 53.

to the ear, and the other to the eye. Rāma Prāsāda saw the fierce rolling clouds that darkened the whole horizon, and thought he saw in them the dark and flowing tresses of the Mother. The fire of the funeral ground, reducing a corpse to ashes, reminded him of the destructive dance of the Mother. The red glow of the evening sky, with its first stars, wore to his eyes the angry look of the divine Mother. The storm, the hurricane, the flood, death and disease—these are her companions. The cry of jackal is the chorus heard behind her. The funeral ground is her favourite place; her dark skin, stained with blood, he compares to the black waters of the Jumna upon which floats the full blown lotus. In the agonies that rend the whole world he sees the chastising rod of the Mother, but says that he is not in the heart affrighted, for he has taken refuge in her grace. The image of Kālī works his imagination into lofty poetry. He sang:—

Punishment and grace.

*"See! she does not bind her flowing tresses, nor does she wear any apparel. A sweet smile breaks out upon her lips!"

Sometimes he says, †"All the miseries that I have suffered and am suffering I know, Oh Mother, to be your mercy alone" for he knew that chastisement opens the blind man's eyes;—a cruel process, but sure in the end to lead to truth and bliss.

* "ধনী না বাঁধে কবরী, না পরে বাস।
সে বিধুবদনে মধুর হাস॥"

† "বারে বারে যত দুঃখ দিয়েছ, দিতেছ, তারা।
সে কেবল দয়া তব জেনেছি মা দুঃখহরা॥"

A mere symbol.

Sitting at the feet of the image, he often knew it to be no more than a symbol, and he yearned for a revealation of his Mother in his soul. Here is one of his songs

*" O mind, why do you indulge in vain thoughts!

"This pompous worship and rituals are in vain,—they only increase the vanity of the soul.

"Pray to Her secretly, that no one may know of it.

" What is the use of making dolls out of metal, stone and earth?

" Don't you, know, O fool, that the whole universe is the image of the Mother?

"You have brought a handful of gram, O shameless one, as an offering to the Mother—to Her who feeds the whole world with delicious food!

"What use, O foolish mind, in making illuminations with lanterns, candle and lamps?

"Let the mind's light grow, and dispel its own darkness, day and night.

---

* "মন তোর এত ভাবনা কেনে ?
এক বার কালী বলে বস্‌রে ধ্যানে ॥
জাঁকজমকে কল্লে পূজা, অহঙ্কার হয় মনে !
তুই লুকিয়ে তাঁরে কর্‌বি পূজা, জান্‌বে নারে জগজ্জনে ॥
ধাতু, পাষাণ, মাটীর মূর্ত্তি কাজ কিরে তোর সে গঠনে।
তুমি মনোময় প্রতিমা গড়ি, বসাও হৃদি পদ্মাসনে ॥
আলোচাল আর পাকা কলা, কাজ কিরে তোর আয়োজনে।
তুমি ভক্তিসুধা খাইয়ে তাঁরে, তৃপ্তি কর আপন মনে ॥
ঝাড়, লণ্ঠন, বাতি দিয়ে কাজ কিরে তোর আলো-দানে।
তুমি মনোময় মাণিক্য জ্বেলে, দাওনা জ্বলুক নিশি দিনে ॥

"You have brought innocent goats for sacrifice.

"Why not say, 'Victory to Kalī!' and sacrifice your passions, which are your real enemies?

"Why these sounds of the drum? Only keep your mind at Her feet and say,—

"Let thy will, O Kalī, be fulfilled, and saying so clap your hands."

In another song he says, "Making pilgrimage, visiting shrines is only a physical labour unto you."

The image of Kalī inspires his songs.

But if Rāma Prasāda condemned empty rituals and the worship of images, it was only at a moment when the mere means were confounded with the end. In fact the image of Kālī was to him a perpetual fountain from which he drew the realisation of the sublime, the terrible and the beautiful in nature; and it inspired in him the most poetic songs that adorn the literature of the Çāktas of Bengal.

The poet of the rural Bengal.

The songs of Rāma Prasāda still reign supreme in our villages. In the pastoral meadows, amidst sweet scents of herbs and flowers, with the gentle murmurs of the river flowing by, or in the rice-fields where sounds of the cutting of grass or reaping of harvest lend a charm to the tranquil village-scene, one may often hear the Mālaçri songs of Rāma Prasāda, sung by rustics in the following strain. *" This brief day will pass, sure

---

মেষ ছাগল মহিষাদি কাজ কিরে তোর বলিদানে ।
তুমি 'জয় কালী' 'জয় কালী' বলে বলি দেও ষড়রিপুগণে ॥
প্রসাদ বলে. ঢাক ঢোল কাজ কিরে তোর সে বাজনে ।
তুমি 'জয় কালী' বলি দেও করতালি, মন রাখি তাঁর শ্রীচরণে ॥

* "নিতান্ত যাবে এদিন, কেবল ঘোষণা রবে গো ।
তারা নামে অসংখ্য কলঙ্ক রবে গো ॥"

it is, oh Mother Kālī,—and all the world will find fault with you that you could not save a sinner like me"! *" My days are spent in vain pleasure ; I have forgotten the only reality in life. When I earned money here and there, my wife, friends, brothers, and sons were all under my control ; but now advanced in years, and unable to earn, they treat me unkindly because of my poverty. When death will come and pull me by the hair, they will prepare a bamboo bier for me, and dismiss me from the house with a poor earthern pitcher, stripped of clothing like an ascetic."

A European critic on Rāma Prasāda.

Sister Nivedita says of the works of Rāma Prasāda, " No flattery could touch a nature so unapproachable in its simplicity. For in these writings we have, perhaps alone in literature, the spectacle of a great poet, whose genius is spent in realising the emotions of a child. William Blake in our own poetry strikes the note that is nearest his, and Blake is by no means his peer. Robert Burns, in his splendid indifference to rank and Whitman in his glorification of common things, have points of kinship with him. But to such a radiant white heat of childlikeness, it would be

---

*" গেল দিন বৃথা রঙ্গরসে, আমি কাজ হারালাম, কালের বশে।
যখন ধন উপার্জ্জন, করেছিলাম দেশ বিদেশে,
তখন ভাই, বন্ধু, দারা, সুত, সবাই ছিল আপন বশে ;
এখন ধন উপার্জ্জন, হল না আর দশার শেষে।
সেই ভাই, বন্ধু, দারা, সুত, নির্ধন বলে সবায় দোষে ॥
যম এসে শিয়রে বসে, ধর্‌বে যখন অগ্রকেশে,
তখন সাজায়ে মাচা, কলসী কাঁচা, বিদায় দিবে দণ্ডীর বেশে ॥"

impossible to find a perfect counterpart. His years do nothing to spoil his quality. They only serve to give him self-confidence and poise. Like a child he is now grave, now gay, sometimes petulant, sometimes despairing. But in the child all this is purposeless. In Rāma Prasāda there is a deep intensity of purpose. Every sentence he has uttered is designed to sing the glory of his Mother."*

The descendants of the saintly poet still live in the village of Kumarahatta. One of them Babu Kali Pada Sen, a great grandson of Rāma Prasāda Sen, is working as an Engineer in Orissa. Rāma Prasāda died in the year 1775 A. D. **The descendants of the poet. His death.**

Before concluding my account of Rāma Prasāda, I quote two more songs of his which are very popular amongst the villages. **Two songs.**

(1)

†"No more shall I call you by that sweet name, 'mother'!

"You have given me woes unnumbered and reserved many more for me, I know!

"I once had a home and family, and now you have made me such that I am disowned by all.

"What other ills may yet befall me I cannot tell.

---

*Kali the Mother page 48.

† "মা মা বলে আর ডাক্‌বনা।
মা দিয়েছ, দিতেছ কতই যাতনা॥
আমি ছিলেম গৃহবাসী, বানালি সন্ন্যাসী,
আর কি ক্ষমতা রাখ এলোকেশী॥

"Who knows but that I may have to beg my bread from door to door? Indeed, I am expecting it.

"Does not a child live when his mother is dead?

"Rama Prasāda was a true son of his mother;

—but you, being the mother, have treated your son like an enemy.

"If in the presence of his mother, the son can suffer so much,

what is the use of such a mother to him?"

(2)

*"O mother, for what offence have I been placed for this long term of life in this prison house of the world!

"I rise in the morning to work; O how hard do I work!

"I wander about in all directions to gain filthy lucre,

না হয় দ্বারে দ্বারে যাব, ভিক্ষা মেগে খাব।
মা ম'লে কি তার ছেলে বাঁচেনা॥
রাম প্রসাদ ছিল গো মায়েরই পুত্র।
মা হ'য়ে হলি গো ছেলেরই শত্রু॥
মা বর্ত্তমানে, এ দুঃখ সন্তানে,
মা থেকে তার কি ফল বল না॥"

*তারা কোন্ অপরাধে এ দীর্ঘ মেয়াদে
সংসার গারদে রাখিস্ বল॥
আমি প্রাতঃকালে উঠি, কতই যে মা খাটি,
ছুটাছুটি করি ভূমণ্ডল॥
বৃথা অর্থ অভিলাষী, মায়ামদে ভাসি।
তারা এলোকেশী জানিস কি কৌশল॥

"O what delusion possesses me !

"And, O mother, how perfect are the enticements by which you bind my soul to this vain world !

"Bringing me down to this world, unnumbered are the troubles you have crowded into my destiny.

"They burn me like fire day and night,

I no longer wish for life, O Mother !"

—— o ——

Other song writers.

After Rāma Prasād, a host of song-writers appeared who imitated his high spiritual strain. Amongst them the following writers attained marked success.

Rāma Krisṇa.

1. Maharaja Rāma Krisṇa of Nattore, son and successor of the far-famed Raṇī Bhavānī of Nattore, and a contemporary of Rāma Prasāda Sen. Maharaja Rāma Krisṇa was one of the famous princely saints of India. We have not succeeded in tracing many of his songs, but the few, that have came down to us, show a high spiritual tone. One is quoted here :—

*"If only my mind can reach realisation, you may do with me whatever you will ; no matter if you place me on a bed of sand. Only recite the name of the divine Mother in my ears.

এনে ভূমণ্ডলে, কতই দুঃখ দিলে
আমার নিরবধি জ্বলে দুঃখানল ॥
আমার বাঁচিতে সাধ নাই ।"

*"আমার মন যদিরে ভোলে,
তবে বালির শয্যায়, কালীর নাম, রেখো কর্ণমূলে ।
দেহ আপন বশী নয়, সে রিপুর সঙ্গে চলে ॥
এনে দে ভোলা, জপের মালা, ভাসাই গঙ্গাজলে ॥"

"This body of mine is so difficult to control; it yields to passion.

"O Bhola, my guide, bring me my rosary; I shall throw it into the Ganges, no more formality."

Kamalā-kānta. 2. Kamalā Kānta Bhattācharyya, born in the last part of the 18th century. He was formerly an inhabitant of Ambikānagara in Kālnā, but removed to Kotalhata in Burdwan in the year 1800. He was the religious preceptor of Maharaj Tejaçchandra of Burdwan. I may here give one of his songs :—

*"In whatever station I may be placed, it all becomes blessed, if I forget thee not. O Mother! this life, the bitter cup of life, is a source of bliss, if I can feel thy grace in my heart. Ashes and clods of earth, or precious jewels, lodging beneath a tree for want of a roof, or a seat on the royal throne,—to Kamalā Kānta all these are of equal value, when in his heart thou dwellest."

3. Dewān Raghunātha Ray, born in 1750 A.D. at the village Chupi in Burdwan. His ancestors held the high function of Dewān in the court of the Maharajās of Burdwan, and on the death of his

---

* যখন যেমন রূপে রাখিবে আমারে।
সকলি সফল যদি না ভুলি তোমারে॥
জনম, করম, দুঃখ, সুখ করি মানি।
যদি নিরখি অন্তরে শ্যামা জলদ-বরণী।
বিভূতি ভূষণ, কি রতন মণি কাঞ্চন।
তরুতলে বাস, কি রাজ সিংহাসন,
কমলাকান্ত উভয় সম সাধন জননি,
নিবস যদি হৃদয় মন্দিরে গো মা॥"

father Dewan Vraja Kiçore, Raghunatha obtained the appointment in due course. He was a profound scholar in Sanskrit and Persian, and composed a considerable number of religious songs in Bengali. He died in 1836.

4. Dewan Rāmdulāla Nandi. He was born at Kalikaccha in Tippera in the year 1785. He acquired a mastery of Sanskrit, Persian and Bengali. He obtained the appointment of Sheristadār in the Noakhali Collectorate under Mr. Haliday; and after some time became the Minister in the Court of the Maharajā of Tippera. Rāma Dulāla died in the year 1851. Here is one of his songs.

Rāma Dulāla.

† "O Mother, I know that you play at magic with our souls.

---

† "ওগো জেনেছি, জেনেছি, তারা,
তুমি জান মা ভোজের বাজি।
যে তোমায় যেমনি ভাবে,
তাতে তুমি মা হও রাজি॥
মগে বলে ফরা, তারা, গর্ড বলে ফিরিঙ্গী যারা,
খোদা বলে ডাকে তোমায়,
মোগল, পাঠান, সৈয়দ, কাজী।
শাক্তে তোমায় বলে শক্তি,
শিব তুমি শৈবের উক্তি,
সৌর বলে সূর্য্য তুমি, বৈরাগী কয় রাধিকাজী।
গাণপত্য বলে গণেশ, যক্ষ বলে তুমি ধনেশ।
শিল্পী বলে বিশ্বকর্ম্মা, বদর বলে নায়ের মাঝি॥
শ্রীরাম দুলালে বলে, বাজি নয় এ জেন ফলে,
এক ব্রহ্ম দ্বিধা ভেবে,
মন আমার হয়েছে পাজি॥"

By whatever name one calls you, you seem to be pleased with it.

The Burmese call you Pharā ; the Europeans call you Lord; the Saiyads, the Pāthanas and the Moguls call you Khodā.

The Çāktas know you as Giver of all strength.

The Çaivas call you Çiva.

The Sauras call you Sun.

The Vaiṣṇavas worship you as Rādhikā.

You are Ganeça to Gānapatyas, Kuvera of the Yakṣas, Viçvakarmā of the artisan class ; and Bador of the boatmen.

Says Ramādulal, this is no miracle ;—
it is quite true that my mind has become debased by thinking the one supreme god to be many."

——o——

IV. The yātrās or popular theatres.

Unlike the *kavi*, a *yatra*-party consists of male performers only, the part of women being performed generally by youths. The old *yatras* were a sort of melodrama,* the dialogues being mainly conducted in songs. There was no scenic representation of any kind. On the bare ground, a large carpet was spread, and the actors appeared upon it, all at one time. They usually began their performance by playing on musical instruments only, unaccompanied by any vocal music. The deep voiced *khol* accompanied by the shrill clang of the *kartal* produced a loud musical chord which summoned the people of

* This word is used in its technical, not popular, sense.

Its defects and incongruities.

surrounding villages to assemble at the place of performance. This loud music would continue for a couple of hours, after which the play would begin in earnest. A green room, so to speak, was reserved for the actors to change their dress. Sometimes one would be observed to throw away his false whiskers, and dress himself as a woman, in full view of the audience; the faces were not very clean shaved, so that while playing the serious part of a princess or a lady of high rank, an actor might often be observed to bear on his chin remnants of the beard or moustache that had adorned his previous masculine part. The performers including those who were dressed as women, would sing in chorus; and the master-singer was always behind them and could sometimes be seen pulling the ear of some erring lad who could not pitch his tone correctly to the high notes of the musical instruments. Another actor, while delivering a speech, might be tempted by the sight of a *hooka*, and in the midst of a pathetic display of feeling, be seen to stop for a moment to snatch a puff of smoke, so that the first line of a song would coincide with the curl of smoke that issued from his mouth. Sometimes we may see the mother of the hero weeping over his dead body; suddenly she springs to her feet, and takes her place in the middle of the chorus, which bursts into a song of grief; at the same moment, the slain hero himself rises, in order to swell the volume of the music! The want of scenic representation was made up for by the simple declaration of the actor that he had now removed to a different place. Thus, Nārada the sage, who happens to be in the heaven of Viṣṇu, declares that he will now visit the

Vrindā groves, and, advancing a few steps from where he stood, begins to describe the scenes of *Vrindavana*, as if he had now actually traversed all the distance between heaven and earth. In these *yatras* of the past, the audience comprised people of all ranks, for it was a free entertainment to which all were welcome, held at the cost of the master of the house. Early comers generally occupied the front places, irrespective of their position, and late comers had the disadvantage of back seats; but people did not mind this. They often stood on their feet enjoying the songs for hours together without seeming to feel the inconveniences to which they were subject.

Redeemed by rich poetry.

Though defective in so many ways—and from a superficial point of view the whole performance was marked by incongruity and want of all æsthetic perception,—yet the old *yatras* had the power to captivate the soul and keep men and women transfixed for hours at a time. The songs describing the scenes of Baikuntha, the heaven of Viṣṇu, of Amarāvati, the heaven of Indra, or of the Alakā, the heaven of Kuvera, couched in rich poetic words and set to pleasing modes of music, made up for all want of painted scenes. They suggested romantic situations, and carried the audience to heights of imagination where no painter's brush could have led them. The outward anomalies, the defective and even grotesque elements, were all forgiven and forgotten. These songs, thrilling with pathos, gave life to the performance, and the audience laughed and cried as though they fully believed in the joys and sorrows of the characters of the play. A very familiar personality in the old *yatras* was

Radha; she would come with flowing tresses frenzied by Krisna's desertion, and address the flowers, Malati and Kunda, as if they were her friends, asking them where her Krisna was. She would then recollect the great love which Krisna bore to her; how he would play with her ringlets, saying "blessed am I in the touch of thy tresses"; how he would himself paint her feet with alta, and bedeck her hair with flowers and garlands, how when looking at her face tears would start into his eyes without any cause, and he would call them tears of joy. He, who could not bear a moment's parting, had now deserted her. The maids were calling him a knave, a hypocrete and faithless lover. But Radha could not bear that Krisna should be reviled by others, though she was dying for love of him.

Radha deserted by Krisna.

The master-singer is generally expert in the theological lore of the Vaisnavas. He comes frequently into the midst of the performers and interprets this love as divine love, making a little commentary aside. Chandravali, who was a rival of Radha, in Krisna love, comes to the Vrinda groves and sees that Radha is lying in a state of unconsciousness, the maids fanning her with lotus-leaves and weeping at her distress. Chandra would not at any other time have cared to see her rival, but now the common grief of parting with Krisna has turned her into a sympathiser and friend. She sees Radha, and sings:—

The master-singer.

The laments of Chandravali

*" How remarkably handsome is Radha! I never saw her so closely before. When she stood by the

*" এতই রূপের রূপসী রাই, আমি নয়ন ভরে দেখি নাই।
যখন বঁধুর বামে দাঁড়াইত, আবার হেসে হেসে কথা কইত,

side of Kriṣṅa, and smiled, and talked, how beautiful did she look! Kriṣṅa, lying on a bed of flowers, would seem to wear her on his bosom, as one wears a precious necklace. Alas, she, the beloved of Kriṣṅa, now lies in the dust! How fine, how peerless are her feet that Kriṣṅa was never weary of praising, those feet that he would softly touch to paint with scarlet *alta*. When these tender feet would trip over the thorny paths of the forest to meet with Kriṣṅa, one could almost have wished to place her own bare bosom on the road, so that she might have stepped on it."

The interpretation. When the singers had sung this song, the master-singer would approach and draw the attention of the audience to the description. He would say—"Rādhā's physical charms are not what the poet refers to. In all the points of this description, one may see that it is the love of Kriṣṅa that is described by the poet as constituting her beauty. Only when she was smiling and talking with Kriṣṅa, would she look charming in Chandrā's eyes, and not at any other time. Chandrā regrets her

---

তখন এইনা মুখে—মুখের কতই যেন শোভা হ'ত।
বঁধু থেকে কুসুম শয্যায়, হৃদয়ে রাখ্‌ত যায়,
বঁধুর সে ধন আজ ধূলায় গড়াগড়ি যায়॥
অতুল রাতুল কিবা চরণ দুখানি,
আল্‌তা পরা'ত বঁধু কতই বাখানি,
এ কোমল চরণে যখন চলিত হাঁটিয়ে,
বঁধুর দরশন লাগি গো অনুরাগে,—
হেন বাঞ্ছা হোত যে পাতিয়ে দেই হিয়ে॥"

Rāi Unmādinī by Kriṣṅa Kamala.

present condition, because she was the object of so much care to Krisña; she offers her own bosom for the treading of Rādhā's feet, when she may go out to meet *him!* In all this she indicates her love for Krisña as the only point that contributes to her beauty. Love for God can alone adorn a man—neither wealth, nor physical charms, nor power."

The pathos created by Krisña's going to Mathurā was the never-ending theme of the old *yatras*, and it was a matter, the lightest touch of which was sure to melt the hearts of all true Bengalis. Yaçodā, the mother of Krisña, wept, and said to her lord Nanda—

* 'O Prince of Gakula, I dreamt a dream; Krisña came to me and disappeared.'

and she details the dream by referring to little incidents which are full of tender pathos.

The shepherd boys sing in chorus.

The grief of the play-mates

† "Have you left us, O Krisña, because we took you for a common play-fellow, and did not pay you the tribute of worship that you deserved at our hands? How often, when playing, we quarrelled and abused you! Did you take these things to heart, and desert us, though we were so deeply devoted to you? We often beat you, or carried

---

*" শুন ব্রজরাজ, স্বপনেতে আজ, দেখা দিয়ে গোপাল কোথা লুকালে"

Svapnavilāsa by Krisña Kamala.

†" তাই ভেবে কি ভাইরে সুবল, ছেড়ে গেছে প্রাণের কানাই;
আমরা সামান্য ভেবে, কখন মান্য করি নাই।

you on our shoulders, and rode on yours. Often we ate first, and gave you the remnants, calling you by all familiar names. Have you, for all these, forsaken us, Oh beloved Krishna?"

Yātrās excelled the theatres.

So the shepherd boys sang; and as they sang they wept, and the audience was moved. All thought themselves in those Vrindā groves, where *Kadamva* trees rose upon the sight fringing the lovely horizon on the banks of the dark-watered Jumna,—those groves that the tears of the milk-maids and the shepherds have hallowed for ever. The *yatras* without any regular stage, without scenery, without the artistic display of costumes, could rouse emotions which now-a-days we scarcely experience, while witnessing semi-European performances given on the stages of the Calcutta theatres.

The Vidyā Sundara yātrās.

The subjects of the *yatras* were mainly episodes in the life of Krishna. There were, however, other subjects also taken up by different parties. The story of Vidyāsundara on the lines of Bhārata Chandra's poem, was adopted by a class of *yatrawalas*, of whom Gopāla Uriyā heads the list. The Vidyāsundara *yatras* had no serious element in them. They were in high favour with the light-brained aristocracy who enjoyed the humour, dances and

---

খেলা বেলায় করি দ্বন্দ্ব, কত যে বলেছি মন্দ,
সে মন্দ কি ভেবে মন্দ, ত্যজেছে ব্রজের সম্বন্ধ ॥
কত মেরেছি, ধরেছি, কাঁধে করেছি, চড়েছি
আপনি খেয়ে, খাওয়ায়েছি, তোতকার করেছি সবাই ॥"

Rāi Unmādinī by Krishna Kamala.

witty sayings in the play, and as I have said on a previous page, the songs and dances of Hira, the flower-woman, formed by far the most important and attractive features of the Vidyāsundara *yatras*.

Gopāla Uriyā was born about the year 1819 at Jajpur in Cuttack. When a boy of nineteen he came to Calcutta, and, being very poor, adopted the calling of a hawker,—selling bananas. One evening he was passing along a lane of Bowbazar Street, where Babu Rādhā Mohana Sarkār, a distinguished noble man, was busy with the rehearsal of a Vidyāsundara *yatra* which he had organised. Gopāla was crying 'good bananas sir,' and only for fun he was called in before the party, where question upon question was put to him. To the surprise of the jovial company, they found that the lad was remarkably witty, and had an excellent voice. He was at once admitted into the troupe, and soon after began to compose songs himself. Becoming trained in music by the favour of his patron Babu Rādhā Mohana Sarkār, he organized a party which far outdid the fame of all other Vidyāsundara *yatrawalas*. He died about the year 1859.

Gopāla Uriyā.

Besides the Vidyāsundara *yatras*, there were the Chandi *yatras*, the Mansār Bhāsān *yatras*, the Rāma *yatras* and other *yatras* which had for the subject-matter of their songs mythological stories from the Mahābhārata

Other yātrās.

There are no authentic records from which we may trace the early history of the *yatrawalas*.

From the time of Chaitanya, *yatras* have flourished in Bengal, and developed their melodramatic character.

A brief history of the yātrā-wālās.

The first great *yatrawala*, of whom we have any information, was Paramānanda Adhikārī, who lived in Bīrbhum more than 200 years ago. The subject of his play was Kāliya Damana. The next *yatrawala*, who earned a reputation in the same subject, was Sudāma Suvala Adhikāri. Lochana Adhikāri, who flourished after Sudāma had left the field, had two favourite subjects, in which he pre-eminently excelled. One was the Akrūra Saṇvada or the advent of Akrūra at Vrindāvana to take away Krișṅa and Valarāma, under orders of the King Kaṁsa of Mathura. The other subject was Nimāi Sannyāsa, or Chaitanya's taking the ascetic's vow. It is said that Lochana made so great an impression on Rājā Nava Kissen of Çobhābāzār and Babu Vanamāli Sarkār of Kumertuli, by his songs, that these noblemen under a sort of spell, made him gifts of immoderate amounts of money. Other noblemen of Calcutta, it is said, did not venture to engage the party fearing lest they also might be led, under infatuation, to pay him rewards beyond their means, as the two other noblemen had done. Govinda Adhikāri, an inhabitant of Krisnanagar, (1798 to 1870,) Pitāmvara Adhikāri of Kātwa and Kalāchand Pāl of Vikrampur, Dacca, were the latter-day luminaries in this field. Premchānd Adhikāri, Ānanda Adhikāri and Jaychandra Adhikāri of Pataihāt obtained celebrity in the Rāma *yatra*. Guru Prasāda Vallabha of Farāsdanga and Lāusen Bāḍala of Burdwan excelled in the Chandi *yatra* and the Manasār Bhāsāna *yatra* respectively.

But we have not yet named the greatest *yatrawala* that Bengal has ever seen. We have reserved a notice of Krisña Kamala Gosvāmi for the more elaborate treatment that he deserves at our hands.

The greatest of them,—Krisña Kamala; his life.

Krisña Kamala was born in 1810 at Bhājanghāta in the district of Nadia. He belonged to one of those few families of Vaidya Gosvāmies in Bengal who claimed Brāhmin disciples. Krisña Kamala's great ancestor Sadā Çiva, a friend of Chaitanya Deva, was reputed for his great piety. Krisña Kamala received his first lessons in Sanskrit grammar at Vrindāvana, where his father Muralidhara had taken him when only six years of age. He was a handsome boy, and by his pleasing manners attracted the notice of a millionaire who desired to adopt him as a son, and make him the heir to his vast fortune. On this, Muralidhara fled from Vrindāvana with his son, who was then only twelve years old.

His poems.

Returning home, Krisña Kamala to please his mother Jamunā Devi, wrote a melodrama on Chaitanya which greatly pleased the village people of Bhājanghata, who marked the author as a young prodigy. When in his twenty-fifth year, his father died, and the poet left Bhājanaghāta and came to Dacca with his patron and disciple Rāma Kiçore. He composed his great *yatra* poem, the Svapnavilāsa in 1835. It was at once taken up and played by the amateur parties of Dacca. The success, this work attained, was unique. The songs of Svapnavilāsa were in the mouth of every one in Eastern Bengal, and even now, though about a century has passed since the publication of the poem, there is scarcely any old man or woman amongst the higher classes of that place who has not at least some songs from the book by heart. In a country where a lyrical element predominates, and where devotional feelings are preferred to action, songs are bound to occupy the same place in the popular estimation, as does drama in other countries where work and not sentiment is the motto. We cannot look for a Garrick here. A Krișṅa Kamala or a Govinda Adhikāri will better fulfil the natural cravings of the soul that longs to hear of lofty sentiment and of the highest flights of love. In the preface to Vichitravilāsa, a subsequent *yatra* poem by Krișṅa Kamala, the author writes about Svapnavilāsa. *"The public probably liked the book; otherwise why should there be a sale of nearly 20,000 copies within so short a space of time?" The sale of 20,000 copies of the book within a few weeks in Eastern Bengal, where a demand for printed books had not yet been created, was quite a phenomenon at that time, and showed the wonderful popularity which the poem had attained.

The best *yatra* by Krișṅa Kamala, however, was his Rāi Unmādini which appeared shortly after the Svapnavilāsa. After this poem had seen the light,

---

*"বোধ হয় ইহাতে সাধারণের প্রীতি সাধিত হইয়াছে, নতুবা প্রায় বিংশতি সহস্র পুস্তক স্বল্প দিনের মধ্যে নিঃশেষিত হওয়ার সম্ভাবনা কি?"

there were produced in succession the Bharatamilana, the Nimāi Sannyāsa, the Goṣṭha and other works.

The Bharatamilana describes that episode of the Rāmāyaṇa in which Bharata meets Rāma in the forest with prayers for his return to Ayodhyā and acceptance of the kingdom. The Nimāi Sannyāsa describes Chaitanya's entering into the holy order of ascetics. All other works relate to episodes of the life of Kriṣṇa. His two best works are the Rāi Unmādinī and the Svapnavilāsa, and in both of them he describes in highly poetic language the woes of the inmates of Vrindāvana and especially those of Rādhā caused by parting from Kriṣṇa. And we may observe that in these poems the author, while giving the noblest expression to the tender feelings of a woman's love, takes the real cue from Chaitanya's life. We have read many speeches in the poems attributed to Rādhā which in reality have been borrowed from Chaitanya-Charitāmrita and other works on Chaitanya, only rendered into more refined forms, as the matter passed out of the hands of biographers into those of a poet. The Rādhā described by Kriṣṇa Kamala typifies and represents the frenzied condition of Chaitanya in divine communion and has been portrayed in a very exquisite form. Kriṣṇa never came back to the Vrindā groves, but the Bhāvasammilana or union in spirit is described by all Vaiṣṇava poets. The significance of this is that a material loss, though fraught with pain for the time being, is bound to prove a spiritual gain to the faithful in the long run. Our souls feel a craving for love, **The conception of union in spirit.**

and imagine that this desire is satisfied by union with some particular individual. But circumstances are not within our control, and when we encounter sorrow in our love, the mind seeks happiness in its own resources, and under favourable condition of spiritual development, may find the fountain of love within itself,—a perennial stream which never dries up. This is the Bhāvasammilana, and in it the lost are found permanently, and the heart satisfied for ever. Nature offers in all directions what seemed to have been lost in a particular spot, and the blessed soul rises from its external sorrow stronger, freer, and happier, realising union which can never be interrupted. The Vaiṣṅava poets were always averse to tragedy; but as they did not find it mentioned any where in the sacred texts that Kriṣṅa ever returned in the flesh to the Vrinda groves, they created this Bhavasammilana in its place,—the ever-blissful subjective union, in which the mind, freed from the trammels of its material environment, revels in a delight, the fountain of which is within one's self.

We have already on pages 532-536 and 728-730 quoted passages from Kriṣṅa Kamala's works. I give below an extract from his *Sankritan* poems in which the shepherd-boys importune Yoçodā to allow him to go with them to the forest.

The importunities of the playmates of Kriṣṅa.

*" Make Kriṣṅa ready, O mother Yoçoda, to go with us to the fields !

" The time is already up—the time for our sport.

---

*ও মা যশোদা দে মা দে সাজায়ে,
তোর শ্যামচাঁদ লয়ে যাই বনে।

"How long must we delay our woodl-and games?

"Give us your Krişṅa, mother, for the day. You ask, what care shall we take of him?

"We shall carry his flute and his rod; and we shall place him in our midst.

"He is so merry! He dances as he goes!

"When the rays of the sun are strong, we shall take him to the cool shadow of a tree, and let him rest; and we shall do our best to give him pleasure.

"If the way is thorny, we can carry him on our shoulders.

"And if we see him pale, we shall give him the fruits of the forest to eat.

"If he goes not with us, whom shall we adorn with wild flowers under the cool shadow of the *tamala* tree?

"Whom shall we crown with peacock feathers, and whose fine hair shall we plait with the *bakula* buds?

খেলার বেলা যায় মা বয়ে,
কখন যাবে গোচারণে।
ওমা সুধাও, সুধাও গো, তোর শ্যামসুধাকরে,
কানাইর বেণু বেত্র লয়ে আমরা যাব ব'য়ে,
মাঝে নেচে চলে নীলরতনে;
দিবাকরকর প্রবল হইলে,
লয়ে কালশশী বসি তরুতলে,
কমল বল্লভে ও প্রাণবল্লভে,
শোয়াইয়া সেবি রাখালগণে।
সাধের কানাই না হলে, কদম্বের মূলে, কারে
সাজাইব বনফুল দিয়ে।

" The sound of whose flute shall charm our ears, and whose embrace shall cool our bodies ?

" The peacock, the cuckoo, the bee, the *Sadi* and the *Suka* in the forest-bowers are waiting with heads uplifted to catch the sound of Krisṇa's flute.

" Help him to dress in his yellow cloth in the manner in which he appears peculiarly charming, O mother, and allow him to come with us.

" In the green pasture under the *kadamva* tree, we shall make him sit, and weave a garland with the *kunda*, the *sephalika*, the *ketaki*, the *mallika*, the *nagakesara*, the *tagara*, the *champaka*, the blue lily and the *kadamva* flower, and put it round his neck.

শিখিপুচ্ছকুলে. বকুলমুকুলে, চূড়া বেঁধে দিব কার
চিকণ চুলে।
কার বংশীরবে শ্রবণ জুড়াবে,
কার আলিঙ্গনে অঙ্গ শীতল হবে।
শিখি-সারি-শুক-মধুকর-পিক
সকলে উৎসুক আছে উর্দ্ধমুখে।
ধড়া ক'রে বেঁধে দেগো, পীতাম্বরে, পীতাম্বর।
বনফুলে সাজাইব আমরা নিয়ে বনান্তর ॥
গোচারণ স্থলে, কদম্বের মূলে,
বসাইয়া সাথে দিব সাজাইয়ে ;
কুন্দ সেফালিকে, কেতকী, মল্লিকে,
নাগকেশর, টগর, চম্পকে,
নীল শতদলে, কদম্ব মুকুলে,
গেঁথে হার গলে দিব পরাইয়ে।

"Do not hesitate, O mother, but allow him to go with us !

"Look at the cows ; they will neither graze, nor drink, if they see not the sweet face of Krișṅa.

"They will not even low, so long as they do not hear Krișṅa's flute,—but will remain as mute as statues.

"When the flute of Krișṅa is sounded, how quick and great is the response from all quarters.

"The sages see their highest visions, the stone melts and the Jumna stops her course.

"Your son, O mother, has magic arts ! If he sounds his flute, the very cows understand and instantly obey his command."

Krișṅa Kamala lived the high life worthy of a true Vaișṅava. He died in 1888, at the advanced age of 78, but all his best works had been written

---

নিঃসন্দেহে দে মা কানাই, ধরি তোর যুগল চরণে,
ওমা ধেনু না দেখিলে কানুর বিধুমুখ,—
অধোমুখে রয় গো, মুখে না লয় তৃণগণে।
যখন শুনে বেণুরব, করে ধেনু রব,
নহিলে নীরব রয় সকলে।
কানাই যখন করে বেণু ধ্বনি, ত্রিভুবনে হয়
জয় জয় ধ্বনি,
মুনিগণ' মন করে আকর্ষণ, পাষাণ গলে, হয়
যমুনা অচল।
তোমার কুমার মাগো, না জানি কি গুণ জানে,
বেণুর সঙ্কেত করে বনে চরায় ধেনুগণে।"

within the first fifties of the 19th century; hence we include him within the range of our treatise. When Kriṣṅa Kamala was brought to the Ganges, at Chinsura and his last moment arrived, his eldest son Nitya Gopāla Gosvāmī wept like a child, lamenting that after the death of the master of the house, he would be quite unfit to govern it. The dying poet, who had till then retained his senses and power of speech, addressed his weeping son and said*:—"My son, do not weep. I really never knew that I was the master of the house. I knew you all to belong to God and as such it was my duty to offer my humble services to you all my life. Though you were my children, I kept away from my mind the vanity of knowing myself as the master. Guide yourselves in the light of this principle, and you will be ever happy."

The dying poet's words.

Yātrā poems with prose.

We have a few *yatra* poems interspersed with prose by authors who lived in the 17th and 18th centuries. Some of these are mentioned below:—

1. Duti Saṇvāda by Rāma Vallabha.
2. Vidyā Sundara Gāyan. The name of the author is not known.

Here is a song of Hirā, the flower-woman from this work.

---

*"বৎস, কাতর হইও না। তোমরা গিরিধারীর; এই স্থানে এতাবৎ আমি তোমাদের সেবা করিয়াছি, পালন করি নাই। প্রতিপালনের কর্ত্তা গিরিধারীকে জানিও। এই ভাব লইয়া সংসার করিও; কষ্ট পাইবে না।"

From the biography of Kriṣṅa Kamala,
by his son Nitya Gopāla Gosvāmī.

* "I am but one, still to how many do I give pleasure !

"All is incomplete where I am not.

"When I do not go to the good damsels of the neighbourhood, interviews with their lovers can not be arranged, and the pain caused by separation kills them.

"If I do not come to the garden, the flowers and buds are all plucked by unknown hands."

3. Manasā Mañgala Gāyan. This works begins with a conversation between the manager of the *yatra* party, and a constable of the Rājā's palace where the *yatra* is to be held.

† "*Const.* Who are you making an uproar here, at this late hour of the night ?

Manager. We are *yatrawalas*, and pray who are you, brother, yourself ?

Const. I am the Rājā's constable.

---

* "একলা প্রাণে ক'দিক যায়, পড়েছি বিষম দায়।
যে দিকে না চেয়ে দেখি, সে দিকে সব ব'য়ে যায়॥
পাড়াতে না গেলে পরে, বিরহিণী প্রাণে মরে,
মালঞ্চে না গেলে পরে, কুসুম কলি সব লুটে ন্যা'য়॥"

† "জমাদার। তোমরা কোন লোক হে, মাহারাজকা নগরমে এত্‌তা রাতমে ঝুমঝাম্ কিয়া ?

যাত্রাওয়ালা। হে, আমরা যাত্রাওয়ালা গাইন হে। আরে ভাই, তোম্ লোক কোন্ হে।

জমাদার। আরে হাম্ মহারাজকা জমাদার হে।

Manager. And, answer me! Where are you going, at this late hour of the night?

Const. I am going to call Kalua, the sweeper of the palace.

[*Enters Kalua, the Sweeper.*]

Song (in Hindi).

"I do not know who it is that calls me.

"For the whole day I have been in attendance at the palace.

"I have swept the roads, and removed all dirt and filth.

"Why I am called again I do not know."

Farcical episodes. In old *yatras*, farcical episodes were introduced, by way of relief, in intervals of a serious play, and the above indicates the way they were introduced.

A *yatra* performance usually commenced at 4 A.M., and ended at noon, thus lasting for 8 hours or more; of this, as I have said, the first one or two hours were spent in playing a high pitched clamarous music, the intention of which was to advertise the commencement of the performance to the

---

যাত্রাওয়ালা। আরে রাতমে কাহা চল্‌তে হো।

জমাদার। আরে হাম্ কালুয়া হাড়ী বোলানেকো আনে চলতা হায়।

কালুয়া হাড়ীর গান।

"মেরা কোন্ বোলা হে চিন্‌তে নারি,
সারা রোজ হুজুরমে দিয়ে হাজিরি।
ঝাড়ু ভি দিয়া, সাফ্‌ ভি কিয়া,
ফের কিস্তরে বোলাতে হে বুঝ্‌তে নারি॥"

villagers. The farcical scenes which were introduced at intervals were generally called সং, and the children who accompanied their mothers to the place of performance, and who could not understand anything of the main play, were greatly interested in সং. In fact they would doze the whole of the time that was occupied in the enactment of the serious portions of the performance, and hailed these farcical scenes with great delight, noting each point with gaping mouths, and sometimes indicating their high gratification by the merry sounds of juvenile laughter.

——o——

V. The three great poets with whom the age closed—Dāçarathi—Rāmanidhi Gupta—Içwara Gupta.

Before we close the narrative of our old literature, and enter upon that which is stamped with English influence, we propose to say something about a few more writers of the old school, and notice the folk tales prevalent in the country from ancient times. Let us first deal with the three poets who lived in the early part of the 19th century. Though by the time they flourished, English rule had become settled in the country, yet their writings bear no traces of European influence. They belonged to the old school and exercised a great influence on contemporary society and literature. These three poets are 1. Dāçarathi Rāi 2. Rāmnidhi Gupta and 3. Içwara Chandra Gupta.

Dāçarathi Rāi.

Dāçarathi Rāi was born at Vandāmura in Burdwan in the year 1804. His father Devī Prasāda Rāi was a man of small means. So the young poet lived with one of his maternal uncles at the village of Pilā where he ultimately settled. He got a smattering of Bengali and became an apprentice in the office of an indigo-planter at Sākāi on a monthly pay of Rs. 3. Here he fell in love with a low-caste woman of ill fame. Her name was Akṣaya Pātini, and she was commonly called Akā Vāi. This woman had organised a party of *kaviwalas* for whom songs and speeches were now composed by our poet. This made him very unpopular at home, and on one occasion in an open competition of extempore verse-making he was lashed by the taunts of a rival *kaviwala*. The mother and uncle of Dāçarathi insisted on his leaving his mean occupation, associated as it was, with an ignominious passion. Dāçu could not withstand the importunities of his relations, least of all, of his mother; for inspite of the low calling that he had adopted, he was a good Brāhmin and his family enjoyed considerable respectability in the neighbourhood. Dāçu left the party of *kaviwalas*, and became the author and inventor of a peculiar kind of doggerel—called *Panchali*. These *Panchalis* took for their main subject those incidents in Kriṣṅa's life which in the popular belief of Bengal were indispensable to songs. But Dāçu adopted other subjects also favoured by the moderns, and possessing contemporary interest. Such for instance are his poems on Widow marriage, on the Lily and the Bee, and other subjects.

Panchali.

The popularity of these poems, which he made it his profession to recite and sing, was immense throughout the country, and though he had started by charging only Rs. 3 a night, for reciting and singing one of his *Panchalis*, he was able to increase his fee to Rs. 150 per night, and the number of engagements that he made was so large that he had to refuse many. He grew rich in his old age, made a nice garden-house at Pĩlā on the bank of the Ganges, and lived comfortably till his death in 1857.

Dāçu Rāi's *Panchali* shows an amazing command over the Bengali language. For one who had had no Sanskrit education and had acquired only an indifferent knowledge of Bengali, his works deserve high praise. Alliteration and punning were his *forte*, and his verses, which flow with remarkable facility, sparkle with humour and wit. The words that he chooses are generally Sanskritic, though not pompous, and the effect produced on the ear by their combination is singularly pleasing. When he is vulgar, we know that he is addressing the mob, to whom the grossest obscenities would be welcome, and he spares no jokes, no hit, however indecent, to pander to their vile tastes. He was essentially a poet of the masses. By his swift doggerels, full of alliterations, by his obscenities, by the display of wit which was often of the coarsest kind, we know that the scum of the society were gathered to hear him, and his aim was to please them at any cost. His poems are full of display—of words, of thoughts, and of wit. They prove that he was trying to create an impression, and was always conscious of his brilliant talent. Take for instance this passage :—

Alliteration, punning and vulgarities.

* "Faith adorns a scholar ; lightning adorns the cloud ; the husband's love adorns a woman ; the sacrificial ashes adorn an ascetic ; the crops adorn the earth ; its own lustre adorns a jewel ; the fruits adorn a tree ; water adorns a river ; the lily adorns water ; and the bee adorns a lily ; his sweet hum adorns the bee ; the eyes adorn the body ; and charity adorns a kind-hearted man, if he gives it with sweet words."

These couplets while scarcely bearing more than any commonplace sense, are, however, remarkable for their jingling alliteration—the rhyming being singularly happy. The poet goes on with his catalogue of what adorns what, for pages, and it appears that unless one forces him to stop, he will never end this strain. Many such verses would be delivered extempore during a single performance, and bear evidence of being carried to the utmost limit of the poet's command over the language, because he was being clapped, cheered, and encouraged to continue. The mob was delighted by the free display of his verbal resources,

Goes on, being clapped and cheered.

---

* "পণ্ডিতের ভূষণ ধর্ম্মজ্ঞানী, মেঘের ভূষণ সৌদামিনী।
সতীর ভূষণ পতি, রত্নের ভূষণ জ্যোতি।
মৃত্তিকার ভূষণ শস্য, যোগীর ভূষণ ভস্ম,
বৃক্ষের ভূষণ ফল, নদীর ভূষণ জল,
জলের ভূষণ পদ্ম। পদ্মের ভূষণ মধুকর,
মধুকরের ভূষণ গুণ্‌ গুণ্‌ স্বর,
উভয়ে উভয় প্রেম বদ্ধ
শরীরের ভূষণ চক্ষু, যাতে জগৎ হয় দৃষ্ট।
দাতার ভূষণ দান করে, বলে বাক্য মিষ্ট॥"

and the poet lost all sense of proportion under the encouragement he received.

He describes many incidents in Krişņa's life. The Prabhāsa scene, for instance, had been worked up to the tenderest pathos by earlier poets. Dāça-rathi, then, began by describing how a Brahmin, who was grovelling in abject poverty, went to Krişņa owing to pressure from his wife to beg for alms, and came back dissappointed. The story is told with much artistic effect, and we can understand how the audience would enjoy it. But the serious portion of the Prabhāsa scene must follow, and the thoughtful amongst the audience were sitting waiting for it. The poet however dragged the incidental story of the Brahmin beggar to such an inordinate length, that the whole time was taken up by it, and he began and ended his Prabhāsa with this single incident introduced by way of diversion and originally meant to supplement the main subject. Dāçarathi had no sense of proportion. In the atmosphere of the vulgar he lost all idea of time and place, and if he claims a place in literature, it is only by right of his sparkling and artistic language, which makes his shortcomings and scurrilities half-pardonable in our eyes. The art of writing and appreciating literature was no longer confined to the higher classes. The crowd also began to feel that Bengali literature was theirs. It was the season, as it were, for a flood-tide in our letters, and the evil was inevitably mingled with the pure to cover the whole range of the Bengali language.

Without any sense of proportion.

The suggestive hits of a sharp wit, the majestic sweep of Sanskrit metres, the lofty spirit of self-sacrifice and higher ideals attracted the upper classes of society; but the coarser elements to suit the taste of the mob were inevitable, and thus the grotesque found place side by side with beauty, indecency with humour and the absurd with the natural. Dāçarathi Rāi was essentially a poet for the masses. In his poem on the Lily and the Bee, the bee, as the lover, being angry with the lily, declares himself an ascetic, and betakes himself to the forest,*—"the lover of the lily, like the sage Çukadeva, went in pensive mood, and gave heed to no one calling him." This poem is an inexhaustible fund of jest and wit, though towards the end it grows extremely vulgar.

The Lily and the Bee.

But I am afraid I have not done justice to Dāçarathi by calling him a poet for the masses only. Curiously enough, he is the author of many songs which breathe lofty religious sentiment and may almost be placed side by side with those of Rāma Prasāda and other saintly poets; with his perverse life, his vulgarities and his conceited style of writing, this element was certainly most inconsistent; yet he was a man capable of pious sentiment and devotional feeling; and whatever may have been his ways and manners, there was an under current of faith in him which comes unmistakably to light in his religious songs. The song beginning with.—† "None is accountable, O Mother, for my sins.

His religious songs.

"With my own hands I dug a tank, and in it I have drowned myself."—

---

* "চলিলেন পদ্মিনী স্বামী যেন শুকদেব গোস্বামী
ডাকলে কথা ক'ন না কারো সনে।"

† "দোষ কারু নয় গো মা
আমি স্বখাদ সলিলে ডুবে মরি শ্যামা।"

—glistens as it were with the tears of true remorse of a penitent soul. I quote below another song.

† "Find out a means, O divine Mother, for this humble soul, that it may finally rest at thy feet.

"Mayst thou grant me this boon, that at my death, the five elements, that constitute this mortal frame, may join the five places favoured by thee.

"May the etherial portions of my body fill the space of thy holy temple, and the clay of this clay-vessel form a part of thy sacred image as made by the potters.

"May my breath mix with the air of the fans with which the priests fan thy image.

"May my fire be mingled with the sacrificial fire kindled for thee, and the watery portion of my body be joined to the water with which the feet of thine image are washed.

"By thus being resolved and thus dedicated, O Mother, may I never come back to this world to be born and to die."

---

† "দুর্গে, কর মা এ দীনের উপায়, যেন পায়ে-স্থান পায়।
আমার এ দেহ পঞ্চত্বকালে, তব প্রিয় পঞ্চস্থলে,
আমার পঞ্চভূত যেন মিশায়।
শ্রীমন্দিরে অন্তর আকাশ যেন যায়।
এমৃত্তিকা যায় যেন ত্বৎপ্রতিমায়, মা মোর পবন তব চামর
ব্যজনে যায়, হোমাগ্নিতে মমাগ্নি যেন মিশায়।
আমার জল যেন যায় পাদ্যজলে, যেন ভবে যায়, বিমলে,
দাশরথির জীবন মরণ দায়। "

Another song that he is said to have composed on the eve of his death may be taken as a sort of last will and testament. He addresses his brother Tinakaḍi, familiarly called Tinu, in the song.

*"Go back, all of you, and yourself also, dear brother Tinu.

"I came alone and alone must I go.

"It is not in my power to return home with you, nor have I any wish to do so.

"I bequeath to you all my property—my house, my lands, and garden-house and all the effects that I possess. You are now their sole proprietor.

The last song.

"Use this inheritance with discretion and wisdom: and be pleased, O brother, to look after my poor widow and maintain her.

"You seem to think that I am alone and helpless. But I have no need of pity at this moment. I am serene and happy in the arms of my divine Mother."

---

*"তোরা ফিরে যা ভাই তিনু রে,
আমি যাব না, যেতে পারব না,
ভবে এসেছি একা, আমার একা যেতে হবে রে।
আমার যত কিছু টাকা, কড়ি,
ঘর দরজা, বাগান বাড়ী,
সকল ধনের অধিকারী, তিনকড়ি ভাই তুমি রে।
হয়ে বিচক্ষণ, ক'রো রে রক্ষণ,
ঘরে র'ল বিধবা রমণী, তারে অন্ন দিওরে।
তোমরা সবে ভাব একা,
আমি কিন্তু নইরে একা,
বসে আছি আমি মায়ের কোলেরে।"

I give below a list of Daçarathi's works :—

Daçarathi's works.

1. Janmāṣṭami of Çrī Kriṣṇa.
2. Nandotsava.
3. Çrī Kriṣṇer Gosthalīlā.
4. Çrī Rādhikār Darpachūrṇa.
5. Vastra-harana.
6. Nava-nārikunjara.
7. Kalanka-bhanjana.
8. Māna-bhanjana.
9. Akrura Samvāda.
10. Māthura.
11. Duti-samvāda.
12. Nanda Vidāya.
13. Uddhava Samvāda.
14. Rukminī Harana.
15. Satyabhāmār Vrata.
16. Satyabhāmār Darpachūrṇa.
17. Sudarçana Chakra and Garuḍer Darpachūrṇa.
18. Draupadir Vastra-harana.
19. Durvāçar Pāraṇa.
20. Çrī Rām Chandrer Vivāha.
21. Rāmer Vana-gamana o Sitā-haran.
22. Sitā Anveṣana.
23. Tarani Sen Vadha.
24. Lakṣṇmaner Çaktiçela.
25. Rāvana-vadha.
26. Rāma Chandrer Deçāgamana.
27. Lava Kuçer Yuddha.
28. Dakṣa Yajña.
29. Bhagavatī ebaṁ Gangār Kondala.
30. Çiva Vivāha.
31. Āgamani.

32. Kāçi Khanda.
33. Bhagīratha kartrik Gangā Ānayana.
34. Mārkander Chandi.
35. Mahiṣāsurer Yuddha.
36. Kamale-Kāminī.
37. Vāmana Bhikṣā
38. Prahlāda Charitra.
39. Çākta o Vaiṣṅaver Dvandva.
40. Vasante Viraha Varṅana.
41. Viraha.
42. Kali Rajār Upākhyān o Chāri-yiār.
45. Navin Chānd o Sonāmani,
46. Stri Puruṣer Dvandva.
47. Nalinī Bhramarokti.
48. Venger Viraha.
49. Miscellaneous songs.
50. Pañchālir Vyakhyā.

In an exhaustive compilation of Daçarathi's works lately published by the Vangavasi Office, Calcutta, we altogether counted 50,000 lines.

Rāma Nidhi Gupta.

Rama Nidhi Gupta, popularly known as Nidhu Babu, was born at Chāñptā in the year 1738. His father was a physician, and earned a small pittance by his profession. At the birth of the poet, the family had removed from Chāñptā to Kumartuli and settled there. Ram Nidhi received a sound education in Persian and Bengali, and acquired, besides, a smattering of English. His father placed him under the care of a European missionary, but the boy paid only little attention to the English language which his parents wanted him to learn, and devoted his whole time to the

His family history. His life and songs.

cultivation of Indian music. Being possessed of a sweet voice he very soon attained fame as a singer and became musically highly accomplished. When twenty years of age he obtained an appointment in the Collectorate at Chāprā where he worked for few years. Music as a science was cultivated with great zeal in Northern India during the decline of the Moslem power. The Mahomedan Chiefs and Nawābs lost their warlike qualities and became addicted to pleasures of all sorts, and highly favoured music. At Chāprā Rāma Nidhi came in contact with a well-known Moslem singer and under his instruction, coupled with his natural proclivities, soon acquired poficiency in Mussulmān music. He came back to Bengal with a resolve to compose songs in Bengali after Sari Miā whose favourite tune—the *tappa* was very popular at the time in the North Western Provinces.

Nidhu Bābu saw that Bengali songs, the Vidyā Sundara alone excepted, had always hitherto related to religious matters. Our love songs had for their theme amours of Rādhā and Krisṅa and formed part of the theological literature of the Vaiṣṅavas. Nidhu Bābu introduced a novelty; in him the higher emotions of love stood on their own basis, requiring no justification by religious reference. Out of this conviction he sang and his utterances have a directness and sincerity which make him unique amongst our song-writers. His style is not marked by any elaboration. The brief and clear expression of thought is always his object,—never the laboured or fantastic conceits of language.

His *tappas*, as his songs are generally called, after the scale adopted by him, have human love for their subject, and the high spirit of idealism which breathes through them, coupled with the charms of a novel melody, elicited the appreciation of the educated community of Bengal. His verses were never popular in the sense in which those of Rāma Prasāda and Daçarathi had been so. The latter commanded appreciation amongst all sections of Bengali Society, but Nidhu Bābu's *tappas* were mainly admired by the higher classes, who knew something of music as a science and had the culture to enter into the spirit of his exceedingly refined ideas, expressed as these were with laconic brevity. The masses still had the notion that no song was worth hearing which did not bear some explicit reference to religion in it. In a collection of songs published in 1905 by Bābu Durgā Dās Lāhiḍi the number of Nidhu Bābu's songs inserted is 472, and this does not indicate one-tenth of the number composed by him. They are generally brief,—ordinarily taking not more than eight lines, while there are many that have four lines only. But however short they may be, one is sure to find a complete idea in each of his songs. A lively emotion or a fine thought is put into charming language and they are as suggestive as they are brief. They remind us of the short and sweet love-lyrics of Robert Burns.

Nidhu Bābu never says any thing vulgar. He has always an elevated notion of love and gives us only the highest forms of tender sentiment. I here quote a few examples;—

*" I love you, not that you may love me in return !

" It has become my very nature to love you and you alone.

" I long for a sight of the smile on your lips, and for that I come here every day,

" O, do not mistake me, dear ! I come to see you, not that you may see me !"

(2)

†" How shall I tell her how deeply I love her ?

" On seeing her I feel a gladness that words can not describe.

" When she is not present, my eyes fill in tears, and when she comes I feel like one who has found a precious jewel, and knows not where to hide it."

(3)

‡" How am I to forget her :—

" Have I not offered my soul to her, knowing her for my own ?

---

*" ভাল বাসিবে বলে, ভালবাসিনে।
আমার স্বভাব এই, তোমা বই আর জানিনে।
বিধুমুখে মধুর হাসি, দেখ্‌তে বড় ভালবাসি,
তাই দেখে যেতে আসি, দেখা দিতে আসিনে॥"

(২)

†" কত ভালবাসি তারে, সই, কেমনে বুঝাব,
দরশনে পুলকিত মম অঙ্গ সব।
যতক্ষণ নাহি দেখি, রোদন করয়ে আঁখি,
দেখিলে কি নিধি পাই কোথায় রাখিব॥"

(৩)

‡" তারে ভুলিব কেমনে,
প্রাণ সঁপিয়াছি যারে আপন জেনে।

" How can I forget that image which with love's brush I painted on my heart with the utmost care?

" They tell me ' she has forgotten you; why do you not then forget her?'

" I shall forget her only when death destroys my memory."

(4)

*" Even before my death, my heart is set aflame.

" May this anguish, that burns me, leave her untouched.

" In my heart I have built a funeral fire, and my grief supplies the fuel.

" I am being consumed in the fire of my love. But may she rest in peace!"

(5)

†" When she is absent I plan to be angry with her; but when again I look upon her face, I forget myself.

আর কি সে রূপ ভুলি, প্রেমতুলি করে তুলি,
হৃদয়ে রেখেছি লিখে, অতি যতনে,
সবাই বলে আমারে, সে ভুলেছে ভুল তারে,
সেদিন ভুলিব তারে, যে দিন লবে শমনে।"

(৪)

*না হতে পতন তনু, দহন হইল আগে।
আমার এ অনুতাপ তারে যেন নাহি লাগে।
চিতে চিতা সাজাইয়ে, তাহে দুখ তৃণ দিয়ে,
আপনি হতেছি দগ্ধ, আপনারি অনুরাগে॥"

(৫)

†সাধিলে করিব মান কত মনে করি,
দেখিলে তাহার মুখ তখনি পাসরি।

"Those eyes, that had resolved to turn away from her, surrender themselves, so soon as she approaches, losing all self-control."

(6)

*" Oh why is there this yearning in my heart to see him ?

" If I miss him for a moment, tears come to my eyes,

" The tongue of slander pursues me, and I glory in it.

" This evil repute seems to me like an ornament.

" My very life is leaving me for love. But he alas, cares nothing for me ! His conduct is indescribable. Why do I love him ? You ask me. I myself know not why !"

(7)

†" How happy I should be, if only my beloved would love me in return !

" The scentless *kinsuka* flower would then become sweet-scented.

অভিমানে কহে আঁখি, আর না হইব সুখী,
দরশনে হণ পুনঃ অধীন তাহারি ।

(৬)

* " তারে দেখিতে এত সাধ কেন
তিলেক না হেরি যদি সজল নয়ন ।
আভরণ করিয়াছি লোকের গঞ্জনা,
তাহার কারণে মরি, সে নহে আপনা ।
তাহার রীতের কথা অকথ্য কথন
তবে যে ভুলেছে মন, জানি না কি গুণে ॥ "

(৭)

† " তবে প্রেমে কি সুখ হ'ত
আমি যারে ভালবাসি সে যদি ভালবাসিত

"The thorny *ketaki* would grow without thorns.

"The sandal tree would have flowers, and the sugar-cane would bear fruits."

But how can I convey the impression made on the mind by these *tappas* when they are sung? It appears as if a voice were heard out of the regions of blessedness where self is completely immerged in love.

Nidhu Bābu married a girl wife in the village of Sukhachara when he was only twenty. A son was born to the pair in 1765. The child died, when only three years old, and his mother survived him only a few months. Soon after the death of this wife Nidhu Bābu married again. His new bride was a resident of Jorāsānko in Calcutta. But she also died a few months after her marriage in 1768. Nidhu Bābu was only thirty years old at the time; but he could by no means be persuaded to marry again. Twenty years passed from this time, and in the year 1788 the widower was compelled by friendly intervention to take a third wife from the village Varijahāti in the district of Howra. He became the father of four sons and two daughters by this marriage. He died in 1825 at the age of 87.

Died in 1825.

Içvara Gupta.

Dāçarathi was pre-eminently a poet of the masses. Rāma Nidhi's love songs were appreciated and sung by that section of the community which delighted in higher music and in the literature of refined

---

কিংশুক শোভিত ঘ্রাণে, কেতকী কণ্টক বিনে,
ফুল হতে চন্দনে, ইক্ষুতে ফল ফলিত॥"

sentiment. Içvar Chandra Gupta was the idol of the educated Bengali Hindus of his period. He was a great figure,—in fact the most remarkable literary personality of his age. It was his encouragement that inspired Bankima Chandra, Rangalāla, Dinavandhu and other young aspirants to literary fame who all served their first apprenticeship in Bengali by writing in the monthly *Prabhâkara* edited by Içvar Chandra.

His life.

Curiously enough, this writer was no scholar, though his voice was so authoritative in the Bengali literature of his time. In his early years he neglected his studies, and was given up for a lost child.

Içvara Chandra was born in 1811 at Kāñchrāpārā in the district of Twenty-four Parganas. His father Hari Mohan Gupta was not a man of means; he earned the small pittance of Rs. 8 a month as clerk in an indigo factory at Selidaha; but he had some small landed property in his native village, and the family was mainly dependent upon this.

Içvara Chandra showed courage, so early as five years of age. One night the lad was passing through a place supposed to be haunted by ghosts; it was a dark night, and a tall man, passing by, tumbled over him. The child was not daunted by what others of his age would certainly have taken for a ghost, but he boldly stood up and asked 'Who are you, my man?.' When he was ten years old, his mother died. His father lost no time in taking a second wife. The step-mother was introduced to young Içvara Chandra, who threw a brick at her by way of first greeting, expressing his great indignation at the conduct of his father. His uncle was so angry at this behaviour that he gave him a sound thrashing with his shoes. Young Içvara sulkily bore the punishment and shutting himself up in a small room, did not come out for the whole day.

Married to an ugly girl.

His father Hari Mohan Gupta not only gave him a step-mother whom he did not like, but married him, when only fifteen, to Durgāmani Devi, an ugly idiotic girl who stammered in her speech. The reason for his father's favouring this girl was that her pedigree was noble,—a point which at one time carried high favour with Hindu fathers.

Içvara Chandra's career in school soon came to a close, and he became notorious for his negligence in his studies and for his rowdisms. All gave him up for lost, and he had no better opinion of himself,

A lost child and soreness of heart

He was unfortunate in life,—in his early years as a motherless child, and in manhood as the husband of a wife who was no companion, but rather a troublesome burden, always keeping afresh a disappointment than which in youth nothing can be greater.

The result is the soreness of heart and spirit of satire which characterise his poems. He became a misanthrope and took revenge upon the world by jeering unsparingly at all classes of people. He found no happiness in the nuptial tie, and Bābu Bankima Chandra Chatterjee, his distinguished biographer writes of him :—

*"He was lacking in that education of soul which the company of women gives to a man; he

---

*"যে শিক্ষা স্ত্রীলোকের নিকট পাইতে হয়, তাহা তাঁহার হয় নাই; যে উন্নতি স্ত্রীলোকের সংসর্গে হয়, স্ত্রীলোকের প্রতি

lacked in the edifying influence which admiration and love for the softer sex causes in youthful minds. Womankind was the subject of his constant abuse."

But we shall deal with the merits of his literary composition in their proper place.

A born poet.

It is said that when only three years old, he composed a couplet, to the great admiration of his relations, describing the sort of life he was leading in Calcutta.

*" Mosquitoes by night and flies by day.

This is Calcutta life, say what you may!"

Though his education was practically *nil*, yet on one occasion as his companions were reading poems in Persian, he sat quietly by and listened with attention to their contents, when explained in Bengali. He retired and soon came back with some sparkling verses in Bengali embodying the spirit of the Persian poems, which highly pleased his companions who took him to be a young prodigy. This poetical trait developed so remarkably in him, that when he was only 11 years old, he could compose songs that were accepted with compliments by professional musicians who put the lad to constant tasks in poetical composition,

---

স্নেহ ভক্তি থাকিলে হয়, তাহা তাঁহার হয় নাই। স্ত্রীলোক তাঁহার কাছে কেবল ব্যঙ্গের পাত্র।"

The memories of Içvara Chandra Gupta
by Bankima Chandra Chatterjee.

*" রেতে মশা দিনে মাছি
এই নিয়ে, ভাই, কলকেতায় আছি "

which it was the joy and pride of young Içvara Chandra to execute to the best of his ability.

But an illiterate man by sheer dint of inborn genius could not be expected to attain more than a rustic fame and the applause of his personal friends. An opportunity however soon presented itself which paved the path to his receiving some education and bringing his remarkable talents to the notice of the enlightened public. His maternal uncles lived at Jorāsānko, where the Tagore family were at the time, as now, pioneers in education and in all progressive movements in Bengal. Içvara Chandra's singular poetic powers attracted the attention of Babu Jogendra Mohan Tagore, and the poet became a friend and companion of that enlightened nobleman. He received a good education here, and conjointly with his noble friend and patron started the weekly *Sanvad Prabhakara* in March, 1830. This journal soon reached the highest popularity in Bengal, and Içvara Chandra's genius supplied the public, through its columns, with an unceasing fountain of satirical and serio-comic pieces in prose and poetry for many years. It was in this journal that the juvenile writings of some of the greatest writers of Bengal such as Bankima Chandra and Dinabandhu Mitra were accorded a place by him, for he was never slow in appreciating talent in young writers and in giving them the encouragement they deserved. Içvara Chandra's noble friend and patron died in the year 1832. Disheartened by this blow of fortune, the poet stopped *Prabhakara* for some time, but it re-appeared as a bi-weekly in 1836, and in 1839 he

Receives education.

Starts a weekly.

made it a daily paper. Besides the *Prabhakara* he edited the *Samvad Ratnavali* which was started in 1849. He translated the Bhāgavata into Bengali verse and also the *Provodha Chandroday Natak* which he called *Vodhendu Vikasha* in Bengali. He was a voluminous versifier; it is said that he composed more than 50,000 couplets. Içvara Chandra died in February, 1858.

Thus the wayward lad and spoilt child lived to wield great influence in the literary atmosphere of Bengal, immediately before it became charged with European influence. He was pre-eminently a poet of the old school, and with him died the last echoes of the age of Bhārata Chandra and Jaya Nārāyaṅa Sen. Satire was his *forte* and bright wit sparkles in his lines directed against what was false and artificial in society. At home he was a genial friend and his company was sought for by the wealthy and talented alike. He kept no accounts and could have amassed a fortune, had he desired to do so. His income from the *Prabhakara* was great; and besides he was endowed with monthly pensions and honorariums from many rich men in Bengal; he spent money heedless of the morrow, and was always ready to help the needy. No friend was refused a loan when he wanted it and many did not repay, but the poet never asked his money back. In the sketch that Bankima Chandra draws of him we find it mentioned that Içvar Chandra distributed prizes and rewards amongst young men who showed skill in literary composition, and young Bankima Chandra who was destined at a subsequent time to win far greater laurels than

His character.

his patron, was also the recepient of prizes from him.

So lived and died Içvara Chandra,—one of the most remarkable men of his time in Bengal. He was a born satirist and a born poet. He adorned whatever he touched with his brilliant wit. When he would vilify a rival, his style would sink into the grossest and most atrocious obsceneties. This had grown to be the fashion amongst the literary men of this time. Içvara Chandra's scathing attacks on his rival Gauri Çaṇkara Bhattâchâryya, commonly known as Gurgure Bhattâchâryya, in the *Sombad Prabhakara*, and the latter's charges in answer published in his journal the *Rasaraja*, form a literature of the worst type that ever saw light ; and Mr. Lang, the popular Christian missionary, whose name is inseparably connected with the indigo disturbances, felt the necessity of moving the authorities to enact a law against obscene writings, owing to these perverse and scurrilous publications.

Vulgar satires.

Yet, in spite of such writings Içvara Chandra often disclosed in his poems a highly religious turn of mind. He was not great enough to introduce innovation in taste and free himself from the vices of the age. In the collection of his poems by Bâbu Maṇindra Chandra Gupta, we find no less than 70 pieces devoted to religious subjects, and all of them bear evidences of their writer's spirituality and faith.

Specimens of his writings.

We give below some specimens of his writing.

(a). From the poem "Festivity in the month of Pausa."

*"The young wife has scarcely time to braid her dishevelled hair. If per chance she spoils a curry, the mother-in-law and sister-in-law are furious with her. They say 'What hast thou done? It takes one's breath away to see the extent of your folly. Your mother could not teach you anything better than this? If we went without food for years, still we would not touch this curry. The beautiful face of the young wife, sweet and lovely as a full blown lotus, is drowned in tears; her sorrows she can not express, and she bears those rebukes though her heart is bursting with grief."

The young wife.

This is a true picture of young wife; peculiarly placed as she is in Hindu society, she must suffer all the ills of life patiently without a word, till she grows to be herself the mother of children, and has a chance to maltreat some other young wife placed in her charge, by way of retaliation.

(b). On the widow marriage act, which had been passed, it will be remembered, in the teeth of the opposition of the orthodox community.

[It should be borne in mind that Hindu widows are not allowed to wear shell-bracelets nor allowed to take fish or meat of any kind.]

---

*" সাবকাশ নাই মাত্র এলোচুল বাঁধে
ডাল ঝোল মাছ ভাত রাশি রাশি রাঁধে।
কত থাকে তার কাঁচা, কত তার পুড়ে।
সাধে রাঁধে পরমান্ন নলেনের গুড়ে।

বধূর রন্ধনে যদি যায় তাহা এঁকে।
শ্বাশুড়ী ননদ কত কথা বেঁকে॥
হ্যালো বউ কি করিলি দেখে মন চটে।
এই রান্না শিখেছিস মায়ের নিকটে॥

Widow-marriage.

*" All are saying, let not the reformers, determined as they are to save the young widows, take up the case of elderly matrons—our wrinkled-faced greyhaired grandams. Who so bold as to dare approach them with an offer of shell bracelets and fish?"

(c). The first kiss of love.

The first kiss.

†"A fount of the utmost happiness, that a lover's heart can wish for, is in the first kiss of love.

" We hear of the nectar in Indra's heaven for which the very angels are suppliants, a drop of which fills their minds with celestial joy,

" for which the demon Rāhu periodically swallows the moon.

" But the nectar—sweet nectar, I do not covet in preference to this first kiss of love."

বধূর মধুর খনি মুখ শতদল।
সলিলে ভাসিয়া যায় চক্ষু ছল ছল॥
আহা তাঁর হাহাকার বুঝিবার নয়।
ফুটিতে না পারে কিছু মনে মনে রয়॥"

*"সকলেই এইরূপ বলাবলি করে।
ছুড়ির কল্যানে যেন বুড়ি নাহি ত'রে॥
শরীর পড়েছে ঝুলে, চুল গুলি পাকা।
কে ধরাবে মাছ তারে, কে পরাবে শাঁখা?"

†"প্রণয় সুখের সার, প্রথম চুম্বন।
অপার আনন্দপ্রদ, প্রেমিকের ধন॥
আছে বটে অমৃত অমরাবতী পুরে।
প্রামোদিত করে যাহে যত সব সুরে॥
উথলয়ে প্রেমসিন্ধু পানে এক বিন্দু।
যার আশে গ্রাসে রাহু পূর্ণিমার ইন্দু।
সে ক্ষুধার সুধা মাত্র নাহি এক ক্ষণ।
যদি পাই প্রণয়ের প্রথম চুম্বন॥"

" Or look at wine, the favourite drink of the Asuras, even a touch of whose cup fills the mind with pleasure,

" drunk with this, the yādavas fought and died,

" wine that kept Vala Rāma in a never ruffled cheerful mood—now become a familiar article with the civilised world ;

" even that drink—wine, sweet wine,—I covet not in preference to this first kiss of love."

‡" Diamonds are found in the mines of Golakanda,—

" On the tops of the mount Sumeru are mines of gold and silver,—

"In the sea near Ceylon the pearls called Gajāmuktā are found in abundance,—

---

† অসুরের সুধা প্রিয় পেয় সুরারস মাত্র।
রসনা সরস গাত্র পরশিলে পাত্র ॥
যার লাগি হল ধ্বংস যদুবংশগণ।
স্বভাবে অভাব সদা রেবতী রমণ ॥
অদ্যাবধি মদ্য মাত্র পানীয় প্রধান।
বিদ্বজ্জন খাদ্য মাঝে সদ্য বিদ্যমান ॥
এমন মধুর সুরা নাহি চায় মন।
যদি পাই প্রণয়ের প্রথম চুম্বন ॥

‡ গলকুণ্ড দেশে আছে হীরার আকর।
রজত কাঞ্চনময় সুমেরু শেখর ॥
নানা রত্ন পরিপূর্ণ রত্নাকর জলে।
গজমুক্তা মূল্যযুক্তা অনেক সিংহলে ॥

"If Kuvera, the god of wealth were to come with all these and offer them to me,

"I would cast them all away for this my love's first kiss."

Biographical sketches.

But Içvara Chandra will always be admired for the pains he took to collect biographical accounts of some of our early poets, as Bharata Chandra, Rama Prasada and some of the old *kaviwalas*. He travelled in various places of Bengal to unearth valuable materials, and regularly published in *Samvad Prabhakara*, the accounts which he gleaned by his patient research. Much of the information that has come down to us about the lives of our great literary worthies is based upon these accounts.

Kavi songs.

Içvara Chandra composed many songs for the Kavi parties. In them we find the same ready wit and the sound realistic pictures of domestic life in Bengal, given with that remarkable fidelity which characterises his other writings.

Growing out of date.

His poems are growing obsolete and the great popularity which they once enjoyed is now a thing of the past. The humour of our elders has lost much of the old flavour owing to the more fastidious taste that prevails now. Some of the witty sayings once admired appear to us puerile and it is to be feared, that 50 years hence, Içvara Chandra's

কুবের লইয়া যদি সেই সমুদয়।
আমারে প্রদান করে হইয়া সদয়।
ক্ষেপণ করিব দূরে প্রহারি চরণ।
যদি পাই প্রণয়ের প্রথম চুম্বন॥"

poems will only be read by a few students of Bengali who would desire to trace the history of its progress.

Içvara Chandra's style bears evident traces of Bhārata Chandra's influence; and the influence of his own is stamped on the works of Hema Chandra who succeeded to his high place in Bengali poetry, a quarter of century after. Most of the social satires of Hema Chandra have a ring of Içvara Chandra's celebrated verses on 'our old Çiva' as Mr. Marshman was humourously called by him.

His influence on Hema Chandra.

Içvara Chandra's prose is far from being happy. It is highly pedantic, and has even an element of grotesqueness in it.

The Folk-literature of Bengal.

Bengal possesses a rich folk-literature, very little of which has yet been put into writing. The grandmothers may be heard to tell these stories to their grandchildren every evening in remote villages, —stories which have come down from a very early age. The Rev. Lāl Behāri Dey published some of these stories in English, but those gleaned by him from the resources available in towns represent only a very small fraction of such literature, and the most beautiful of these were not accessible to him, as, being a Christian, he could not have full command of the resources of the Hindu home. Lately Babu Dakṣiṇā Ranjana Mitra Mazumdār has published two volumes of folk-tales in Bengali. He has attempted to reproduce them in the very language of the rustic women from whom he collected them. In some cases he recorded the

Dakṣiṇa Babu's collections.

stories by a phonograph at the time they were delivered; so that their language remains remarkably faithful to the narration of the villagers. The language owes not the least colouring or refinement to modern literary Bengali. The dialect spoken in the country five hundred years ago, of which specimens are to be found in the written literature of the period, remains unchanged in the colloquial language of our backward villages, not subjected to the influences of the outside world; and Dakṣiṇā Babu's collection has not only preserved the spirit of the old folk-lore unpolished by the touch of the compiler, but has retained even those old and quaint forms with all their mannerisms, which best indicate the genius of our tongue.

As specimens of old dialect.

There are altogether 16 stories in the two volumes. Some of them are meant simply to amuse the children, which is the primary object of all nursery tales. There are others, like the stories of Mālanchamālā and Kānchanamāla, which though sufficiently wild and romantic to amuse the young, have also deeper meanings to interest more thoughtful readers. The characters of the heroines of these stories possess a living interest. The ideals of chastity and devotion to the husband, which they hold up, open vistas, as it were, into the domestic life of the Hindu women of past days, and enable us to see the workings of their souls—the purity of their hearts and the wonderful spirit of sacrifice which actuated them in there every-day conduct. The pathos created by Mālanchamālā's sufferings, her sacrifices, and devotion to her husband are matters difficult to be conveyed to those whose idea

Mālanchamālā.

of wifehood is different from that which governs Hindu women. The Hindu wife in those days bore all kinds of ills from her husband with untiring patience; she lived with her co-wife, to whom often the husband was devoted and bore her neglect and his contempt in a surprising spirit of resignation; and inspite of all maltreatment cherished only the best feelings for her husband. All this was sometimes done with a grace,—a saintliness and devotion which place her sorrows above our pity. They may be looked upon almost in the light of martyrdom. The supernatural element prevails in the story of Mālanchamālā, with all imaginable excesses of wild fancy, and this constitutes its interest for the young; but as we proceed, the griefs of the heroine becomes the all-absorbing subject of the readers. Her woes claim a tear at every page. She like Behulā restores her husband to life; she saves him from the flames of the funeral pyre; follows him like a shadow; and, all unseen by him, ministers to his every comforts. She was married to him when he was a mere child. The child grows up, but Mālanchamālā does not show herself to him till he becomes a handsome youngman and has married a princess. Many years of fasts, and vigils, heart-rending anguish, and cruel treatment from her royal father-in-law, who does not allow her to live in his palace because she is of an inferior caste, are rewarded with this, that her husband marries the princess and lives in the palace of his new bride's father. And this husband had been the apple of her eye; in the funeral ground, in the deep shades of the wilderness she had saved him from death, undergoing unheard of hardships,

Her great love.

and bringing to him all the ministering care of a guardian angel! The young wife looks through a window in the moonlight and sees her husband and his new bride happy together. Mālanchāmālā—chaste, devoted and faithful to her husband, as fidelity itself, peeps through the lattices of the window, and sees her husband in the arms of the princess; it was like Enoch Arden peeping into the room of Phillip and discovering Anne as his wife; but our Mālanchamāla is no earthly woman; she is heavenly in every sense of the word. She sings:—

"Live in happiness, O Prince; live in happiness, O Princess.

"If I am a chaste woman, my words will not be in vain.

"Let your ancestors in heaven, O Prince, watch the candles that light up this chamber and preserve you from all ill.

"May the children, that are born to your new wife, walk beneath royal umbrellas for fourteen generations to come!

"O Forests, O trees, O land, O waters, keep guard! Let me know when they awake, that I may steal away unseen by either.

"Let the towers of the palace, where my husband reigns, endure for ever.

"Let the sun and the moon be as guards of his city.

"May my royal father-in-law's palace and the throne of my husband be victorious for ever.

"And may the shell-bracelets of the Princess and her vermilion mark, the signs of her wifehood, —endure for ever.

"Grant me this boon, O God. I brought up my husband with great pain, and now what can I covet more than to see him happy with a princess?

"Though I die and am reduced to dust I shall ever rejoice at this sight of the happiness of my husband.

"If I die now and am transformed into a bird or a lower animal, or whatever else may befall me, I care not, as I have seen my beloved happy."

This song is couched in the idioms of at least five centuries back.* The story has been worked into such life-like details, that the woman Mālanchamālā does not here pose as a great heroine. She does not seem to attempt at reaching any inaccessible height. Her woes give rise to great pathos, but with all these she continues to attract us, as an unassuming lovely village-girl that she is.

Our Bengali folklore shows how peculiarly situated a Hindu wife might be in the midst of environment and influences favourable to the development of a spirit of sacrifice, devotion and fidelity. Her growth was often as natural as that of a flower, and is quite faithfully portrayed in the old literature of the country, and even in this unassuming folklore, where nothing has been put forward for the sake of display. The story of Kānchānamālā also shows the familiar ideal of the Hindu wife. Her husband neglects her, but she persists in her devo- **Kānchanamālā.**

* Thakur Dadar Jhuli by Daksina Mitra p. 195.

tion. For selfish reasons her husband comes reluctantly at a certain crisis to obtain her permission for undertaking a sea voyage, promising her, as a reward, a necklace of pearls, a fine pair of shell-bracelets and vermilion to adorn her forehead. But she answers, "You are my necklace of pearls; you are my shell-bracelets and vermilion mark; I do not want any other. Only take me with you my husband, I shall be at your bidding and be happy." These stories are interspersed with songs in language which is generally very antiquated. Many facts about old Hindu society and about the sea-voyages undertaken by the merchants of Bengal are to be found in these stories; and there are other elements which indicate Bhuddistic influences, such as instances of the wonderful powers of Siddhās, and descriptions of Tāntrick rites. There are some stories on which Mahomedan influence has evidently left its impress, as for instance in the story of Madhumālā, the introduction of fairies is certainly no creation of the Hindu fancy.

Buddhistic and Moslem influences.

The songs with which those stories abound are sung to the favourite village metre known as Bhātiāl *sura.* This rythem and cadence is peculiarly distinctive of Bengal; it has nothing to do with the refined melodies of Sanskrit or Persian music. There are six *Ragas* and thirty six *Raginies*—42 chief scales or musical modes of the Hindus; but the Bhātiāl *sura* is not included in the range of this higher musical system. Bhātiāl is the cadence of the rustics, and its plaintive and appealing notes, so unassuming and simple, go straight to the heart and create their own pathos, without possessing any of those niceties of sound which characterise the *Ragas* and *Raginies*. The power of the Bhatial to strike the tender cords of the human soul, was found out by the Vaiṣṅavas who refined and enriched it with modulations and made from it that soul-captivating air—the Manohara Sāi. The writers of religious songs adopted it with peculiar modifications to form the *Baul sura* which produces emotions peculiar to an ascetic mood.

Supplementary Notes,

TO

CHAPTER VI.

I. Miscellaneous Poems.
II. Mainly on style, literary tastes, and language.
III. Early prose-literature.

We must remember that during that period when the Bengali language was being most rapidly developed and its literature was growing, the Hindus had already lost their political supremacy. By far the larger section of the Hindus lived in villages, and for them henceforth history lay almost entirely in the story of their social changes. Descriptions of society and its revolutions are found in many works of the Vaiṣṅavas. We have also, however, a small number of works on political history. Some of those written in poetry are noticed below. We reserve our treatment of the historical works written in prose for our account of Bengali prose, upon which we have not yet touched.

I, Miscellaneous Poems.

(a) Historical poems.

1. Rājamālā, a history of the Rājās of Hill Tippera. This work was undertaken at the command of Mahārājā Çri Dharma Mānikya (1407—1439 A.D.) by two Brahmin scholars of his court—Cukreçvara and Vāṅeçvara who were inhabitants of Assam. Durlabha Chandāi a hoary headed old man, a courtier and the leader of the Chandāi community at the time, had much information about the early history of Tippera; and Çukreçvara and Vāṅeçvara

frequently consulted him while compiling the Rāja-mālā. It also appears that there existed in fragmentary condition, earlier works on the same subject from which much help was received. Those to which reference is made in the Rājamālā are (1). Rājamālikā (an earlier work on the Tippera Rājās), (2). Yogini Mālikā, (3). The Lakṣmaṅa Malika (probably a history of Rājā Lakṣmaṅa Sen of the Sen dynasty of Bengal) and (4). Vārunya Kālirnaya. The Rājamālā was written in simple metrical verse.

We have also seen a small treatise, evidently very old, in which the history of the Tippera Rājās, traced from Duryya, son of Yayāti of the Lunar race, is embodied briefly in verse.

2. *Maharastra Purana* by Gangārāma. This is an historical work in Bengali verse, which gives an account of the Maharatta raids in Bengal led by Bhāskara Pandit in 1741 A. D. These raids, commonly known in our country as the *Vargira hangama*, gave rise to a feeling of general unrest and panic, inspiring the well-known nursery song, sung up to the present day by mothers to lull naughty children to sleep. This couplet which, like all nursery songs, does not convey any clear meaning, runs as follows— **Mahārāstra Puraṅa.**

*"The child is asleep, the whole village is relieved.

---

*"ছেলে ঘুমাল, পাড়া জুড়াল, বর্গী এল দেশে ।
বুলবুলীতে ধান খেল, খাজনা দিব কিসে ?"

"The Maharatta raiders have overun the country.

and the Bulbulis (*Turdus jocosus*) have eaten up the crops.

"How shall we pay the rent?"

Gangārāma wrote his historical poem in 1750 A. D.,—seven years before the battle of Plassey. His account of the raids seems to be a faithful one. The author describes how Ālivardi Khān, the Nawāb was suddenly attacked by Bhāskara Pundit at Burdwan and made a captive there for a short time. This is borne out by a statement in Tarikhi Yusufi, though in Mitākṣarin, Tarikhi Bāngālā, and in the accounts of Mr. Holwel we do not find this incident mentioned. Gangārāma gives a great many facts about the Maharatta raids which will be found interesting to the readers of the history of Bengal.

3. *Samser Gazir gan.* This poem, which runs through 4,000 couplets, describes the life and achievements of Samser gazi who was originally a robber, and who grew so powerful as to dethrone a king of Tippera and proclaim himself its chief for a time. Samser gazi lived 200 years ago, and the poem commemorating his exploits is sung by the rustic folk of Tippera to this day. It is said that Samser used to carry the vast riches, he obtained by looting, to the depths of the jungle in the Udayapura hills. He would then dismiss the carriers and with the help of a carpenter make deep cavities in the trunks of large Çāl trees, where he stored his hoards, and after carefully closing them up with blocks of timber, and effacing all marks of the work, he would cut off the head of the poor artisan, thus removing all chances of detection.

In this way absolute secrecy was secured. It is said that even now stray wood-cutters, while applying their axe to the trunks of Çāla trees in the deep forest, sometimes unexpectedly find themselves in possession of treasure stored up there by the famous robber. The Samser Gazir gān was composed shortly after his death.

4. *Chaudhuri's Ladai*, a poem describing the fight between the two Zeminders, named Rājanārāyaṅa Chaudhuri and Rājachandra Chaudhuri. The fighting took place at Babupur, seven miles to the north of Noākhāli, about 100 years ago, when British rule was not yet settled in that quarter. Rājanārāyaṅa was the more powerful of the contending rivals. He is said to have founded a town by cutting down a great jungle which had belonged to Sindur Kāzi. The town was called Rājagānja. The author of the poem was a Mahomedan, as appears from his preliminary verses in praise of Khodā. There is an interesting account in the poem, of Rangamālā, a beautiful damsel who is said to have played an important part in the affairs.

Chaudhuri's Laḍai.

5. *The Raids by Kookis of Hill Tippera on the villages of the plains.* This poem was written about a century ago, and is still reproduced from memory by many old men of the Tippera district.

Raids by Kookis.

6. *Dara Sekh.* This is a poem by Dvija Rāma Chandra. It gives an account of the misfortunes of the Prince Dārā, the eldest son of Jāhāngir.

Dārā Sekh.

7. A poem on *Pratapa Chand* who claimed the the *gadi* of Burdwan, by Anup Chandra Dattā, an inhabitant of Çrikhanda. The peom was written in 1844 A.D.

Pratāpa Chānd.

Short historical treatises.

There are numerous small poetical treatises, written about a century ago, describing the flood of the Dāmodara and its devastating effects on the villages of Birbhum; and on Bābu Rājkumar Sen of Kirtipaçā who died of poison administered to him by Kiçore Mahālanavis, his Dewan, and on various other subjects of minor importance. The poem on the flood of the Dāmodara was written by Napher Chandra Dās in 1823.

---

(6) Metaphysical and other works.

Māyā Timira Chandrikā.

1. *The Maya Timira Chandrika* by Rāmagati Sen, which I have already mentioned on page 682, is a work treating of the processes of Yoga. He begins the poem in the form of an allegory, much on the lines of the well known Sanskrit work *Prabodha Chandrodaya Nataka.* The poem begins as follows:—

*"The mind goes in a fit of anger to the soul—that Prince whose capital town is the body and whose palace is the heart; false vanity is his

---

*" কোপে অতি শীঘ্রগতি মন চলি যায়।
যথা বসে নানা রসে সদা জীবরায় ॥
তনু যার সুবিস্তার দিব্য রাজধানী।
হৃদি তারি রমাপুরী তথায় আপনি ॥
অহঙ্কার হয় যার মোহের কিরীটী।
দম্ভ-পাটে বৈসে ঠাঠে করি পরিপাটী ॥
পুষ্পচাপ উগ্রতাপ লোভ, অনিবার।
দুই মিত্র সুচরিত্র বান্ধব রাজার ॥

crown; pompous arrogance keeps his royal company; lust and greed are his two dear friends. The heavenly maidens peace, forbearance and kindness do not visit the palace, having been insulted. There ignorance reigns supreme as the favourite queen, pandering to all the foolish desires of the Prince, who is found steeped in the well of foul passions."

After this the various processes of Yoga are detailed in the poem, on the merits of which we can not pronounce any judgment.

Yoga Sāra.

2. Yoga sāra or the essence of Yoga. As the name implies, this book describes Yoga, leading to the emancipation of the soul, and attainment of the stage of beatitude, step to step. The author's name is not found in the book; he introduces himself by his title Gunarāj Khān. He undertook the work at the command of a rich man named Çachipati Majumdār.

Hāḍamālā and other poems on Yoga.

3. Hāḍamālā, a poem relating to Yoga. The author's name is not known.

4. Jnāna Pradipa by Saiyad Sultān who calls himself a disciple of the saint and Fakir named Sāhā Hosen. Though a Mahomedan, the author

---

শান্তি, ধৃতি, ক্ষমা, নীতি, শুভশীলা নারী।
মান করি রাজপুরী নাহি যায় চারি ॥
পতিব্রতা ধর্ম্মরতা অবিদ্যা মহিষী।
পতি কাছে সদা আছে রাজার হিতৈষী ॥
নারী সঙ্গে রতিরঙ্গে রসের তরঙ্গে।
এইরূপে কামকূপে জীব আছে রঙ্গে ॥"

acknowledges the God Çiva as the authority in all matters relating to Yoga.

5. Tanu Sādhana—a poem on Yoga. The author, who was a Mahomedan, writes elegant Bengali and has a profound respect for the tenets of the Hindu Çāstras.

6. *Jnana Chautisa*. This poem contains only 152 couplets. The author Saiyād Sultān explains the metaphysical truth embodied in the symbol of Çiva and Çakti and describes the processes of Yoga. This book was written in 1780 A.D.

There are other small treatises on Yoga, a brief notice of which is to be found in the catalogue of old Bengali Mss. published by Munsi Abdul Karim in the Sāhitya Pariṣad Patrikā issued from Calcutta.

The above poems were written within the last 200 years; the latest of them comes up to the middle of the 19th century.

Kaçī Khanda by Jayanārāyaṅā.

Translation of Kāçī Khanda by Jayanārayaṅa Ghoṣāla. Passing from the subject of metaphysics, we shall here take up a work of translation, which deserves a somewhat elaborate notice. It was compiled by its illustrious author with the help of many distinguished Pundits.

From a copper-plate inscription prepared by Rājā Kāli Çankara Ghoṣāla of Bhukailasa—son of Rājā Jayanārāyaṅa, we glean the following particulars about the poet. Jayanārāyaṅa was born in October, 1752. He received a sound education in Sanskrit, Persian, Hindi, English and French. He inherited from his father a vast property which comprised the villiages of Govindapur, Garya and Behālā. He obtained the title of Mahārājā from the emperor of Delhi for his patriotism and munificience, and founded a college at Benares which was called Jayanārāyaṅa College after him. He built a temple moreover for the worship of the image of Karunā Nidhāna (Krişṅa) at Banares in 1790. He enjoyed the confidence of Warren Hastings, and helped the Government of the East India Company in their work of Survey and Settlement in various provinces of Bengal. Jayanārāyaṅa died in 1818 A.D. at Benares in his 66th year.

The translation of Kāçī Khanda was however the joint work of several scholars and one of its chief contributors was a Kāyastha nobleman named Narasinha Deva Ray who bore the title of Çūdramaṅi. The translation took many years for its completion. Here is the account given by Jayanārāyaṅa himself as to how the arduous work was gone through.

The history of this compilation.

*" Dwelling at Benares, which is situated on the five noble streams of the Ganges, I was desirous of writing something in praise of the holy city. I thought of translating the Sanskrit work Kāçī-Khanda into Bengali, but found none who could

---

*" কাশীবাস করি পঞ্চ গঙ্গার উপর।
কাশী গুণ গান হেতু ভাবিত অন্তর॥
মনে করি কাশীখণ্ড ভাষা করি লিখি।
ইহার সহায় হয় কাহারে না দেখি॥
মিত্রশত চৌদ্দ শক পৌষ মাস যবে।
আমার মানস মত যোগ হইল তবে॥

help me in the undertaking. In the month of January in 1792, an opportunity presented itself for the fulfilment of my wishes. Çrijukta Narasinha Deva Rāy of the Çūdramaṅi family and an inhabitant of Pātuli, visited the city of Benares With him came Jagannātha Mukerjee, and in the month of February the work was commenced by us jointly. Rāma Prasāda Vidyā Vāgīça, a learned Sanskrit scholar, explained the text and Narasinha Rāy prepared his drafts of the translation in prose, based on the interpretations given by the former. Jagannātha Mukerjee turned them into metrical verse; Narasinha Rāy corrected the rhymes and prepared fair copies; when forty chapters were thus completed, the learned Vidyā Vāgīça died, in September, and Jagannātha Mukerjee went home to

---

শূদ্রমণি কুলে জন্ম পাটুলি নিবাসী।
শ্রীযুক্ত নৃসিংহ দেব রায়াগত কাশী ॥
তার সঙ্গে জগন্নাথ মুখুয্যা আইলা।
প্রথম ফাল্গুনে গ্রন্থ আরম্ভ করিলা ॥
শ্রীরামপ্রসাদ বিদ্যাবাগীশ ব্রাহ্মণ।
ভাঙ্গিয়া বলেন কাশীখণ্ড অনুক্ষণ ॥
তাহারে করেন রায় তর্জ্জমা খসড়া।
মুখুয্যা করেন সদা কবিতা পাতড়া ॥
রায় পুনর্ব্বার সেই পাতড়া লইয়া।
পুস্তকে লিখেন তাহা সমস্ত শুধিয়া ॥
এইমতে চল্লিশ লাচাড়ি হৈল যবে।
বিদ্যাবাগীশের কাশী-প্রাপ্তি হৈল তবে ॥
ভাদ্রমাসে মুখুয্যা গেলেন নিজ বাটী।
বৎসর স্থগিত ছিল গ্রন্থ পরিপাটী ॥

Bengal, for one year. Owing to these causes, the book could not make any progress. In the mean-time Narasiñha Rāy removed himself from the house which he occupied at Benares to Bāngālitolā; there he found a companion and friend in Valarāma Vāchaspati who was a profound scholar. Jointly with Vakreçvara Panchānana, another Pundit, they finished the translation of 75 chapters,—Vakreçvara contributing two chapters one on Kaçi Panchakroçī and the other describing a journey through the city. The work now again came to a stand-still for various reasons. After this, however, we happened to meet with a Pundit named Umāçañkara Tarkālankāra. Though by the will of Providence this excellent man is blind in both eyes, yet he is possessed of some very admirable qualities. He is a native of Kāçīpur and a thoroughly truthful man of a highly religious

---

পরন্তু বাঙ্গালীটোলা গেলা যবে রায়।
বলরাম বাচস্পতি মিলিলা তথায়॥
পচত্তরী অধ্যায় পর্য্যন্ত তার সীমা।
বক্রেশ্বর পঞ্চাননে সমাপ্ত গরিমা॥
কাশী পঞ্চক্রোশী আর নগর ভ্রমণ।
এই দুই অধ্যায় পঞ্চাননে সমাপন॥
পরে সম্বৎসরাবধি স্থগিত হইলা।
শ্রীউমাশঙ্কর তর্কালঙ্কার মিলিলা॥
যদ্যপি নয়ন দুইটী দৈবযোগে অন্ধ।
তথাপি তাহার গুণে লোকে লাগে ধন্ধ॥
ইষ্টনিষ্ঠ বাক্‌নিষ্ঠ কাশীপুরে জন্ম।
পরানিষ্ট পরাঙ্মুখ বিজ্ঞমর্ম্মি-মর্ম্ম॥

temperament. He never dreams of doing harm to any one, appreciates merit in others ; and is a true advocate of noble ideas. The blind Pundit became eager to help in the completion of the work. His father Rāma Chandra Vidyālañkāra is also a learned Pundit of a quiet and obliging disposition. With the latter I travelled for six months, in search of good and reliable manuscripts. The accounts of different festivities held in the different parts of the year are given in Bengali poetry, literally translated from the Sanskrit texts. Viṣṅu Rāma Siddhānta, a high-minded scholar and a friend of the blind Pundit, helped us with a right interpretation of these Sanskrit texts, and Narasiñha Rāy finally published the work when completed. The description of the city of Benares and of the origin of this work added to the book, is my own. In it I have given a faithful account

---

লোক উপকারে সদা ব্যাকুল অন্তর ।
গ্রন্থের সমাপ্তি হেতু হলেন তৎপর ॥
শ্রীযুক্ত রামচন্দ্র বিদ্যালঙ্কার আখ্যান ।
তর্কালঙ্কারের পিতা সুধীর বিদ্বান ॥
নিজে তার সহিত করিয়া পর্য্যটন ।
ছয় মাসে বহুগ্রন্থ করি সঙ্কলন ॥
ঋতু মাস তিথি বার বর্ষ যাত্রা যত ।
পদ্যেতে আনিয়া সংস্কৃত অভিমত ॥
তর্কালঙ্কারের বন্ধু বিষ্ণুরাম নাম ।
সিদ্ধান্ত আখ্যান, অতি ধীর গুণবান্ ॥
পদ্ধতি ভাষাতে করিলেন পরিষ্কার ।
রায় করিলেন সর্ব্ব গ্রন্থের প্রচার ॥

of my own observations. Rājā Jayanārāyaṅa of the family of Ghoṣāla, here ends his account."

The translation of Kāçī Khanda is complete in 11,200 lines; it forms a record of patient labour, carried on by half a dozen scholars for many years. In the Bhaṅitā (signature) at the end of each chapter we find the name of Rājā Jaya Nārāyaṇa, given no doubt by way of courtesy, having regard to the high position and munificence of this scholarly nobleman who initiated and maintained this undertaking, as the patron of the scholars. The main portion of the work was done by Narasiñha Deva Rāy of Pātuli whose descendants now dwell at Bañsberia in the district of Hughly.

But the chief interest of the work lies in the supplementary account of the City of Benares which the Rājā himself gives in Bengali verse. Literal translations from the Sanskrit have little value in this country. The learned do not care to read translations instead of the original texts, and those who do not know Sanskrit, do not care to read literal translation, in which they do not find an adequate or modernised expression of the thoughts to which they are accustomed. The translation of Kāçī Khanda is thus a lost labour, though the labour that produced it was great.

But the supplementary account of the City of Benares is full of interest. In simple and unassum- **A description of the city.**

নগর বর্ণন মোর গ্রন্থের কারণ।
প্রত্যক্ষ বৃত্তান্ত তাহা যথার্থ বর্ণন॥
ঘোষাল বংশের রাজা জয়নারায়ণ।
এইখানে সমাপ্ত করিলা বিবরণ॥"

ing language the Rājā, who was a pious man, jotted down notes in verse of what he saw in the Holy City, a hundred years ago. He begins his description of 'the abode of Çiva,' as Kāçī is called, with a few poetic lines in which its semicircular shape, as observed from the Ganges, is compared to the crescent moon on the forehead of Çiva. He next gives a short notice of the bathing ghātas—the Parçvnāth ghāta, the Asi ghāta, the Vaidyanāth ghāta, the Nārada Pānde's ghāta and so on. There were then altogether 53 bathing ghātas at Benares and all of these are faithfully noticed. Though the notes are short, the writer makes them interesting by his witty remarks in many of them. He then proceeds to give a description of the Postās (embankment), the chief amongst which is the Mirer Postā; it is 120 ft. in height and 600 ft. in breadth. Hurriedly taking a note of the great houses, some of which were seven stories high, he gives an account of the Dhārāras or pinnacles. The pinnacle named Çri Madhava Rāyer Dharārā rises to a height of 172 ft.; at 135 ft. there is a seat for visitors, from which a bird's-eye view of the City of Benares may be taken. *"Like the cliffs of Mount Sumeru, it appears as if the Dharārā might pierce the heavens." At the time when the Rājā lived at Benares, this Dharārā was used by the desperate and unhappy as a place for committing suicide. The Rājā has given a list of the people who killed themselves during his time by throwing themselves down from

The Ghātas.

The Postās.

Dhārārās

A place for suicide.

---

*"সুমেরুর দুই শৃঙ্গ যেমত প্রকাশ।
মনে লয় তার চূড়া ভেদিল আকাশ॥"

the above-mentioned seat in Dharārā. A young Kṣetri with his lady-love had disappeared for three days, and on the fourth, they were found dead in close embrace on the ground-floor of the temple; they had evidently thrown themselves down from the great height, after enjoying each other's company for three days. But death does not always come to the unfortunate, though he may sincerely wish for it. *"Another person ascended the great height and threw himself down, but he fell on the top of a tree and catching hold of a branch reached the ground safe and quietly glided into his own chamber."

Warren Hastings stayed in the garden house adjoining this temple for a time when he was in that City for carrying on hostile operations against Chait Singh, Rājā of Benares.

The lighting of the roads.

Instead of the modern centralisation of municipal arrangements, there was the mutual agreement of honest and public-spirited citizens:—†"In the Mahājantolā the lanes were so dark that neither the sun nor the moon could look within them. At night the residents here kept lights in their windows for the convenience of the passers-by."

---

*" অন্য এক জন সেই ধরারাতে চড়ি।
দৈবক্রমে তথা হইতে তরুপরে পড়ি ॥
তরুডাল সহ পুনঃ হইয়া ভূমিষ্ঠ।
অনায়াসে নিজ ঘরে হৈল প্রবিষ্ট ॥"

†" মহাজন টোলী মধ্যে রাস্তাতে সর্ব্বথা।
দিনকর হিমকর করহীন তথা ॥
একারণ নিশাযোগে, পথিকের প্রীতে।
দীপ-শিখা করে সবে নিজ খিড়কিতে ॥"

The writer of the sketch made notes of all that he saw; the short lines call up living pictures before one's imagination. Regarding the Buddhist Lāmās (Priests) he says:

The Lāmāṣ.

*"The ascetics called Lāmās who outwardly profess renunciation are in reality full of worldliness. They transact a prosperous loan-business and trades of various kinds; and everyone of them is immensely rich, having residential houses like palaces."

The various amusements and religious festivities of Benares, the mode in which the citizens passed their evenings in idle gossip lounging on the banks of the Ganges, and other matters chiefly of social and domestic interest have been briefly noted. A chapter is devoted to the silk industry for which the Benares weavers have always been so famous. We find in this chapter a list of various kinds of cloth which used to be manufactured there,—the far-famed Benares Sāḍi, the fine silken stuff coloured with various dyes, a piece of which used to sell for Rs. 200, velvet of the first quality, striped silk with which turbans were made, silk adorned with gold embroidery and so on. He concludes his remarks under this head by saying,—†" They show admirable skill in making artistic designs on cotton with coloured silk threads, but they can not produce

Social gatherings.

Silk industry.

*" লামা সন্ন্যাসীর কত শত মঠ।
বাহে উদাসীন মাত্র, গৃহী অন্তঃপট ॥
সদাগরী মহাজনী ব্যবসা সবার।
এক এক জনার বাড়ী পর্ব্বত-আকার ॥"

†" সাদাতে রেশম পাড়ি কত রঙ্গ করে।
শুদ্ধ সাদা অত্যুত্তম করিতে না পারে ॥"

fine cotton pieces of the first quality." While writing these lines, the Rājā evidently had in mind the unapproachable muslins of Dacca.

The temples.

Next he proceeds to describe the temples. The accounts are vivid and life-like. He begins with a description of the temple of Ahalyā Bāi, the famous Maharatta queen, who spent three lakhs of rupees on building a beautiful shrine at Benares. Next he describes the temple of Viṣṅu Mahādeva, Kānchī and others. The architectural points of the edifices are mentioned, and the use served by their important apartments is also described at some length.

Lanes of the city—a scene of bloodshed

The lanes of Benares were at one time scenes of bloodshed, assassination and plunder. The Ahir Rājputs are described as always carrying swords with them. *"Each looks like a king of death (যম). If he happens to have a grudge against a man, he does not feel the least scruple in wounding him. Every month there is deadly strife, and many heads roll on the ground as a result."

Our author's account of the Hindu women who visited the shrines or lived holy lives in the city, during his time, verges on the poetic :—

---

*" ....যমের আকার ॥
যার সঙ্গে যাহার আক্রোশ রোষ থাকে।
অনায়াসে নির্ঘাত আঘাত করে তাকে ॥
এইমতে প্রতি মাসে প্রায় হয় দ্বন্দ্ব।
ক্ষণমাত্রে গড়াগড়ি যায় কত স্কন্ধ ॥"

The Hindu women.

*"Some of them wear bracelets made of the horns of rhinoceros, mounted in gold which look like dark clouds lined by lightning. Their lovely tresses that hang loosely down their backs are peerless; over the breasts of some hang necklaces of bright pearls, which look as though over the peaks of the Himālaya flowed the white stream of the Ganges."

But the Rājā knew where to stop. At this stage of his description, he suddenly cuts it short by saying :—

†"The sight of women should create in the mind feelings of respect; never should any unholy thought be entertained."

This account of Benares giving a topography and other details about the city of a particular period will increase in value, in course of years, and will possess the same interest as the account of Jeruselem by Mandevile, Brahmakhanda by Vyāsa, and Navadwipa by Narahari Chakravarty.

The interchange of customs and ideas bet. Mahomedans & Hindus.

Hindus and Mahomedans had now lived in Bengal for long years in close proximity and on terms of peace and unity, and they were naturally

---

*" গণ্ডারের চুড়ী কারু কনক-রচিত।
ঘোর ঘন মাঝে যেন তড়িত জড়িত ॥
কি উপমা দিব যেই পিঠে দোলে বেণী।
....
কারু উরোদেশে মুক্তা-মালার দোলানী।
হিমাচলে আন্দোলিত যেন মন্দাকিনী ॥"

†" এ সব দর্শনে ভক্তি মনেতে হইবে।
কদাচিৎ অন্যভাব মনেতে নহিবে ॥"

influenced by one another in many respects. In Kṣemānanda's Manasā Mangala, written more than 300 years ago, we find a passage in which it is told that in the steel-house made for Lakṣmindhara, along with many other charms to ward off evil influences, a copy of the Korān was kept. Many a Mahomedan offered *puja* at Hindu temples, as the Hindus offered *sinni* at Mahomedan mosques. In the N. W. P. the Hindus celebrated the Mahorum festivals with as great enthusiasm as the Mahomedans. Mirza Hosen Āli, a native of the Tippera district, who lived a hundred years ago, not only composed songs in praise of the goddess Kāli, but worshipped her at his house with great *eclat*; and Gariv Hosen Chaudhury of Dacca, a contemporary of the Mriza, another Mahomedan zeminder, was a devout worshipper of Çitala Devī, the goddess of small pox, worshipped by the Hindus.* Gol Mahāmud is to-day the leader of a professional party of singers in Tippera who sing only praises of the goddess Kāli, and his party carries the palm in this respect and gets engagements in preference to Hindu parties at the houses of the orthodox Hindus. Hindus have borne Mahomedan names and the Mahomedans are often called by Hindu names and such instances

*Gariv Husen Choudhury, when only 24, had gone a-hunting in the jungles on the banks of the Boori Ganga, where he chanced to see an image of Citala Devi in clay placed on the sand bank, and calling her a witch, aimed a shot at the clay image, as a mark of his contempt. The bullet fell on one of the eyes of the image, and disfigured that side of the face. That night Gariv Husen caught fever, and the symptoms of small pox quickly followed. The goddess is said to have appeared to him in a dream and told him that she would spare his life, but take one of his eyes, as he had done hers. Gariv Husen recovered with the loss of an eye, and since then turned into a devout votary of the goddess.

are very common in this country even now. In the Statesman of the 17th November 1910, there is a leader on an article from the pen of the Hon'ble Mr. Mazhal-ul-Haque on this mutual assimilation by the Hindus and the Mahomedans of the customs and thought of each other. The article appeared in the magazine—"Modern Behar." We quote from the Statesman,—"From the begining the Musalman invaders adopted wholesale the customs of the Hindus, says Mr. Mazhar-ul-Haque, and when these went entirely against their religious ideas they so adapted them as to give a semblance of conformity to their own religion. From birth to death at every stage of life, the Mahomedan in India perform ceremonies which are of purely Hindu origin. When he is born, the songs sung are not of Musalman conception but those in which allusions to Çrī Krişņa are frequent. The series of ceremonies which are performed during pregnancy are adopted from the Hindus, and the symbols of Hindu religions and philosophical ideas play the most important part. At marriage the ceremonies are even more Hinduised. In Islam the simple reading of the Nikāh is quite sufficient to complete the marriage contract, and unnecessary and wasteful ceremony has always been expressly discouraged. But the Indian Musalman goes through a long series of festivities and ceremonies, most of which are bodily importations from the Hindus, while others are adapted with slight modifications to give them some colour of Mahomedanism. The custom, in connection with marriage ceremonies to which Mahomedan ladies attach the greatest importance, is of purely Hindu origin: so, too, is the line of vermilion and the dot on the forehead, while the bridal songs are all in Hindi, a language which is certainly not the mother-tongue of the Musalmans. Funeral rites, too, can be easily traced to a Hindu origin, and widow re-marriage, which is not only permitted but enjoined by Islam, is considered a disgrace in Muslem as well as in Hindu society. The mutual participation in religious festivals is a phenomenon which strikes even the European observer, though perhaps none have had the experience of Mr. Mazhar-ul-Haque himself, who relates that in his childhood at Mohorum time, he has seen Hindus weeping as copious tears at the recital of the incidents of Karbalā, as any pious Shiā would do. But perhaps the most striking instance of the sympathy of ideas to which Mr. Mazhar-ul-Haque refers is the well-known sight of Hindus revering the shrines of Musalman saints and martyrs in the same degree as, if not in a greater degree than, Musalmans themselves. Mr. Mazhar-ul-Haque repudiates the idea that this is to be attributed merely to the superistitious nature of the Hindu. "It is to be ascribed to a deep truth ingrained in "the human nature and discovered by Hindu "philosophers." No man is absolutely bad or good. Some are more, others less so. If a man was adored by his own people who know him well, the good in him must have predominated over the bad, and, acting on this principle, the Hindus adore and worship the good qualities of the man and not the man himself. "To me," says Mr. Mazhar-ul-Haque, "this worship of the Musalman "saints and pious men by the Hindus reveals "another side of their lovable nature, and my "heart goes out to them in gratefulness and "fraternal love."

The Mahomedans of Rājshahi have the monopoly of *Bhasan gan* or songs on Manasā Devi. In Chittagong this fusion of ideas and interchange of customs and usages seems to have reached its highest point. In a Bengali poem called the Bheluā Sundarī, written by Hāmidullā of Chittagong, we read that the Brahmins who had assembled to find out an auspicious day for the hero's journey abroad, consulted the Korān for the purpose. The hero, who was the son of an orthodox Hindu merchant, obeyed the injunctions 'as if they were laid down in the Vedas' and started on his voyage, 'praying to Āllāh' for his safety! Even at the present time the lower clases of Hindus in Chittagong use the expression *Allar hukum* (command) in the same sense as '*Deo volente.*' Aptavuddin, another Mahomedan poet of Chittagong who wrote a poem called the Jāmil Dilārām in 1750, writes that his hero, who was a Mahomedan, went to the nether worlds to seek a boon from the Saptarṣies or the seven sages of the Hindus.

A common god.

When the two communities mixed so closely, and were so greatly influenced by one another, the result was that a common God was called into existence, worshipped by Hindus and Mahomedans alike. His name was formed by compounding an Arabic word with a Sanskrit word. He was called Satya Pir. There are many poems on Satya Pir in old Bengali, some of which are noted below:—

Satya Pir.

1. Satya Pirer Pānchāli by Fakir Chānd, an inhabitant of Cuchiā in Chittagong, written in 1734.

2. Satya Pir by Rāmānanda.

3. Satya Pir by Çankarāchāryya written in 1636 A.D. A complete Ms. of this poem has been recovered by Babu Nagendra Nath Vasu from Mayurbhanja. It is a voluminous work and is divided into 15 chapters. The book discloses a curious fact about the origin of the god Satya Pir. It is a legendary account, but by comparison with the story in another work on Satya Pir by Nāyek Mayāj Gāji, we glean the fact that the Emperor Hosen Shāh of Gauḍa who tried to ensure the good will of his Hindu subjects, was the originator of the Satya Pir-cult, which made Hindus and Mahomedans join hands in worshipping a common God. Though in Orissa Satya Nārāyaṅa and Satya Pir are reckoned as the same God, they do not appear to be identical in Bengal. There is not a village in Bengal where Satya Nārāyaṅa is not worshipped once evey week, but in these *pujas* the Mahomedans do not join with the Hindus.

Poems on Satya Nārāyaṅa are to numerous to be mentioned here, as there is hardly a village in Bengal in which there is not a poem on the God; they scarcely deserve any notice being generally very short. We have quite a heap of Mss. on the subject giving short stories to illustrate the might and the grace of the deity: but none of them has risen to the dignity of a poem except the Hari Līlā by Jaya Nārāyaṅa and Ānanda Mayī about which we have already written, on pages 683-687. Amongst these Mss. we may mention one by Kavi Chandra containing a description of a river trip from Hugli to the Bay of Bengal with short notices of the places lying on both sides of the river. This account may be found interesting by students of Geography as it was written more than 200 years ago.

Hymns to Çiva and Sarasvati by Mahomedan poets.

In a work called Yāmini Vahāl by Karimullā—an inhabitant of Sitākundu in Chittagong (1780 A.D.), the heroine, a Mahomedan, is represented as praying to the God Çiva and in another work named Imam Yātrār Puthi, the Mahomedan author has a hymn addressed to Sarsvati, the goddess of learning, beginning with the lines—

*" Hail O Sarasvati, thou art my mother.

" Thy helpless child invokes thee ; will thou not hear."

Karamali.

Karam Ali, a leading poet of Chittagong, sang exquisitely on Rādhā and Krisna. One of his *padas* runs thus :—

†" Rādhā wept and said, who amongst you, O my maids will bring Krisna to me ?

" Vrindā, my friend, help me by bringing him here from Mathurā."

" My heart burns with the fire of love.

" The cuckoos on yonder boughs coo pleasantly.

---

*" আয় মা সরস্বতি, তুমি আমার মা ।
মা অনাথ বালক ডাকি শুনে শুনে না ॥"

†" কান্দ্যা কান্দ্যা বলিতেছে শ্রীমতী রাই ।
আন্যাদে, আন্যাদে মোর নাগর কানাই ॥
শুন আয় বৃন্দা দূতী বলি তোমারে
মথুরায় গেল হরি আন্যাদে মোরে ॥
প্রেমানলে দহে মোর হৃদয় অন্তরে ।
বৃন্দাবনে বসিলে, দেখি কোকিল কুহরে ॥

"How can I describe the agony that are caused by their notes.

"O maids of my heart, tell me who was so cruel as to cause the moon of the Vrindā groves to depart from here!

"No more do the bowers resound with the sweet notes of his flute calling 'Rādhā Rādhā.'

"Alas! am I become as nobody to him? O how sorrowful am I, when I think upon this!

"The poet Karam Āli says "Hear me Rādhā, Krisña is always in thine heart, enjoy the spiritual union, and do not weep."

There are short poetical treatises on music in old Bengali literature, mainly written by the Mahomedans. **Musical treatises.**

1. Rāga Mālā or an account of the various modes of Indian music with a poetical description of the presiding deity of each, and with songs in illustration by Āli Miān, Aloāl, and Tāhir Mahmud.

2. Tāla nāmā—a similar work containing songs by Saiyad Ainuddin, Saiyad Murttajā, Nasiruddin, Ālāol, Gāyeja, Dvija Raghu Nāth, Bhava-

---

কে হরিল প্রাণ দূতি, ব্রজের শশী।
বৃন্দাবনে রাধা বলে ডাকে না বাঁশী ॥
সেই সে মনের দুঃখ কইতে নারি কার ঠাঁই।
অভাগী রাধারে দিয়ে বুঝি শ্যামের কাজ নাই ॥
কহে শ্রীকরম আলি শুন গো প্যারী।
ধ্যানে ভজ নাগর কানাই, কেঁদনা শ্রীমতী রাই ॥
নিকটে আছেন তোমার প্রাণের হরি ॥"

Karam Āli.

nanda Āmin, Hira Maṅi and other writers. This book was compiled in 1840.

3. Sṛiṣti Pattana—a work on Indian music compiled by Dāneça Kāji, Nasir Mahamud and Baksh Ali. This book also gives an account of various modes of Indian music, with a number of songs in illustration of each.

4. Dhyāna Mālā by Ali Rāj. Ali Rāj was a fine poet. In this book he gives a detailed account of various modes of music—of the six Rāgas and 36 Rāginies with directions as to the hour and season suited for singing each, and accounts of the deities presiding over them. The songs given in illustration are all composed by Ali Rāj.

5. Rāga Tāler Puthi—a poem on Indian music compiled by Jivan Ali and Rāma Tanu Achāryya.

6. Rāga Tāla by Champā Gāzi.

7. Pada Saṁgraha—This work also deals with music. It is besides a compilation of songs by different poets of whom Lāl Veg contributes a large number.

8. Jubiā—a short treatise containing only 20 songs. These used formerly to be sung on the occasion of Mahomedan marriages.

(c) Stories.

We have a pretty large number of stories written by Mahomedan writers, most of them composed in the latter part of the 17th and in the earlier half of the 18th century. In most of them the decadent taste which marks the age of Bhārata Chandra is prominent. Though the heroes and heroines are generally Hindus, yet the inspiration of these poems seems to have come from Persian tales and poems.

Lor Chandrāni.

Under this head we should begin with Lor Chandrāni by Daulat Kāji,—a poem mentioned by Ālāol in his Padmāvati. Ālāol himself completed the book, for Daulat Kaji had not lived to finish it. The supplementary portion of Lor Chandrāni was contributed by Ālāol in the year 1657. Daulat Kāji's work was composed early in the 17th century. He had undertaken to write the poem at the command of Uzir Āsraf Khan of the Court of Runta Dharma-Rājā of Rosāng (Chittagong) whose capital is described as situated on the eastern bank of the river Karnafuli. The supplementary portion by Ālāol excels the original poem of Daulat Kāji in poetical merits.

Sapta Payakar and other stories.

Sapta Payakar by Ālāol—This poem contains seven stories, each said to have occupied one night in its narration.

Ranga Mālā by Kavir Mahmud.
Rejoān Sāhā by Samser Āli.
Bhāva Lābha by Sāmsuddin Chhiddik.
A passage in this poem runs as follows :—

"O my mind, on the ocean of this world, you have put out for trade but could win no profit.

"You forgot your real master and did not serve him as you should have done.

"The riches you sought are within you. How foolish are you to seek them elsewhere!

"Call upon Him who is the soul of your soul and He will give you relief.

"The poet Chhiddik here tells how he spent his life in vain pursuits, when he should have been serving his Master."

Eusuf Jelekhā—a Bengali rescension of Persian poem of Mahābbat nāmā by Ābdul Hākim.

Layeli Majanu—a famous Persian tale rendered into Bengali verse by Daulat Uzir Baharam.

Yāmin Jelāl and Chaitanya Silāl—a love-story by Mahomed Ākbar.

(*d*) Buddhist poems recovered from Chittagong.

Buddha Ranjikā. Bauddha Ranjikā by Nīla Kamala Dās. This is a translation of the Burmese work Thāḍu Thāng into Bengali metrical verse. The date of composition of this work is not known, but the Ms. is more than 100 years old. Nīla Kamala Das translated it under orders of Rāni Kālindī, wife of Rājā Dharma Baks of the Chittagong Hill tracts. It gives an account of Buddha's life from his birth to the time of his preaching the doctrine of Nirvāṅa. It is the only book yet found in old Bengali literature in which Buddha's life is described.

Nīlār Vāra Māsa. Nīlār Vāra Māsa. Who this Nīlā (Līlā) was no one knows; but the Bengali ladies still observe a fast on a particular day of April in memory of Līlāvatī. From the poem under notice it appears that Nīlā's husband turned a Buddhist monk renouncing his home, and Nīlā passed through unheard of hardships to get him back and win him to the sweets of a domestic life. The poem has come down to us as a rustic song; but though woven into crude rhymes, it has a deep pathos which explains to us the impression that the woes of Līlā must once have made on the popular mind. Līla's husband is described as having been an inhabitant of Nanda Pātana in Sulluk. His father's name was Gangādhara and his mother's name Kalāvati.

Mss. brought to light by M. Abdul Karim.

The works by Mahomedan writers noticed under the head 'Miscellaneous works' have been mainly brought to light by the researches of Munsi Abdul Karim, late Head Master of the Anwārā School in Chittagong. We have not been able to see these Mss., but brief notices of them have from time to time appeared in the Vangiya Sāhitya Parisat Patrikā from which our accounts are gleaned. The Mss. may be traced with the help of Munshi Abdul Karim. Considering the fact that a large number of these Mss. is being destroyed every year by white ants, worms and fire, as they are generally preserved in wretched straw-built huts, immediate efforts should be made to recover them. Otherwise we may only rise to the consciousness of the necessity of preserving them when it will be already too late.

Moslem writers of Radhā-Krisņa songs.

The works mentioned above disclose plenty of songs by Mahomedan writers on Rādhā and Krisņa, which show that the love songs of the Vaisņavas were appreciated beyond the pale of their own society, and inspired even that race of *Iconoclasts* who had once gloried in breaking up Hindu temples. The soil of India favours the growth of toleration and sympathy in religion, and it is no wonder to find that those who came with the sword became, in course of time, united to us in love and good will.

The works of Mahomedan writers mentioned in this book are all written in more or less sanskritised Bengali, and not in that style known as Musulmāṅni Bāngālā, which shows an admixture of Urdu, Persian and Arabic words with corrupt Bengali.

Works written in Musalmāni Bāngālā.

A vast literature of the rustic Mahomedans is to be found written in Musalmāni Bāngālā, and there are many works of this class, some of which may be traced back to the 16th century. But for various reasons we have not found it convenient to include books written in Musalmāni Bāngālā in the present work.

II. Mainly on style, literary tastes and language.

The Sanskrit metres in Bengali.

The chief feature of the poetical literature dealt with in this chapter is its wealth of *chhandas* or metres adopted from Sanskrit. Though in the earlier epochs some of our writers had tried to introduce Sanskrit metres, their attempts were marked with that crudeness which often characterises the products of beginners. Bāhrata Chandra has done yeoman's service to our literature by enriching it with various Sanskrit metres, some of which he imitated to perfection in Bengali. His *totaka* and *bhujanga prayata* are almost faultless—a success which could not have been anticipated in a language that seemed so unsuited as our own for the rich and varied metres of Sanskrit, especially as there is no distinction between long and short vowel sounds in its syllables. Rāma Prasāda was the first to attempt some of the Sanskrit metres in high-flown Bengali, and though his efforts were not crowned with a full measure of success, yet he discovered the innate strength of our language, which gave promise in his writings, of happier developments. In the Vidyā Sundara by Rāma Prasāda we often find the right accent of vowels not adhered to, as required by the particular metre that he attempted. For instance in his *totaka* in the line ধনি মুখ চিবুক ধরে যতনে the উ is untenable in মু and বু owing to its short sound. In the Hari lilā by Jaya Nārāyana, another clever poet, who tried his hand at Sanskrit metres in Bengali compositions, we find his *bhujanga prayata* faulty in many places, as for instance in the lines বসিয়া সুবর্ণের পীঠে হাসিছে। প্রবালাধরে মন্দ মন্দ ভাসিছে,—the ই in the second and the eleventh letters and the আ in the tenth letter of the 1st line are incorrect, and in the second line the 1st, the 7th, the 10th, and the 11th letters do not conform to the rules required by the metre: the first three ought to have short sounds and the last (the 11th) a long sound. Numerous instances of such faults may be found: but it was surely a bold step for writers to attempt Sanskritic metres in a language which had no long short and vowel-sounds in its current forms. But Bharata Chandra had a remarkable aptitude for hitting on the most appropriate words, and though he had to struggle against these disadvantages, yet he put the materials at his command to the best possible use. His remarkable power of choosing elegant expressions is best evidenced by the fact that though he successfully introduced some of the

Bhārata Chandra's signal success,

noblest Sanskrit metres into Bengali, yet there is no trace of any struggle on his part for this end. He creates pictures in words, as for instance, in his description of Çiva's great wrath, to which I have already referred on page 668. This could not have been grander in any other language. When we peruse his poems we are so powerfully captivated by his descriptions, that we quite forget that they were wrought in one of the most difficult metres of Sanskrit, with a perfection hitherto unequalled in Bengali. Bhārata Chandra's writings have suffered considerably in the hands of his copyists who were ignorant of the rules of Sanskrit verse. They occasionally tampered with the readings, and copyists as a class have always done so in regard to all other poems, with this difference that in the case of works written by other poets they have occasionally improved on the orignal by such changes, whereas in the case Bhārata Chandras's works they have invariably done more harm than good, as the change of a single syllable would disturb his scheme of metre, a matter of which ordinary copyists had no knowledge.

Çiva's anger in bhujanga prayāta.

I quote below the famous lines in the *bhujanga prayata* describing Çiva's anger. Now in the printed books we find শিঙ্গা in the second line for শিঙা, নন্দী in the 17th line for নন্দি (ই having been changed to ঈ, as the word forms a compound with ভৃঙ্গী). The metre contains 12 letters in each line and runs thus - – ⌣ - - ⌣ – – ⌣ – –. The text should be reduced to the following form for a right exposition of the metre :—

*ম হা রু দ্র রূ পে ম হা দে ব সা জে ।

ভ ভ ম্ভম্ ভ ভ ম্ভম্ শি ঙা ঘো র বা জে ॥

ল টা পট্ জ টা জূ ট সং ঘ ট্ট গ ঙ্গা ।

ছ ল চ্ছল্ ট ল ট্টল্ ক ল কল্ ত র ঙ্গা ।

ফ ণা ফণ্ ফ ণা ফণ্ ফ ণী ফ ণ্ন গা জে ।

দি নে শ প্র তা পে নি শা না থ সা জে ॥

ধ ক ধ্বক্ ধ ক ধ্বক্ জ্ব লে ব হ্নি ভা লে ।

ব ব ম্বম্ ব ব ম্বম্ ম হা শ ব্দ গা লে ॥

দ ল ম্মল্ দ ল ম্মল্ গ লে মু ণ্ড মা লা ।

ক টি ক ট্ট স দ্যো ম রা হ স্তি ছা লা ॥

---

*মহারুদ্ররূপে মহাদেব সাজে ।
ভভম্ভম্ ভভম্ভম্ শিঙা ঘোর বাজে ॥
লটাপট্ জটাজূট সংঘট্ট গঙ্গা ।
ছলচ্ছল্ টলট্টল্ কলকল তরঙ্গা ॥
ফণাফণ্ ফণাফণ্ ফণীফণ্ন গাজে ।
দিনেশপ্রতাপে নিশানাথ সাজে ॥
ধকধ্বক্ ধকধ্বক্ জ্বলে বহ্নি ভালে ।
ববম্বম্ ববম্বম্ মহাশব্দ গালে ॥
দলম্মল্ দলম্মল্ গলে মুণ্ডমালা ।
কটি কট্ট সদ্যোমরা হস্তিছালা ॥

প চা চ র্ম্ম ঝূ লী ক রে লো ল ঝো লে।

ম হা ঘো র আ ভা পি না ক ত্রি শূ লে ॥

ধি য়া তা ধি য়া তা ধি য়া ভূ ত না চে।

উ ল ঙ্গী উ ল ঙ্গে পি শা চী পি শা চে ॥

স হ স্রে স হ স্রে চ লে ভূ ত দা না।

হু হু ঙ্কা র হাঁ কে উ ড়ে স র্প বা ণা ॥

চ লে ভৈ র বা ভৈ র বী ন ন্দি ভৃ ঙ্গী।

ম হা কা ল বে তা ল তা ল ত্রি শৃ ঙ্গী ॥

চ লে ডা কি নী যো গি নী ঘো র বে শে।

চ লে শাঁ খি নী পে তি নী মু ক্ত কে শে ॥

পচাচর্ম্ম ঝূলী করে লোল ঝোলে।
মহাঘোর আভা পিনাকে ত্রিশূলে ॥
ধিয়া তাধিয়া তাধিয়া ভূত নাচে।
উলঙ্গী উলঙ্গে পিশাচী পিশাচে ॥
সহস্রে সহস্রে চলে ভূত দানা।
হুহুঙ্কার হাঁকে উড়ে সর্পবাণা ॥
চলে ভৈরবা ভৈরবী নন্দিভৃঙ্গী
মহাকাল বেতাল তাল ত্রিশৃঙ্গী ॥
চলে ডাকিনী যোগিনী ঘোর বেশে।
চলে শাঁখিনী পেতিনী মুক্ত কেশে ॥

গি য়া দ ক্ষ য জ্ঞে স বে য জ্ঞ না শে।

ক থা না স রে দ ক্ষ রা জে ত রা সে ॥

অ দূ রে ম হা রু দ্র ডা কে গ ভী রে।

অ রে রে অ রে দ ক্ষ দে রে স তী রে ॥

ভু জ ঙ্গ প্র য়া তে ক হে ভা র তী দে।

স তী দে স তী দে স তী দে স তী দে ॥

Rhyming added.

Besides closely following, as far as possible in Bengali, some of the noble Sanskrit metres, Bhārata Chandra performed a much more arduous task by making the couplets composed in Sanskrit metres rhyme with one another. Sanskrit verse does not require this, but the readers of Bengali during this period considered it to be an indispensable condition of poetical compositions. With all these self-imposed restrictions in his poem Bhārata succeeded in hiding the art he had employed, and the verses run clear and limpid reflecting the merry and sublime sentiments of the poet's soul.

গিয়া দক্ষযজ্ঞে সবে যজ্ঞ নাশে।
কথা না সরে দক্ষরাজে তরাসে ॥
অদূরে মহারুদ্র ডাকে গভীরে।
অরে রে অরে দক্ষ দে রে সতীরে ॥
ভুজঙ্গ-প্রয়াতে কহে ভারতী দে।
সতী দে সতী দে সতী দে সতী দে॥"

Long after Bhārata Chandra, Valadeva Pālit, a poet who wanted to revive the old taste for artistic poetry, which had, however, in his time grown to be a thing of the past, employed in his Bengali poem called Bhartṛihari Kāvya, all the chief metres of Sanskrit. He was a true student imbued with a refined classical taste and his Sanskrit vocabulary was immense. With all these qualities, however,

Valadeva Pālit.

he failed to make any impression in the literature of his period. Bhārata had been essentially a poet of his age which had demanded in Bengali poetry a close conformity with the rules of Sanskrit rhetoric; alliteration and other figures of speech were prominent characteristics of the period, and the school begun by Bhārata Chandra served as a model to a host of writers; he had besides been a born poet, who adorned all that he touched, and if he em-

His attempts to revive Ssnskrit metres.

ployed Sanskritic metres, it was because a keen appreciation of the beauty of their sound so completely possessed his soul that he could not resist their flow in his Bengali poetry. Valadeva, however, wrote with the pedantic object of showing himself learned, and he succeeded in this end, for his readers certainly gave him a certificate that his ingenuity elicited their admiration; but the laurels which adorn the brow of a true poet were not reserved for a writer of his conceit and pedantry. I quote below two extracts from the writings of Valadeva Pālit to illustrate the metres Mālinivritti (containing fifteen letters in each line) running thus: ⏑ ⏑ ⏑ ⏑ ⏑ ⏑ — — — ⏑ — — ⏑ — —) and Vaṁçasthavila (containing 12 letters in each) running thus: ⏑ — ⏑ — — ⏑ ⏑ — ⏑ — ⏑ — respectively.

Mālinivritti :—

"ফুল সম সুকুমারী, দীর্ঘকেশী কৃশাঙ্গী
অচপল তড়িতাভা সুন্দরী গৌরকান্তি ;
মধুর নববয়স্কা পদ্মিনী অগ্রগণ্যা
যুবক-নয়ন-লোভা কামিনী কামশোভা ॥"

Vaṁçasthavila :—

"তথায় ভীমাসিত-বর্ম্ম-ভূষিত
প্রচণ্ড আভাময় চক্র মস্তকে।
সবিদ্যুতাগ্নি প্রলয়োন্মুখাভ্রবৎ
কৃপাণ-পাণি প্রহরী ব্রজে ভূমে ॥"

The lines in the Mālini *chhanda* are nearly correct. In the third line of the stanza in Vaṁçasthvila the writer commits a mistake in compounding সবিদ্যুতাগ্নি which should have been সবিদ্যুদগ্নি. There are, besides, some other inaccuracies also. Valadeva Pālit, when putting Bengali verse in Sanskrit metre, omits to conform to the rule observed by the preceding Bengali writers, *viz.*, that all metrical verses should rhyme. Strictly speaking the words প্রচণ্ড আভাময় are untenable in a Bengali poem which requires, that after the first word in a line containing three letters there should be a corresponding word containing three letters.

Payāra Chhanda.

The bulk of the old poetical literature of Bengal is in the metre called the Payāra. It consists of 14 letters in each line, and there is a cæsura after 8 letters. If the first word in a line of Payāra consists of two letters, either the second must have four letters or the second and the third must have two letters each. If the first word has four letters, the second word must have either four letters or the second and the third words, two letters each. If the first word has three letters, the second word must have three letters as well. That verse is defective which violates this rule, though all the letters counted in a line may come up to 14. The first line rhymes with the second and the two rhyming lines make an entire stanza. The word Payāra has been evidently derived from the word Pada. The word 'Pāyā' in Bengali which means the foot of a bedstead, or 'Tripāyā' which means a three-footed light-stand, illustrates the similar forms derived from the word Pada.

Tripadī.

The next favourite metre of the old poets was the Tripadī. The Tripadī was a verse of the Rig Veda containing three padas or hemistiches. The verses were called Tripada Riks (*vide* Pānini IV, 1, 9). This metre which is traced to the Rig Veda was adopted in Prākrita and through that channel passed into Bengali. In Tripadī as in the case of Payāra, there was in the early times no hard and fast rule about the number of letters, but gradually as the study of metre reached perfection, the number of letters in each hemistich, of which there are three making a half stanza, was fixed. The first two half-lines which rhyme, contain six letters each, and the third half-line which rhymes with the 6th contains eight letters. Jayadeva introduced this Sanskritic metre though without observing any definite number in the letters. Rhyme was no necessary condition. The half-stanza 'রতিসুখসারে, গতমভিসারে মদনমনোহরবেশম্'—sounds as the keynote to the modern Tripadī in Bengali. In the next half-stanza, however. '—ন কুরু নিতম্বিনি, গমনবিলম্বন মনুসর তং হৃদয়েশম্'

and its offshoots.

the first half-lines do not rhyme. They consist besides of seven letters each, and the third half-line of eight letters. In Prākrita, the verses like চরণ-গণবিপ্প, পঢ়মলইথপ্প or সত্তা দীহা জানেহী, কণ্ণাতিণ্ণামানেহী" (Pingala) illustrate that the Tripada and the Dvipada metres first traced in the Rig Veda had branched off into many quaint forms in the Prākrita language. The Dvipada and Tripada metres attained perfection in Bengali ; and various metres in this tongue, such as the *Dīrgha Tripadī, †Laghu Tripadī, ‡Bhanga Tripadī, §Dīrgha Chaupadī, ||Hinapada

---

*" কালীদহের জলে, কুমারী কমলদলে.
গজ গিলে উগারে অঙ্গনা ॥"

Chandi by Kavikañkaṅa.

†" থাক, থাক. থাক. কাটাইব নাক. আগেতে রাজারে কহি ।
মাথা মুড়াইব. শালে চড়াইব, ভারতে কহিছে সহি ॥"

Vidyāsundara by Bhārata Chandra.

‡" ওরে বাছা ধূমকেতু. মা বাপের পুণ্যহেতু,
কেটে ফেল চোরে, ছেড়ে দেহ মোরে. ধর্ম্মের বাঁধহ সেতু ।"

Vidyāsundara by Bhārata Chandra.

§" এক কাণে শোভে ফণিমণ্ডল, এক কাণে শোভে মণিকুণ্ডল.
আধ অঙ্গে শোভে বিভূতি ধবল, আধই গন্ধ কস্তুরীরে ॥

Annada Mañgala by Bhārata Chandra

||" হর মম দুঃখ হর ।
হর রোগ, হর তাপ, হর শোক, হর পাপ, হিমকরশেখর শঙ্কর ॥"

Annadā Mañgala by Bhārata Chandra.

Tripadī, *Mātrā Tripadī and †Mātrā Chatuṣpadī, &c., have been formed in Bangali by an archaic manipulation of the Dvipada and Tripadī metres, as also by an artistic combination of them.

The earlier Tripadī.

The earlier Tripadī metres were of a crude form. There was neither that elegant rhyming nor that fixity in the number of letters in each line which have rendered it now-a-days one of the most lovely metres in our tongue. We quote the following extracts from the Mahabhārata by Kavīndra Parameçvara, written 400 years ago, to show how quaint in form it was in those days.

and its example.

"শিশু হতে পুত্র, দেবগুরু পূজন্ত,
নাহিক যে পরস্পর ভেদ,
বিপ্রতর্পন্ত, সতত করেন্ত,
অভ্যাস করন্ত ধনুর্ব্বেদ ॥

সতত সত্য ছাড়ি অসত্য না বোলেন্ত।
প্রতিবর্গের, প্রাণ সমসর,
বিচিত্র যোদ্ধা মহাবীর ॥
মাদ্রী গর্ভে হৈল, মোহর প্রিয় পুত্র,
নকুল কোমল শরীর ॥
বহুশত্রু ক্ষয়, করিল পুত্র মোর,
পুনি কি দেখিমু নয়নে।
কহ ত গোবিন্দ, হাহা শিশুপুত্র,
নকুল চলিয়া গেল বনে ॥"

---

*" ঝন ঝন কঙ্কণ, নূপুর রণ রণ।
ঘুনু ঘুনু ঘুঙ্ঘুর বোলে।"

Vidyāsundara by Bhārata Chandra.

†"হে শিবমোহিনি, শম্ভ-নিসূদনি, দৈত্যবিঘাতিনি, দুঃখহরে ॥"

Annadā Maṅgala by Bhārata Chandra.

In all the earlier works we find Tripadī adopted in Bengali verses for the purpose of conveying sentiments of grief ; it was considered to be the fit metre by the poets of old school for giving expression to feelings of mourning or of any dire loss, and it was called নাচাড়ী which is no doubt a corrupt form of the word লহরী.

Folly in alliteration and puns.

The artistic school of Bhārata Chandra greatly improved the resources of our language, and contributed to that elegance for which it has now won universal praise ; but their attempts often produced abortive results also in the craze for alliteration, evinced not only by poets but by writers of prose during this period. Alliteration and puns on words became a notorious literary folly, many writers having carried them to abnormal excesses. One can hardly imagine how a sane man could have produced a composition like the following ;—

"রে পাষণ্ড ষণ্ড, এই প্রকাণ্ড ব্রহ্মাণ্ডকাণ্ড দেখিয়াও কাণ্ডজ্ঞান শূন্য হইয়া বকাণ্ড প্রত্যাশার ন্যায় লণ্ডভণ্ড হইয়া ভণ্ড সন্ন্যাসীর ন্যায় ভক্তি-ভাণ্ড ভঞ্জন করিতেছ এবং গবাপণ্ডের ন্যায় গণ্ডে জন্মিয়া গণ্ডকীস্থ গণ্ডশিলার গণ্ড না বুঝিয়া গণ্ডগোল করিতেছ ."

Even gifted writers like Içvara Chandra Gupta were not free from the great folly of the age, and we find his prose writings often disfigured by too much indulgence in alliteration. In the Çiçu Vodhaka, an elementary book for children, that used to be read in the Pathaçālās half a century ago, there is much useful and instructive information for the boys to which no one can take objection, but there is an atrocious model letter in it which must have been contributed by a pedantic Sanskrit scholar, the silliness of which, not to speak of its wicked taste, passes all limit of decency, specially as it has been incorporated in to a juvenile reader. We need not dwell upon the letter which is an example of a wife writing to her husband, but to show how a spirit of alliteration prevailed in the age, we quote its first lime.

" শ্রীচরণ-সরসি দিবানিশি সাধন-প্রয়াসী দাসী "

Not only in regard to alliteration but in puns on words also, the fashion ran to excess. We quote below passages from various writers to show the sort of puns which characterised the writings of the day. Examples of them are only too numerous in the writings of standard authors of this period :

"ও বীণে, লবিনে, জানকী-প্রাণকান্তের নাম বিনে।
যে পথে আছে কাল রবিসুত রে, সে পথে যেন রবিনে॥"

Dāçarathi.

" যতই কাঁদে বাছা বলি সর সর
আমি অভাগিনী বলি সর্ সর্
বল্লেম নাহি অবসর কেবা দিবে সর
অমনি সর্ সর্ বলে ফেলিলাম ঠেলে "
" যদি না পাই কিশোরীরে কাজ কি শরীরে "
" উপেখিলে রাই স্থান অখিলে নাই "

Krisṇa Kamala.

The typical writer of the age like Butler's Hudibras

"...............could not ope
His mouth, but outflew a trope."

But artificiality can never completely crush nature. Like those tiny weeds and plants whose rootlets pierce through adamantine rocks and draw their sap from stones, the literature of an age held in the iron grip of rhetoric, has yet strange offshoots which, though humble, discover a strength not possessed by the great,—sufficient to assert the victory of nature over all the forces and appliances employed to thwart her. Some of the Kaviwālās, who were almost illiterate, composed songs in unassuming and artless language, which charmed even the highly educated of this age of rigid classic taste by their simplicity. The Umā *sangita*, of which I have already spoken in a foregoing chapter, composed by writers of meagre education, discloses a style in which simple and elegant words produce, without any attempt at puns or alliteration, a far greater effect on the emotions than all the grandiloquent phraseology at the command of a poetic master of rhetoric could do.

How nature asserts herself.

Not only some of the Kaviwālās, but also Nidhu Babu, who was a man of light and leading, preferred simple words and a plainness of style which strikes us by its contrast with the spirit of pedantry that guided contemporary writers.

When Sanskrit metres were being so closely adopted in Bengali poems, and learned scholars were trying to place the art of writing poetry hopelessly out of reach of the common mortals by imposing subtle rules on all forms of versification, Dāçarathi Rāy's new school of doggerel, called Pānchāli, asserted itself in bold defiance of all metrical rules,—rhyming being the only condition in their composition. He certainly took his cue from the sort of verses made extempore by the Kaviwālās as sequel to their songs. The Bengali poetry of a very early age had been called Pānchāli. This was a period

Daçarathi's Pānchāli—a departure from classical model.

when the metre Payār had not been fossilised into 14 letters with the rules of cæsura and the arrangements of words in each line to which I have already referred. Panchāli was the metre for the masses. The last letter of the first line agreed with the last letter of the second line; and no other restraint was put upon it. Sometimes we get couplets of the following nature:—

"পরিধানের সাড়ী দিল ময়নামতি জলত বিছায়্যা।
যোগাসন করিল ময়না ধরম স্মরণ করিয়া॥"

Manik Chandra Rājar Gān.

The first line contains 20 letters and the second line 19. There are also numerous instances of very short lines, as "তার বদলে ছয় মাস কাল খায়" (13 letters).

Dāçarathi revised the Pānchāli with this difference that without conforming to the rules of the Payār, Tripadi, or any other kind of Bengali metre, he had still a way of rhyming of his own, and the expressions that he particularly chose were not crude or inelegant as in their earlier prototypes, but were generally of a refined character, though simple and colloquial. The Pānchāli suited the understanding of illiterate audiences who were taken by surprise by the wonderful rapidity and flow of doggerel-rhyme, which took a wild course, owing to its freedom from the restraints of any regular metre. I quote a few verses from Dāçarathi's Pānchāli.

"রাজার মায়ের এমনি গুণ—11 (letters)
ভাল করুণ বা না করুণ—10 (letters)
না গেলে পরে মন্দ করবেন রাগে—13 (letters)
উনি বল্‌ছেন পাবে অশ্ব—10 (letters)
আমি বল্‌ছি পাব ভস্ম—9 (letters)
পোড়া কপালে জোড়া নাহি লাগে—11 (letters)

The first line rhymes with the second, the third with the sixth and the fourth with the fifth, so he follows no fixed code. Besides this, while going on with his verses in the above strain, he suddenly introduces a quite different form, which shows some affinity with the Tripadi, more often breaking its rules, however, than conforming to them.

When the rules of metre had put such complex restraint on metrical compositions, the Pānchāli and the extempore verses of the *Kaviwalas* opened out a new channel for the free expression of the thoughts and sentiments of our masses for whom Bengali had already became too learned,—not so much in its vocabulary as in its artistic forms and in the subtle conditions of its metre.

Learned discussions.

This was an age when a display of classical learning was made through the vehicle of the vernacular, and as a matter of course it was most in evidence in the discussions of scholarly Brahmins on various points of philosophy and literature. On these occasions there were animated scenes in which the Brahmins, in the enthusiasm of advocating their own points, often dragged their opponents by the locks of hair that dangled behind their shaven heads, or otherwise offered what appeared like affronts of a personal nature. These of course never reached any very immoderate excess. The lock was really pulled to draw the attention of the opponent to the points which his rival Pundit had so enthusiastically tried to establish. In a heated scene of this nature box after box of snuff was emptied of its contents in a few moments, and the discussion sometimes continued day and night. There was invariably a judge or mediator where two Pundits argued, and his duty was not only to give the final verdict, so that the vanquished might not argue any more, but also to interrupt when any irrelevency or want of moderation marked the controversy. The Pundits were generally called to a rich man's house on the occasion of Çrāds and other religious ceremonies, and those who excelled in open controversy with their rivals were entitled to special rewards, though many would not accept any gift whatever, priding themselves both on their scholarship and their poverty. This system of inviting the Pundits by rich men is still preserved in Bengal *in form*; but with the decadence of the spirit of patronising Sanskrit learning, the matter has lost the great importance and interest which it once possessed. In rich men's houses, the well-known Pundits not only of Bengal, but of the whole of India, used to be assembled for the discussion of Philosophy, Logic, Poetry, Astronomy, Theology and other subjects. Thus learning received a social impetus, and even fresh life on such occasions. Opportunities were frequently offered to Pundits for such meetings, so that during a period when there were no facilities of communication, and no proper conveyances for undertaking long journies, this system kept alive a continual interchange of high thoughts and thus contributed to the preservation and development of classical learning. The Pundits led very simple lives, without coveting earthly fortunes or caring for luxury of any kind, and were quite indifferent to praise or blame—often really devoted to a high spiritual life and to the cause of learning. The following passage from

The meeting of the learned.

And its great usefulness.

Jaya Nārāyaṇa's Hari Līlā shows what the discussions of the Pundits were like. The poet describes a meeting on a festal occasion.

The description of a meeting

*"The learned Brahmins received letters of invitation and hastened to attend the meeting.

"They were present there with the sole object of furthering the cause of their religious doctrines and were not prepared to accept any gifts.

"Their faces beamed with intelligence, and dressed in white garments, they seated themselves on scarlet-coloured Bhutan seats.

"They wore the sacred Ganges' mud on their foreheads; and white sacred threads adorned their breasts.

"As soon as they took their seats they commenced an animated discussion.

"The Logicians stepped forward to discuss the question of conclusions from given premises, and the evidence of the senses, pointing out the connection between proof and the thing proven.

---

*"ব্রাহ্মণ পণ্ডিতগণে, পাইয়া পত্র নিমন্ত্রণে,
উপনীত সভা আরোহণে।
কেবল অধিষ্ঠান মাত্র, দান নিতে নহে পাত্র,
ধর্ম্ম সংস্থাপন কারণে॥
তেজসপুঞ্জ সুকিরণ, শুক্লবর্ণ সুবসন,
ভালেতে গঙ্গামৃত্তিকা ফোঁটা।
শুক্ল যজ্ঞোপবীতে, রক্ত ভোট আসনেতে,
বসিতেহি বিচারের ঘটা॥
অনুমান প্রত্যক্ষেতে, পরস্পর সম্বন্ধেতে,
তার্কিক ঘটায় নানা তর্ক।

"They cited Kusumānjali as their authority and tried to establish the fact of the divine existence by various methods of argument.

"In a discussion about words and topics, containing long compound words of which each would take half an hour to recite, the grammarians began to find fault with one another's arguments, and made home-thrusts against their opponents, basing their discourses chiefly on the supplement by Gopinātha.

"In another quarter sweet discourses on rhetoric were going on. Their subject was figurative allusions and the suggestions they contained. They drew illustrations in support of their theories from the Kāvya Prakāça.

"There were fair fights on literary subjects also. The mediators were often called in to give their verdict in respect to the interpretations given by

---

প্রমাণ কুসুমাঞ্জলি, নানা মতে ব্রহ্ম বলি,
একে আর ঘটায় সম্পর্ক ॥
শব্দ পদার্থ বিচারেতে, এক দণ্ড সমাসেতে,
কার কত নিন্দিত ঘটাইয়া ।
বৈয়াকরণিয়া সবে, বিচার কর্কশ রবে,
গোপীনাথ পরিশিষ্ট লইয়া ॥
মধুর বাক্যের বাণী, অলঙ্কার শুনি ধ্বনি,
এক দিগে কহিছে রসেতে ।
ধ্বনি বাক্য কয়ে কয়ে, ব্যঞ্জনাদিক লয়ে,
কাব্য প্রকাশ উদাহরণেতে ॥

opposing parties, of the meanings of lines from the Raghu, the Bhatti, the Çiçupāla Vadha and the Naiṣadha Kāvya.

"Those who discoursed on the Purāṇas quoted chapter and verse from Vaçiṣtha, and others, who elected Astrology as the subject of their discourse discussed particular conjunctions of planets and their aspects, positions, and influences in regard to human life. Their chief authority was the Suryya Siddhānta.

"The Vedāntists held that the supreme soul pervades all; virtue and vice, which appear to us as such from a superficial point of view, are merely phenomenal. All alike spring from Him. There is nothing hostile or friendly. Such ideas are merely

---

নানা ছন্দে শ্লোক পাঠ, সাহিত্যে বিচার ঠাট,
কত মত বর্ণনা ভাবের।
রসিক বিবুধগণে, মধ্যস্থ পণ্ডিত মানে
রঘু, ভট্ট, মাঘ, নৈষধের॥
পৌরাণিক পণ্ডিতে, নানা মত প্রসঙ্গেতে,
বিচার করিছে ভাবি মনে।
বশিষ্টাদি বেদ জানে, স্তন্‌ফ ভাবগণে,
অস্ত প্রত্যন্তর লিখি।
দশা বিদশা বসতি, জানায় সাধু প্রতি,
সূর্য্য সিদ্ধান্তের মত দেখি॥
সকলেতে ব্রহ্মময়, বেদান্তে এমত কয়,
পাপ পূণ্যালয় নিরঞ্জন।
শত্রু মিত্রময় তিনি, জ্ঞান ভেদে ভিন্ন মানি
শঙ্করাচার্য্যের এ লিখন॥

illusive. He alone is really root of all. This is the view, the Vedantists argued, that was held by Çankarāchāryya; also the great law-giver Çula Pāni, Manu, and others have openly avowed this truth."

The education of women.

Amongst respectable people the women-folk not only received a sound education in Bengali, but often acquired a good knowledge of Sanskrit also. Ānandamayī's education made her a match for any ordinary Sanskrit-knowing Pundit; and of her literary compositions, bearing evidences of great pedantry, we have already spoken in full. Yajneçvari, a poetess who composed songs for a Kavi party, lived in the beginning of the 19th century, and some of her songs show creditable command over the language. Gangāmaṅi Devī, a sister of the poet Jaya Nārāyaṅa Sen and a native of Vikrampur in Dācca, composed a large number of songs, which the women of that place sing up to now, during marriage festivities.

Arabic, Persian, and Hindi.

In the courts of the Hindu Rājās it was considered an indispensable acquirement for a scholar to have a knowledge of Arabic, Persian and Hindusthāni. The Pundits who scrupulously avoided all court-influences, considered a knowledge of any other language than Sanskrit as profane, just as they would not touch a non-Hindu or a low caste Hindu for fear of contamination.

পড়িলে বিপত্তিকালে, দোষ যদি ঘটে বলে,
ধর্ম্মশাস্ত্র মতে পাপ নহে।
স্মৃতিশাস্ত্রে লেখা এই, শূলপাণি মত এই,
মুক্তকণ্ঠ হৈয়া মনু কহে॥"

But those Brahmins, who did not soar so high in their fancied greatness and cared for the favour of the Rājās, acquired Bengali, Persian, Arabic and Hindusthani along with Sanskrit, and Bhārata Chandra Rāy Guṅākara was a man of sound culture in all these tongues. In describing a conversation between the Emperor Jāhāngīr and Rājā Mān Sinha, our poet says :—

*" It would be fit in the nature of things to give the gist of the conversation, that took place between Rājā Mān Sinha and the Emperor in Arabic, Persian and Hindusthani, for it must have been carried on in a mixed language. I have studied these languages and can write in them; but the account would scarcely be intelligible to ordinary people. Besides, by giving the discourse in different languages I should destroy the effect on the reader's mind of my own poetry, and it would lose much of its simplicity. So I must be content with borrowing only, occasionally, words from those languages in my Bengali."

But though he curbed his desire in this instance to display his varied scholarship, he did not always use such discretion. He adopted a heterogenous

* " মানসিংহ পাতসার হইল যে বাণী।
উচিত যে পারশী, আরবী, হিন্দুস্থানী॥
পড়িয়াছি সেইমত বর্ণিবারে পারি।
কিন্তু সে সকল লোক বুঝিবারে ভারি॥
না রবে প্রসাদগুণ না হবে রসাল।
অতএব কহি ভাষা যবনী মিশাল॥"

language in a certain short poem for the purpose of display. The following extract will show what such efforts were like.

> "শ্যামহিত প্রাণেশ্বর. বারদকে গোয়দ কুবর,
> কাতর দেখে আদর কর, কাহে মরুরো রোয়কে।
> বক্তুং বেদং চন্দ্রমা, চুঁ লালা চে রেঁমা,
> ক্রোধিত পর দেও ক্ষমা, মেটিমে কাহে শোয়কে ॥"

Change undergone by words in use and meaning.

Some of the words that were largely used in the 18th century have grown obsolete. The word 'মেনে' for instance, which we meet with frequently in Bhārata Chandra's poems, is no longer used in writing. The word seems to have no meaning; it was only used to emphasise a statement or merely to fill up a space in a line of verse which did not come up to the fixed number of letters required by the metre. The words নেহা, পেখিল, রঘরণী দোহে, এথায়, এবে, এড়িল are not now used in prose-writings; they are confined to poetry.

There are numerous words in Bengali which have lost their original Sanskritic significance. The word পীরিত is derived from প্রীতি-love, but the former word in colloquial Bengali has been degraded in sense, and implies an illicit love. It was the promiscuous mixing of men and women in the lower orders of Vaiṣṇava society, which by leading to immorality, caused the degeneration in the meaning of this word. But at the time of Chandi Dās, and even of the poets of a subsequent age, the word was still true to its original significance in current Bengali and implied a pure sentiment. Chandi Dās wrote short discourses using the word to imply a highly refined and austere feeling. The word রাগ has two meanings in Sankrit ; it means colour and attachment. In Bengali it has come to signify fits of anger, probably owing to one's face and eyes being reddened under passion. But at the time of Chaitanya, 400 years ago, the Bengali word had not yet lost its original meaning. In the Kaḍcnā by Govinda Dās we find it used in the sense of love or attachment, as in the line "রাগে ডগমগ প্রভু করে সম্বরণ." There is no difference in Sanskrit between the words রাগ and অনুরাগ. In Bengali, the one implies anger, and the other love, though the words রঞ্জিত and অনুরঞ্জিত—participal adjective-forms of the two words respectively—have retained their Sanskritic significance. The Bengali word derived from Sanskrit ভর্ত্তা (lit. one who maintains), a husband, has been degraded in Bengali and is not used in decent society, though I can not make out the reason why The word ভাণ্ডারী (lit. a store-keeper) does not possess its original elevated sense ; it now generally means with us a menial servant. The word ভাস্বর in colloquial Bengali means the husband's elder brother ; but in Sanskrit it means shining, splendid. The Hindu women of Bengal consider it sacrilegious to name the elder brothers of their husbands. When he is to be mentioned, they refer to him by some qualifying adjective. The word ভাস্বর, originally 'shining,' must have been thus reduced to its present restricted meaning. The words শ্রীযুক্ত and শ্রীমান (endowed with *Cri*—fortune) in Sanskrit have the same meaning, but in Bengali শ্রীযুক্ত is used in regard to elders or equals, and শ্রীমান্ invariably to junior relations. The word রৌদ্র in Sanskrit means 'fierce,' though there is a rare use of it in that tongue implying sun-shine. In Bengali রৌদ্র is the commonest term to signify sun-shine, and except scholarly folk, no one knows that originally its meaning was fierce. The word মহোৎসব has been restricted in Bengali to imply that particular festivity of the Vaiṣṅavas in which cooked food is indiscriminately distributed amongst the poor, who assemble there without invitation. The word literally means a great festivity, and in Sanskrit it is always used in that sense. Similarly the word সঙ্কীর্ত্তন, which in Sanskrit means reciting or singing, has been restricted in Bengali to a particular kind of singing of God's name by a procession party of the Vaiṣṅavas.

Bengali sculptors.

We find frequent references to sculptural work done in Bengal on stone in which the artisans of Navadvipa excelled. Rājā Jaya Narayaṅa in his Kāçi Khanda says that many orders of stone images for the temples at Benares were executed by Nadiā artisans. In the Bhakti Ratnākara we find the name of one renowned sculptor to be Nayana Bhāskara, a resident of Hālisahar in Twenty-four Parganas.

III. Early Prose Literature.

Bengali, a mixed language.

A people who had lost their political supremacy, and had no voice in the administration of their own country,—who had retired to quiet village-life and pastoral occupations, and had scarcely any occasion to commune with the rest of the world,—what need had they for cultivating prose? Outside their quiet homes they came to towns only for trade or to transact litigation in courts, and had to deal with a heterogenous people who would not recognise pure Bengali as a medium of communication. In their correspondence or documentary writings the Bengalis had to adopt a mixed language, into which not only Persian and Arabic but even Portuguese elements had entered in no inconsiderable degree; for these people were a great power in Bengal, more than two centuries and a half ago; and we read the following account of their language, having been adopted, for business purposes, by Europeans and Bengalis alike. We quote from Mr. Marshman's history of the Çri Rāmapur Mission Vol. I.* The writer refers to incidents occurring in 1759.

Portuguese elements.

"Portuguese came in with the Portuguese power two centuries and a half before, and survived its extinction. It was the Lingua Franca of all foreign settlements around the Bay of Bengal and was the ordinary medium of conversation between the Europeans and their domestics; while Persian was the language of intercourse with the native courts. Even in Calcutta Portuguese was more commonly used by the servants of the company and the settlers than the language of the country. The charter granted to the East India Company at the beginning of the 18th century contained a provision that they should maintain one Minister at each of their garrisons and superior factories, and that he should be bound to acquire the Portuguese language within a twelve-month of reaching India. Clive, who was never able to give an order in any native language, spoke Portuguese with fluency. The use of this language has since died out in

* pp. 21—22.

Bengal so completely that the descendants of the Portuguese now speak Bengali from their cradle. Yet down to so late a period as 1828, the Governor of Çri Rāmapur, a Norwegian, received the daily report of his little garrison of 30 sepoys from the Native Commandant, a native of Oudh in Portuguese."

A small number of words subjoined in the foot-note* are some of the remnants retained in Bengali of the great admixture of Portuguese which our language must have once borne in business and domestic colloquies.

The nature of the mixed language.

The prose, in which business transactions were conducted in Bengal, was thus a medley of many different languages, and it was to this point that Mr. Halhed one of the first Bengali grammarians refers with regret. In the very nature of things a pure Bengali prose could not grow up. The Maho-

*Bengali.	Portuguese.	Bengali.	Portuguese.
জোলাপ	... Jalapa.	রেস্ত	... Resto (fund)
টোকা	... Toca (to note down).	স্থরতি	... Sorte.
		আনারস	... Ananaz.
নোনা	... Annona (fruit).	আয়া	... Aya.
		আলকাৎরা	... Alcetrao.
পিপা	... Pipa.	কপি (শাক)	... Couvi.
পেরেক	... Prego.	কাকাতুয়া	... Catatua.
ফর্ম্মা	... Forma.	কিরীচ	... Cris
ফিতা	... Fita.	কেদারা	... Cathedera.
বোয়া	... Boia.	গরাদে	... Grade.
বরগা	... Verga.	গির্জ্জা	... Igrija.
বাল্‌তি	... Baldi.	চাবি	... Chave.
বোতাম	... Botao.	জানালা	... Janella.

medans did not recognise it in their courts, and the people had no power to assert their own tongue in the field of business. As long as Mahomedans held the supreme power, Arabic and Persian were recognised by all as the chief languages of the Court, and in the mixed dialects, which grew up, an admixture of these two languages was held to be a point of glory. Says Mr. Halhed in the preface to his grammar published in 1778 :—

"At present those persons are thought to speak the compound idiom (Bengali) with the most elegance, who mix with pure Indian verbs the greatest number of Persian and Arabic nouns."

What this prose was like may be seen from the documentary writings still prevalent in courts. The court language still favours a preponderence of Persian and Arabic elements in Bengali, as in 'টাল মাটালে আদায় না করায়' or in 'ওয়াদা কার্ত্তিক মাসে টাকা আদায় করিব.' Curiously enough remnants also of Sanskrit elements still persist in the language of the courts, reminding us of the ancient days of Hindu supremacy, when all court transactions were carried on in Sanskrit. The form 'কস্য কর্জ্জ পত্রমিদং কার্য্যাঞ্চাগে' has preserved, though in a ridiculously corrupt style, some of the legal terms of the Hindu age. In ordinary letters written by the gentle folk of Bengal there was a large admixture of Persian words. Mr. Beveridge published some letters of the Mahārājā Nanda Kumāra in the National Magazine of September, 1872, written to Radhā Krisṅa Ray and Dinanatha Sāmantaji in August, 1756. We quote an extract from one of these letters.

"অতএব এ সময়ে তুমি কমর বাঁধিয়া আমার উদ্ধার করিতে পার, তবেই যে হউক, নচেৎ আমার নাম লোপ হইল, ইহা মকররর, মকররর জানিবে, নাগাদি ৩রা ভাদ্র, তথাকার রোয়দাদ সমেত মজুমদারের লিখন সম্বলিত মনুষ্য কাসেদ এথা পোঁছে তাহা করিবা, এবিষয়ে এক পত্র লক্ষ হইতে অধিক জানিবা।"

Causes leading to the development of modern prose.

I may add here, that the chief causes that have contributed to the development of Bengali prose in modern times are (1) the preference of Bengalis to live in conjested cities, (2) the establishment of Post offices all over the land, (3) the easy means of communication afforded by railways and steamers, helping the unification of different provincial dialects by eliminating provincialisms, (4) the great efforts of Missionaries and of Government, particularly in the earlier periods of British rule, to spread education amongst the masses.

The early Bengali prose-works.

But though circumstances did not favour the development of Bengali prose before the advent of the English on the field, and though Mr. Nathenie! Prassy Halhed could not lay his hand upon any prose-work in Bengali, as he tells us in his preface, such works, nevertheless, did exist in the country in his time, and long before it, though they did not possess that importance which would render them accessible to any casual enquiry. I shall here notice some of the books that have come down to us, as specimens of early Bengali prose.

The Çuṅya Puraṅa.

1. The Çunya Puraṅa is one of the earliest works in Bengali, upon which we have already written (page 30). It was composed in the 10th century and though it was recast in subsequent times, the few prose portions which it contains have

retained their antiquated form. The sentences are like short riddles and sound more like poetry than prose. Here is a specimen.

*"Who is the scholar in the western gate ? Çvetāi with four hundred followers. Chandra, the Police Officer......the messenger is not afraid of thee. Chitra Gupta keeps a register." The portion left out is unintelligible. There is a very considerable portion of prose-writing in the book in this style.

Deva Dāmara Tantra.

2. Along with this writing may be placed the specimen of prose which we have found in the Deva Dāmara Tantra, running as follows "গোঁসাই চেলা সহস্র কামিনী ডোমা, চাঁড়াল পাই মুই আকাটন বিষ হাতে এ গুয়া পান খাইয়া।" We avow our inability to translate or interpret this.

3. A small prose treatise ascribed to the poet Chandi Dās, who lived 500 years ago, has come down to us. It is called Chaitya Rupa Prāpti. The booklet seems to interpret in mystic language the incantations and riddles of the Tāntrikas. The Ms. copy in our possession was written in the year 1674. The preliminary sentence runs thus:—

Chaitya Rupa Prāpti.

"চৈতন্যরূপের রা চ অধরূপ লাড়ি। রা অক্ষরে রাগ লাড়ি। চ অক্ষরে চেতন লাড়ি। র এতে চ মিশাল। হবে এক অঙ্গা লাড়ি। রাগ রতি। লাড়ির নাম সুধা॥ সেই লাড়ি সাতইস প্রকার।"

---

*"পচ্চিম দুআরে কে পণ্ডিত। সেতাই যে চারিসত্ত গতি আনি লেখ্যা॥ চন্দ্র কোটাল যে বসুয়া ঘটদাসী। দূত নাহি ডরাই তুম্মাক দেখিআ। চিত্রগুপ্ত পাঁজি পরিমান কর এ দূত জমর বিদ্যমানে॥"

Çunya Purāṅa.

Prose works by Sahajiyās.

A host of writers of the Sahajiyā cult wrote short treatises in prose or introduced prose passages in their poetical works. We briefly notice them below.

1. Dvādaça Pāta Nirṅaya written early in the 16th century by Nilāchala Dās.

2. Āchraya Nirṅaya by Chaitanya Dās.

3. Rupa Gosvāmir Kārikā. Rupa Gosvāmi, who is said to have written this book, was born in 1489 A.D. He was a contemporary and follower of Chaitanya Deva. The Ms.-copy with us was written in 1675.

4. Rāgamayi Kaṅā by Kriṣṅa Dās Kavirāja who lived in the middle of the 16th century.

5. Ātma Tattva Jijnāsā.

6. Dāsyadāsatattva Bhāvartha. The copy with us was written in 1685 A.D.

7. Ālamvana Chanrikā by Kriṣṅa Dās Kavirāja. The Ms.-copy found was prepared in 1655 A.D. and the composition of the treatise must have been at least half a century earlier.

8. Upāsanā Tattva—the Ms. is dated 1755.
9. Siddhi Tattva—the Ms. is dated 1755.
10. Trigunātmikā Do.
11. Ātma Sādhanā.
12. Bhoga Patala.
13. Deha Bheda Tattva Nirupana.
14. Chandra Chintāmaṅi by Prema Dās.
15. Ātma Tattva Jijnāsā Sāratsāra by Kriṣṅa Dās.
16. Sādhanā Traya.
17. Çikṣā Patala.

18. Siddhānta Tikā by Damu Ghoṣe Gosvāmi.

19. Kriṣṅa Bhakti Parāyaṅa.

20. Upāsanā Nirṅaya.

21. Svarupa Varṅanā.

22. Rājamāla by Narottama Dās.

23. Deha Kaḍacha by Narottama Dās.

24. Champaka Kalikā. This book describes the incidents of the release of Sonātana Gosvāmi from prison.

25. Ātma Tattva.

26. Pānchānga Niguḍha Tattva.

27. Hari Nāmer Artha.

28. Goṣthi Kathā.

29. Siddhi Patala.

30. Jijnāsā Praṅāli.

31. Javā Manjuri.

32. Vraja Kārikā.

33. Rasa Bhajana Tattva copied in 1650.

34. Vrindāvana Parikramā copied early in the 18th century.

35. Vedādi Tattva Nirṅaya.

36. Vrindāvana Lilā copied in the middle of the 18th century.

We have, besides, in prose a vast number of treatises on medicine and on the genealogies of old families written within the last three centuries.

Of the books, mentioned in the above list, Nos. 6, 7, 9, 10, 12, 14, 18, 25, 27, 28, 29, 30, 31, 32, 34, 35, 36 are written in prose and the rest are in prose and poetry combined. Genealogical works are numerous, and in many of them we find elaborate passages in prose. We quote below a

Genealogical works in prose.

specimen of prose from one such work on the Bārendra Brahmins of Bengal.

*" Ādi Sur was a powerful King. He brought to his capital five Brahmins of five different Gotras:—Nārāyaṅa of Çāndilya Gotra, Dharādhara of Bātsya Gotra, Susen of Kāçyapa Gotra, Gautama of Bharadvajā Gotra, and Parāçara of Savarṅa Gotra.

" The whole of Bengal was made pure by the holy influence of these Brahmins, and after the country had been thus improved, Ādi Sur, the King died."

One thing strikes us here. Prose was more often adopted by the Sahajiyā Vaiṣṅavas than by other sects for the exposition of their doctrines. Nos. 32, 34, and 35 show elaborate specimens of prose. The Sahajiyās who were, as we think, originally a Buddhist sect, imbibed this taste for writing in prose from a very early age, when the Buddhists used to elucidate their views in prose in the Prākrita language.

Logic and Law in prose.

We have come upon translations of Bhāṣā Parichchada—a work on Logic, and of Vyavasthā Tattva, a book on Hindu Law, copied in 1773, which show that prose was adopted at least two centuries ago, for dealing with highly metaphysical

*" আদিশূর রাজা বড় প্রতাপযুক্ত রাজা। আদিশূর রাজা পঞ্চগোত্রের পঞ্চ ব্রাহ্মণ আনয়ন করিলেন:—যথা নারায়ণস্ত শাণ্ডিল্যঃ সুষেণঃ কশ্যপস্তথা, বাৎস্যো ধরাধরো দেবঃ ভরদ্বাজস্ত গৌতমঃ সাবর্ণস্ত পরাশরঃ—এই পঞ্চগোত্রে পঞ্চ ব্রাহ্মণ আনয়ন কর‍্যা গৌড়মণ্ডল পবিত্র কর‍্যা আদিশূর রাজার স্বর্গারোহণ।"

subjects. We quote a passage from the Bhāṣā Parichchada.

Bhāṣā parichchada.

*"The disciples of the sage Gautama approached him with these words. How, master, may our deliverance be obtained? Graciously enlighten us on this point: Gautama said—'deliverance may be obtained by a knowledge of the predicaments.' The disciples wanted to know what were these predicaments, and Gautama replied:—'Seven predicaments may be enumerated. *viz:*—(1) Substance, (2) quality, (3) action, (4) genus, (5) difference, (6) co-inherence, and (7) non-existence.' "

The language of the treatises in the list just given is invariably very simple, though owing to our ignorance of the special terms and technicalities used by the Sahajiyā Vaiṣṅavas, much of their writings is unintelligible to us. The sentences are generally short and rarely loaded with compounds. Here is a passage which may be taken as a specimen of the sort of style used by them. We quote from the *Karika* by Rupa Gosvāmi who lived 400 years ago, †"Victory be to Rādhā and Kriṣṅa! First of all a classification of subjects; proceeding

---

*" গৌতম মুনিকে শিষ্য সকলে জিজ্ঞাসা করিলেন, আমাদিগের মুক্তি কি প্রকারে হয়? তাহা কৃপা করিয়া বলহ। তাহাতে গৌতম উত্তর করিতেছেন। তাবং পদার্থ জানিলেই মুক্তি হয়। তাহাতে শিষ্যেরা সকলে জিজ্ঞাসা করিলে, পদার্থ কতো? তাহাতে গৌতম কহিতেছেন। পদার্থ সপ্ত প্রকার। দ্রব্য, গুণ, কর্ম্ম, সামান্য, বিশেষ, সমবায়, অভাব। তাহার মধ্যে দ্রব্য নয় প্রকার।"

†" শ্রীশ্রীরাধাবিনোদ রায়। অথ বস্তু নির্ণয়। প্রথম শ্রীকৃষ্ণের গুণ নির্ণয়। শব্দগুণ, গন্ধগুণ, রূপগুণ, রসগুণ, স্পর্শগুণ, এই

with the enumeration of the qualities, we should note five points :—perception of sound, of smell

Kārikā. of colour, of taste and of touch. These belong to Rādhā and Kriṣṅa alike. The first perception belongs to the ear, the second to the nose, the third to the eyes, the fourth to the tongue and the fifth to the skin. These five perceptions create a desire for love."

Kāminī Kumāra. In *Kamini Kumara*, a poem written in the middle of the 18th century, we find a passage written in simple prose, showing a contrast with the subtle and abstruse style of the learned men of the period. We quote the passage below.

*"When the merchant again and again swore in this manner, the lady smiled and addressed Sonā and said, "Well, my servant. This thief has thus foresworn himself several times, and has surrendered himself entirely to us. Suppliant for mercy as he is, he should not be further molested. In his present predicament, he deserves to be treated with indulgence because he is so helpless. This is what the sacred books enjoin. The number

---

পাঁচ গুণ। এই পঞ্চ গুণ শ্রীমতী রাধিকাতেও বসে। শব্দগুণ কর্ণে, গন্ধগুণ নাসাতে, রূপগুণ নেত্রে, রসগুণ অধরে, ও স্পর্শগুণ অঙ্গে। এই পঞ্চ গুণে পূর্ব্ব রাগের উদয়।"

*"সদাগর অতিকাতরে এইরূপ পুনঃ পুনঃ শপথ করাতে সুন্দরী ঈষৎ হাস্য পূর্ব্বক সোণাকে সম্বোধন করিয়া কহিলেক। 'ওহে চোপদার এই চোর এতাদৃশ কটু দিব্য বারম্বার করিছে ও নিতান্ত শরণাগত হইয়া আশ্রয় যাচিঞ্চা করিতেছে, অতএব শরণাগতে নিগ্রহ করা উচিৎ নহে বরং নিরাশ্রয়ের আশ্রয় দেওয়া

of our servants besides is not sufficient; though he may not be trusted with any responsible work, what harm if he be appointed to prepare *silims* of tobacco for us? That would be a great service in the present state of things. Sonā said 'well said, my master; let him be kept as a servant.' Kāminī thus taking the sense of Sonā addressed him thus: "Well, thief, the highly criminal act that you have committed, deserves a severe punishment, but owing to your solicitations, humility and promises we excuse you this time. You must now become our constant attendant obeying our commands in all respects. Whatever we may be pleased to order, it will be your duty to execute promptly. If you play the truant, you will at once be brought before the king without mercy; on the other hand if you can please us by your obedience and prompt execution of our orders, we promise to

---

বেদ বিধি সম্মত বটে। আর বিশেষত আমাদের অধিক ভৃত্য সঙ্গেতে নাই, অতএব অন্যকর্ম্ম উহা হইতে যত হউক, আর না হউক, কিন্তু এক আধ ছিলিম তামাক চাহিলেও ত সাজিয়া দিতে পারিবেক। তাহার আর তো কোন সন্দেহ নাই তবু যে অনেক উপকার। সোণা কহিলেন 'হাঁ থাকে থাক।' কামিনী এইরূপ সোণার সহিত পরামর্শ করিয়া সদাগরকে কহিতেছেন। "শুন চোর তুমি যে অকর্ম্ম করিয়াছ তাহার উপযুক্ত ফল তোমাকে দেওয়া উচিত, কিন্তু তোমার নিতান্ত নূন্যতা ও বিনয়ে কাকুতি মিনতি এবং কঠিন শপথে এ যাত্রা ক্ষমা করিলাম। এক্ষণে আমার সর্ব্বদা আজ্ঞাকারী হইয়া থাকিতে হইবেক, আমি যখন যাহা কহিব তৎক্ষণাৎ সেই কর্ম্ম করিবে, তাহাতে অন্যথা করিলে তদ্দণ্ডে রাজার নিকট প্রেরণ করিব, তাহার আর কথা নাই। কিন্তু

consider your case favourably in future. When the merchant heard this he thought. "By Rāma, it is a great relief, I am out of danger now." He folded his hands, and said to Kāminī, 'Sir, the great relief you have given to your most humble servant by granting him pardon is a proof that in a past life you were one of his kith and kin, or else how can this act of favour at the hands of a stranger be explained? Now, by God, I say you are my God-father, I accept you as my master. Whatever order you may graciously be pleased to make, it will be my duty as a humble servant to execute to the best of my powers, and if required even with my life.' Kāminī said, 'What work will you do here? There is not much to be done. I would simply put you in charge of my *huka* for the present; one word more, how long shall I address

---

যদি কর্ম্মের দ্বারায় আমাকে সন্তোষ করিতে পারহ, তবে তোমার পক্ষে শেষ বিবেচনা করা যাইবেক।" সদাগর এই কথা শুনিয়া মনে মনে বিবেচনা করিলেক, যে রাম বাঁচা গেল, আর ভয় নাই। পরে কৃতাঞ্জলি পূর্ব্বক কামিনীর সম্মুখে কহিতেছে, "মহাশয় যে ঘোর দায় হইতে এ দাসের প্রাণ রক্ষা করিলেন ইহাতেই বোধ হয় আপনি জন্মান্তরে এ দীনের কেহ ছিলেন, তাহার কোন সন্দেহ নাই, নতুবা এমত উপকার পর পরের যে তো কখন করে না। সে যাহা হউক আজি হইতে কর্ত্তা তুমি আমার ধরম বাপ হইলে, যখন যে আজ্ঞা করিবেন এই ভৃত্য কৃতসাধ্য প্রাণপণে পালন করিব। কামিনী কহিলেক, ওহে চোর তুমি আমার আর কি কর্ম্ম করিবেক, কেবল হুকার কর্ম্মে সর্ব্বদা নিযুক্ত থাকহ, আর এক কথা তোমাকে চোর চোর বলিয়া সর্ব্বদা বা কাঁহাতক ডাকি. আজি হইতে আমি তোমার নাম রামবল্লভ

you as a thief, I give you a name; I shall henceforth call you Rāma Vallabha.' The merchant said 'So be it sir.' After such conversation Kāminī said, 'Now my Rāma Vallabha, do kindly prepare a *silim* of tobacco for me.' Rāma Vallabha immediately prepared a *silim* and bringing the *huka* held the pipe before Kāminī. Rāma Vallabha being appointed to the work soon became an expert in the art, and it became the subject of his constant thought, so much so that if Kāminī called him while dining or while asleep, saying 'Where have you gone, my Rāma Vallabha?' He would immediately answer, 'Sir, I am preparing tobacco.'''

For conveying the humour of the passage an introduction to the story is necessary. The young merchant Kumāra, the husband of Kāminī, went to a distant country for trade immediately after his marriage. There he fell in love with a young princess and was admitted into the Rājā's harem in the guise of a maid-servant. There he stayed for a fairly long time, till his wife Kāminī became anxious about his safety, and started in the

---

রাখিলাম। সদাগর কহিলেক 'যে আজ্ঞা মহাশয়।' এইরূপ কথোপকথনান্তে ক্ষণেক বিলম্বে কামিনী কহিলেক 'ওহে রাম বল্লভ একবার তামাক সাজ দেখি।' রামবল্লভ 'যে আজ্ঞে' বলিয়া তৎক্ষণাৎ তামাক সাজিয়া আলবোলা আনিয়া ধরিয়া দিলেক। এই প্রকার রামবল্লভ তামাক সাজা কর্ম্মে নিযুক্ত হইলে পরে, ক্রমে ক্রমে তামাক সাজিতে সাজিতে রামবল্লভের তামাক সাজায় এমত অভ্যাস হইল যে রামবল্লভ যদ্যপি ভোজনে কিম্বা শয়নে আছেন ও সেই সময়ে যদি কামিনী বলে—'ওহে রামবল্লভ কোথায় গেলে হে'—রামবল্লভের উত্তর 'আজ্ঞে তামাক সাজিতেছি॥'

guise of a prince with her maid, Sonā, who was also dressed as a young man. After a weary search—they traced out Kumāra, and learning all about him went to the palace of the Rājā, whose daughter had kept him in her vicinity as a lover. Kāminī, who was a very beautiful woman, played her part as the young prince so well, that the Rājā offered his daughter in marriage to her. After the marriage was over, she at once detected the guilty man, her own husband, and brought the matter to the notice of the Rājā, playing her mock-anger with admirable tact. The Rājā in great consternation offered the thief to his false son-in-law saying that he might inflict any punishment on him that he liked,—at the same time he begged him to pardon his daughter. Kāminī, on the pretext of going away for a short time on business, marched homewards with her husband who thought her to be the prince and had not recognised her as his loyal and loving wife. This passage describes what took place after she had taken the thief into custody. She gave him the name of Rāma Vallabha, because it was held sacrilegeous in those days for a Hindu wife to utter the name of her husband.

Before we close the account of our early prose, we should note some points about it. Though the above passage is connected with the incidents of an illicit love, which forms the subject matter of the poem Kāminī Kumāra, the author of which belongs to the depraved school of Bhārata Chandra, yet the rest of our early prose which we have noticed, shows that it was mainly employed for the purpose of metaphysical and religious writings.

The translation of the Sanskrit work on Logic called the Bhāṣā Parichchada, in simple Bengali, was indeed a bold attempt, for even in the present advanced development of our prose literature, the subject is considered to be too intricate for Bengali, especially as it would be most difficult to translate the technical words of Sanskrit Logic. The same may be said of the various translations of the Hindu Law-books compiled in prose two centuries ago.

The development of poetical literature helping the cause of prose.

We find mention in a poem named Kirtī Latā by Rājā Prithvi Chandra of Pākur, of an author named Rādhā Vallabha Çarmā who translated most of the Hindu Law-books before the battle of Plassey. All this shows that though prose-writing was not much in favour with the authors of past ages in Bengal, yet on account of the high development which our language had already attained through its vast poetical literature, there would be no difficulty experienced by any author in attempting translation into Bengali prose the most abstruse and metaphysical of Sanskrit works. This fact also explains why our prose has developed so wonderfully within the last half century. The literary language was already in a highly prepared state, so it needed no great effort to bring our prose to a considerable degree of perfection within a comparatively short time.

In early times prose was classified in Bengali as a sort of metre. With what justification they [illegible] it so is not known; but prose passages are

'The prose metre.'

generally found introduced by the word গদ্য ছন্দ. In a poem in praise of Chandi Dās by the poet Vaishnava Dās we find the line—"যাকর নিরমল গদ্য পদ্যময় গীত" which indicates that prose passages also along with poetic used to be sung or chanted. This is substantiated by the fact that the genealogical accounts of the noble families of the Hindu community in Bengal used to be chanted by Kulāchāryyas, though a considerable portion of them was written in prose. The Kathakatās even in our own day show unmistakably how prose passages may be used for the purposes of vocal music. Most probably it was owing to this adaptability of prose to the purposes of song, as found in Bengali, that they called it গদ্য ছন্দ—the prose metre. The authors of early prose in many cases used to include their *bhanita* or signature in the same form in which they did so in their poetical compositions. The last lines of the passage from Kāminī Kumāra quoted above run as follows :—

**Kali Krisna Das* (author of the poem Kāminī Kumāra) *says* that Rāma Vallabha in course of time became so clever and practised a hand at the art of preparing tobacco, that he would not wait till his full name was pronounced. As soon as 'Rāma' came out of Kāminī's lips, Rāma Vallabha was ready with his tobacco."

When a whole paragraph was finished the sign of punctuation was ।। ; but after the completion of the sentence, the sign generally used was ।.

---

*" কালীকৃষ্ণ দাস বলে, পশ্চাৎ রামবল্লভের এমনি কস্ত হইল যে, কামিনীকে আর পষ্ট রামবল্লভ বলিতে হয় না, 'রাম' বলিবা মাত্রেই রামবল্লভ তামাক সাজাইয়া মজুত।"

CHAPTER VII.

THE MODERN AGE.

I. (a) The epoch ushered in by European workers—civilians and missionaries.

(b) Dr. Carey and his colleagues.

(c) Bengali works written by Europeans.

(d) A new ideal in the country.

II. (a) The College of Fort William.

(b) The Pundits of the College—Mrityunjaya—Rāma Rāma Vasu—Chandi Charan Munsi—and Rājiva Lochana—Their Bengali works.

(c) The Rev. K. M. Banerjee and other authors who followed in the wake of European writers—a list of their publications.

III. General remarks chiefly indicating the characteristics of the new age and its contrast with the earlier one.

IV. (a) Decadance of the high spiritual ideal in Hindu society and the advent of Rājā Rāma Mohana Roy.

(b) A comprehensive review of his life and work.

(c) The writers that followed Rājā Rāma Mohana Roy — Devendra Nātha Tagore. — Akṣaya Kumāra Dutta and others.

I. (a) The new epoch ushered in by European workers,—civilians and missionaries.

Early prose—of a minor importance.

Whatever remnants of prose we may be able to unearth from old records and manuscripts in order to vindicate the glory of our past literature, it must, for the sake of truth, be admitted that they were too insignificant to deserve prominent mention in a history of literature. Disconnected from the story of the later development of prose, that has grown up like a rich harvest during the British rule, they would scarcely deserve more than a passing notice.

Bengalis hitherto content with village-life.

I have said more than once in the foregoing chapters that the heart of Bengal lay in her villages,—contented as these were with their never-ceasing fountain of domestic and spiritual happiness. Our people did not hitherto care for the world outside the pale of their homes. They worked and sang, prayed, fasted and had visions of God. They heard the bird Kokil coo from the mango boughs in spring, and saw their favourite flower, the lotus, bloom in their tanks in autumn; and blithely did they sing about all these, and about the sweets of home life. They were content with loving their kith and kin, their mothers, wives and children, and thought that God revealed Himself to them in domestic tenderness. They pursued the nicities of Logic or indulged in abstruse metaphysical contemplations, and disciplined their mind that they might take a quiet and ungrudging view of the iils of life and encounter nobly the supreme penalty of nature when in due course it would come upon them.

But this village life underwent a sudden disturbance. Political changes were of little importance to the people. They heard from gossips that the *Badsah,* who ruled from the throne of Murshidābād, had been ousted by the English, and that a great battle had been fought at Plassey, but this did not seem at all any important news to them. Now, however, for the first time in history, a set of people came with the distinct object of improving them spiritually and morally. The Mussalmāns had not done so,—not even the great Ākbar in his dream of a political empire. The Portuguese, the Burmese and the Maharattas had all overrun the country during successive ages. They came to loot or judge criminals—restore rights or seize them ; that was in the eyes of the Hindus the true function of their foreign sovereigns. The Mussalmāns had come with the Korān, but often with a dagger also, as an alternative for the acceptance of their faith ; those that failed to be convinced were sometimes forcibly served with beef and made converts.

A call from outside.

But here came a people who showed real anxiety to ameliorate the condition of the people. Bent on high motives of philanthropy and love, they did not apply force but used gentle persuasion. Besides they showed a great anxiety to give to our countrymen the sort of education which they had not yet had, notwithstanding their higher flights in theology and metaphysics. A class of philanthropic men, whose mission was the propaganda of the great love of their master, Jesus Christ,—the missionaries in the earlier stages of British rule did for our country and her literature what we can not too highly eulogise. They approached with love and so touched the heart of the people. Dr. Carey called us semi-barbarians in a letter to a friend, but he had no contempt for the people ; it was a *bonâ fide* statement which we may very well excuse, when we know that he was truly inspired with the spirit of Christian love for his fellowmen and did not mean to abuse. This love touched the heart of the Bengalis. In fact the ardour, with which the missionaries and even some members of the Civil Service commenced their self-imposed task of educating the masses and ameliorating their condition, elicits our unqualified respect and admiration. The first Bengali types in the country were those em-

Halhed's Grammar.

ployed in printing a Bengali grammar by Mr. Nathenial Prassy Halhed who was a Civilian and oriental scholar and "was so well acquainted with the language as sometimes to pass in disguise as a Native."* The grammar was printed in 1778 A.D. in a press at Hugli. The punches of the fount were prepared by Mr. Wilkins who rose to great distinction as an oriental scholar, and published a translation of the Gitā which was the first Sanskrit work made accessible to the scholars of Europe by translation. Mr. Wilkins, who was afterwards decorated with knighthood, belonged to the Service of the East India Company, and in his researches in the field of Sanskrit lore was a recipient of the distinguished patronage of Warren Hastings. Wilkins made it the mission of his life to improve the condition of the masses of Bengal by giving them a general education for which printing was essentially necessary. In his zeal to do so, he acquired the art of punch-cutting and prepared a set of Bengali punches with his own hands, after he had been seven years in this country, and in this stage he also trained another hand to do the same work. Panchānana Karmakāra and his relation and assistant Manohara Karmakāra belonging to the caste of blacksmiths, were instructed in the art of punch-cutting by Mr. Wilkins; and the worry and trouble attending the enterprise for years would have been considered not worth undergoing, had not Mr. Wilkins proceeded with a true Christian spirit of patient philanthrophy. In fact the amelioration of the condition of

Punches by Wilkins.

* A descriptive catalogue of Bengali works by J. Lang, p. 20.

the people, amongst whom he was called upon to work, had become the all-absorbing matter of his thought. Through the labours of Panchānana Karmakāra and his relative and colleague Manohara the art of punch-cutting became domesticated in India. We do not, however, mean to say that the art of printing in a crude form was not known in Bengal before Charles Wilkins came to the field. We have come across a Ms. nearly 200 years old which was printed from engraved wooden blocks. But the art was not in general use; a stray endeavour for decorative purposes does not prognosticate a system or a regular cultivation of the art, so we may rightly pass over it.

Panchānana and Manohara.

Crude printing known, 200 years ago.

The next notice that we have of printing in Bengali is that of the printed Code of Regulations drawn up by Sir Elija Impey on which all subsequent legislation has been based. The regulations were translated by Mr. Jonathan Duncan, afterwards Governor of Bombay, and were printed at the Company's Press' in 1785. The great Cornwallis Code of 1793, translated into Bengali by Mr. Forster, who was in his time the most distinguished European scholar of Bengali, was printed at the same press but from an improved fount, which continued to be the standard of Bengal types, till a neater and a smaller fount was prepared by Dr. Carey.

Early printing.

Next to Sir Charles Wilkins, Natheniel Prassey Halhed and Graves Chamney Haughton came a host of European scholars in Bengali and other oriental languages, many of whom belonged to the Çri Rāmapur Mission, but none of them was so

Dr. Carey.

conspicuous in his efforts to improve the resources of Bengali prose or help the circulation of Bengali printing as was Dr. Carey.

(b) Dr. Carey and his colleagues.

He had started in life as a cobbler. When, however, by his great diligence, piety, scholarship and strength of character he had raised himself to a position of eminence as missionary, he was dining one summar day in 1786 with the Governor General, the Marquis of Hastings, at Barrackpur Park, opposite Çri Rāmapur and, "overheard one of the guests, a general officer, making enquiry of one of the Aides-de-Camp, whether Dr. Carey had not been a shoemaker, on which he stepped forward and exclaimed, 'No Sir, only a cobbler!'" "Carey might be seen" writes John Clark Marshman "walking eight or ten miles to Northampton with his wallet full of shoes upon his shoulders and then returning home with a fresh supply of leather to fulfil his engagements with a Government contractor."

This man came subsequently as a missionary to Bengal and felt a true Christian love for the people around him who appeared to him to be sunk in superstition, vice and idolatory. He learnt Sanskrit, Bengali, Persian and Maharatti, not with a view to know the people or profit by the wisdom contained in oriental books, but with the object of bringing a large mass of humanity, whom he sincerely believed to be grovelling in darkness, to light. We may regret that Dr. Carey failed to observe the religious life in Bengal which,

Your affect. Bro.
W. Carey.

Mahabharata, written about three centuries ago, have been received not only from Chittagong, Noakhali, Dacca, Mymensing, Tippera, and Sylhet, but also from various parts of Western Bengal. We have with us one old manuscript of the poem recovered from the village of [illegible] Pargana [illegible], and several other copies are found in the library of Babu Nagendra Nath Vasu, obtained by him from Pattrasayer and other villages of Birbhum. A manuscript of this poem [illegible] years old was collected by the late Mr. [illegible] from a village in the district of Rangpur. We may conceive from all this how extensively popular Kabindra's Mahabharata was in those days. Amongst the other translators of the Mahabharata, the influence of [illegible] the greatest on [illegible] and Kasi Das—the two great humanisers who [illegible] masses on the beauties of the classical epic in comparatively recent times. There are a host of other early Eastern Bengal poets on the subject of the Mahabharata; these works will be found mentioned in the body of this book.

Krittibas the earliest writer of the Ramayana, got his education in Eastern Bengal, somewhere on the banks of the Padma, as he has himself informed us in his auto-biography. His ancestors had belonged to [illegible], and the family was driven to Phulia by the oppression of [illegible] in the year [illegible]. Sanjaya and Gangadas, whose poems have been already mentioned [illegible]

[illegible] in connection with [illegible] wrote [illegible] works on the Ramayana and the Maha-[illegible] inspite of superstitions, was permeated with a noble purpose and a spirit of true devotional fervour. But we can by no means ignore or underestimate the great pains and the indefatigable industry that mark his endeavours to improve the lives of the Bengalis by spreading education and by disseminating the truths of the Gospel among them. To him we pre-eminently owe the rapid development of Bengali prose before Rājā Rāma Mohana Roy took up the work right earnestly.

His efforts to print the Bible.

The difficulties in the way of Dr. Carey were many and great. It was his greatest ambition in life to publish a translation of the Gospel in Bengali. When after years of hard and unremitted labour, he had brought the translation of the New Testament almost to completion, he estimated the cost of printing at Calcutta of 10,000 of copies at Rs. 43750. This was quite beyond his means, and he thought of getting the book printed in England. At first he proposed to obtain punches from Caslon, the eminent letter-founder in London, calculating that the cost of each punch would be 5*s.* only; but he was wrong; the cost of the punches was a guinea a piece. So he gave up the idea of getting the book printed in England, though before doing so he had made another attempt to engage the services of a letter-founder whom he knew at Derby. In 1798 he read an advertisement that a letter-foundry was established for the 'country language' at Calcutta. Dr. Carey lost no time in corresponding with the projector of the scheme, and found that the punches of the foundry were cut by Panchānana, who had been trained by Sir Charles

Wilkins. Soon after a printing press constructed of wood was advertised for sale and Dr. Carey immediately purchased it for £40. Panchānana was once more found out and his services engaged by the the Çri Rāmapur Mission. Here Panchānana completed a fount of 700 separate punches for Devanāgri letters and their compounds. Panchānana was now an old man, so his worthy colleague Manohara, already mentioned, was called in to assist him and "was subsequently employed for forty years at the Çri Rāmapur press and to his exertions and instruction, Bengal is indebted for the various beautiful founts of the Bengali, Nāgri, Persian, Arabic and other characters which have been gradually introduced into the different printing establishments."*

All this was due to the indefatigable industry of Dr. Carey and his colleagues. They were determined to publish the Bible in Bengali, and this Carey was ultimately able to do. Imagine his great delight when on the 18th of March, 1803, Mr. Ward set the first types with his own hands and presented him with the first sheet of the Testament. We find the following account of him in the notice of his career published by the British and Foreign Bible Society at his death in 1834. "The extent of his zeal may be judged by the fact that, in conjunction with his colleagues, he has been instrumental in giving to the tribes of Asia the sacred scriptures in whole or in part in between 30 and 40 different languages." He acquired Bengali with a thoroughness which we scarcely find in any other

He acquires Bengali.

* History of Cri Ramapur Mission Vol. I., p. 179.

foreigner who has studied our language. He had employed Pundits to help him to acquire knowledge of Bengali, and when they declared that he was fit to address the people he commenced preaching; and in 1794 we find him devoted to this task in the jungly tracts of Sundarvans. He writes on the 16th January, 1798, "I spoke in Bengali for nearly half an hour without an intermission." "But" says he later on "I recollect that after I had preached or rather thought that I had, for two years (in Bengali), a man one day came to me and declared that he could not understand me, and this long after my flattering teachers had declared that every one could understand me. I feel the impression which that poor man's remark made on me to this day."*

But we presume that it was his peculiarity of accent in pronouncing the letters ড়, ঢ় etc. which must have made his speech in some cases unintelligible to people. Reading his Bengali works on various subjects, one is struck with his wonderful command over the idioms and colloquial forms of our dialect so difficult for a foreigner to acquire. Dr. Carey was not, however, the man to be daunted by failures. He composed a short and simple marriage service in Bengali for meeting the growing demand of such formulæ, as there was already a good number of native Christians, whose marriage ceremonies were to be celebrated according to the new rites for which there was yet no guide in the vernacular. He besides composed songs in Bengali and we find one of his friends writing about himself and Dr.

* Memoir of Dr Carey by Eustace Carey.—p. 503.

Carey "This morning brother Carey and I took our stand like two ballad-singers and began singing in Bengali before one of Çiva's temples."* Of course now-a-days a European Missionary singing a Bengali song is no strange spectacle in this country; but Carey was the pioneer in all such matters and he was inspired by a real zeal to bring the people who, according to his notions, erred in religion, to the creed which he considered to be the only true one; and Hindus have always judged of a people by the sincerety of their faith and not by the loftiness of their doctrines, of which their own Çastras furnish sufficiently great and noble examples. Before these sincere souls took up the task of propagating their religious faith "there had been no indication that the conquerers of Bengal possessed any religion at all, excepting the hoisting of the flag on Sundays and the official attendance of the few at the Sunday morning service" and it was the earnest endeavour of Carey, Marshman, Martyn and their colleagues to remove this impression. They spared no pains to bring the lost sheep to the fold. In the Sundervans Dr. Carey lost a son, but he could induce no person, not even a Mahomedan, to make a coffin, and the distress, to which he and his wife were put, can hardly be adequately described. All this he underwent with a patient and even a glad heart., because though the people opposed him, he wanted to do good to them,—to return good for evil, as the great master had enjoined upon all true followers of his creed. This great love attracted the people and all difficulties, all problems—however insur-

The result of self-sacrifice.

* Memoir p. 129.

mountable or intricate—are overcome by love. The best men of the land during the first epoch of the British rule were drawn to Christanity by the noble examples of philanthropic love displayed by the Christian missionaries. They were not attracted by the inherent qualities of Christanity so much as by the examples of suffering for love before them. It was owing to these traits of disinterestedness in the life of early missionaries that men like the Rev. K. M. Banerjee, the Rev. Lāl Behari De, Michael Madhu Sudana Datta, Govinda Chandra Datta and last though not the least of this glorious band, Dr. K. C. Banerjee had embraced Christanity. For nearly a century the enlightened Hindus were dazzled by the glare of western civilisation; and showed no inclination to admit that anything could have been noble or great in the past of their own nation. The great personality of Chaitanya Deva and his heavenly love, the poems of Chandi Dās and the lays of other Vaiṣṇva poets, the songs of Rāma Prasāda, the vivid and noble portraitures of domestic life found in Kavi Kañkana's poems and the exquisite touches and elegance of Bhārat Chandra's style could now command no attention from the educated young men of Bengal; in fact, Bengal with her wealth of noble ideas lay far off, though so near, and Europe, removed from us by land and sea became nearer and dearer to the new generation of the Hindus who came in touch with the missionaries. In the domestic circle the parents became anxious for children who under the spell of missionary influeuce failed even to admire the patient and self-sacrificing love for religion which had marked the Hindu women of the past, and revolted

Young men of Bengal anglicised.

against all that was old and had been sacred in popular estimation. The gods had now become to them mere earthen clay, the temples were unholy and the hallowed precincts of their homes a hole of superstition. Their noble literature was no more than a miserable scribbling and shreds of paper which they should consign to the fire or to worms. The songs of Rādhā and Krisña which, were expressed in the highest language of poetry, and were hitherto a fountain of joy and inspiration to the rich and the poor alike, now became horrible to them ; and one of our greatest countrymen of that age was known to declare that Krisña, the supreme soul, was worse than a sweeper. The Hindu shrines had once been desecrated by Mahomedans who had thrown beef and other unholy things into them to destroy their sanctity: but they had only half succeeded, for thousands of hearts had remained true to them. But now our own people, the educated classes, lost faith in the temples, and looked upon them as pandemoniums and the gods enshrined in them as Beelzebubs and Molochs, whether they believed in Christanity or not. The victory of the missionaries was complete. The secret of their success, I beg to repeat, lay in the circumstance of their approaching us with love. They had shown a system of organised philanthrophy hitherto unknown to the country. Their charity, devotion, zeal and sympathy had drawn away those who were the natural ornaments of our society, and poor Bengal may consider this love to have been the greatest of her disasters, since more than the sword it upset time-honoured hoary institutions and alienated true hearts.

True love never spends itself in a single channel. Dr. Carey and his colleagues did not consider their work done by merely propagating the truths of Christianity. They wanted sincerely to give our countrymen education, according to their own standards, in all departments of knowledge; and the wonderful activity displayed by them in their labour of love draws forth our greatest admiration, when we consider that the Government of the East India Company, afraid of disturbing the conservative views of our people in the earlier stages, did not assist but often obstructed them. There is not a subject in which these Europeans did not come forward to write books in Bengali in order to spread education amongst the masses.

Dr. Carey's Bengali works.

Dr. Carey wrote the following books in Bengali besides numerous treatises on Christianity and the translation of the Bible.

1. A Dictionary of the Bengali language in three volumes, quarto size, containing 80,000 words—the work of thirty years. The original price was Rs. 120. This book came out in 1815—25.

2. A Bengali Grammar published in 1801. It had passed through four editions before 1855.

3. Kathopakathana or Colloquies, published in August, 1801.

4. Itihāsamālā, or garland of stories, published in 1812. It contains 150 short stories at that time current in Bengal.

The last two books form a rich mine of idioms of the spoken dialect of Bengal, from which Tek

Chand Thākur took the cue for his style in the composition of his masterpiece in Bengali—the Ālāler Gharer Dulāla. Dr. Carey writes in the preface to his Kathopakathana : " That the work might be as complete as possible, I have employed some sensible natives to compose dialogues upon subjects of domestic nature and to give them precisely in the natural style of the persons supposed to be speakers.'' So he did not write the whole of the book himself, but the dialogues, other than those written on domestic subjects, are his composition, and they do him a great credit. He had a high regard for Bengali as a language. He says of it in the aforesaid preface, "This language......current through an extent of country nearly equal to Great Britain......when properly cultivated, will be inferior to none in elegance and perspicuity." He wanted not only to educate and elevate the masses of Bengal, but also to develop, as best he could, the resources of a language for which he had a great respect. The style of his colloquies inspired many of our countrymen to write in the current dialect, and not only do we find it imitated in a pre-eminent degree in Ālāler Gharer Dulāla and Hutum Pechār Naksā, but even in the style of a Bankima Chandra and Dina Vandu Mitra. I quote a passage from his colloquies. Dr. Carey appended an English translation which I adopt with some modifications.

Specimens of colloquial style.

*"Yesterday at 12 o'clock my youngest wife had cooked the dinner, and my children had first eaten

---

*" কাল দুপুর বেলা ছোট বৌ রাঁধিতেছিল, ইহার মধ্যে

their rice. At that moment the middle woman came in and set up a quarrel."

"None of the women of your house can bear to see any good happening to another."

"What can I say? There is no place where I can go and stay for 4 or 5 days, and allow the breeze to blow on my face (enjoy peace)."

"Why don't you go to your brother's house and stay there for a few days?"

"What, go to their house! If I were to go to their house, do you think I should be preserved from these abusive women? There is not one of them who can bear to hear of my brothers. My husband scarcely stays at home at all, on account of their quarrels. When he does come, he himself abuses and scolds."

"Formerly you lived on such good terms. Strange, you are always differing now."

আমার ছ্যালা আগে ভাত খাইয়াছিল, ইহার মধ্যে মাধ্যা মাগী আসিয়া দ্বন্দ্ব আরম্ভ করিল।"

"তোরগো বাড়ীর ম্যায়াগুলা কেহ কাক ভাল দেখিতে পারে না।"

*"কি করিব, এমন ঠাঁই নাই যে সেখানে গিয়া থাকিলে দশ পাঁচ দিন গায় বাতাস লাগে।"

"কেন? তোর ভাইদের বাড়ী দিন কতক যা না কেন?

"তাদের বাড়ী যাব কি? তাহা হইলে কি ভাইখাগীদের কাছে রক্ষা আছে? আমাদের ভাইদের নাম শুন্‌তে পারে না কেউ। কর্ত্তা যিনি তিনি দ্বন্দ্ব ডাকাডাকির জন্য বাড়ী প্রায় থাকেন না। যখন আইসেন তখন গালাগালি তিরস্কার করেন।"

"If I could only give my daughters in marriage, I would take seven mustard seeds and bathe (an idiom in Bengali signifying great relief of mind). I would offer betel to Kulai Chandi and send *puja* to Suvachani."

"Where do you think of marrying your girls? In the country or outside it?"

"I cannot say what God intends. I think it would be well to marry them near home."

"What do all the brothers' wives say? What say the uncles and aunts? What all agree upon is proper."

"As it happens I will go home; if the evening comes I shall be scolded."

"তোদের সংসারে এমন ঐক্য ছিল, এখন এমন অনৈক্য হইয়াছে।"

"ম্যায়া ছুটার বিয়া দিতে পারিলে আমি সাতটা শরিষা দিয়া স্নান করি, কুলাই চণ্ডীর বাড়ী গুয়া পান দিই, শুবচনী পুজা করি, মনস্কামনা সিদ্ধ করিলে হয়।"

ম্যায়ার বিবাহ কোথায় ঠাওর হইয়াছে? দেশের মধ্যে না বিদেশে দিবা?

"ঈশ্বরের মনে কি আছে বুঝতে পারি না; আমার ইচ্ছা দেশের মধ্যে হইলেই ভাল হয়।"

"তোমার যারা সকলে কি বলে? ম্যায়ার মামা, মামী কি বলে? পাঁচটার যে মত সেই কর্ত্তব্য।"

"সে যেই হউক, আমি বাড়ী যাই, বেলা গেলে এখনই গালাগালি দিবে।"

The colloquy under the head "Quarrels of Women" beginning with "Where have you been, gossip? Is none of the business of the evening in your mind?" presents to us a disagreeable scene, which, assuming that some pundit wrote it for Dr. Carey, though he himself appends an English translation, should not, for the sake of decency, have found a place in a missionary's book. We find slang of a most revolting type used freely in that dialogue, and we wonder how Dr. Carey could have published it in his own name. This goes to show that even a European missionary of such spotless reputation as Dr. Carey's was, could not escape from that corrupt taste of the age which marks the writing of Içvara Gupta and Gauri Çankar Bhattāchāryya.

We quote below two more extracts from Dr. Carey's Bengali writings, which will illustrate his great command over the language. I take both of them from his Itihāsamālā or Garland of Stories.

The story of a thief.

I. *" Once upon a time a thief was running away with the articles stolen from a house, and was passing by the fields adjoining the village. A ploughman, who happened to see him, said, 'Would you mind returning those things to the rightful owner? If you do not, I shall have you punished in the court of the king.' The thief replied, 'Mind your

---

*" এক চোর কোন গৃহস্থের কতকগুলি দ্রব্য চুরি করিয়া গ্রামোপান্তে যাইতেছিল ; সেই সময়ে এক কৃষক তাহাকে দেখিয়া কহিল, 'তুই যে লোকের দ্রব্যাদি লইয়া যাইতেছিস্ তাহাকে ফিরিয়া দে, নতুবা রাজ নিকটে দণ্ড হইবে।' চোর উত্তর

own business, fool. If you show any undue enthusiasm in this matter I shall make you suffer capital punishment at the hands of the king.' The ploughman, who was naturally very angry at the audacity of the thief, caught hold of him with the stolen articles and brought him before the king to whom he related the whole story. When the king asked the thief what he had to say in reply, he answered, 'Great king. I saw that this man was sitting with these articles in a jungle: I told him that he looked like a thief and threatened to bring him before your majesty, if he would not return the articles to the owner. But the man abused me for saying so. Be pleased to judge this thief as he deserves.' The king asked if there was any eyewitness to substantiate the statement of either; but both of them declared that there was none. The king ordered his officers to take away both of them, and, after tightly binding each to a corpse, to burn them at separate places. He desired, moreover, that his order should be quickly executed.

করিল, তুই আপনার কর্ম্ম কর, অতিরিক্ত কহিলে রাজার অগ্রে তোর প্রাণদণ্ড হইবে।' কৃষক ইহা শুনিয়া ক্রুদ্ধ হইয়া দ্রব্যের সহিত চোরকে ধরিয়া রাজার সমীপে সমস্ত গিয়া নিবেদন করিল। অনন্তর নৃপতি চোরকে আসিয়া জিজ্ঞাসা করিলে, সে উত্তর করিল, 'হে মহারাজ আমি দেখিলাম যে এই লোকে ঐ সকল দ্রব্য লইয়া বন মধ্যে বসিয়া রহিয়াছে। তাহাতে আমি কহিলাম যে তুমি চোর হইবা। যাহার দ্রব্য আনিয়াছ তাহাকে দিয়া আইস, নতুবা তোমাকে মহারাজের নিকট লইয়া যাইব তাহাতে ইনি আমাকে কটুবাক্য কহিলে, আমি ইহাকে এখানে ধরিয়া আনিলাম। ইহার বিচার করিতে আজ্ঞা হউক।'

After publicly passing this sentence, he brought the officers into his private chamber, and instructed them to keep a secret watch upon these men after they had been bound to the corpses as directed. They were instructed to listen to the conversation of the two and report it to him at once. The officers accordingly took the two men to the river side, where they bound them to two different corpses; and on the pretext of going away to bring fuel for burning them, hid themselves close by, so that they could overhear without being seen. The two men thinking they were left to themselves, now felt sure that death was inevitable, upon which the ploughman said to the thief, 'Well, thief, you are a remarkably clever fellow, you have succeeded in bringing death and ruin upon me though I am innocent.' The thief said in reply, 'I begged you not to adopt the course you took, saying that if you quarrelled with me your life would pay the forfeit. For my part, I am a thief, and death is just the punishment that I deserve. But you are going to lose your life

---

তদনন্তর রাজা কহিলেন, 'উহার কেহ সাক্ষী আছে?' তাহাতে উত্তরে কহিলা 'সাক্ষী কেহ নাই।' অনন্তর ভূপতি ভৃত্যের দিগকে আজ্ঞা করিলেন, যে এই দুই জনকে লইয়া নদী তীরে দুই শবের সহিত পৃথক পৃথক দাহ কর, ইহাতে বিলম্ব না হয়। পশ্চাৎ নির্জ্জনে ঐ দাসের দিগকে ডাকিয়া কহিলেন 'ঐ দুইজনকে দুই শবের সহিত পৃথক পৃথক বন্ধন করিয়া গুপ্তবেশে নিকটে থাকিয়া উভয়ের কথোপকথন শুনিয়া আমাকে কহিবা।' পরে দাসেরা সেই দুই লোককে নদীতীরে শবের সহিত বন্ধন করিয়া কাষ্ঠাদি আনিতে যাই ইহা কহিয়া অস্পষ্টরূপে নিকটে থাকিল, তাহাতে ঐ দুই ব্যক্তি আপন মরণ নিশ্চয় বুঝিয়া কৃষাণ চোরকে

out of sheer foolishness.' The officers overheard the conversation and at once reported to the King who, on knowing the facts, inflicted a suitable punishment on the thief and duly rewarded the ploughman."

How 23 fish disappeared.

II. *" A husbandman went with his plough to the fields one day, and got 24 fish from a neighbouring canal. He came back to his home and, after having made over the fish to his wife for cooking, returned to his duties. His wife prepared a curry with the fish and wanting to know the taste of her preparation took a sip from it. She found that it tasted well, and then she thought, 'But I don't know how the fish tastes ; let me eat one.' So she ate a fish, and then she thought 'But still I donot

---

কহিল যে 'হে চোর তুই এতবড় বুদ্ধিমান, বিনাপরাধে আমার প্রাণদণ্ড করিলি !' ইহাতে সে প্রত্যুত্তর করিল 'আমি পূর্ব্বে তোমাকে বারণ করিয়াছিলাম যে আমার সহিত বিবাদ করিলে তোমার প্রাণ যাইবে, আমি চোর, আমার মৃত্যু অবধারিত আছে। তুমি না বুঝিয়া প্রাণ হারাইয়াছ। রাজ-ভৃত্যেরা এই কথোপকথন শুনিয়া রাজ-সমীপে সমুদায় কহিল। রাজা সমস্ত বৃত্তান্ত অবগত হইয়া চোরকে উপযুক্ত দণ্ড করিয়া কৃষককে তুষ্ট করিয়া বিদায় দিলেন।"

*" এক কৃষক লাঙ্গল চষিতে গিয়া কোন খানে গোটা চব্বিশেক মৎস্য ধরিয়া গৃহে আনিয়া আপন গৃহিণীকে পাক করিতে দিয়া আপনি পুনর্ব্বার চষিতে গেল। তাহার গৃহিণী সে মৎস্য কয়টী পাক করিয়া মনে বিবেচনা করিল, যে মৎস্য পাক করিলাম কিন্তু কি প্রকার হইয়াছে চাখিয়া দেখি। ইহা ভাবিয়া কিঞ্চিৎ ঝোল লইয়া খাইয়া দেখিল যে ঝোল সুরস

know how that one on the dish would taste, and she ate the second fish also. In this manner she proceeded till she had finished all but one; and when her husband came home, she presented him with a dish of rice and a single fish. The husbandman wondering said 'what is the matter? I got 24 fish; what about the rest?' His wife gave him the following account of the fish.

"You brought 24 fish. A kite fell upon them and took away eight; sixteen remained.

"I took them to the tank for washing and eight swam away in the water; eight remained.

"I got two bundles of fuel in exchange of two fish.

হইয়াছে। পরে পুনর্ব্বার মনে ভাবিল মৎস্য কিরূপ হইয়াছে, তাহাও চাখিয়া দেখি, ইহা ভাবিয়া একটা মৎস্য খাইল। পুনর্ব্বার চিন্তা করিল ওটী কিরূপ হইয়াছে, তাহাও চাখিতে হয়; ভাবিয়া সেটীও খাইল। এইরূপে খাইতে খাইতে একটীমাত্র অবশিষ্ট রহিল। পরে কৃষক ক্ষেত্র হইতে বাটী আইলে তাহার গৃহিণী সেই মৎস্যটী আর অন্ন তাহাকে দিলে, কৃষক কহিল 'যে একি? চব্বিশটী মৎস্য আনিয়াছি, আর কি হইল?' তখন তাহার স্ত্রী মৎস্যের হিসাব দিল।

মাছ আনিলা ছয় গণ্ডা,
চিলে নিল দুই গণ্ডা,
বাকী রইল ষোল।
তাহা ধু'তে আটটা জলে পলাইল॥
তবে থাকিল আট।
দুইটায় কিনিলাম দুই আটি কাঠ॥

" Your good neighbours ought to have a share.

" I presented them with six ; and then only two remained.

" I ate one to see how it tastes ; there remained only one.

" Look for that on the dish.

" If you are a true man eat the bone and keep the flesh (for me).

" Because you have got such a wife as myself, you are furnished with a true account."

A friend of Bengali writers.

The above two extracts illustrate the easy and simple style which is to be found in some of the text books compiled for the college of Fort William in which Dr. Carey taught the Bengalee, Hindusthāni, and Mahārathi languages. He not only contributed very considerably himself to Bengali prose literature, but always befriended those who took good vernacular work in hand. For instance we find that Thākur's Bengali and English Diction-

---

তবে থাকিল ছয়।
প্রতিবাসীকে চারিটা দিতে হয়॥
তবে থাকিল দুই।
তার একটা চাখিয়া দেখিলাম মুঁই॥
তবে থাকিল এক।
ঐ পাত্তপানে চাহিয়ে দেখ॥
এখন হইস যদি মান্সের পো।
তবে কাঁটাখান খাইয়া মাছখান থো॥
আমি যেঁই মেয়ে।
তেঁই হিসাব দিলাম ক'য়ে॥"

ary, an admirable work of scholarship, was compiled for the Fort William College in 1805 at the suggestion of Dr. Carey. He employed Rāma Rāma Vasu and Rājiva Lochana to write Pratāpaditya Charita and Krisña Chandra Charita respectively, the former of which appeared in 1801, and the latter in 1805.

Thus lived Dr. Carey in Bengal from 1793 when he first landed here till his death in 1834,—one of those rare spirits who, crossing the barriers of their national prejudices, by dint of that all-embracing brotherhood which every true Christian should feel for all men, worked without a thought of reward or personal aggrandisement. He and his colleague Mr. J. Marshman had nothing to bequeath to their children at death, but enough as heritage to the suffering race whose cause they espoused, not under obligation or extraneous mandate, but according to the dictates of their own consciences through which their God spoke to them. Amongst his other colleagues the name of Yates, W. Marton (of whom the Rev. J. Long says 'He is one of the ablest Bengali scholars ever produced in the country'), and the Rev. J. Pearson deserve a special mention as having greatly furthered the cause of our prose literature.

His colleagues.

(c) Bengali works written by Europeans.

The works written in the vernacular language about this time by European writers cover a vast field. We cannot name all of them. We confine ourselves to the following list of works, and our list even here is not exhaustive as we have not included those that deal with Christianity. There is a great literature of translations of the Bible and treatises on Christianity which we cannot undertake to dwell upon at present. The list below is mainly based on the catalogue on vernacular works compiled by the Rev. J. Long in 1855. Most of these works were no doubt written for educational purposes.

Arithmetic.

1. Smith's zemindary papers, printed at the Çri Rāmapore press in 1817.

2. Mr. May's Arithmetical Table selected from those employed in the native schools. It was published in 1817 and called May-Gaṅita.

3. Harley's Arithmetic—Gaṅitāñka. First Edition appeared from Chinsura in 1819.

Dictionary.

1. Bengali Dictionary by Forster,—a Civilian and Sanskrit Scholar. It contains 18000 words. Published in 1719 in two volumes. Price Rs. 60.

2. Miller's Bengali Dictionary, published in 1801. Price Rs. 32.

3. Haughton's Glossary, published in 1825.

4. Haughton's Bengali-to-English Dictionary, published at the expense of the Court of Directors in 1833. It contains 40,000 words. Price Rs. 80.

5. Marshman's Bengali Dictionary. Published in 1827,—25000 words.

6. Marshman's Bengali and English Dictionary, published in 1829. Price Rs. 10.

7. Rev. J. Pearson's School Dictionary, published in 1829.

8. Morton's Dictionary. 600 pages, Quarto size. Published in 1828. Price Rs. 6.

9. Mendie's Abridgment of Johnson's Dictionary (Bengali and English). First Edition appeared in 1822.

10. Rozario's Dictionary—1837. Price Rs. 6.

Ethics and moral tales.

1. Dr. Gilchrist's Bengali translation of Æsop's Fables—in 1803.

2. Upadeçakathā or moral tales by Stewart—in 1820.

3. Satguṅa O Viryya (95 anecdotes illustrating virtue and valour). Price Re. 1-8 as. compiled by a Çrī Rāmapore Missionary in 1829,

4. Æsop's Fables translated by Marshman.

5. Hitopadeça by Yates. Published in 1841.

6. Pārasika Itihāsa by Kneane.

Geography.

1. Bhugola Evaṁ Jyotiṣa (dialogues on Geography and Astronomy) by Pearson. Published in 1824.

2. A Map of the world in Bengali by G. Herklotts (1825).

3. J Sutherland's Geography of India.

4. Pearce's Bhugola Vrittanta (Geography)—in 1818.

5. Sandy's General Geography in Bengali—in 1842.

Grammar.

1. Halhed's Bengali Grammar—in 1778.

2. Carey's Grammar—in 1801.

3. Murray's English Grammar translated into Bengali by Rev. J. Pearson—in 1820.

4. Sir C. Haughton's Grammar. Price Rs. 15. Published in 1821.

5. J. Robinson's Bengali Grammar (a translation of Carey's Anglo-Bengali Grammar). Pages 109.

6. Keat's Bengali Grammar (Ket-Vyakaraṅa). Published in 1820. Pages 59. Price 2 as. From 1820-1854 upwards of 15,000 copies were sold.

7. Wenger's Bengali Grammar. Pages 156. Price Re. 1-4 as.

History and Biography.

1. Goldsmith's History of England translated into Bengali by Felix Carey in 1819. Pages 412.

2. Captain Stewart's Moral tales of History with selections of historical subjects such as—glimpses of the early days of England, with moral instruction, historical anecdotes—illustrative of friendship, industry, justice, pride, anger ; the arrival of the English in India, the Rules of the permanent settlement.

3. Itihāsa Samuchaya or Epitome of ancient history by Pearson. Pages 364. Price Re. 1. This book gives an account of the history of Egypt, Assyria, Babylon, Medea, Persia, Greece and Rome.

4. Prāchīna Itihāsa by Pearson. Published in 1830. Pages 623, compiled from Rollin and Anquetel; it gives brief account of the Egyptians, Assyrians, Babylonians, Medes and Persians, Grecians, Romans, treating of manners, customs, buildings, natural productions, laws, Government and history of those States.

5. Vaṅga Deça Purāvritta translated from Marshman's History by Wenger. Pages 284.

6. Dharma Pustaka Vrittānta by Mrs. Hæberlin. Published in 1846. Pages 252 with 27 woodcuts.

7. Kāla Kramika Itihāsa by G. Pearce, published in 1838. Pages 89 with 10 wood cuts.

8. Daniel Charita by Morton. Pages 345 —in 1836.

9. Purāvritta Saṁkṣepa by J. Marshman;— 1833. Pages 515. Price Rs. 3.

10. Bharata Varṣiya Itihāsa by J. Marshman. Two Volumes, 1831. Price Rs. 8.

11. Tucker's History of the Jews translated into Bengali by J. Kempbell. Pages 257. 1845.

12. Mahammad Jivana Charita by Rev. J. Long. Pages 121. Founded exclusively on Arabic authorities as given in the works of Sprenger, Weile, and Caussin de Perceval—treats of Geography, Natural History and religious state of Arabia previous to Mahammad's time, Mahammad's youthful days, his

trading, when 40 years old he announces a new faith, opposition of his relatives, becomes a warrior, his polygamy, messages to foreign rulers, regulations for his followers: death in the midst of his plans. "The second part now in the press will take in the spread of Moslemism, the Korān, Moslemism as at present, the festivals and sects of the Mahomedans."

Medicine.

1. Carey's Bengali Anatomy (Hāḍavali Vidyā) Pages 638. Price Rs. 6. Published from the Çrī Rāmapore press in 1820. Designed in 1818 to form the first part of a Bengali Encyclopædea, to consist chiefly of translation of 'esteemed compendiums of European art and science.'

2. Bachelor's Medical Guide. Pages 358. Price Re. 1.

Mensuration.

1. Robinson's Bengali Mensuration (Bhumi Parimāṅa) 1850. The author was an Inspector of Government Schools in Assam and the neighbouring districts. This work gives the elements of land-surveying and rules for finding the areas of 16 plain figures. 'It contains 10 problems—to find the area of a square, of a rectangular parallelogram: an oblique-angled parallelogram, a trapezium, a circle, ellipse, two sides of right-angled triangle, a triangle, a right-angled triangle.'

Readers.

1. Yule's Spelling book—Çiçu Vodhodaya. A spelling book with short sentences and verses for reading.

2. Haughton's Selections, containing 10 stories from the Totā Itihāsa, 4 from the Vatriça Siṁhāsana and 4 from the Puruṣa Parikṣā. Published in 1822. Price Rs. 10.

3. Kṣetra Bhāgana Vivarana or Agri-horticultural Transactions, by J. Marshman, pages 730. Published in 1831 in two volumes.

4. Çiçu Çikṣā or Object Lessons—by J. Weitbrecht, in 1852.

5. Praçnāvali—by J. Long. This book contains questions on the animal, vegetable and mineral kingdoms, taken from objects in this country—designed to call forth the curiosity of the young people, and show them the wonders existing in common objects around them.

Natural Philosophy.

1. Padārtha Vidyā Sāra or Natural Philosophy and History by Yates, compiled from Martinet's Catechism of nature, William's Preceptor's Assistance and Bayley's Useful Knowledge, designed as an easy entrance to the path of science—treats of the properties of matter—the firmament and heavenly bodies, air, wind, vapour, rain, earth, man, animals, birds, fishes, insects, worms, plants, flowers, grass, grain, minerals and miscellaneous productions. Published in 1825.

2. Yate's Padārtha Vidyā—1824. Pages 91.

3. Kimiya Vidyā Sāra or Chemistry by Mack, pages 337—price Rs. 2-8 as,—treats of Chemical forces, Caloric, Light, Electricity, Chemical substances, Oxygen, Chloride, Bromine, Hydrogen, Nitrogen, Sulphur, Phosphorus, Carbon, Boron, Selenium, the steam engine.

Miscellaneous.

1. Rev. J. Pearson's Pāthaçālā Vivarāṅa—a translation of the more important part of Dr. Bell's instruction for modelling and conducting schools. Published from Chinsura in 1819.

2. Patra Kaumudi, composed by the Rev. J. Pearson, contains 286 letters on familiar subjects, commercial and familiar correspondence, forms of leases, zemindary accounts and other forms in common use. First edition 1819, sixth edition 1852; 8,500 copies sold within this period.

3. Pāthāvali by the Rev. J. Long—extracts chiefly from native works, on the life of a shepherd astronomer, Punjab salt mines, silk worms, Moslem saints, frog in a tone, printing the wonderful veil, the transparent watch, the tower of Pandua, ghātamurders, steam engines, women devoted to Christ, a wonderful spring, the gold and silver of Scripture, balloons, Rāma Mohana Ray, productions of India-tin, lead and copper of Scripture, human body, Siamese twins, breathing, sagacity of elephants, etc.

4. Samvāda Sāra or selections from the native press by Rev. J. Long, 1853; pages 198. Price 6 as.

5. Yates' Prose selections, vol. I, 1847, pages 428. Price Rs. 5.

6. Prose selections from Bengali literature by Yates, vol. II, Octavo size, pages 407; gives 18 tales of a parrot, 9 letters from the Lipimālā, 14 stories from Vatriçā Siṁhāsana, notices of Indian kings from the Rājāvalī, the History of Rājā Kriṣṇa Chandra Ray of Krishnagar, 16 moral tales from the Puruṣa Parikṣā, 5 chapters of the Hitopadeça, 9 moral essays from the Jnāna Chandrikā and 9 from the Jnānārṅava, 4th chapter of Pravodha Chandrikā, chapters against idolatry from the Tatta Prakāça, History of Nala from the Mahābhārata, specimens of Rāma Mohona Ray's hymns, selections from two native newspapers.

7. Vākyāvali (Idiomatical exercises, by J. Pearson, pages 294, Price Re. 1. A phrase-book with examples of words alphabetically arranged; "very useful for either natives wishing to learn colloquial English idioms or Europeans wishing to know Bengali dialogues." Forms of letters and notes; appeared in 1819.

8. Sāra Saṁgraha by Yates, 1845.

We have quite a large number of Law books translated into Bengali by European writers. Forster's translation of the Regulations of 1793, a work about 400 pages,—is a curiosity both as to style and typography. We have besides the Regulations of 1802—1809, pages 504, translated by Turnbull and Sutherland. Ditto 1816—1821 by Wynch; the Navavidhāna or abstract of miscellaneous Regulations of 1793—1824; Dewani Āin Sāra and Rjā Samparkiya Āin (in two volumes) by Marshman, any many other works of this nature.

9. In 1818 a Bengali Encyclopædea was commenced at Çrī Rāmapore, but only one part, Carey's Anatomy, was completed. In 1828 the society for translating European sciences with H. Wilson as president started the Vijnāna Sevādhi, a serial on the plan of the Library of useful knowledge. It reached 15 numbers embracing Indian Geography, Hydrostatics, Mechanics, Optics, Pneumatics and Broughām's discourse on the advantage of Science.

10. Virgil's Æneid. First book translated into Bengali by J. Serjeant. a Civilian and a student of Fort William College, pages 65 ; it came out in 1805.

11. Shakespeare's Tempest, translated into Bengali by Monckton, a student of the Fort William College.

12. First Part, Robinson Crusœ. Pages 261. Translated into plain Bengali by the Rev. J. Robinson, illustrated by 18 wood-cuts. A second edition was published in 1855.

13. Pilgrim's Progress, translated into Bengali in two volumes by Felix Carey.

14. Gladwin's Pleasant stories, translated into Bengali, by George Gallowway in 1840.

15. Mylius' School Dictionary, translated by J. Lavandier.

16. History of a lion.

17. Life of Fatik Chānd by the Rev. J. Lawson.

18. Madhu's conversation,—by the Rev. W. Morton.

19. Lamb's Tales from Shakespeare, translated by Dr. Roer.

20. Memoir of Pitāmvar Singh by the Rev. W. Ward.

News-papers and Magazines.

"On the 31st of May, 1818, the first newspaper ever printed in any oriental language, was issued from the Çri Rāmapore Press; it was called the Samāchāra Darpāṅa or the 'Mirror of News.' It was started jointly by Dr. Marshman and Dr. Ward.

In February, 1818, Dr. Marshman published the Dikdarçana, a monthly journal, in which amongst other subjects, there was given an account of the life of Rājā Kriṣṅa Chandra of Nadiā.

The Satya Pradipa by Mr. Townsend,—started in 1850, was a most useful paper; it gave a *precis* of news, correspondence, wood-cuts with descriptions of objects in art and nature.

The impetus given by European writers.

The above list shows that European writers, chiefly missionaries, were the pioneers in all departments of vernacular-writing which grew into favour with the awakening of Hindu intelligence under British rule. Every subject, from the principles of Arithmetic, Botany, Astronomy, Anatomy, Chemistry down to Law, is comprised in this list. The extraordinary energy displayed by foreign writers in mastering the idioms and technicalities of our language, and dealing with such widely divergent subjects, is a sure proof of the earnestness of their philanthropic mission. The writer of the present treatise can hardly refrain from giving expression to his gratitude, while reviewing these works, for the impetus given by them to the native mind in acquiring the knowledge so essential for the needs of modern civilisation. They laid the foundations upon which the vast fabric of our present-day-literature is based—a literature which though necessarily lacking in originality, chiefly consisting as it does of translations and compilations, promises to rise to universal esteem under favourable circumstances, when it shall have passed its noviciate in acquiring all that it can assimilate from the vast resources of occidental learning.

(d) A new ideal in the country.

Contact with the west.

In the chapter on the Pauranic Renaissance, we noticed how mythological stories, fraught with a spirit of noble martyrdom and sacrifice, had elevated the minds of the people, and helped in spiritualising them. The Pauranic revivalists had held the earliest torch to enlighten our masses after Buddhism had declined in the country. The efforts of the missionaries and European scholars in giving culture through the medium of Bengali, now again after a lapse of nearly 700 years, served to awaken the Bengali mind to the consciousness of new ideas, the ideal of western civilisation.

The past ideal.

It was as if the home-stayers of Bengal had suddenly left the precints of home and launched out into the wide world. Hitherto the highest and noblest ideas that had inspired the Hindu mind in Bengal had drawn their impetus from home and from domestic life. Obedience to parents, loyalty to the husband, devotion to brothers and sacrifices to be undergone for guests, servants and relations, had all been elevated into the highest virtues, and the Purañas had supplied inexhaustible examples, illustrating each of these qualities. Rāma who left the throne and became an ascetic, and Viṣma, who took the vow of celibacy, foregoing his rightful claims to the throne of Indraprastha, typify the highest example of filial obedience. Sītā, Sāvitrī, Damayanti, Çakuntalā, Behulā in the past and hundreds of those in the later age who courted death on the funeral pyre of their husbands, showed that the ideal of nuptial duties in this land was capable of raising women to the highest martyrdom. Hanumāna typifies devotion to a master, and Ekalavya to the religious preceptor. The home was the great sanctuary where sacrifices and martyrdoms were to be undergone for the sake of those sacred ties which bind one to it ; and this would, according to the notion of the Hindus, infalliably lead him to a realisation of the supreme duty which a man owes to God,—culminating in a glorious renunciation of home for the good of the soul and of the world. Indeed, in a place where a joint and undivided family system required a man to live and eat together with all his near kinsmen, it would be impossible to live in harmony without elevating the domestic duties into the highest virtues. Hence no other nation has ever given so high a value to domestic duties, identifying them so closely with the spiritual.

The literature of a race inspired with such ideas has a unique value. Its scope may be comparatively small, but within its own narrow limits, it is deeper and purer than one could expect from a literature covering a wider range. The Bengali literature of the past had been reserved for the Bengalis alone ; a fact which gives it an original character, displaying the subtle turns of the intellectual and spiritual qualities of the race ; and one, who may feel interested in studying our national ideas and aspirations, would do well to read this ancient literature, which, for a century after the English conquest, lay neglected and uncared for,—consigned to the care of the Batatalā publishing agencies of Calcutta.

The old and the new.

From the home to the world—it was a descent from the Himalayas to the plains,—from the lofty spiritual idea permeating the Hindu home,—the visions of beatitude which it was the dream of every great Hindu to attain,—to the matter-of-fact world and to an observation of things that are taking shape and changing all arround ;—from the great examples of Bhiṣma and Rāma—cherished in the heart of every Hindu—the loftiest like the loftiest peak of the Himālayas,—to the stories of Duval's assiduity in learning, and Sir Philiph Sydney's offering his cup of water to the dying soldier ; —from the pursuit and acquisition of Yoga to the knowledge of a Geographical catechism,—to be able to point out Popocatepetl on a map of the globe,—from the celestial songs of Rādhā and Krisṅa, which while gratifying all our yearnings for the loftiest of human love, have kept a door constantly open heaven-wards,—to the stories of Paul and Virginia or of Æneas and Dido: the descent is as great as one from the Himalayas to the plains. But a race of people confined within the narrow grooves of their own thoughts were dragged out to observe the wonders of the world, of which they had hitherto known nothing, nor cared to know,—nipping in the bud all curiosity about the material world by fabrication of monstrous stories to explain the origin of things. To explain earthquakes, they had fabricated the story of Vāsuki, the great serpent who upholds the earth, as shaking his hydra-heads a little. To explain the origin of the universe they had invented the story of the golden egg that burst; with regard to the sea their idea was, that there were seven seas—one of curd, one of wine, one of salt, one of milk, and so forth; and as to the earth, that it consisted of seven islands and had a triangular shape. I do not mean to say that the race, who first formulated the principles of Arithmetic, Trigonometry, Geometry and Astronomy, and from whom the world learned these sciences, was so stupid as not to know the simple truths of Physical Geography; a Bhaṣkarāchāryya or a Varāhāmihira certainly knew them, and many things more, in advance of their age. But after the revival of Hinduism the spirit of inquiry had been directed from the material to the metaphysical world; the masses cared not to know the facts or the laws of the external world, and were content with fables regarding them, because the temporal had no longer any attraction for them. They took the same interest in the outer world as a globe-trotter takes in what he sees. Their knowledge of their surroundings was as superficial and as full of mistakes as that of one who merely passes through a country, thinking that this is not his true home. The Hindus showed the subtlest knowledge with regard to that world which they considered to be the only real one, and their Metaphysics is a mixture of the simple and the complex, in various grades of spiritual thoughts, springing from those of home life—reaching the loftiest range in the conception of the Nirguṅa.

Nothing strikes a man so greatly as his contact with a person who possesses qualities other than his own, and the Bengalis are a race who owing to their keen intellectual powers can at once enter upon a new field, as soon as it is presented to them. European hand-books and manuals took them by surprise. They disclosed a world to them of which they knew nothing. They saw in the civilisation of Europe a success and acquisition of power which struck them with wonder and they became willing disciples of the new teachers. In the passionate sincerity of our race to acquire new knowledge, they forgot their home, their literature, their wonderful success in metaphysical learning, and their great spirituality, and felt that they were dwarfed in the presence of that great materialistic civilisation which, armed with thunder and lightning and with the tremendous power of steam, stood knocking at their door—demanding audience.

"Young Bengal."

Young Bengal, as the new generation of the Bengalis were then called, became thoroughly anglicised in spirit. They exulted in Shakespeare's dramas and Milton's poetry; they read Schiller's Robbers and Goethe's Faust; they could name all the English dramatists of the Elezabethan age—Marlow, Philip Massinger, Ford, John Webster, Ben Johnson and Shirley and reproduce from memory lines from still earlier dramatists and from Holinshed's chronicles which Shakespeare had improved on, in many a noble line. They grew mad after Shelley's Epipsychidion, Keat's Hyperion and even after Chatterton's Death of Charles Bodwin. Poor Chandi Dās, poor Vidyāpati and Kavi Kañkaṅa!, the tears of your departed spirit fell on the big towns of Bengal which lay under the charm of European influence,—mixed with nocturnal dews and unheeded by Young Bengal, who despised their own country from the bottom of their hearts and yet posed as representatives of the people in public meetings!

The College of Fort William.

The College of Fort William established by Lord Wellesley in 1800 was an institution, which having directly in view the imparting of knowledge of different languages and other subjects to the European candidates for the Civil Service, proved to be a bond of sympathy and good will between the rulers and the ruled. The test of proficiency was high and severe. It was laid down that "Before any Civilian could obtain a degree, he was required to demonstrate his knowledge of the native languages by holding in regard to the service in Bengal, four disputations in the Persian or Bengali language before all Calcutta in an august assembly comprised of the natives of rank and learning, Rājās, Foreign Ministers, Pundits and Munsies." It was further ordained that "no promotion was to be given in the public service throughout India in any branch of the service held by Civilians except through the channel of the College."

A knowledge of the vernacular essential for the Rulers.

This College was a place where the European candidates for the Civil Service, European professors and some of the best Indian intellects met on terms of intimacy. It was not a meeting between officers and their subordinates which necessarily becomes formal for the discharge of official functions, but of those who made it a great point of their earnest endeavours to understand one another mutually. The study of the oriental languages, a high standard of proficiency in which was made compulsory, enabled the Civilians to comprehend the inner feelings and ideals of the vast population whom they were called upon to rule. The College of Fort William produced the most salutary results, creating a sympathetic attitude in European minds towards the native community, and both sections derived great profit from an interchange of thoughts. In the case of our countrymen, this result was manifest in the adoption of European manners and in the preference given to the civilisation of the west, and in the case of the European Civil servants, in their sympathetic attitude towards the people of this country, and in the hearty interest taken in all the movements of reform calculated to improve the condition of the latter.

The vast range of college-studies.

"The range of studies marked out for the students in the College was very extensive. It embraced the modern languages of Europe, the Greek, Latin and English Classics; Gcography and Mathematics; general History, Botany, Chemistry and Astronomy; Ethics and Jurisprudence, the laws of nations—of England, and in reference to Indian studies the Arabic, Persian, Sanskrit Hindustani, Bengali, Telegu, Mahratta, Tamil and Canarese languages and the history of the antiquities of Hindustan and the Decan............ The college was considered one of the most important departments of the State, and the Senior members of the Government were required in virtue of their office, to take a share in its management. Lord Wellesley proposed to erect a spacious and magnificent edifice for the institution in the immediate neighbourhood of Calcutta at Garden Reach, suitable for the accommodation of all professors and 500 students with a public hall, library, chapel and other requisite apartments."

"Such was the grand institution which, Lord Wellesley projected to qualify the public functionaries for their official duties. It was the noblest and most comprehensive plan of usefulness which had been devised since the Factory had grown into an Empire."

"The incitements to exertion in the College of Fort William were of the highest and most effective nature and its moral, economical and religious discipline such as was admirably calculated to promote all that was virtuous and useful in civil society.*

"Several of those who attained the highest posts in the empire, and many, who, if they did not reach such a proud eminence yet departed with the esteem of the high, and confidence of the lowly, laid the foundation of future success within the precincts of the College. The well-known names of Macnaghton, Bayley, Jenkins, Haughton, Prinsep and others, are sufficient to prove the justness of this observation."†

* Memoirs of Dr. Buchanan Vol. I, Page 208.
† Calcutta Review, Vol. V.

(b) The Pundits of the College.

The movement for undertaking literary and scientific works in Bengali prose, mainly initiated by the Europeans, served to evoke the zeal of the enlightened native community who pursued it with great vigour and activity. Some of the best prose works, on the lines indicated in the vernacular writings of Europeans, were compiled by the Pundits of the Fort William College, where Dr. Carey, as a professor of the vernacular languages, wielded a great influence, and was ever ready to render all possible help to all undertakings to promote the cause of vernacular literature. The works written by Bengali authors in this period mainly follow European models in style, and the best of them, making all possible allowances, scarcely possess the worth of second class literary productions, whereas most of the others, while embodying rudimentary information in all departments of useful knowledge, are mere translations of European works—mostly school-books.

The Pundits of the Fort William College, as I have said, wrote many Bengali prose works about this time which enjoyed great popularity not only with the native community but with the Europeans, specially the candidates for Civil Service Examination who had to read them as text-books in that College.

Mrityunjaya.

"At the head of the establishment of Pundits," (at the Fort William College) writes J. C. Marshman in his history of Çri Rāmapur Mission, stood 'Mrityunjaya, who although a native of Orissa,*

* Mrityunjaya Tarkâlankara was born in 1762 A. D. at Midnapur.

usually regarded as the Bœotia of the country, was a colossus of literature. He bore a strong resemblance to our great lexicographer not only by his stupendous acquirements and the soundness of his critical judgments but also in his rough features and unweildy figure. His knowledge of the Sanskrit classics was unrivalled, and his Bengali composition has never been surpassed for ease, simplicity and vigour. Mr. Carey sat under his instruction two or three hours daily while in Calcutta, and the effect of this intercourse was speedily visible in the superior accuracy and purity of his translations. In the English preface to the Probhoda Chandrika, Marshman says of Mrityunjaya as "one of the most profound scholars of the age."

Of the Bengali works written by Mrityunjaya, his *Prabodha Chandrika* is a monument of learning; it contains dissertations on Hindu Astronomy, Rhetoric, Law, Logic, Philosophy and other branches of learning of which the author was a perfect master. He makes a curious hotch-potch of the whole by combining the serious with the comic. The metaphysical subjects are huddled up with colloquies of artizans and rustics, and the whole is treated without much care for arrangement or system. The book was written in 1813. An edition of it appeared in 1833 after the author's death. Marshman further says in the preface, "the book is written in the purest Bengali of which indeed it may be considered one of the most beautiful specimens............Any person who can comprehend the present work and enter into the spirit of its beauties may justly consider himself master of the language." Mrityunjaya Tarkālankāra wrote *Rajavali* in 1808. It traces the history of India from the earliest time down to Timur. Mr. Ward in his work on the Hindus bestows a high encomium upon this book. It contains some of the traditions about ancient Hindu kings which may be of much help to the students of Indian history in substantiating thereby some of the informations derived from copper-plate inscriptions and other historical sources. The book is written in a simple style, though some of the expressions used by the learned author appear quaint to us, owing to lapse of years. Mrityunjaya's third work *Vatrica-siñhasana* is a collection of tales illustrative of Vikramaditya's romantic self-denial and liberality to a beggar, to a Brahmin, to a scholar, to the poor, to a pundit and to an enemy.

Though the Pundit lived in close touch with his distinguished European students, and was highly admired by them for his learning and character, he was an orthodox Hindu all his life. His pamphlet called "a defence of idolatry" shows the sweep of his scholarly arguments and the sincerity of his conviction in defending the creed of his forefathers. Mrityunjaya translated the Sanskrit work Hitopadeça into Bengali. The book appeared in 1801. "It treats of friendship, discord, war and peace in 42 fables, in which after the manner of Æsop, animals are introduced to teach Ethics. The original, like Telemachus, was written for the ethical instruction of a king's son at Palibothera."

Mrityunjaya also translated from Sanskrit a treatise on the Hindu law of inheritance.

Next to Mrityunjaya, we find Rāma Rāma Vasu— a Kayastha held in high esteem by the Europeans at Fort William College, for his great learning in different oriental languages. Says Dr. Carey about him "a more devout scholar than him I did never see." Rāma Rāma Vasu was born towards the end of the 18th century at Chinsura. He got his early education in a *pathacala* at the village of Nimtā, a place in Twenty-four Parganas already noted as the birth-place of the old poet Krisna Rāma. "Rāma Basu" writes Dr. Carey "before his 16th year became a perfect master of Persian and Arabic. His knowledge of Sanskrit was not less worthy of note.......... He was of a peculiar turn of mind. Though amiable in manners and honest in dealings he was a rude and unkind Hindu if any body did him wrong." Rāma Vasu was appointed as a Pundit in the Fort William College in 1800, but owing to difference of opinion, resigned his post shortly after.

Rāma Rāma Vasu.

Rāma Vasu's *Pratapaditya Charita* published in 1801 at Çri Rāmpur was one of the first works written in modern prose. "Its style, a kind of Mosaic, half Persian half Bengali, indicates the pernicious influence which the Mahomedans had exercised over the Sanskrit-derived languages." * We find the following account of the book in the descriptive catalogue of books by the Rev. J. Long. "The first prose work and the first historical one that appeared was the life of Pratāpāditya, the last king of the Sāgara island by Rāma Vasu, (page 156)." The Rev. J. Long also condemns this style

* Calcutta Review 1850.

of the book as corrupted by an admixture of Persian, but this estimate, I must say, is not just, for in the descriptions of wars and court-affairs the language could not in those days avoid a mixture of Persian in which all court affairs were managed even in the States under the control of Hindu Rājās. The great Sanskrit scholar and poet Bhārata Chandra himself, who introduced some of the choicest Sanskrit metres in Bengali, could not describe war or court scenes without having recourse to Persian words. In describing domestic or religious matters Rāma Vasu generally avoided Persian and Arabic words. His style is quaint and affected; at any rate as one of the earliest specimens of modern Bengali prose we may often excuse his faults, and be prepared to admit that he wrote a connected story in an interesting and lively manner. The other works by Rāma Vasu were his (1) *Lipimala*, or a guide to letter-writing containing a number of models for letters. This treats also of business, religion, and Arithmetic,—printed at the Çri Rāmapur Press in 1802. (2) *Attack on Brahmins*. Rāma Vasu was a friend of Rājā Rāma Mohana Roy who had kindly revised the Ms. of *Pratapaditya Charita* before it was published. From some of his writings it appears that he favoured the views of his enlightened friend.

Chandi charaṇa and Rājiva Lochana.

Two other works written by Pundits of the Fort William College respectively are (1) *Tota Itihasa* by Chandi Charan Munsi, which appeared in 1826, (2) *Krisna Chandra Charita* by Rājiva Lochana Mukhopādhāya, which came out in 1805. The style of both these works is elegant. We quote an extract from Rājiva Lochana's Kriṣṇa Chandra Charita. Rājā Kriṣṇa Chandra of Navadvipa, an account of whom we gave in a foregoing chapter, is the subject of this memoir. The Rājā, called by the Rev. J. Long 'The Augustas of the East' was a great friend of the English, and had been chiefly instrumental in persuading Mirzāfar and other leading men of Bengal to form a secret alliance with them on the eve of the memorable battle of Plassey. The extract refers to the defeat of Sirājuddaullā, his destitution and miserable end.

Kriṣṇa-Chandra Charita.

*"The English next came to the field of Plassey and began to fight. The soldiers of the Nawāb saw that their great generals were fighting in a half-hearted manner and that the volley of fire opened on them by the English was killing hundreds of them. In deep dismay many died fighting desperately. Mohana Dās, a general of the Nawāb saw that the fighting was not conducted as it should be, and informed the Nawāb that some of his generals had conspired against him and were trying to bring ruin upon him. The Nawāb wonderingly asked how that could be? Mohana Dās

---

* " পরে ইঙ্গরাজের যাবদীয় সৈন্য পলাসীর বাগানে উপনীত হইয়া সমর আরম্ভ করিল। নবাবী সৈন্য সকল দেখিল যে প্রধান ২ সৈন্যেরা মনোযোগ করিয়া যুদ্ধ করে না এবং ইঙ্গরাজের অগ্নিবৃষ্টিতে শত শত লোক প্রাণত্যাগ করিতেছে। কি করিব ইহাতে কেহ উষ্মা ক্রমে যুদ্ধ করিয়া প্রাণত্যাগ করিতেছে। যুদ্ধ ভাল হইতেছে না ইহা দেখিয়া নবাবের চাকর মোহন দাস নামে এক জন সে নবাব সাহেবকে কহিলেক আপনি কি করেন আপনার চাকরেরা পরামর্শ করিয়া মহাশয়কে নষ্ট করিতে বসিয়াছে। নবাব কহিলেন সে কেমন। মোহন

submitted that the Commander-in-Chief Mirzāfar Khān had made a secret league with the English and was not fighting. Mohana Dās wanted an army to lead to the field to destroy them and warned the Nawāb against placing confidence on any one at such a critical hour. He advised his master besides to keep a close watch, and guard the eastern gate with the remaining army. The Nawāb was alarmed at this information, and placed Mohana Dās at the head of 25,000 soldiers, and gave him every encouragement to fight at Plassey. Mohana Dās began to fight with remarkable zeal, which alarmed the English; Mirzāfar saw that matters would not stand well for him, if Mohana Dās should gain the victory over the English, and the present Nawāb

The assassination of Mohana Dās.

দাস কহিল সেনাপতি মিরজাফরালি খান ইঙ্গরাজের সঙ্গে প্রণয় করিয়া রণ করিতেছে না অতএব নিবেদন আমাকে কিছু সৈন্য দিয়া পলাশীর বাগানে পাঠান আমি যাইয়া যুদ্ধ করি। আপনি বাকী সৈন্য লইয়া সাবধানে থাকিবেন পূর্ব্বের দ্বারে যথেষ্ট লোক রাখিবেন এবং এইক্ষণে কোন ব্যক্তিকে বিশ্বাস করিবেন না। নবাব মোহন দাসের বাক্য শ্রবণ করিয়া ভয়যুক্ত হইয়া সাবধানে থাকিয়া মোহন দাসকে পঁচিশ হাজার সৈন্য দিয়া অনেক আশ্বাস দিয়া পলাশীতে প্রেরিত করিলেন। মোহন দাস উপস্থিত হইয়া অত্যন্ত যুদ্ধ করিতে প্রবর্ত্ত হইল। মোহন দাসের যুদ্ধেতে ইঙ্গরাজ সৈন্য সশঙ্কিত হইল। মীরজাফরালি খান দেখিলেন এ কর্ম্ম ভাল হইল না যদ্যপি মোহন দাস ইংরাজকে পরাভব করে আর এ নবাব থাকে তবে আমাদিগের সকলেরি প্রাণ যাইবেক অতএব মোহন দাসকে নিবারণ করিতে হইয়াছে। ইহাই বিবেচনা করিয়া নবাবের দুত একজন লোককে পাঠাইলেন। সে মোহন দাসকে কহিল আপনাকে নবাব-

continue to reign, the lives of all of them would be forfeited. So it appeared to him of vital importance to check Mohana Dās. Apprehending dire disaster, Mirzāfar sent a messenger who declared himself as bearing a message from the Nawāb to Mohana Dās. He said that it was the order of the Nawāb that the general should at once appear before him. Mohana Dās said that it was not possible for him at that stage of the fight to leave the battle-field. The carrier of the false message said, "How is it that you do not obey the Nawāb?" Mohana Dās now felt sure that it was all a trick. Why should the Nawāb call him at such an hour? So he at once beheaded the man and resumed the fight. Mirzāfar was terror-struck; he thought all hope would be gone if things were allowed to continue in that manner any longer. So he called in a relation of his own, and ordered him to go as a soldier of the English and kill Mohana Dās. That person immediately took a gun with him and going close to Mohana Dās fired at him; So fell Mohana

Flight of the Nawāb.

সাহেব ডাকিতেছেন শীঘ্র চলুন। মোহন দাস কহিল আমি রণ ত্যাগ করিয়া কি প্রকারে যাইব। নবাবের দূত কহিল আপনি রাজাজ্ঞা মানেন না। মোহন দাস বিবেচনা করিল এ সকল চাতুরী. এসময় নবাবসাহেব আমাকে কেন ডাকিবেন ইহা অন্তঃকরণে সিদ্ধান্ত করিয়া দূতের শিরশ্ছেদন করিয়া পুনরায় সমর করিতে লাগিল। মীরজাফরালি খান বিবেচনা করিল বুঝি প্রমাদ ঘটিল পরে আত্মীয় একজনকে আজ্ঞা করিল তুমি ইঙ্গরাজের সৈন্য লইয়া মোহন দাসের নিকট গমন করিয়া মোহন দাসকে নষ্ট করহ। আজ্ঞা পাইয়া একজন মনুষ্য মোহন দাসের নিকট গমন করিয়া অগ্নিবাণ মোহন দাসকে মারিল সেই বাণে

Dās. The army of the Nawāb dispersed and fled and victory was obtained by the English.

Joy of the people at the Victory of the English.

"Sirājuddaullā heard all and saw that there was no way to escape, so he thought it prudent to beat a retreat. He embarked on a boat and fled. Mirzāfar Āli Khān brought all this to the notice of the English General, and going to the Fort of Murshidābād hoisted the English flag from which all knew that the noble people of England had gained the victory. They were all so delighted at the event that they began to shout for joy and play on various instruments of music. People of the higher class went in great numbers with presents to the English General, who received them cordially, and ordered that those officers who were already discharging State functions should all be reinstated. He distributed tokens of his favour, moreover,

---

মোহন দাস পতন হইল। পরে নবাবী যাবদীয় সৈন্য রণে ভঙ্গ দিয়া পলায়ন করিল, ইঙ্গরাজের জয় হইল।

পরে নবাব স্রাজেদৌল্লা সকল বৃত্তান্ত শ্রবণ করিয়া মনে মনে বিবেচনা করিলেন কোন মতে রক্ষা নাই, আপন সৈন্য বৈরী হইল, অতএব আমি এখান হইতে পলায়ন করি। ইহাই স্থির করিয়া নৌকাপরি আরোহন করিয়া পলায়ন করিলেন। পরে ইঙ্গরাজ সাহেবের নিকটে সকল সমাচার নিবেদন করিয়া মীরজাফরালি খান মুরসীদাবাদের গড়েতে গমন করিয়া ইঙ্গরাজি পতাকা উড়াইয়া দিলে সকলে বুঝিল ইঙ্গরাজ মহাশয়দের জয় হইল। তখন সমস্ত লোক জয়ধ্বনি করিতে প্রবর্ত্ত হইল এবং নানা বাদ্য বাজিতে লাগিল। যাবদীয় প্রধান প্রধান মনুষ্য ভেটের দ্রব্য দিয়া সাহেবের নিকট সাক্ষাৎ করিলেন।

among them. They placed Mirzāfar Āli on the throne of Murshidābād and instructed the officers to carry on official work with care, so that the empire might flourish and the poor might not suffer. The officers began to work as they were bidden.

The sad end of the Nawāb.

" After his defeat the Nawāb in the course of his flight became oppressed with hunger ; for three days he had had no meal, and when on the fourth day his boat was passing by the abode of a fakir he ordered a man to go to him and tell him that a certain man was very ill and that he wanted to eat food at his place. The fakir hearing this came near to the boat, and recognised the Nawāb, who looked exceedingly pale. He thought "once upon a time

---

সাহেব সকলকে আশ্বাস করিয়া যিনি যে কর্ম্মে নিযুক্ত ছিলেন সেই ২ কর্ম্মে তাঁহাকে নিযুক্ত করিয়া রাজপ্রসাদ দিলেন। মীরজাফরালিকে নবাব করিয়া সকলকে আজ্ঞা করিলেন, তোমরা সকলে সাবধানপূর্ব্বক রাজকর্ম্ম করিবা যেন রাজ্যের প্রতুল হয় এবং প্রজালোক দুঃখ না পায়। সকলে আজ্ঞানুসারে কার্য্য করিতে লাগিলেন।

পরে নবাব স্রাজেদৌল্লা পলায়ন করিয়া যান। তিন দিবস অভুক্ত অত্যন্ত ক্ষুধিত, নদীর তটের নিকট এক ফকিরের আলয় দেখিয়া নবাব কর্ণধারকে কহিলেন এই ফকিরের স্থানে গিয়া তুমি ফকিরকে বল কিঞ্চিৎ খাদ্য সামগ্রী দাও একজন মনুষ্য পীড়িত কিঞ্চিৎ আহার করিবেক। ফকির এই বাক্য শ্রবণ করিয়া নৌকার নিকট আসিয়া দেখিল অসুস্থ নবাব স্রাজেদৌল্লা বিষন্ন বদন। ফকির সকল বৃত্তান্ত জ্ঞাত হইয়া বিবেচনা করিল, নবাব পলায়ন করিয়া যায় ইহাকে আমি ধরিয়া দিব। আমাকে

the Nawāb oppressed me and now the time for retaliation has come. I shall bring him up to Mirzāfar." But with joined palms he said "I am arranging the dinner quickly, so that you may continue your journey as soon as possible after partaking of it." The Nawāb was highly pleased with the courteous reception thus given him by the Fakir, and went to his house in great confidence. The fakir began to make arrangements for the meal, but in the meantime he had sent a secret message to an officer of Mirzāfar reporting that the Nawāb was fleeing and that he should lose no time in seizing him. As soon as the officer got this information, he hastened to the fakir's abode with a body of men, seized the Nawāb and sent him to Murshidābād."

Fort-Willam College dissolved in 1854.

Fort William College with its glorious record of usefulness in various departments of knowledge —and with what particularly interests ourselves, its labours in the cause of Bengali prose literature

---

পূর্ব্বে যথেষ্ট নিগ্রহ করিয়াছিল তাহার শোধ লইব। ইহাই মনমধ্যে করিয়া করপুটে বলিল আহারের দ্রব্য আমি প্রস্তুত করি, আপনারা সকলে ভোজন করিয়া প্রস্থান করুন। ফকিরের প্রিয় বাক্যে নবাব অত্যন্ত তুষ্ট হইয়া ফকিরের বাড়ীতে গমন করিলেন। ফকির খাদ্যসামগ্রীর আয়োজন করিতে লাগিল এবং নিকটে নবাব মীরজাফরালিখানের চাকর ছিল তাহাকে সম্বাদ দিল, যে নবাব স্রাজেদৌল্লা পলায়ন করিয়া যায়, তোমরা তাহাকে ধর। নবাব মীরজাফরালি খানের লোক এ সম্বাদ পাবা মাত্র অনেক মনুষ্য একত্র হইয়া নবাব স্রাজেদৌল্লাকে ধরিয়া মুরশিদাবাদ আনিলেক।"

gradually decayed in importance from the time of the foundation of Haileybury College in 1807, till its final extinction in 1854.

The Bengali prose works written by various authors early in the 19th century, though occasionally encumbered with compound words and quaint and high flown style, often show great erudition, as the writers were all learned Pundits. They enriched the prose literature by translations either from English or from the Sanskrit, Arabic and Persian languages. These works were generally compiled with great care; and considering the disadvantages from which the early labourers in any field must always suffer, we may excuse many of their inevitable short-comings. Personally, we have hitherto neglected the literature of this period being repelled, on the one hand, by the quaint bombastic style of our learned countrymen, and by the errors in idiom, on the other, into which European writers of Bengali have so frequently fallen. But this was an age in which Bengali prose had been taken up in earnest by men who spared no pains to contribute to its development; and there is surely much in these writings which will repay careful perusal by the writers of Bengal, at the present day.

———o———

(c) The Rev. K. M. Banerji and other authors who followed in the wake of European writers. A list of their publications.

Foremost amongst those who laboured in the field of Bengali prose under the influence of English education and the missionaries, was the Rev. K. M. Banerji.

Born in 1813 at Calcutta, this scholar was trained in the Hindu College and was one of the most diligent pupils and admirers of Dr. Razario whose influence upon "Young Bengal" was unbounded in his time. His pupils were imbued with European tastes, and though many of them rose to great eminence in later times, nearly all of them despised the orthodox religion and by their unrestrained conduct created great alarm in the minds of the Hindus. The comrades of Mr. Krişṅa Mohana Banerji, in the enthusiasm of their reformation, used to throw bones and meat into the neighbouring houses, and then cry out that it was beef which they had deliberately thrown there to pollute the homes of their Hindu friends. Krişṅa Mohana in his youth was unsparing in his abuse of those who happened to hold a different view from himself in matters of religion and used to call the illustrious Rādhā Kanta Deva, who was one of the leaders of the orthodox community, by the name of Gādhā Kanta, the word '*gadha*' meaning an ass.

K. M. Banerji.

Krişṅa Mohana embraced Christianity in 1832, and after the hey-day of his youth had passed, was held in high esteem by Europeans as well as by our countrymen for the soundness of his views, his great scholarship and his coolness of temper.

His Encyclopaedea Bengalensis.

His chief work in Bengali was the *Vidya Kalpa Druma* or Encyclopædea Bengalensis. It was started under the patronage of the Government in 1846, and dedicated by permission to the Governor-

General of India. The following are some of the subjects which the Encyclopædea was designed to embrace—

(1). Ancient History—Egypt, Babylon, Greece, Rome, India. Manners, Customs, opinions etc., of the Egyptians, the Babylonians, the Greeks, the Romans, the Hindus and other Asiatic nations.

(2). Modern History—of Europe, England, India, Bengal, America, etc.

(3). Science, Geography, Mathematics, Natural Philosophy, Astronomy, Metaphysics, Moral Philosophy, etc.

(4). Biographies of eminent men,—politicians, scholars, etc., European and Asiatic, ancient and modern, more after the form of Cornelius Nepos, than the more elaborate work of Plutarch.

(5). Miscellaneous readings containing detached pieces of various kinds adapted to the comprehension of the people of Bengal. Anecdotes, orations, speeches, accounts of travels and voyages.

Thirteen volumes of the projected Encyclopædia came out, *viz* :—

1. History of Rome Vol. I.
2. Do. do. Vol. II.
3. Geometry Vol. I.
4. Do Vol. II.
5. Miscellaneous extracts Vol. I.
6. Do. do. Vol. II.
7. Biography (containing the lives of Confucius, Plato, Alfred, and Vikramāditya).
8. History of Egypt.
9. Geography

10. Moral tales.
11. Watt's On The Mind Vol. I.
12. Do. do. Vol. II.
13. Life of Galileo.

The Encyclopædea contains much useful information for the enlightenment of the Bengal public who had hitherto had no knowledge of the outside world, but it shows no original research in any field by the compiler, consisting, as it does, mainly of translations from standard European writers. The Vidyā Kalpa Druma by Dr. K. M. Banerji and the *Vividhartha Samgraha* by Dr. Rājendra Lāl Mitrā (started in 1851) are two monuments of patient labour giving that up-to-date information in Science and Art which was so essential for the dessimination of useful knowledge amongst our countrymen in the earlier half of the 19th century.

A list of publications.

There was at the time quite a legion of Bengali works on the aforesaid lines, most of which have sunk into oblivion, after their brief day of usefulness in enlightening the masses of Bengal; and we can only name some of them to show in what direction the wind blew in our literature. For the list furnished below we have had to depend mainly upon the descriptive catalogue of Bengali books by the Rev. J. Long published in 1855.

Vocabulary

1. A Dictionary by Rāma Kamala Sen (Grand father of the illustrious Keçava Chandra Sen) pp. 1534. "A work of great research—the result of 15 years' labour—a translation of Todd and Johnson containing the meanings in Bengali of 5800 English words—a perfect chaos of materials for future lexicographers and a work of great

industry with Rādhā Kanta's famous Çavda Kalpa Druma." The price of the book was Rs. 50 per copy.

2. Çavda Sindhu—translation of the Amara Koṣa in Bengali by Pitāmvar Mukerjee of Uttarpārā, 1909.

3. Rāma Kiṣana's vocabulary—English, Latin and Bengali, 1821.

4. Anglo Bengali Dictionary by Tārā Chānd (75,000 words). Price Rs. 6.

5. Dictionary by Jaya Gopāla.

6. Do. by Lakṣmi Narayaṇa.

7. Çavda Kalpa Tarangini by Jagannāth Mallik.

These three works, all published in 1838, give suitable Bengali substitutes for the Persian terms prevalent in courts.

8. Dictionary by Jaya Nārāyaṇa Carmā, (16,000 words), 1838,

9. Ratna Hāldar's Vangabhidhana (6224 words) 1839.

10. Anglo Bengali Dictionary by Rādhānath De & Co. A vocabulary giving the meaning of words relating to Grammar, Heaven, Earth, the Body, Natural Objects, Apparel, Minerals, and Agriculture, 1850.

11. *Parasikabhidhana* or Persian and Bengali Dictionary by Jaya Gopāla, 1840;—contains about 2500 Persian words arranged alphabetically with the Bengali meanings.

Grammar. 12. Gangā Kiçore Bhattāchāryya's Vyākaraṅa.

13. A Bengali translation of the Mugdhavodha by Mathurā Mohana Dutta of Chinsura, 1819.

14. Bhāṣā Vyākaraṅa, 1823.

15. Rāma Mohana Ray's Vyākaraṅa, 1833.

16. Vraja Kiçore's Bengali Grammar, 1845.

17. Bhagavana Chandra's Bengali Grammar, 1845.

18. Sanskrit Grammar in Bengali by Devendra Nāth Tagore, 1845. Part I "Extends to Pronouns—gives the rules of Sandhi and the declensions written after the European system of Philology,—simple, well illustrated by examples," published by the Tatta Vodhini Sabhā.

19. Çyāmā Charaṅa's Anglo Bengali Grammar, pages 408—the most elaborate grammar that had appeared up to that time. Government patronised it liberally taking 100 copies at Rs. 10 per copy;—contains much information on the prosody of Bengali poetry.

History. 20. History of India by Govinda Chandra Sen, 1836.

21. History of Bengal—a translation of Marshman's history, pages 337, 1840.

22. Vāngālā Itihāsa by Içhvara Chandra Vidyāsāgara from the battle of Plassey down to Lord William Bentinck's administration, 1849.

23. History of the Punjab by Rājā Narāyaṅa Banerji, pages 194, gives much information respecting the Punjab, Kaçmir, Kabul, Kandahār and

the country of the Shikhs, derived from the Rāja Tarangini, Āin-Ākvari, Seyar Mutākharim, Prinsep's Life of Ranjit Singh, Lawrence's adventure in the Punjab and MacGregor's Çikhs.

24. Rome Purāvritta by K. M. Banerji, pages 610.

25. Bhāratvarṣer Itihāsa by Vaidya Nāth Banerji. Two volumes, pages 352, 1848. Compiled from Manu, Yajnavalka, the Rāmāyaṇa, the Mahābhārata, the Rājāvali, Book's Gazetteer, Marshman's History of Bengal, etc. One object of this book was to oppose the views given in Marshman's India which the author thinks are too much against the Brahmins and in favour of Christianity. The books treats of the Chronology of ancient Hindu King's, their residences, mode of government, origin of caste and other matters;—a defence of Hindu character.

26. Bharatvarṣer Itihāsa by Gopāla Lāl Mitra, pages 201, 1840.

27. Rājāvali by Çyāma Dhana Mukerjee. 1845.

---

28. Life of Bhavāni Charaṇa, "editor of the Chandrikā and the great leader of the Pro-suttee party." "A curious piece of biography" I find the following notice of the subject of this memoir in John Clark Marshman's History of Çrirāmpur Mission. In 1821 a native newspaper was started in Calcutta which maintained great influence in native circles for many years. It was designated the Chandrikā, and was edited by Bhavāni Charaṇa, **Biography.**

a Brahmin of great intelligence and considerable learning, though no Pundit, remarkable for his tact and energy which gave him great ascendency among his fellow countrymen. The journal was intended to check the liberal tendencies of the age, and it soon became the organ of the orthodox Hindus. During the life of its able and astute editor, it was considered the great bulwork of the current superstitions. Its success was owing not only to the popularity of the opinions which it advocated, but also to the charm of pure and simple style."*

29. Satya Itihāsa, pages 239, 1830. Sketches of Semiramies, Sesostris, Homer, Lycurgus, Socrates, Demosthenes and Alexander.

30. Jivana Charita by Içvara Chandra Çarmā, 1849. Lives of Copernicus, Galileo, Newton, Herschell, Grotius, Linœus, Duval, Thomas Jenkins, S. W. Jones.

Moral tales and other subjects.

31. Ajnāna Timira Nāçaka, 1838. By Vaidya Nāth Āchāryya of Kānchanpāra.

32. Praçasti Prakāçika, 1842. By Krisña Lāl Deb, compiled from original Sanskrit of Vararuchi of the Court of Vikramāditya ; gives rules according to the Çāstras for writing letters—the colour and size of the paper, the titles of letters and mode of address. Some curious things are to be found in this work, such as,—a person is to write to a young girl in red paper with red ink, to a great man in gold-coloured letters, to a man of middle rank in silver, to a

* Vol. II, p. 241.

common man on copper or tin coloured paper, before marriage on vermilion; a letter to a great man is to be six finger-breadths long, to a person of middle class 18 inches; receiving a letter from a Rājā or Guru it is to be laid on the head, from a friend on the forehead; from a wife on the breast.

33. Jnāna Kaumudi, on letter-writing by Rameçvara Banerjee of Gopālapur.

34. Lipi Mālā by Rāma Rāma vasu, 1802.

---

34. Paçvāvali (Animal biography) by R. C. Mitra.

35. Pākhī Vivaraṅa—on birds, by R. C. Mitra pages 660, 1834.

36. Padārtha Vidyā by P. C. Mitra, 1847.

37. Vividha Pātha—Miscellaneous readings, 1847.

38. Patradhara by Jaya Gopāla Tarkālankāra, 1821.

39. Vānarāṣṭaka, 1834. By Rājā Kali Kissen. A man disguised as a male-ape questions Rājā Vikramāditya.

40. Strī Çikṣā Viṣayaka (on female education) by Goura Mohana De, 1818, gives evidence in simple language in favour of the education of Hindu woman "from the examples of illustrious ones both ancient and modern and particularly of Indian females, such as Rukmini, Khanā, Vidyālankār (?) who gave lectures at Benares on the Çāstras. Sundarī of Faridpur skilled in Logic, Ahalyā Vāi who conversed in Sanskrit and erected many buildings.

41. Strī Durāchāra—a reply to the above in the language of fierce ire published in 1840.

42. Hita Kathā—100 ethical stories by Rāja Kiçore of Pulāsati.

43. Jnāna Pradīpa—moral tales by Gauri Çankara Bhattāchāryya, 1848.

44. Jnāna Ratna—selection of morals by Prema Chānd Rāy, 1842, gives tales and anecdotes to illustrate the following subject:—Duty to parents and teachers—Knowledge and folly.

45. Jnāna Chandrikā—selection of ethical pieces, 1838, by Gopāla Mitra.

46. Nitī Kathā—Moral tales by Rāma Kamala Sen, prepared at the suggestion of a Revd. gentleman who was the father of a late Lieutenant-Governor of the North-Western Provinces.

47. Manoranjana Itihāsa by Tārā Chānd Datta, 1819. "The school-book Society alone had sold 18,000 copies" of the book before 1854. The writer was in the employment of the late Captain Stewart of Burdwan.

---

48. Rājā Kāli Kissen's—"A lithography of an Orrery," 1826.

49. Geography and eclipses by the same author, in 1836.

Geography. 50. Elementary Geography published by the Tatta Vodhini Sabhā, 1840.

51. Bhugola by Kṣetra Mohana Datta, 1840.

52. Geography of Asia and Europe by the Rev. K. M. Banerji, 1848.

53. Sandeçavali—(Indian Gazetteer), pages 346, by Rama Narsinha Ghoṣa.

54. Map of the world—the first specimen of a map engraved in Bengali,—executed by a Bengalee Kaçi Natha under the superintendence of C. Montague. 1821.

---

55. Geometry by K. M. Banerjee, 1846. **Geometry.**

56. Bhuvana Parimaṅa Vidya (Land surveying) by Vraja Mohana, 1846.

---

57. Chittotkarṣa Vidhana—a philosophical work by the Rev. K. M. Banerji, pages 600 in two volumes, 1849–50. **Miscellaneous.**

58. Phrenology by Radha Vallaba Das, 1850.

---

59. Bramly Vaktrita or Dr. Bramly's speeches by Udaya Charana Adhya, 1836.

60. Atma Rakṣa by Raja Kriṣṅa Mukherjee. Compiled from Nidana, 1849.

61. Dravya Guṅa by Içvara Chandra Bhattacharyya, 1835.

62. Auṣadha Kalapavali by Madhu Sudana Gupta, 1849, pages 244.

63. Jala Chikitsa (water cure) by Prema Chand Chaudhuri, 1850. The writer professes having experienced wonderful benefits from Hydropathy; he points out its advantages to others in the various uses of water applied internally and externally to different parts of the body for costiveness, fever,

rheumatism, measles, small-pox, dysentery, etc. He fortifies his arguments by quotations from the Hindu medical Çastras.

Periodicals and Magazines.

1. Dikdarçana by Çriramapore Missionaries, 1818.

2. Gospel Magazines, 1823.

3. Brahmanical Magazine by Rama Mohana Ray, 1821.

4. Çastra Prakaça, 1851.

5. Jnanodaya by R. C. Mitter, 1831.

6. Vijnana Sevadhi by Ganga Charana Sen, 1832.

7. Jnana Sindhu Taranga by Rasika Mallick, 1832.

8. Four-anna Magazine, 1833.

9. Vidya Sara Saṁgraha, 1834.

10. Vidya Darçana by Akṣaya Kumara Datta, 1834.

11 Vidya Darçana by Prasanna Kumara Ghoṣe.

12. Kaustabha Kiraṅa by Raja Narayaṅa Mitra, 1846.

13. Jagatvandhu Patrika edited by the students of the Hindu College, 1846.

14. Satya Sancharini by Çyama Charṅa Bose, 1846.

15. The Kayastha Kiraṅa, 1846. It gives translations from the Puraṅas and advocates the claims of Kayasthas to wear the Brahmanical thread.

16. The Durjana Damana Navami by Thākur Dās Bose, (Tri-monthly), 1846;—opposed Young Bengal, defended idolatry, had as its symbol the picture of a cross fastened by a charm to signify that it would restrain Christian influence.

17. Hindu Dharma Chandrodaya by Hari Nārāyaṅa Gosvāmi.

18 Jnāna Sanchāriṅī—organ of the orthodox community, 1847.

19. The Kāvya Ratnākara, edited by the students of the Hindu College, 1847.

20. Muktāvali by Kali Kānta Bhattachāryya. Commenced at the instigation of Rāja Nārāyan of Andul, opposed the right of Kāyasthas to wear the Brahmanical thread, 1848.

21. Bhakti Suchaka by Rāma Nidhi, 1848.

22. Rasa Ratnākara by Jadu Natha Pal, 1849.

23. Satjnana Ranjana by Govinda Chandra Gupta, 1849.

24. Duravikṣanikā by Dvārikā Natha Mazumder, 1850.

25. Dharma Marma Prakāçikā from Konnagar, 1850.

News papers.

1. Bengal Gazette by Gangādhar Bhattāchāryya, 1816.

2. The Çri Rāmapore Darpaṅa, 1818.

3. The Kaumudi, edited by Rāma Mohana Ray and Bhavāni Banerjee, 1819.

4. Chandrikā by Bhavāni Charan, 1822. It was for many years the native "Times of Calcutta."

5. Timira Nāçaka by Krisña Mohana Dās, 1823.

6. Vanga Dūta by Nīla Ratana Hāldār, 1825.

7. Sudhākara by Prema Chānd Ray, 1830.

8. Prabhākara by Iṣvara Chandra Gupta, 1830.

9. Sabha Rājendra by Maulvi Ālimolla, 1821.

10. The Jnānānveṣaṅa by Rasika Mallik and Dakṣina Mukherjee, students of the Hindu College, 1831.

11. The Ratnākara by Vraja Mohona Sinha, 1831.

12. The Sāra Saṁgraha by Veni Madhava De, 1831.

13. Ratnāvali by Jagannatha Mullik, 1832.

14. Sudhāṁçu by Kalī Kinkara Datta, 1835.

15. Divākara by Gangā Narayan Bose, 1837.

16. Saudāmini by Kāli Chandra Datta, 1838.

17. Guṅākara by Giriça Chandra Bose, an ex-student of the Hindu College, 1858.

18. The Mrityunjaya by Pārvatī Charaṅa Datta, 1838.

19. The Rasarāja by Gauri Çankara Bhattāchāryya, 1839.

20. Aruṅodaya by Jagannārāyaṅ Mukherjee, 1839.

21. The Murshidābād Patrikā, 1840.

22. Jnāna Dīpikā by Bhagavata Charaṅa, 1840.

23. Sujana Ranjana by Govinda Chandra Gupta, 1840.

24. Bharata Vandhu by Çyāmā Charaṅa Banerjee, 1841.

25. Niçākara by Nīlāmvara Dās, 1841.

26. The Bhringā Dūta by Nīlakamala Dās.

27. Rāja Rāni by Gangā Narayaṅa Bose, 1844.

28. Jayadā Dīpaka by Maulvi Āli, 1846.

29. The Mārttanda, 1846.

30. The Jnāna Darpaṅa by Umā Kanta Bhattacharyya, 1846.

31. The Pāṣandakiraṅa by Içvara Chandra Gupta, 1846.

32. Rungpur Vārttavaha by Nīla Ratan Mukherjee, 1847.

33. Jnāna Sancharinī from Kānchḍāpaḍa, 1847.

34. Sudhi Ranjana by Içvara Chandra Gupta, 1847.

35. Ākkala Guḍum by Vraja Nātha, 1847.

36. The Dikvijaya by Dwaraka Natha Mukherjee, 1847.

37. Jnananjana by Chaitanya Charaṅa Adhikāri, 1847.

38. Sujana Vandhu by Nivaraṅa Chandra De, 1847.

39. The Manoranjana by G. C. De, 1847.

40. The Jnana Rātnakara by Viçvamvara Ghoṣe, 1848.

41. Dinamaṅī (scandalous), 1848.

42. The Ratna Varṣaṅa by Madhavā Chandra Ghoṣe of Bhowanipur, 1848.

43. Rasa Sāgara by Rāma Gopala Banerjee of Kidderpore, 1848.

44. The Aruṅodaya by Pānchānana Banerjee, 1848.

45. Rasa Mudgara—advocated Hinduism, by Kṣetra Mohona Banerjee 1849.

46. The Mahajana Darpaṅa by Jaya Kali Basu, 1849,

47. The Satya Dharma Prakāçika—an organ of the Kartā-bhajās.

48. Varaṅaçi Chandrodaya.

49. The Bhairāvananda, 1849,—both edited by Umā Çankar Bhattāchāryya, a blind scholar who helped Rājā Jaya Nārāyaṅa in his translation of Kāçi Khanda.

50. Vardhamāna Chandrodaya by Rāma Tārana Bhattāchāryya, 1850.

51. Vardhamāna Samvāda, 1850.

III. General remarks chiefly indicating the characteristics of the new age and its contrast with the earlier one.

The growth of the modern literature.

These are some of the products of the literary labours of our countrymen in the vernacular tongue under the intellectual stimulus of the first contact with Europe. They continued the work with an ardour which has grown without intermission, and our present day literature is the richest among the vernaculars of India in quality and in its many-sided activity. The lists I furnish embrace the literature of a period ending 1850, but it is only at and after the middle of the 19th century that we can see the full harvest grown from the seeds sown at the beginning. The works on various subjects written in Bengali after the model of European works abound like "leaves by the streams of Vallombrosa," and it will be a hard task for the historian of the present epoch of our literature to make his selection from amongst the very considerable materials which will be at his command.

Bengali literature, previous to the advent of the Europeans on the field, was mainly in the hands of the Vaiṣṇavas and Çāktas. The songs of Kriṣṇa Kamala who belonged to the former and of Rāma Prasāda who belonged to the latter sect, are the last great utterances of the two cults, the echoes of which will ring in the ear of future generations of Bengalis for ages to come. The *yatrawalas*, *kaviwalas*, and *panchalikars* drew profusely from the vast resources of our past lore, and having put the old sentiments in modern garb appealed to our masses. But with these people the last echoes of our past literature have nearly died out. There are still *kirtanas*, *kathakatas* and *yatras*, but they no longer contribute to the rich literature of the past. They only recite what the old masters have sung or said, and are mere relics of institutions which were once a living force in the country.

The representative character of our past literature.

The old literature of Bengal was a truly representative literature; Bhārata Chandra's writings and Ālāol's style, though so artificial and loaded with classical figures, were yet accessible to the masses of Bengal. The literature of the Bengalis belonged essentially to them all,—not to the literate merely, but to the whole race. For hundreds of years its ideas had been made familiar to the whole country by innumerable ways and means. The whole race had assimilated these sentiments which found expression in their literature; and even the finished expressions, and the highly coloured metaphors that had characterised the productions of latter-day Sanskritic Bengali were not unintelligible to the people. The best evidence of this statement will be found in the fact that very low classes of men and even those who are thoroughly illiterate, have preserved up to the present, works like the Padmāvat which are still being printed for them. This shows great advancement on the part of the people in mastering a highly wrought literary style, and the past literature of Bengal was the medium through which the words of her poets and scholars were communicated to the lowly, the humble and the poor, who, often without knowing the alphabet, could understand the most difficult points in the Hindu philosophy or poetry under the educative influences of their own heredity and environment.

The old school upset.

But towards the end of the 18th century the Vaiṣṇavas and the Çāktas were practically driven out of the field. Our vernacular literature passed into the hands of Europeans; and they trained a class of people to write manuals and school books after the manner of their own standard works. Mr. Wilkins trained Panchānana Karmakāra in the art of punch-cutting, but this was not all; it was the Europeans and chiefly the missionaries who trained the Pundits to write Bengali,—not as they would have it, but as their European masters wanted it.

The Vaiṣṇavas and the Çaktas, who had hitherto been at the helm of our literature, inspite of their occasional indulgence in ornamental style, always meant their works for readers who would understand them. But the great Sanskrit scholars, the Bhattāchāryyas, as the *Tol* pundits were called, had hitherto nothing to do with vernacular literature. They were now considered fit to write in the vernacular tongue on account of their proficiency in Sanskrit. Their classical accomplishments, however, proved an utter disqualification for the purpose.

We have seen that the specimens of early Bengali prose that have come down to us were all written in simple language. They were generally used for the interpretation of the doctrines of particular creeds or of Sanskrit texts. So the writers found it expedient to adopt popular language.

The Bhattāchāryyas

But the Bhattāchāryyas not accustomed to write Bengali showed the defects and faults of untrained hands. They affected a pedantic style which sounded strange to the Bengali ear. In their efforts to display their great learning they wrote in a ridiculous style which was difficult not only to foreign people but also even to Bengalis themselves. The pedantry of the old school of poetry, though sometimes carried to excess, had in it elements which suited the genius of our language. It was absurd in some places, but it was a natural though a peculiar growth. The pedantry of the Bhattāchāryyas on the other hand—the vollies of high sounding compounds that they poured out—were unbearable in our language. It was as if giants had been let loose; and the artistically decorated gardens, into which they had found entry, could ill bear their heavy and unwieldy tread.

Specimens of their style.

We quote here a few specimens of their style. The great Pundit Mrityunjaya of the Fort William College, whom Dr. Marshman compared to Johnson in all respects, wrote in his Pravodha Chandrikā.

'কোকিল কলালাপ বাচাল যে মলয়াচলানিল সে উচ্ছলচ্ছীকরাত্যচ্ছ নির্ঝরাম্ভঃ কণাচ্ছন্ন হইয়া আসিতেছে।*

In a translation of the Government Regulations and Laws entitled the Ādalata Timira Naçana, by one Rāma Mohana Ray (he could not have possibly been the illustrious Rāma Mohana Roy) printed in 1828, we find a preliminary prayer in prose, addressed to God as follows:—

†"বারংবার অপার জগদুদয়স্থিতিসংলয়াদি সাধারণকারণ মানস-বাক্‌পথাতীত পরমাদ্ভুত বিবিধবিচিত্রচিন্তাতীত পরাৎপরানন্ত বৈভবানুক্ষণ বিস্তারক অবিরত্যাধ্যাত্মিকাধিবহুবিধতাপকলাপ-কবলিত-বিকলিত-মানস-মানবসমূহনিস্তারক পরমকারুণিক মনুজাণ্ডজ বিবিধস্থলচরজলচরাকাশচর কীটপতঙ্গাদিজীবকৃত

---

*"The Malaya breeze, resounding with the warbles of the cuckoo, is becoming drenched with the transparent particles of the over-flowing sprays of water."

†"To him who is the cause of the creation, of the preservation and of the final dissolution of the universe which occurs again and again in cycles—who is beyond all comprehension and whom no language can express,—no thought however subtle can reach,—to Him who is the saviour of all men, ground down and distressed by Providential and physical and other evils, who is mercy itself and the one great equitable Judge of the deeds

সতত সদসদ্বিচারক জগদেকনিয়ামক বিশ্বোপকারার্থ দিনকর-নিশাকরাসংখ্যেয় তারকাদ্যনিশবিভ্রমকারক সদাচারনিরত সর্জ্জমানমোদক তৎকর্ত্তৃক নিখিলকার্য্যানুদৃষ্টা শ্রবণমননদ্বারা অকিঞ্চিঃস্বরূপাভাসমাত্র রূপকাখিলাধ্যক্ষের প্রতি গণণাতিরিক্ত প্রণতিপূর্ব্বক বিশিষ্টশিষ্ট সদসদ্বিচারকমহাশয়সমূহ সমীপেষু বহুতর বিনয়পুরঃসর নিবেদন।"

All this is a single sentence, which moreover is not yet complete; it appears like some monstrous sea-reptile coiling into a thousand folds and dragging itself to an appalling length.

The author of "Praphulla Jnānanetra" is Içāna chandra Banerjee. This writer grievously errs in every sentence in spelling, yet poses as a great and erudite scholar. His address to Hare Krisṅa Addy in the dedication shows that, however inferior may be his qualifications, he desires to surprise the readers by his pedantry. **Praphulla Jnāna-netra.**

"আপনকার সাহার্য্যতরণী কত্তৃক গভীর তিমির দুস্তার অজ্ঞানার্ণব হইতে নিস্তার পাইয়া"

(which means,—'being enabled to cross the illimitable and the deep sea of ignorance by the boat of thine help).'

---

virtuous or otherwise of men, of the oviparous, acquatic, and amphibious animals, of worms and birds,—to Him who is the great law-maker of the universe, who for the good of the world created the moving celestial bodies—the sun, the moon and the innumerable stars, who observes all, and only a glimpse of whose attributes is obtained by our perception of sight, hearing etc.,—after offering numberless salutations to that great Master of the universe, next with humility and respect do I approach the benevolent judges of right and wrong with the prayer that—,"

Sarvāmoda Tarangini.

In "Sarvāmoda Tarangini" written in 1850,—a work expounding theistic principles, we find "সর্ব্বোপাস্য সর্ব্বশক্তিমান সর্ব্বান্তর্য্যামী সর্ব্বস্বামী সর্ব্বভূতের কর্ত্তা পাতা বিধাতাকে সর্ব্বতোভাবে প্রণাম পূর্ব্বক সর্ব্বামোদতরঙ্গিণী নামক গ্রন্থ প্রকাশ করিতেছি।"

Represen-tative character lost

The whole literature of the period abounds with such absurd instances of pedantry. They are specimens of composition by untrained hands. Those who were the natural leaders, so long acknowledged to be the masters of the vernacular style of composition,—at whose hands and by whose disinterested and self sacrificing labour Bengali literature had flourished and attained distinction,—the Vaiṣṅava and Çākta writers were ousted from the field, and in their place the Tol pundits, who knew nothing of our past literature, whose study was confined to Sanskrit, were called in to write Bengali books; the result was that their unwieldy style and its uncouth form struck a discordant note to the spirit of our language. Besides, the subject-matter which they chose was all upon the model of European books. This naturally failed to appeal to our masses unacquainted with the new spirit which was inspiring the authors of our modern prose. Modern literature thus lost that representative character which the yellow leaves of the old Mss. had so pre-eminently possessed. A foreign plant was, as it were, engrafted on an old tree and it required years for the graft to grow and become a true and living branch of our literature.

and the link broken.

The old school had been a homogeneous creation; one would hear the echoe of Vidyāpati, who died 400 years ago, in Bhārata Chandra who lived 250 years after. The choes of Chandi Dās's songs, sung 500 years ago, were traceable in the lays of the modern *kaviwala* ; and the joys and sorrows, pain and pleasures, embodied in the Bengali literature extending over a period of 700 years worked in the minds of the whole Bengali race and found a ready response from every soul. The niceties and even the pedantry of our past literature proved no barrier, as I have said, to our masses in enjoying the productions of the artificial school of poetry which grew up under circumstances natural to the soil. But now the link was suddenly snapped. Our old literature was, as it were, walled up, and a new one substituted which the people found inaccessible to them, and thus Bengalis ceased for half a century to understand the written Bengali of this age,—a time required by the masses to train themselves up to the new style and to the new subject matter. Even now the works of some of our best modern poets, wrought in the simplest of terms, seem unintelligble to a large section of the people, because of the European ideas in them with which they are not familiar ; and yet these readers can scale all the heights of the mystic metaphors of Bhārata Chandra and Ālāol.

Admixture of Persian.

Persian scholars no less than Sanskrit-knowing pundits contributed their share towards making the style of modern prose in its early stages, cumbersome and corrupt to a degree ; and we have found such specimens of writing in Rāma Rāma Vasu's Pratāpāditya printed at Çrirāmapore Press in 1800 A.D. Lipimālā or model letters by this author shows a style which was in current use in the country for long years. The epistles on mercantile and state affairs show a greater preponderance of Persian words, whereas the correspondence of a domestic and personal nature and those on religious subjects were generally free from such admixture. The addresses to high personages contained stereotyped sentences which were full of corrupt Sanskrit words. The form seems to have come down from a very remote age. Here is a curious specimen of the usual form of one Rājā addressing another. We take the extract from the Lipimālā.

Lipimālā.

"রাজাধিরাজ হিন্দুস্থানমাঝ যাহা দর্পময় ক্ষমা অতিশয় সরলান্তকরণ রূপ হেমবরণ শক্তিমন্ত ধীর অতি মহাবীর আত্ম-লোকপাল বৈরীমর্দ্দকাল শ্রীমান গুণধর মহারাজ রাজেশ্বর রাজচক্রবর্ত্তীর সাহায্য লিপি লেখা যাইতেছে।"

When Bengali literature had been thus placed in inexpert hands and committed to pedantic follies from which there seemed no way of its resuscitation, the European writers of Bengali cut a new channel of their own and made the style of vernacular prose flow into it; it was thus saved from the mazy and intricate paths of involved sentences and compound words in which it had entangled itself. The European writers naturally chose simple and short sentences and colloquial words and obliged the pundits to write in a similar style. However high a pundit might soar in the atmosphere of classical learning, he certainly knew the colloquial dialect of his country, though he had hitherto treated it with great contempt and had never thought of adopting it as a medium for literary composition. We find Dr.

The colloquial style favoured by the Europeans.

Carey employing Pundits to write a portion of his colloquies in Bengali, and even Mrityunjaya, the great scholar was made to introduce a colloquial style into his Pravodha Chandrika. Side by side with his উচ্ছলচ্ছিকরাত্যচ্ছ নির্ঝরাম্ভ কণাচ্ছন্ন হইয়া আসিতেছে" we find :—

* "স্ত্রী কহিল, গুড় হইলেই কি রাঁধা হয়? তৈল নাই, লুন নাই, চাউল নাই, তরকারী পাতি কিছুই নাই। কাঠগুলি সকলি ভিজা, বেসাতি বা কিরূপে হবে * * * কুটনা বা কে কুটিবে, বাটনা বা কে বাটিবে? তৎপতি কহিল, আজ কি ঘরে কিছুই নাই, দেখ দেখি খুদ কুঁড়া যদি কিছু থাকে তবে তার পিঠা কর, এই গুড় দিয়া খাইব। ইহাতে তাহার স্ত্রী কহিল, বটে পিঠা করা বুঝি বড় সহজ? জান না, পিঠা আঠা; যেমন আঠা লাগিলে শীঘ্র ছাড়ে না, তেমনি পিঠার লেঠা বড় লেঠা, শীঘ্র ছাড়ে না। কখনো ত রাঁধিয়া খাও নাই। আর লোকদের মাউগের মতন মাউগ পাইয়া থাকিতে, তবে জানিতে।"

The great Pundit Mrityunjaya, who could discourse on all the six systems of Hindu philosophy, would hardly have condescended to adopt the despised *patois* of the country and choose such an humble subject for treatment, had it not been set

* "The mistress of the house said 'Is molasses the only thing required for cooking? There is no oil, no salt, no rice, no vegetable of any kind: the fuel is wet. What about the spices? My son's wife is out of health and cannot work. Who will grind the spices and who prepare the vegetables? Her Lord said, 'Look closely; is nothing available in the house? See, woman, if you can find out some refuse rice and make cakes with it. We shall take them with molasses.' The mistress said, 'Indeed, is the preparation of cakes so simple then? They say that the making of cakes is like putting gum in the hands, if once it sticks, it takes a good deal of time to clean it off. Cake preparation takes much time and is full of trouble. You never cooked anything in your life, husband, therefore you speak so foolishly. Had you had an ordinary woman for your wife you would by this time, no doubt, have had much bitter experience.'"

on him as a task by the European masters of Fort William College.

The European's Bengali.

It was unavoidable that European's writing in Bengali would now and then commit mistakes of idiom. Instances of translating 'গোপাল উড়ের যাত্রা' as 'the flying journey of Gopala' and 'বীচি বিক্ষেপ হইতেছিল না' as 'did not shed its seeds' or 'bad humours of the body' as 'শরীরের দুষ্ট রসিকতা' and similar writings which would amuse every Bengali, abound in the prose writings of the foreign scholars; and if they had had occasion to cultivate our language with the earnestness with which we are acquiring English, it is certain that we should have had as ample materials at our command to amuse ourselves as the ridiculers of "Babu English" have at theirs.

Errors in idioms.

We find in the Sarasamgraha by the Rev. Yates D. D, a very good scholar of Bengali, such lines as "ভ্রমণের দ্বারা তাহাদের মন প্রফুল্ল ও উত্তম হইতে পারে এবং অনেক অনেক বিবেচনার কথা উপস্থিত হইতে পারে." The writer confounds চিন্তা with বিবেচনা in the last line. In a Bengali vocabulary the difference in meaning of the two words is not indicated; and it is only to be known by a mastery of the idiom, hence this writer fell into such an error.

In a grammar of the Bengali language by the Rev. J. Keith, we find the following curious specimen :—

নিত্যবৃত্ত ভূতকাল।

একবচন	বহুবচন
আমি করা যাইতেছিলাম	আমরা করা যাইতেছিলাম
তুমি করা যাইতেছিলা	তোমরা করা যাইতেছিলা
তিনি করা যাইতেছিলেন	তাহারা করা যাইতেছিলেন

In Satguṅa O Viryyer Itihāsa written in 1829 by a Çrirampur missionary, we come across the following sentences on the title page :

"সকল লোকের হিতার্থে বাঙ্গালা ভাষায় তর্জ্জমা করা গেল। তাহার একদিকে ইংরাজী ও এক দিকে বাঙ্গালা"।

General excellence of style.

But inspite of these unavoidable defects met with now and then in the use of Bengali idioms, the vernacular style of the foreign writers commended itself generally for its simplicity, closeness of argument, and directness as contrasted with the high flown unmeaning jargons of scholarly pedants ; and the latter had gradually to adopt the simpler style of the European which erred occasionally in idiom, but was, generally speaking, correct and elegant.

Indirect benefit.

The indirect benefit derived from the writing of vernacular works by Europeans was great, for they controlled Bengali prose ; and though it was taken out of the hands of the Vaiṣṅavas and the Çāktas, it came once more to competent hands, who made it a vehicle of thought and not a show thing to be admired for artistic excellence or rendered too abstruse for popular understanding by pedantic follies.

Europeans ceased to take the great interest in the vernacular literature as they had done in the first half of the 19th century, only when the native hand grew sufficiently strong to take up the work in right earnest, and this our country men ere long did, even beyond all expectations of their friendly patrons.

Scientific and technical terms.

The great zeal of the European writers of Bengali prose is evidenced by the fact that Mr. Felix Carey coined scientific and technical terms for writing on those subjects in Bengali. How far he succeeded in his attempt is not the question, but it shows the ardour of his soul in attempting to bring the vernacular language of Bengal up to the standard of the advanced languages of the world. In the descriptive catalogue of Bengali by the Rev. J. Long, we find the following reference to this fact,—"Goldsmith's History of England (Bengali translation of) came out in 1819. Pages 412, by Felix Carey, an able Bengali scholar, the history closes with the peace of Amiens in 1802. A useful glossary of technical and difficult words was appended, though some names are rendered curiously. Admiral of the Blue is Nilpatakādhyernava, Whig is Svātantra Pakṣapāti." "Haḍāvali or Anatomy by Carey. The glossary of the technical terms by the translator Felix Carey, a good Bengali scholar, is of use to translators."

Books in colloquial style.

Under European influence a taste for writing in the colloquial language came into considerable favour; and writings like Ālāler Gharer Dulāla and Hutum Pechār Naksā, which are usually supposed to be our first attempts at witty writing in the colloquial dialect, were preceded and anticipated in style by numerous works which served as models to Tek Chānd Thākur and Kāli Prasanna Siṁha in later times Some of these earlier works reached a high level of success and were very popular at one time. Nowhere in the whole range of colloquial literature of this epoch, do we find a better sample of style or display of naive humour, and of scathing satire than in the Nava Bābu Vilāsa or sketch of a modern Babu by Pramatha Nāth Çarmā, published in 1823. The Rev. J. Long in 1855 wrote

The ablest satire of the time.

of this book as "one of the ablest satires of the Calcutta Babu as he was thirty years ago. New editions of the work are constantly issuing from the press. The Babu is depicted as germinating, blossoming in flower, in fruit. The Babu under Guru Mahāçaya, under the Munsi, devoted to licentiousness and his lament for past folly. It is a kind of Hogarth's Rake's Prayers." The book was analysed at length in the Quarterly Friend of India, 1826.

I quote below an extract from this book. There is no need for any comment on the corrupt taste which prevails in it—which was the vice of the age and the spirit of the time.

* " Then came dancing girls—three or four parties of them—a glorious band,—those who generally appear in the foremost row of a marriage procession and, riding on Taktārama (a state *palkee*), dance to the admiration of the on-lookers. When all had joined the party, the Babu with his Chādar on his neck, as a sign of humility, and with clasped palms, addressed Baknā Piary and other dancing girls,—the best of their kind, reputed far and wide, and worshipped by the public, and said

* " আর যাহারা বিবাহাদি সময় রাস্তায় সর্ব্বাগ্রে তক্তারামায় আরোহণ করিয়া নৃত্য করে, এমত নর্ত্তকী প্রায় তিন চার সম্প্রদা আইল; তৎপরে সকলের আগমনান্তর বাবু জনসমাজ পূজ্যা বারাঙ্গনাগ্রগণ্যা বকনা পেয়ারী প্রভৃতির নিকট গললগ্নকৃতবাস হইয়া করপুটে কহিলেন " আপনারা স্নান করুন" তৎপরে অন্ত ভক্তগণ আসিয়া বাবুর আজ্ঞামত আতর মর্দ্দন করাইলেক, কাঁচা-গোল্লা দিয়া মাথা ঘসাইয়া দিলেক, নির্ম্মল পুষ্করিণীর জল ক্রীড়াচ্ছলে কুতুহলে ভৃত্যগণের বহুসমাদরে ভক্তগণেরা গোলাপ জলে শরীর ধৌত করাইলেক। সেই সময়ে এক গাটি বস্ত্র

"Be pleased now to take a bath." The other admirers of these fair creatures appeared on the scene and at the request of the Babu rubbed perfumes on their delicate persons, and with Kānchāgolla (a rich pudding) cleaned their long black hair; the servants with a feeling of great reverence took them to tanks, and in a sportive spirit poured water upon their heads, and then come the admirers who bathed them with rose-water. At this stage the tailor came and produced a bundle of fine clothes. There were in the bundle beautiful Sāḍies made by the far-famed weavers of Çāntipur, Amvikā, Vādāgāchhi, Dacca, Chandrakonā, Khāsvāgān and other places. Some of these fine stuffs had beautiful borders in imitation of Kashmir shawls, others with borders in which the figures of crabs were neatly woven with the threads, and others where the amulet was imitated. These elegant borders were of different colours, purple, blue and crimson. The Barānagar striped Saḍies looked particularly gay. These clothes were distributed by the tailor among the worthy votaries of the terpsichorean art. Then in the pleasure garden the Babu and his friends seated themselves on costly seats with the accomplished

The reception to the dancing girls.

আনিয়া উপস্থিত করিলেন। শান্তিপুর অম্বিকা, বাদাগাছি ঢাকা, চন্দ্রকোণা, খাসবাগান, বরাহনগর প্রভৃতি নানা স্থানের শাড়ী, শালপেড়ে, কাঁকড়াপেড়ে, লালপেড়ে, নীলপেড়ে, তাবিজ-পেড়ে, বরানগরের, দূরে ব্যক্তিবিশেষে ২ প্রদান করিলেন। তৎপরে আনন্দকাননে অপূর্ব্বাসনে সর্ব্বজন প্রফুল্ল বদনে বেশ্যাসমবিধানে উপবিষ্ট হইলেন, সেই আসনে ভৃত্যগণেরা নানাবিধ সুখাদ্য মিষ্টান্ন মদ্য মাংস আনিয়া প্রস্তুত করিলেক; ইতিমধ্যে এক নির্ব্বোধ পূর্ব্বদেশীয় বাঙ্গাল ব্রাহ্মণ কহিলেক, যে ভোজন কালে পৃথক পৃথক স্থানে করিতে হইবে। এমন সময়ে খলিফার কুলপুরোহিত

hirelings. The servants brought to them various kinds of sweetmeats, meat and wine in profuse quantities, when a fool of an East Bengal Brahmin said that there should be separate seats at dinner. Hearing this the high priest of the Babu—the jewel of the forehead of all *pandits*—stepped forward and said 'O thou the most despised of all mortals, dost thou not know the sacred books, dunce and illiterate as thou art? This is a Bhairavi *chakra* (a circle of the Tantricks), as people of various castes are present here and women have joined us. In a Bhairavi *chakra* no caste distinction should be observed. You want authority! Here it is :—

Upsetting of caste-rules in the Chakra.

Recites a Sanskrit couplet here which means ;—

'Those who join a Bhairavi *chakra*, whatever caste they may belong to, should be considered for the time as the best of Brahmins. They should all drink wine, till they turn tipsy and reeling fall to the ground and rise to drink again. If they do so they shall be free from all future births and attain final emancipation.'

"When authority had thus been quoted all were quite satisfied and the Hindus, Mahomedans and

---

শিরোমণি কহিলেন "ওরে নরাধম মূর্খ শাস্ত্র জানিনি না, এক্ষণে এস্থল ভৈরবী চক্র বলা যায়, ভৈরবী চক্রে জাতিবিচার নাই। প্রমাণং যথা—

আগতা ভৈরবীচক্রে সর্ব্বে বর্ণাঃ দ্বিজোত্তমাঃ
পীত্বা পীত্বা পুনঃ পীত্বা পুনঃ পততি ভুতলে
উত্থায় চ পুনঃ পীত্বা পুনর্জ্জন্ম ন বিদ্যতে'

ইত্যাদি প্রমাণ শুনিয়া সকলে হৃষ্টচিত্ত হইল। হিন্দু মুছলমান

women of ill fame sat together with a clear conscience, and began to eat various preparations of meat and other dainties with profuse quantity of wine."

A Serio-comic aspect.

The *Pundits* took up Bengali prose under the direction of European writers of Bengali; and under their direction also the former had to come down from high flown bombasts to colloquial simplicity. The best works produced by the *Pandits* during this epoch of our literature are characterised, on the one hand, by ascent to obscure heights and, on the other, by descent to slang;—from the cloudy region of philosophical dissertations to the housewife's harangue with her husband on the question of the preparation of cakes. There was no *via media*. When the theme soared high, it became mystic,—the phalanx of compound words scarcely left a loop-hole for the ordinary reader's understanding to penetrate into it; but when it came down from these heights it grovelled in the mire of vulgarity; street scenes were described in terse, forcible but exceedingly corrupt style; all limits of decency were exceeded on,—coarse and flat jokes passed for humour, and the Bengali prose of the period presented a seriocomic aspect which puzzles us in its seriousness and almost repels when it tries to amuse.

The good result.

But the advent of the *Pandits* into the field of Bengali, though associated in the earlier stages of its modern prose with uncouth efforts verging on

---

বেশ্যা সাধারণ তাবতেই নির্ম্মলান্তঃকরণে একাসনে বিবিধ মদ্য মাংস প্রভৃতি নানা দ্রব্য ভোজন করিলেন।"

Babuvilas, Page 38.

the ridiculous, was not an unmixed evil. Their productions materially aided the cause of Bengali style in the long run. The *pundits* had a perfect command over the Sanskrit vocabulary and Sanskrit grammar and aimed at a pure grammatical style which was gradually introduced into Bengali prose, mainly through their influence and by their writings. Under the salutary control of the European scholars these *pundits* were trained to write in a simple style and they no longer despised the colloquial dialect from which they gradually imported a large number of simple and elegant expressions into the written language. Modern prose was developed both in purity of style and in resources of words by the efforts of these scholarly writers, and abundant proofs of this are to be found in the standard works of the 19th century, written by them. In the prose works of Içvara Chandra Vidyāsāgara we have that crowning success in prose composition to attain which the *pundits* had been struggling for half a century. The high sounding compounds were reduced in his writings to simpler and more elegant forms, the coarse and the vulgar element was entirely eliminated ; and living at this distance of time, as we do, we cannot help being struck with the inimitable grace and purity of his style. He saved our prose alike from pedantry and vulgarity and adopted a golden mean which only a finished master of Sanskrit and gifted literature could have been capable of achieving.

The high price of printed books.

The printing of Bengali books was a costly affair in those days. We have seen that Dr. Carey calculated the cost of printing ten thousand copies of the Bengali New Testament at Rs. 43750, and that even, at the wrong estimate of the cost of a punch as 5*s.* whereas it was really a guinea. Considering the enormous expenditure on printing as also the very limited sale of Bengali books, we should not be surprised at the high price set on many of the books of this period; for instance Mitter's Bengali Dictionary was published in 1801, "equal to an 8vo of 50 pages"; the price was Rs. 32. Tara Chand Chakravarty's Anglo Bengali Dictionary; pages 25, price Rs. 6. "The original price of Krişňa Chandra Charita by Rajiva Lochana Rs. 5 only for 120 pages. It barely paid its expenses then, so limited was the demand for Bengali books."

Journals edited by students.

The energetic devotion displayed in the cause of learning by the students of the Hindu College under the influence of Dr. Richardson and Mr. D'Rozario is evidenced in the list of Bengali newspapers and magazines of this period already given on a foregoing page. Along with a hundred other channels into which that energy flowed for promoting the cause of learning, no less than four journals (Nos. 13, 19 pp. 908-909 and Nos. 10 and 17 p. 911,) were edited and conducted by the students of the Hindu College.

The excellence of the Hindu method in arithmetic.

It is curious to observe that when the English were introducing European educational methods into our schools, they were frequently struck with the excellence of the Hindu method of teaching already current in our Pāthaçālās, and this they freely admitted. An English writer in the London Asiatic journal, 1817, bestows a high panegyric on the arithmetical rules set to doggerel rhymes by Cubhankara who is said to have been "the Cocker of

RAJA RAMA MOHANA ROY.

Specially photographed for Mr. Ramananda Chatterjee from the oil painting in British Miuseum. By kind permission of Mr. R. N. Chatterjee.

Bengal." "These rules" wrote another English reviewer in the middle of the 19th century "have been chanted for 150 years in 40,000 schools. Thus the Hindus took the lead in a practice which have been since introduced into our infant schools." In the May-Gaṅita printed at Çrirāmapore in 1817, the author, Mr. May, says of the Çubhankari Aryyās in his preface to the book :—"It is remarkable that many coincidences may be traced between them and the most improved kind of arithmetical tables adopted in the schools in Britain on the new model."

IV (a) Decadance of the high spiritual ideal in Hindu Society, and the advent of Rājā Rāma Mohana Roy.

A touch from outside.

When Buddhism had sunk into depraved Tantrik rites, sophistry and atheism, the Hindu Society awaited but a touch from outside for blossoming into that living faith which is so pre-eminently observed in the lives of Chaitanya and Nānaka. The Renaissance brought about by the great Çankara required only a touch with the faith of Islam to develop the creed of faith into the creed of love, which in the 16th century showed itself in the glories of renunciation and the spiritual ecstasies of so many ardent souls. Similarly also when towards the end of the 18th century, the religion of the Hindus was more or less reduced to superstitious practices, and empty ceremonies, and ritual, Hindu society required only a touch from outside to be restored to a realisation of high spiritual truths. The Christian Missionaries awakened the spirit of research into religious truth once more in the minds of our countrymen, who were never found slow to respond to a call for putting forth their best activity in the cause of religion.

Ostentation in religion.

The simple ways taught by Chaitanya Deva, of reciting the name of God and of praying to Him in the spirit of true renunciation had gradually fallen into disfavour. Pompous processions and great festivities accompanied with dances of *nauch* girls and display and flourish of materialistic grandeur now attracted people to religion, which had, however, lost its serious character, and become a source of amusement to the vulgar. The great devotees had already begun to realise the uselessness of a multiplicity of religious rites, and the vanity which in many cases prompted the ostentation of religious festivals in Bengal. Rājā Rāma Krisṅa expressed the idea in one of his songs that he would fling away his rosary into the waters of the Ganges as soon as true devotion for the divine Mother should dawn on his mind,—thus showing an utter disregard of formal observances in religion; and Rāma Prasada, already quoted on page 716, said of himself that he was a fool to worship an image of clay, when his divine Mother was manifesting herself throughout the whole universe He said how foolish it was to kill goats before the image instead of sacrificing the passions—his real enemies, and that it was but so much energy wasted to visit the sacred shrines. If one's mind is fixed on the lotus feet of the Mother, there he will feel all the sanctity of the Ganges and of the holy cities of Benares and Gaya.

Severe codes for petty offences.

Violation of petty rules was regarded as a great sin in the code of the Brahmins. "That infidel who has not cleansed his teeth before sunrise, has no right to worship God."* "One who takes Putikā (*Basella lucida* on the twelfth day of a lunation is worse than a murderer of Brahmins." "One who takes a meal while touching the seat with his feet is to be reckoned as a beef eater."†

"If one raises a cup of water with his left hand and drinks therefrom he commits the offence of him who drinks wine."‡

These were some of the rules for the guidance of a Hindu householder's life. "Murder, theft or perjury, though brought home to the guilty man by a judicial sentence, so far from inducing loss of caste, is visited in their society with no peculiar mark of infamy or disgrace. A trifling present to the Brahmin commonly called Prāyaçchitta, with the performance of a few idle ceremonies, are held as sufficient atonement for all those crimes; and the delinquent is at once freed from all temporal inconvenience as well as dread of future retribution."§

---

* "উদিতে জগতীনাথে যঃ কুর্যাদ্দন্তধাবনম্ ।
স পাপিষ্ঠঃ কথংক্রতে পূজয়ামি জনার্দ্দনম্ ॥"

Smriti.

† Raja Rama Mohana Roy's Bengali works edited by Raja Narayan Bose p. 620.

‡ Raja Rama Mohana Roy's Bengali works, published from the Panini Karyalaya, Allahabad, page 228.

§ Raja Rama Mohana Roy's English works, published by Cri Kanta Roy vol. I, p. 203.

The plant Tulasi is sacred with the Vaiṣṅavas and the Bel tree with the Çaivas. When regarded in the light of simple devotion and as possessed of emblematic significance, these plants have a charm for the Hindus which is indescribable. When the pious wife lights the evening lamp at the foot of the sacred Tulasi, the darkness of evening yields to that quiet light glittering through the leaves, and the vermillion-marked forehead bends low in the act of making obeisance to the deity whose symbol it is, the small scene breathes poetry to the soul which feels in its presence as before some alter; but when the atrocious Brahminic code lays down "the great sinner who seeing a *Bilva* tree or a *tulasi* plant does not instantly bow down, will be sent to hell and be afflicted with leprosy,"* —the poetry and spirituality of the whole vanishes, and our mind revolts against such ordinances and feels strongly against Brahminic tyranny. The horrid hook-swinging festivity called the Chaḍaka, the custom of throwing children to the Sāgara, human sacrifices offered to Kāli and other atrocious ceremonies performed under the sanction and control of the Brahmins compelled our enlightened rulers to check them by enacting new laws, and if the missionaries were unsparing in their abuses of our religion and called us semi-barbarious, they were justified in their condemnation of the crimes that pervailed in the lower stratum of our society.

* "বিল্বং বা তুলসীং দৃষ্ট্বা ন নমেদ্যো নরাধমঃ ।
সযাতি নরকং ঘোরং মহারোগেণ পীড্যতে ॥

Skanda Purāṅa.

The pure faith promulgated by Chaitanya was now giving its last flicker. In the lower order of the Vaiṣṅava community men and women mixed promiscuously and, interpreting the emblematical religion in the light of gross sensualism, preached unrestrained licentiousness; and the cries of those who were forcibly made to play *sutties*,—though subdued and unheard owing to the noisy music deliberately kept to drown them, rose to heaven where the Lord heard them though men would not. The missionaries drew attention to these matters. Such were some of the superstitions and crimes that pervaded the whole of our society at the moment we are considering. Young men of the new generation, who had not fathomed the depths of religious life that still pervaded the quiet villages of Bengal inspite of their superstitions, ran to the extreme, and in the general sweep of their reformatory procedures turned their backs upon good and evil alike, indiscriminately condemning all in their own society. They did not wish to reform but aimed at totally upsetting society, which, though in its lower grades showed Brahminical craft and oppression, had in its great heights—on its topmost pinnacles, an unequalled glory which is conspicuous in the doctrines of love and renunciation inculcated by the Vedanta.

Leanings towards Christianity.

Young men saw wrongs on all sides and did not care to hear of the speculative theology of the Hindus or to keep the patience to scale its great height themselves. They felt that Christianity was better than their own religion owing to the moral principles which were a living force amongst its votaries. "Young Bengal" showed a decided leaning towards the new creed.

Rājā Rāma Mohana Roy,

At this juncture stepped forward Rāma Mohana Roy, born at the village of Rādhānagar in the district of Hughli in the year 1774,—the year in which the great Rāma Prasāda Sen died at Hālisahara.

(b) A comprehensive review of his life and work.

A born fighter.

As I look upon the portrait of Rājā Rāma Mohana, with his huge turban on his head, his loose flowing garments, his dark eye brows bent in serious thought and his brilliant eyes with their meditative look,—a voluminous book held tightly in his right hand and lips which display determination and the power of persuasive eloquence,—the high forehead beaming with intellectuality,—his tall robust figure erect to its full height,—he appears to me rather as a warrior bound for the battle field, than as a pious religious man—the part he chose to play in life.

He was in fact a born fighter. The combative element is not only found throughout his stupendous writings in English, Bengali, Sanskrit and Persian, but even in the hymns he offered to God. He could not forget the fighting and controversial spirit even when he was addressing praises to the Deity. Referring to the rite of *Prana pratistha* or "endowment of animation" and that of subsequently throwing the clay image in the water after the *puja* is over, Rāma Mohana sings in one of his hymns "O deluded mind, whom do you invoke, and whom do you cast away." Again, dealing with the swinging ceremony in the Dolotsava he sings: "You want to swing him who moves the sun, the moon and the stars! How vain your efforts are! He who feeds the beasts, and birds, fishes and men, how absurd it is to think of feeding him ! The Deity who pervades the whole universe, with what propriety can you say to him 'stay here' (refers to the *mantra* ইহ তিষ্ঠ &c.)

"It is vain, if you do not accept the truth ; it is like taking food through the nose when you are endowed with a mouth."*

When half a century before, Rāma Prasāda had composed songs in this strain, there had been a sincerity in his utterances, and there was no polemic spirit in them ; he was actually engaged in all the multifarious ritual of Hindu worship, and passing through them as an orthodox Hindu, he only refreshed his consciousness of the clay image as an emblem by referring to the monotheistic views which he really held and realised through all the rites to which he had to conform outwardly. But Rājā Rāma Mohana had given up all such Hindu practices and declared them idolatrous. His hymn to the Deity in the passages quoted above

---

* "মন একি ভ্রান্তি তোমার
আবাহন বিসর্জ্জন কর তুমি কার ?
চন্দ্র সূর্য্য গ্রহ যত,
যে চালায় অবিরত,
তারে দোলাইতে কত করহ যতন।
পশুপক্ষী জলচরে, যে আহার দেয় নরে,
চাহ সেই পরাৎপর করাতে ভোজন।
যে বিভু সর্ব্বত্র থাকে
ইহ তিষ্ঠ বল তাঁকে।"
"সত্য সূচনা বিনা সকলি বৃথায়
যেমন বদন থাকিতে অদন করা নাসিকায়।"

sounds the trumpet of battle; and though he apparently applied to himself the word 'deluded', it is really meant for those who held views in religion other than his own.

Throughout all his writings this combativeness is obvious. He probably felt it necessary for the times, believing that people had begun to accept the image as God Himself and forget that it was a mere emblem.

As a combatant he was superior to most who came in contact with him, not only by the strong and forcible manner in which he marshalled his arguments, based on a learning which was most extraordinary, but in the equanimity of temper that he preserved throughout all controversy. Seldom or never did he resort to the language of abuse so freely indulged in against him by his opponents. He was master of many languages,--Hebrew, Greek, Persian, English, Sanskrit, Arabic Hindusthani and Bengali, and knew something of French besides. The missionaries found in him a scholar who could point out flaws in their translations of the Bible and refer them to the original text in Hebrew, or Greek.* His antagonists were generally brought to their knees by the solid learning of the Rājā who, with all respect for the scriptures of different religions, assailed his opponents with ample quotations from the books held sacred by them, and beat them on their own ground in the most effective way. In

His European admirers.

* "He argues the matter very fairly and quotes with great ease and fluency the passages of both Old and New Testaments explaining some maltranslations of Hebrew which Trinitarians sometimes urged in their favour."

Monthly Repository, 1822.
Page, 754.

fact his giant intellect struck every one with the sense of his superiority, and the testimonies of admiration left by Europeans are even more laudatory than those which he received from his own countrymen. Sir John Bowring, while greeting him with an address of welcome from the Unitarian Society of London, said "I recollect some writers have indulged themselves with inquiring, what they should feel, if any of those time-honoured men, whose names have lived through vicissitudes of ages, should appear among them. They have endeavoured to imagine what would be their sensations if a Plato, or a Socrates, a Milton or a Newton, were unexpectedly to honour them with their presence. I recollect that a poet, who has well been called divine, has drawn a beautiful picture of the feelings of those who first visited the scenes of the southern hemisphere, and there saw, for the first time, that beautiful constellation, the Gold Cross. It was with feelings such as they underwent, that I was overwhelmed when I stretched out in your name the hand of welcome to the Rājā Rāma Mohana Roy."*

Dr. Booth, an American physician of London, wrote to Mr. Estlin on the 27th November, 1833, "I have studied his (Rājā Rāma Mohana Roy's) writings with a subdued feeling since his death and risen from their perusal with a more confirmed conviction of his having been unequalled in past or present time."† The Rev. J. Scott Porter said in a funeral sermon on the death of the Rājā—preached

* Monthly Repository, June, 1831. (Vol. V, pages 417-20.)
† Last days of Rama Mohana Roy by Mary Carpenter Page 174.

in the meeting-house of the first Presbyterian congregation, Belfast, on the 10th of November, 1833 :—"Never have I known a person who brought a greater variety of knowledge to bear upon almost every topic on which he conversed, never one whose remarks were more original, solid and useful........, —one of the most extraordinary men whom the world has witnessed for centuries." * The Rev. J. Fox spoke of the Rājā in his sermon delivered at Finsbury Chapel, South Place, on Sunday October 14, 1833, "His presence has passed away as a poetic image fades from the brain!........... And, 'being dead, he yet speaketh with a voice to which not only India but Europe and America will listen for generations."† The Rev. R. Aspland preached a funeral sermon in the New Gravel Pit Meeting, Hackney, in the course of which he said "the name of Rāma Mohana Roy will endure as long as the history of religious truth."‡ Lieutenant-Colonel Fitzclarence, latterly Earl of Munster, wrote (in his Journal of a Route across India through Egypt to England in the years of 1817 and 1818). "The most extraordinary Brahmin....... His learning is most extensive, as he is not only conversant with the best books in English, Arabic, Sanskrit, Bengali and Hindusthani but has even studied rhetoric in Arabic and English, and quotes Locke and Bacon on all occasions."§ The English editor of the *India Gazetta* referred to him while writing about his controversy with Dr. Marshman as "a most gigantic combatant in the theological

* Last days of Rama Mohana Roy Page 223.
† do. do. do. 242.
‡ do. do. do. 207.
§ do. do. do. 40.

field."* Many English writers wrote verses on his death, and those by Miss Dale, Miss Acland, Mrs. Thomas Woodforde, the Rev. W. J. Fox, and Dr. Carpenter, quoted in 'The Last Days of the Rājā Rāma Mohana Roy' by Mary Carpenter, are not only exquisite as pieces of poetic composition, but also breathe those sentiments of profound love and respect, which his great personality raised in the minds of all who came in contact with him. The tender care with which he was attended by the ladies at Stapleton Grove during his last illness, and their tears at his death, lend deep pathos to the description of the scene of his death at Bristol; and our heart goes forth in gratitude to those kind friends of a foreign clime who not only appreciated the noble qualities of the great Indian but felt for him a veneration which annulled all distinctions of birth and associations.

In his controversies with the Çrirāmapore Missionaries, some of whom went the length of calling him a heathen, his mild answers bearing the impress of superior reasoning power, showed that he was a far better Christian in spirit than his adversaries; and the impression they made on the mind of the distinguished William Roscoe, who poured over the Rājā's Precepts of Jesus with admiring delight, amply testifies to the great appreciation of his writings throughout the whole of Christendom. Mr. Recorder Hill writes about his encounter with the celebrated Robert Owen† :—" one of the guests was Robert Owen who evinced a strong desire to

Robert Owen's defeat.

* Last days of Rama Mohana Roy, Page 17.
† do. do. do. 111.

bring over the Rājā to his socialistic opinions. He persevered with great earnestness, but the Rājā, who seemed well acquainted with the subject and who spoke our language in marvellous perfection, answered his arguments with consummate skill, until Robert somewhat lost his temper,—a very rare occurrence which I never witnessed before. The defeat of the kind hearted philanthropist was accompanied with great sauvity on the part of his opponent." Dr. T. Boot wrote about the Rājā to Mr. Estlin, in November 1833 :—"to me he stood in the single majesty of, I had almost said, perfect humanity, no one in past or present ever came to my judgment clothed in such wisdom, or humility." Another Englishman spoke of him as "a rare combatant. We are constrained to say he has not met with his match here." "It is well known" writes Mary Carpenter (p. 252) "that Mr. William Adam a Baptist of Çrirāmapore, who endeavoured to make him a convert to orthodoxy, concluded his task by acknowledging himself a convert to the true Evangelical opinions of the Rājā." The greatest philosopher of England at the time, Jeremy Bentham, gave him a cordial reception and addressed him as "intensely admired and dearly beloved collaborator in the service of mankind." "Your works," wrote Bentham to the Rājā, "are made known to me by a book in which I read a style which, but for the name of a Hindu, I should certainly have ascribed to the pen of a superiorly educated and instructed Englishman" and in the same letter while praising the great work of James Mill on the History of India, Bentham remarked, "though as to the style I wish I could with truth and

Other European admirers.

sincerity pronounce it equal to yours."* The poet Campbell was also one of his great admirers. When he landed in England the Rājā met with a reception which only the most exalted men of Europe could expect to receive. He was presented to His Majesty the King by the President of the Board of Control and had a place assigned to him among the foreign ambassadors. The highest honours were publicly accorded to him. "Persons most remarkable for their social standing and literary eminence sought his society and highly esteemed the privilege of intercourse with him. He was received into our English homes not only as a distinguished guest but as a friend."† During his short stay at Paris he was more than once at the table of Louis Philippe. Wherever he went he had to attend meetings according him a most hearty and cordial reception. Mary Carpenter writes that she had herself met some of those "who still treasured the remembrance of the Rājā; one of these, now a grayheaded man, recollected when a young midshipman on arriving at Calcutta, going to visit the magnificent residence and grounds of the Brahmin who was even then celebrated. It was in the Circular Road at the Eastern extremity of the town. He did not see the master of the mansion, but he picked up in the large aviary a relic in remembrance of the distinguished man which he still treasures."‡

Reception in Europe.

A midshipman's recollections.

Social and religious reformation he chose as the chief object of his pursuit. His evidence before

---

* Bowring's works of Bentham, vol. X; page 586.
† Mary Carpenter's life of the Raja, page 65.
‡ Do. do. page 67

Evidence before the select Committee.

the Select Committee of the House of Commons in England regarding the Judicial and Revenue system of India and his essay on the European colonisation show a masterly grasp of the subject as also the vast range of his study and minute observation in every detail of the administrative questions of the country, upon which the British press bestowed at the time their highest encomiums. His writing materially assisted the Government in enacting legislation for the administration of the country on a more solid and efficacious basis. His letter on the question of education preceded the memorable minute of Lord Macaulay and sounded the key note of the future educational policy of the Government.

On Education.

In fact in every department of thought, calculated to advance the cause of his countrymen, his great intelligence and zealous advocacy of all that he considered right have left a powerful impress. In all movements, whether of social or political nature, the start that he gave to the enlightened Hindu Society of Bengal has kept it going forward up to the present. Thoroughly acquainted with the political conditions in Europe, the sympathy of his great mind went forth to the cause of liberty and freedom, wherever it was at stake. His humane feelings were also as cosmopolitan. When on one occasion he attended divine worship at Carter Lane Chapel, the Minister was reading a letter from a clergyman in that quarter describing the sufferings of the poor people in the west of Ireland, then in a state of lamentable distress. Writes Mr. Poter on the occasion "the tears that fell from his, (Rājā's) eyes declared how deeply

Broad sympathy and cosmopolitan views.

he was moved by the reciter."* He materially contributed to the fund collected for affording them relief.

For women the sympathy of his heart was ever in readiness; and one, who reads his arguments in favour of the abolition of Suttee, cannot but be struck with the great humanity with which he advocated the cause, as also with the high reverence in which he held Indian women. When a pro-Suttee champion declared woman-kind as weak, frail and irreligious, his honest indignation burst forth in a glorious speech in which the sufferings, the devotion and the firmness of Hindu Women are so vividly represented, that no poet could do it in better language or in more effective form. He suffered all kinds of persecution, intolerance and abuses from his opponents who even tried to waylay and belabour him, but reading his answers to the charges made against him by orthodx Hindus, and even by the clergy, one is struck with his gentle and persuasive eloquence, his kindly words indicating a sweet and unruffled temperament. These are found in sharp contrast to the foul and wanton abuse of his antagonists. He himself says in some of his answers that as a child frets, when the well-meaning doctor gives him medicine, but the doctor heeds it not, even so does he treat those who without understanding his good intentions are crying down his works. He was never weary of arguing in favour of what he considered to be the truth. Such an untiring champion of truth is scarcely to be met with now. Mr. Arnot writes of him,

Good for evil.

* Miss Carpenter's "Last Days of Raja Rama Mohana Ray," page 225.

Vindicates the unity of God.

"During the greater part of the period of Rāma Mohana Roy's residence at Calcutta, the whole powers of his mind were directed to the vindication of the doctrine of the unity of God. In this, he maintained, the sacred books of the Hindus and Mussalmans, Jews and Christians agreed; and that all apparent deviations from it were modern corruptions. He propagated it day and night by word and writings, with the zeal of an apostle and the self-denial of a martyr. He was ever ready to maintain it against all gain-sayers, from the believer in thirty three millions of God to the denier of one, for both extremes are common in the East. The writer remembers finding him at his Garden House near Calcutta, one evening, about 7 o'clock, closing a dispute with one of the followers of Buddha, who denied the existence of the Deity. The Rājā had spent the whole day in the controversy, without stopping for food, rest or refreshment, rejoicing more in confuting one atheist than in triumphing over hundred idolators: the credulity of the one he despised; the scepticism of the other he thought pernicious; for he was deeply impressed with the importance of religion for the virtue and happiness of mankind."*

Rejects miracles.

His pro-Christian tendencies are well known. Yet he would not agree with the missionaries in their orthodox views. When the Çrī Rāmapur missionaries advanced their arguments in support of them iracles of Christ, the Rājā quietly remarked:— "His miracles were less stupendous than those of the Hindu who drank up the ocean and discharged

* "Last Days in England" by Miss Mary Carpenter, page 299.

it from his body."* Though attacking the idolatrous practices of the Hindus, the Rājā boldly declared his profound respect for the Hindu philosophy before his European friends. An English writer writes, "he (the Rājā) asserts that he has found nothing in European books equal to the scholastic philosophy of the Hindus."† **Respect for Hindu Philosophy.**

He combined in himself the best elements of European and Asiatic ideals. In spirituality he was a Vedantist and in morality he was a follower of Christ.

This extraordinary man, with his noble efforts in all works of reformation, did a great service to the cause of Bengali literature to which we shall refer hereafter. We here briefly give a sketch of his life as narrated by himself.

An autobiographical account.

"My ancestors were Brahmins of a high order and, from time immemorial, were devoted to the religious duties of their race, down to my fifth progenitor who, about one hundred and forty years ago, gave up spiritual exercises for worldly pursuits and aggrandisements. His descendants ever since have followed his example and, according to the usual fate of courtiers, with various success, sometimes rising to honour and sometimes falling; sometimes rich and sometimes poor; sometimes excelling in success, sometimes miserable through disappointment. But my maternal ancestors, being of the sacerdotal order by profession as well as by birth, and of a family than which none holds a higher rank in that profession, have

* History of Cri Ramapur Mission Vol. I, page 238.
† Monthly Repository 1818, Vol. XV, pp. 2-4.

up to the present day adhered to a life of religious observances and devotion, preferring peace and tranquillity of mind to the excitements of wordly grandeur.

"In conformity with the usage of my paternal race, and the wish of my father, I studied the Persian and Arabic languages,—these being indispensable to those who attached themselves to the courts of the Mahomedan princes; and agreeably to the usage of my maternal relations, I devoted myself to the study of the Sanskrit and the theological works written in it, which contain the body of Hindu literature, law and religion.

"When about the age of sixteen, I composed a manuscript calling in question the validity of the idolatrous system of the Hindus. This, together with my known sentiments on that subject, having produced a coolness between me and my immediate kindred, I proceeded on my travels, and passed through different countries, chiefly within, but some beyond, the bounds of Hindustan, with a feeling of great aversion to the establishment of British power in India. When I had reached the age of twenty, my father recalled me, and restored me to his favour; after which I first saw and begun to associate with Europeans and soon after made myself tolerably acquainted with their laws and form of government. Finding them generally more intelligent, more steady and moderate in their conduct, I gave up my prejudice against them, and became inclined in their favour, feeling persuaded that their rule, though a foreign yoke, would lead more speedily and surely to the amelioration of the native inhabitants; and I enjoyed the confidence of several of them even in their public capacity. My continued controversies with the Brahmins on the subject of their idolatry and superstition, and my interference with their custom of burning widows, and other pernicious practices, revived and increased their animosity against me; and through their influence with my family, my father was again obliged to withdraw his countenance openly, though his limited pecuniary support was still continued to me.

"After my father's death I opposed the advocates of idolatry with still greater boldness. Availing myself of the art of printing, now established in India, I published various works and pamphlets against their errors in the native and foreign languages. This raised such a feeling against me, that I was at last deserted by every person except two or three Scotch friends, to whom, and the nation to which they belong, I will always feel grateful.

"The ground which I took in all controversies was, not that of opposition to Brahminism, but to a perversion of it; and I endeavoured to show that the idolatry of the Brahminism was contrary to the practice of their ancestors, and the principles of the ancient books and authorities which they profess to revere and obey. Notwithstanding the violence of the opposition and resistance to my opinions, several highly respectable persons, both among my own relations and others began to adopt the same sentiments.

"I now felt a strong wish to visit Europe and obtain, by personal observation, a more thorough insight into its manners, customs, religion and political institutions. I refrained however, from carrying this intention into effect until the friends who coincided with my sentiments should be increased in number and strength. My expectations having been at length realised in November, 1830, I embarked for England, as the discussion of the East India Company's Charter was expected to come on, by which the treatment of the natives of India and its future government would be determined for many years to come, and an appeal to the King in Council against the abolition of the practice of burning widows was to be heard before the Privy Council; and His Majesty the Emperor of Delhi had likewise commissioned me to bring before the authorities in England certain encroachments on his rights by the East India Company. I accordingly arrived in England in April, 1831."*

His work in England

Rāma Mohana Roy was requested to give his evidence before the Select Committee of the House of Commons on the Judicial and revenue systems of India. He was also examined on the condition of the native inhabitants of India. His answers, as already mentioned, were remarkable as showing his great command over the subjects in which he was thus consulted. Through his earnest attempts

* Miss Carpenter introduced this Autobiographical sketch into her book 'Last Days in England of Raja Rama Mohana Roy' with the following remarks. :—

"The following letter from Rama Mohana Roy himself first appeared in the 'Athenæum' and in the Literary Gazette, from one or other of which it was copied into various papers. It was written just before he went to France. It was probably designed for some distinguished person who had desired him to give an outline of his history; and he adopted this form for the purpose. The letter may be considered as addressed to his friend Mr. Gordon of Calcutta."

the appeal against the abolution of Suttee was rejected on the 11th of July, 1832. After a residence of three years in Europe Rājā Rāma Mohana Roy died at Bristol on the 27th of September, 1833. **and death**

Gods and goddesses of the Hindus.

How far the Rājā's strenuous and self-sacrificing efforts against idolatry may have succeeded will engage us for a few moments. As a heated controvercy was going on in the vernacular tongue on this point, we consider ourselves justified in summarising here the arguments advanced by the other side. From the time of the Riṣis, when Uṣās appeared to them as beautiful nymph of the horizon clothed in purple apparel, down to the days of the Purāṅas, the religious history of India has been one in which monotheism has constantly adopted the garb of allegory, in order to appeal more potently to popular minds; and the vast pantheon of the Hindu gods and goddesses have an emblematical significance which has been repeatedly emphasised by the writers of theological treatises. The Rājā himself admitted "there can be no doubt however, and it is my whole desire to prove, that every rite has its derivation from the allegorical adoration of the deity, but at the present day all is forgotten";* and again "many learned Brahmins are well informed of the pure mode of divine worship."†

The position taken by his opponents was not without a rational basis; and the controversy was as interesting as it was learned. In the spiritual world, as in poetry and even in Mathematics, the symbol

* English works of Raja Rama Mohana Roy, vol. I, page 5.
† Do. do. vol. II, page 127.

is adopted for convenience. As in the geometrical definition of a line or point the basis is taken for granted, or as in the play of Hamlet the historic facts need not be authentic, so in any subject the ground-work may always be called in question; but the stupendous facts which rest upon it are not therefore to be ignored or undervalued. The whole civilisation of the Hindus, their vast poetic literature, their architectural achievements, shrines, temples, the geography of India as revealed to them in a spiritual light—the sacred Ganges, the Godāvari, the Brahmāputra, the snow-topped Himalaya and the Vindhya hills, all are associated with religious stories and episodes, underlying which there is the Vedanta Philosophy which invests external forms with spiritual truth; and the idea of the Supreme Being permeates all that may superficially strike us as irrational. From the lays of Jayadeva, Chandi Dās and Vidyāpati to the Kīrtana and the Āgamani songs of Bengal, our whole vast lore of devotional sentiment is no literary curiosity to our people;—it is a perpetual fountain of faith to the humble as well as to the enlightened. The gods and goddesses of the Purāṇas, like the Uṣās of the Riṣis, represent the attributes of one who attracts us through their familiar forms even as the sun approaches us through a thousand rays of light. This vast religious fabric was not created in a day. It has taken deep root in our soil for hundreds of years. Such gods as these could not be dismissed at a word, however great might be the power that cried to them 'Vanish!' Even when Rājā Rāma Mohana Roy was decrying what he called idolatry in unsparing language, there were already

Europeans who were attracted by it,—nay had adopted the 'idolatrous practices' themselves. The facts disclosed by the extracts quoted below should be judged independently. The comments made on them are what one naturally expects from the biassed persons from whose writings they are taken.

European converts to Hinduism.

"Mr. Twining and Major Scott Waring were joined in their missionary crusade by a colleague in the person of a "Bengal officer," Col. Stewart, generally known in India under the name of "Hindu Stewart." He had abjured Christianity and become a worshipper of the Hindu deities. He exposed himself equally to the ridicule of his own countrymen, by going down in the morning to the Ganges, with flowers and sacrificial vessels, to perform his ablutions according to the Hindu rituals. At a subsequent period, he asked permission to accompany the army in its progress towards the capital of Nepal, that he might have an opportunity of paying his devotion at a celebrated shrine of Çiva which lay on the route. .... The Bengal officer exhibited the most profound respect for the Hindu religion, and entertained the most lofty conceptions of the morals and virtues of the Hindus; and he now came forward to denounce the sacrilegious attack of the missionaries 'on the sacred and venerable fabric of Hinduism.' In his pamphlet called 'The Bengal Officer's Pamphlet' published in 1808, he says, "wherever I look around me in the vast region of Hindu mythology, I discover piety in the garb of allegory: and I see morality, at every turn blended with every fable; and as far as I can rely on my

Hindu Stewart.

judgment, it appears the most complete and ample system of Moral Allegory that the world has ever produced."*

We find from the introduction to Abridgement of Vedanta by Rājā Rāma Mohanā Roy, published in 1816, that he attacked "that system of popular idolatry on which Sir Thomas Munro, and Mr. Lushington, and Mr. Marsh had bestowed the highest eulogium three years before in the presence of the Parliament."†

Mr. W. Ward of the Çrirāmapore Mission seemed to be particularly hostile to any who advocated the cause of Hinduism. In his work on the Hindus, he writes, "The Rev. Maurice has attempted to describe the Hindu ceremonies in the most florid colours. It might have been expected, (idolatry being in itself an act so degrading to man and so dishonourable to God) that a Christian Divine would have been shocked while writing in this manner. If Mr. Maurice thinks there is something in Hinduism to excite the most sublime ideas, let him come and join in the dance before the idol or assist the Bramhins in crying Huree bul : Huree bul ! "‡

Mr. Maurice on Hinduism.

From this Mr. Maurice himself, we quote the following interesting and sympathetic passage. "Mr. Forbes of Stanmore Hill in his elegant museum of Indian rarities numbers two of the bells that have been used in devotion by the Brahmins,

---

* History of the Criramapore Mission by John Clark Marshman, vol. I, pp. 354—56.

† "History of the Criramapore Mission," vol. II, page 128.

‡ Introductory Remarks, Ward's 'on Hindus' vol. II page ixxv.

as great curiosities, and one of them in particular appears to be of very high antiquity, in form very much resembling the cup of the lotus, and the tune of it was uncommonly soft and melodious. I could not avoid being deeply affected with the sound of an instrument which had been actually employed to kindle the flame of that superstition, which I have attempted to unfold. My transported thoughts travelled back to the remote period when the Brahmin religion blazed forth in all its splendour in the caverns of Elephanta: I was, for a moment, entranced and caught the ardour of enthusiasm. - A tribe of venerable priests, arrayed in flowing stoles and decorated with high tiaras, seemed assembled around me, the mystic song of initiation vibrated in my ear; I breathed an air, fragrant with the richest perfumes and contemplated the deity in the fire that symbolised him." Dr. Ward quotes this passage from an article written by the Rev. Maurice in the fifth volume of "Indian Antiquities" and treats it with great contempt. But it is the last part of the article which most of all annoys him. This runs as follows.

"She (the Hindu religion) wears the similitude of a beautiful and radiant cherub from heaven, bearing on his persuasive lips the accents of pardon and peace, and on his silken wings benefaction and blessing."*

Pro-Hindu tendencies of Halhed and Jones.

Dr. Ward also finds faults with Mr. Halhed of the Civil Service, the first writer on Bengali grammar, because he "seems to prefer Hinduism to

* 'Ward's 'on the Hindus,' vol. II. Introduction. Page IXXVI.

Christianity; " and condemns even Sir William Jones for his pro-Hindu tendencies. The great scholar was, according to the critic, " accustomed to study the Çāstras with the image of a Hindu god placed on his table."

The Hindus were never known to possess any proselytising zeal; yet the poetry and devotion which pervaded the allegorical mode of their worship could not fail to commend itself to many an enlightened European who would openly avow his partiality for it. These foreign admirers of our religion were Rājā Rāma Mohana's contemporaries—a circumstance which shows that the Hindu religion in Bengal had not yet sunk into utter grossness as it was represented to have done by its reformers; for, in that case it could not have counted its votaries among the Europeans who lived in the country. Almost a century has pssed since Rāma Mohana Roy breathed his last. The incense still burns in the Hindu temples at the time of the Ārati or evening service: the village *potters* still prepare clay images of the gods. The auspicious sound of the evening conch still resounds beyond the temples across our fields and lawns. The sacred books Bhāgvata, Chandi and other Purāṇas, still find hundreds of listeners, whose love is far more ennobling than if the works had possessed a merely literary interest and how dreary would be the Hindu home without these things! To me it appears that if the allegorical forms of our religion were all swept away, the whole Hindu civilisation, intervening between the period of the Vedas and that of Rāma Kriṣṇa Paramahaṁsa's sayings, would be overthrown, and the spiritual soul of India,

Hinduism in our village-homes.

thousands of years old, would have to be born anew, as a child of to-day, losing the benefit of the rich heritage transmitted by our forefathers through the ages of the past.

The success of the Rājā's mission.

But has the Rājā's mission failed in its attempt to lead our society to a realisation of the truth that symbols are not to be mistaken for realities and that the deity is not to be confounded with them? Every right thinking man must emphatically say 'no' to this enquiry. The enlightened Hindu youth of the present day has reverted to the Vedanta Philosophy; and the movements of the revivalists, though often displaying ridiculous niceties in their metaphysical interpretations, have constantly aimed at taking a rational and sensible view of matters. The modern Hindu is not the Hindu of the old school. In the general awakening of the intellect and in the widening of the search after spiritual truth which followed Rājā Rāma Mohana Roy's advent, the Hindus have not neglected to make their position secure by studying the Çāstras in a new light; it has been a point of their constant efforts to interpret rationally what a great number of people of the preceding generations did blindly.

The Rājā has therefore been directly instrumental in helping the cause of monotheism by founding the Brahmo Samāja, and indirectly by giving a stimulus to Hindu Society, which in its anxiety to defend itself against the Rationalists, soon came forward to propound myths about the gods in accordance with monthiestic principles, for which, however, it had ample authority in its scriptures. Like all great men the Rājā came to minister to a real need of society. It may be that the enlightened people of Bengal would without him have been drawn more irrevocably to Christianity, being dissatisfied with the existing state of their religion. The spirit of the Rājā not only dominates the Brahmo Samāja of to-day, but his influence is distinctly traceable in the general a wakening of the Hindu mind to a consciousness of new ideals in the spiritual world.

The Rājā's work in Bengali prose.

This great man approached his countrymen through the vehicle of his mother tongue. Before Rāma Mohana the prose literature that existed was of very minor importance. The Europeans had already set themselves to the task of compiling Bengali Grammar and vocabularies. They had begun to translate the Gospel, and those placed at the head of the judicial administration had found it expedient to translate the Laws and Regulations into the vernacular. There was a general activity in Bengal among an enlightened though limited circle of men to contribute to our prose literature—an activity which as I have said in a foregoing chapter, was largely due to the energetic efforts of missionaries in bringing home to the people the truths of the Bible, as also to their sincere desire to promote the condition of our countrymen by a diffusion of western education. Rāma Mohana Roy is generally known as the father of the Bengali prose; but we have seen that some of the earliest writings in Bengali, composed in the 10th century A.D, were in prose. Small and even large treatises were written in simple Bengali

'The father of Bengali prose.'

prose before the advent of the Europeans. The assertion of "fatherhood" therefore can not be countenanced. Even before any book had been published in Bengali prose except the Regulations and Vocabularies, Rām Basu's *Pratapaditya Charita* came out in the year 1800. It has been urged by many people that Rāma Mohana Roy in his sixteenth year (1790 A.D.) wrote a book in Bengali prose "against idolatry of all religions." True, he wrote a pamphlet bearing that name, but it was written in Persian with an Arabic preface. The Vedanta Sutra was his first work in Bengali, and this appeared in 1815. In the Vedanta Sutra he himself refers to a translation of Bhāṣāparichchheda in Bengali prose as having already existed before he began to write in Bengali.* We have mentioned several translations of the above work on Logic, while dealing with the old Bengali literature. If one reads the translations of the Bhāṣāparichchheda, the latest of which was written nearly a century before Rāma Mohana Roy's Vedanta Sutra, one will be struck with the similarity of language in the above treatises with the style of Rāma Mohana Roy. The missionaries had taken up Bengali, in right earnest, and they had required no impetus from the Rājā in adopting the vernacular prose as the medium through which to approach the people of Bengal.

But all these considerations hardly detract from the glory which attaches to the name of Rājā Rāma Mohana Roy for his furtherance of the cause of Bengali prose. The literary works by Europeans in Bengali were mostly translations, and whatever credit and reverence may be due to these authors for undertaking a task which required them to over-

* Raja Rama Mohana Roy's Bengali works, P. 267.

come the difficulties of a foreign tongue and master its idioms, their works, judged from the standpoint of pure merit, have, we are constrained to observe, no great attraction. They scarcely rise above the level of school-books. They were pioneers in the field of their labours, so we need not underrate their laudable efforts ; but except awakening the Hindu mind to a sense of its own duty in literature and diverting it into practical channels, their productions have not served any essential or permanent purpose. These works will, in time to come, be looked upon merely as literary curiosities, to be preserved on the shelf amongst old and rare books.

Their Bengali imitators set themselves mostly to the task of compiling and translating English works, which, though extremely necessary at that early period of the diffusion of western education, possess no remarkable merit or permanent interest. The whole of this period in the history of our literature, inspite of its great activity diverted to useful purposes, strikes us as singularly barren of originality ; and the greatest productions then worked out, though they required years of patient and indefatigable industry, are no land-marks in the history of our progress ; and our minds, while full of admiration for the noble band of writers, involuntarily turn to the old literature for the gratification of those desires which true and original composition can alone fulfil. There was much in the prose writings of this age to interest the intellect but little to give pleasure or satisfaction to the soul.

Rājā Rāma Mohana Roy rose on the horizon of our letters at this stage, and all lesser lights grew dim at his advent. The whole aspect of our literature became changed. He wrote the following books in Bengali:—

The Bengali works of the Rājā.

1. Vedānta Sutra. Quarto size, 114 pages, 1815 A.D.
2. Vedānta Sutra, 15 pages, 1815.
3. Talavakāra Upaniṣad, 11 pages, 1816.
4. Īçopaniṣad, 24 pages, 1816.
5. Sahamaraṅa Viṣaya (on the Suttee), part I, 33 pages, and part II, 12 pages 1819.
6. Do. Part III, 21 pages, 1829.
7. Pathya Pradāna, 139 pages, 1823.
8. Brahmanistha Grihasther Lakṣaṅa, 5 pages, 1826.
9. Kayasther Sahita Madyapāna Viṣayaka Vichāra, 4 pages, 1826.
10. Vajra Suchi, 6 pages, 1830.
11. Anusthāna, 13 pāges, 1829.
12. Suvrahmaṅya Çāstrīr Sahita Vichāra, 5 pages.
13. Prārthanā Patra, 3 pages.
14. Ātmānātma Viveka, 17 pages.
15. Brahmaṅā Sevādhi, 38 pages, 1721.
16. Pādri O Çisya Samvāda, 4 pages.
17. Brahma Saṁgita, 116 songs.
18. Brahmopāsanā, 3 pages.
19. Gāyatrir Artha, 7 pages, 1818.
20. Kathopanisad, 34 pages, 1817.
21. Mundakopanisad, 9 pages.
22. Māndukyopanisad, 26 pages, 1819.
23. Gosvāmir Sahita Vichāra, 30 pages, 1818.

24. Kavitkārer Sahita Vichāra, 35 pages, 1821.

25. Bhattācaryyer Sahita Vichāra, 80 pages, 1817.

26. Gauḍiya Vyākaraṅa, 80 pages, 1833.

27. Samvāda Kaumudī, 20 pages.

The English works of Rājā Rāma Mohana Roy have been edited by Jogendra Chandra Ghose, M.A., B.L., and published by Çrīkantha Roy of Calcutta in three volumes.

The Bengali works of the Rājā referred to above, were collected and published by Rājā Nārāyaṅa Vasu and Ānanda Chandra Tarkavāgiça in 1873. The collection contains over 800 pages (quarto size). Most of his Bengali treatises are short; but the vast learning which he displays in each of these productions, together with the closeness of argument and sincere and ardent desire for truth, lends them an importance second to none in our literature. His interpretation of the Vedānta, chiefly based on the commentary of Çankarāchāryyā, gives in lucid Bengali prose what would be impossible for any other person of his age to have done in the vernacular. The intricacies of one of the most abstruse subjects that ever engaged the human intellect,—the difficulties of a language whose prose was not yet properly formed, were all overcome, and the truths of the great Philosophy were brought within the easy reach of every man of ordinary intelligence in a masterly way. The Rājā, like a Riṣi, realised the truths of the Vedanta and expressed them from his own soul through his vernacular writings. We repeat that it would have been impossible for any other man of his age, however

Their merit.

learned, to have reduced such great and abstruse truths to pristine simplicity in a language which as yet was so inadequate to the purpose as our own. It was possible for the Rājā to do so only because he was a himself a seer of these truths like the great sages—the Riṣis of the past.

His controversies similarly display his great powers, his logical acumen, and his vast classical erudition. He gives precedence to reason in every step of his arguments; and it is the light of his own soul that he brings forward, in order to dispel the darkness of superstition and ignorance that prevails all round. Nowhere does he make his motive prominent. He brings forward a whole array of texts from Sanskrit, Hebrew, Persian and Arabic in favour of what he advocates, so that while arguing with a Maulvi he seems to be himself a Maulvi, with a missionary, he appears to be a Christian, and before a Bhattāchāryya he comes in the garb of the Brahmin that he was. While holding a controversy with a Mahomedan, the Rājā quotes from the Korān, with a Hindu from the Çāstras, and with a Christian from the Bible. He does not decry even the most obvious evils on his own authority, but he brings his whole learning to bear upon each topic; and the quotations he makes are of an overwhelming nature and display his minute knowledge of the different theological systems of the world. This power of keeping his personal opinions in the back ground and advancing them merely on the authority admitted by his antagonists, required a colossal range of studies which in his age only Rāma Mohana Roy possessed. This accounts for his unique position and his great ascendency over his rivals in discussion. Another noteworthy feature in his writings is the entire absence of any outburst of feeling. It might have been supposed that a man who so deeply felt the wrongs that prevailed all around, would denounce them in the fiery language of an ardent enthusiast in the cause of reformation. But his great intellectuality and deep conviction made him proceed quietly in controversy, like a doctor in the process of a serious surgical operation; occasions, however serious, did not disturb his temper. This superior control over himself is to be traced distinctly in all his writings. What was said of some of his English works by his English reviewer in the Monthly Repository for September, 1833, applies equally to his Bengali writings also. "The method and coolness with which the Rājā arranges and states his facts, in contrast with the rousing nature of those facts, are as remarkable as anything in the whole affair; and the courtesy with which he accounts, where he can, for the rise and growth of abuses, will not impede, but hasten the rectification of those abuses. The Rājā appreciates too well the nature and operation of free institutions, not to have felt many a throb of indignation, many a pang of grief, when witnessing the oppressed condition of the ryots of his country, and the various kinds and degrees of guilt among his countrymen, which have been originated by British misgovernment: but when the cause can be best served by a plain statement of facts, he can adduce them with all the calmness of a mere observer. That which it makes our spirits sink to read, he states unaccompanied by reproach or entreaty. Suggestions on which we should stake our lives, and which we should be apt to thrust in the face of friend and foe, he offers in their due connection, and with a moderation most likely to ensure them a hearing."

However trivial or puerile were the charges made against him, he listened to every point urged by his opponents with great attention, and in his anxious solicitude to bring conviction of the truth home to the party, he gave a sensible reply to their foolish abuses and revilings prompted by animosity, with a surprising quietness of temper. I quote a passage from his Bengali writing.

Extracts from his Bengali prose.

*" The first argument in support of idolatry, is that the Supreme Being is beyond all power of human comprehension and cannot be expressed by words; hence the necessity of worshipping a Deity endowed with form and other attributes, as Master of the universe. The plain answer to this is :—If a person in his early childhood, before he has had any knowledge of his father, is kidnapped, or by other causes separated from home, would it be proper for him, when growing into manhood, to call some object before him his father? Rather should he not, when observing a

---

*" প্রথমত: এই যাহাকে ব্রহ্ম জগৎকর্ত্তা কহ তিহোঁ বাক্য মনের অগোচর সুতরাং তাহার উপাসনা অসম্ভব হয় এই নিমিত্ত কোন-রূপ গুণবিশিষ্টকে জগতের কর্ত্তা জানিয়া উপাসনা না করিলে নির্ব্বাহ হইতে পারে নাই অতএব রূপগুণ বিশিষ্টের উপাসনা আবশ্যক হয়। ইহার সামান্য উত্তর এই। যে কোন ব্যক্তি বাল্যকালে শত্রুগ্রস্ত এবং দেশান্তর হইয়া আপনার পিতার নিরূপণ কিছু জানে নাই এ নিমিত্ত সে ব্যক্তি যুবা হইলে পরে যে কোন

religious ceremony or engaged in a prayer for the good of his father,—say 'Peace be unto him who has begotten me!' In the same way, it should be understood, though the Divine Being may be incomprehensible to us, that we may always address Him as the creator and preserver of the universe without giving Him fictitious attributes and a fancied name. The quality and nature of many objects of creation,—such as the sun or the moon, are not fully known to us; how is it then possible for us to know the nature of the creator! But observing the objects around us, and the laws which govern the universe, we are conscious of His omnipotence and of His divine dispensation which is good for all: and with such a consciousness we are always quite free to approach him. Our common sense tells us that the creator is mightier than his creation, and that a created object, as forming but a part of the universe, cannot be its master. The

---

বস্তু সম্মুখে পাইবেক তাহাকে পিতারূপে গ্রহণ করিবেক এমত নহে বরঞ্চ সেই ব্যক্তি পিতার উদ্দেশে কোন ক্রিয়া করিবার সময়ে অথবা পিতার মঙ্গল প্রার্থনা করিবার কালে এই কহে যে যে জন জন্মদাতা তাঁহার শ্রেয়ঃ হউক। সেই মত এখানেও জানিবে যে ব্রহ্মের স্বরূপ জ্ঞেয় নহে কিন্তু তাঁহার উপাসনা কালে তাঁহাকে জগতের স্রষ্টা পাতা সংহর্ত্তা ইত্যাদি বিশেষণের দ্বারা লক্ষ্য করিতে হয় তাহার কল্পনা কোন নশ্বর নাম রূপে কিরূপ করা যাইতে পারে। সর্ব্বদা যে সকল বস্তু যেমন চন্দ্র সূর্য্যাদি আমরা দেখি ও তাহার দ্বারা ব্যবহার নিষ্পন্ন করি তাহারো যথার্থ স্বরূপ জানিতে পারি না ইহাতেই বুঝিবে যে ঈশ্বর ইন্দ্রিয়ের অগোচর তাঁহার স্বরূপ কিরূপে জানা যায় কিন্তু জগতের নানাবিধ রচনার এবং নিয়মের দৃষ্টিতে তাঁহার কর্ত্তৃত্ব এবং নিয়ন্তৃত্ব নিশ্চয়

supporters of idolatry urge that the worship of an invisible power is impossible. This argument is curious, since they may observe that their own countrymen and the people of other countries have found it quite possible to pray to the invisible Deity. The second point urged is :—It is not at all worthy of a good soul to leave the ways of their ancestors and of their own people and trample upon old customs.

Ans.—People seem to be carried away a good deal by their love for ancestors and kinsmen. But it is the lower animals only which altogether follow the beaten track of their own kind. How should a man, endowed with a sense of right and wrong, be justified in following a certain path merely because his forefathers adopted it? Blind faith in past

---

হইলে কৃতকার্য্য হইবার সম্ভব হয় সামান্য অবধানে নিশ্চয় হয় যে এই দুর্গম্য নানা প্রকার রচনা বিশিষ্ট জগতের কর্ত্তা ইহা হইতে ব্যাপক এবং অধিক শক্তিমান অবশ্য হইবেক ইহার এক অংশ কিম্বা ইহার ব্যাপ্য কোন বস্তু ইহার কর্ত্তা কি যুক্তিতে অঙ্গীকার করা যায়। আর এক অধিক আশ্চর্য্য এই যে স্বজাতীয় বিজাতীয় অনেকেই নিরাকার ঈশ্বরের উদ্দেশে উপাসনা করিতেছেন ইহা প্রত্যক্ষ দেখিতেছেন অথচ কহিতেছেন যে নিরাকার ঈশ্বর তাঁহার উপাসনা কোন মতে হইতে পারে না॥ ১॥ দ্বিতীয় বাক্য রচনা এই যে পিতা পিতামহ এবং স্ববর্গেরা যে মতকে অবলম্বন করিয়াছেন তাহার অন্যথা করণ অতি অযোগ্য হয়। লোকসকলের পূর্ব্ব পুরুষ এবং স্ববর্গের প্রতি অত্যন্ত স্নেহ সুতরাং এ বাক্যকে পর পূর্ব্ব বিবেচনা না করিয়া প্রমাণ স্বীকার করেন ইহার সাধারণ উত্তর এই যে কেবল স্ববর্গের মত হয় এই প্রমাণে মত গ্রহণ করা পশু জাতীয়ের ধর্ম্ম

authority is inadmissible with a progressing race. But inspite of their advancing this argument, we see that our countrymen never gave such absolute authority to custom in by-gone ages. Amongst the Hindus one born in a Vaiṣṇava family is often seen to change his faith and become a Çakta; and a Çakta is similarly observed to accept the Vaiṣṇava faith; within the last hundred years the people of Bengal have adopted the views of Raghunandana in their religious observances, and in this respect there has been an entire deviation on their part from following the beliefs and practices of their ancestors. We read in history besides that when the five Brahmins first came to Bengal they had socks on their feet, wore coats, and they came riding in bullock carts. Such practices are now considered as sacrilegeous on the part of Brahmins. In olden times a Brahmin would never accept service under a *Yavana* or foreigner, nor learn any

---

হয় যে সর্ব্বদা স্ববর্গের ক্রিয়ানুসারে কার্য্যে করে। মনুষ্য যাহার সং অসং বিবেচনার বুদ্ধি আছে সে কি রূপে ক্রিয়ার দোষ কি গুণ বিবেচনা না করিয়া স্ববর্গে করেন এই প্রমাণে ব্যবহার এবং পরমার্থ কার্য্যনির্ব্বাহ করিতে পারে। এইমত সর্ব্বত্র সর্ব্বকালে হইলে পর পৃথক পৃথক মত এ পর্য্যন্ত হইত না বিশেষত আপনাদের মধ্যে দেখিতেছি যে এক জন বৈষ্ণবের কুলে জন্ম লইয়া শাক্ত হইতেছে দ্বিতীয় ব্যক্তি শাক্ত কুলে বৈষ্ণব হয় আর স্মার্ত্ত ভট্টাচার্য্যের পরে যাহাকে এক শত বংসর হয় না যাবতীয় পরমার্থ কর্ম্ম স্নান দান ব্রতোপবাস প্রভৃতি পূর্ব্ব মতে ভিন্ন প্রকার হইতেছে আর সকলে কহেন যে পঞ্চ ব্রাহ্মণ যে কালে এদেশে আইসেন তাঁহাদের পায়েতে মোজা এবং জামা ইত্যাদি বেশ এবং গোযান ছিল তাহার পরে পরে সে সকল ব্যবহার কিছুই রহিল

language other than the Sanskritic; they were also prohibited from teaching Sanskrit to non-Hindus; but they do all these things now. So it is evident that we have not over zealously persevered in our old customs and manners. Why, therefore, should we be led by an idle prejudice in their favour in the matter of faith itself which concerns the good of our souls and our hereafter.

The third argument in support of idolatry is that the knowledge of the absolute makes a man unfit for all practical purposes. To him good and evil, fire and water, sweet scent and obnoxious stench become all the same as he rises above the phenomenal; such a knowledge is therefore not compatible with the pursuits of ordinary men.

Ans.—What they mean to imply by this is not clear. You, sirs, will admit that Nārada, Sanat-Kumāra, Çuka, Vaçiṣtha, Vyasa, Kapila and other sages had a knowledge of the absolute and invisible Brahma. Nevertheless these sages recognised

---

না আর ব্রাহ্মণের যবনাদির দাসত্ব করা এবং যবনকে শাস্ত্র পাঠ করান কোন্ পূর্ব্ব ধর্ম্ম ছিল। অতএব স্ববর্গে যে উপাসনা ও ব্যবহার করেন তাহার ভিন্ন উপাসনা করা এবং পূর্ব্ব পূর্ব্ব নিয়মের ত্যাগ এমত বাক্যে বিশ্বাস করিয়া পরমার্থের উত্তম পথের চেষ্টা না করা যায়। তৃতীয় বাক্য এই যে ব্রহ্ম উপাসনা করিলে মনুষ্যের লৌকিক ভদ্রাভদ্র জ্ঞান থাকে না, অতএব সুতরাং ঈশ্বরের উপাসনা গৃহস্থ লোকের কিরূপে হইতে পারে। উত্তর। তাহারা কি প্রমাণে এবাক্য রচনা করেন তাহা জানিতে পারি নাই যেহেতু আপনারাই স্বীকার করেন যে নারদ জনক সনৎ-কুমারাদি শুক বশিষ্ঠ ব্যাস কপিল প্রভৃতি ব্রহ্মজ্ঞানী ছিলেন অথচ

fire as fire and water as water; they administered justice, and taught their disciples; so how can you urge that they had lost all consciousness of the phenomenal world? Besides it seems very curious to me that you believe that by worshipping your gods the knowledge of the visible world becomes keener; but by praying to the invisible and absolute Power, people become mad, and lose all consciousness of the external world. The knowledge of the world is not interfered with by a knowledge of the Deity, as a man who has the knowledge of God still continues to live in the world and his eyes and ears continue to perform their functions, and if he lives with his father, son, and others, he continues to fulfil his duties to them and all this is the will of the Supreme being. It is not indicated where a knowledge of God clashes with the knowledge of the world. The sages of the past who were endowed with a knowledge of the true God

---

ইঁহারা অগ্নিকে অগ্নি জলকে জল ব্যবহার করিতেন এবং রাজ-কর্ম্ম আর গার্হস্থ্য এবং শিষ্য সকলকে জ্ঞানোপদেশ যথাযোগ্য করিতেন তবে কিরূপে বিশ্বাস করা যায় যে ব্রহ্মজ্ঞানীর ভদ্রা-ভদ্রাদি জ্ঞান কিছুই থাকে নাই আর কিরূপে এ কথার আদর লোকে করেন তাহা জানিতে পারি না। বিশেষতঃ আশ্চর্য্য এই যে ঈশ্বরের উপাসনাতে ভদ্রাভদ্র জ্ঞান থাকে আর ব্রহ্ম উপাসনাতে ভদ্রাভদ্র জ্ঞানের বহির্ভূত হইয়া লোক ক্ষিপ্ত হয় ইহাও লোকের বিশ্বাস জন্মে। যদি কহ সর্ব্বত্র ব্রহ্মজ্ঞান করিলে ভেদ জ্ঞান আর ভদ্রাভদ্র জ্ঞান কেন থাকিবেক তাহার উত্তর এই যে লোকযাত্রা নির্ব্বাহ নিমিত্ত পূর্ব্ব পূর্ব্ব ব্রহ্মজ্ঞানীর ন্যায় চক্ষু কর্ণ হস্তাদির কর্ম্ম চক্ষু কর্ণ হস্তাদির অবশ্য করিতে হয় এবং

according to your own admission, did nothing less than ordinary people in worldly matters, nay they did it with a more elevated and refined sense of duty. Some of the supporters of idolatry say " Is it proper to discard the view held by all the world and in preference to follow the opinions of one or two men? Was there no scholar born before him? and is there none who is equal to him in learning now? Would they not also arrive at the same conclusions, if there were any truth in this?"

Ans. Though I am pained at these reflections, yet I feel inclined to answer them for the furtherance of my cause. In the first instance, India does not form even one twentieth part of the earth already known to us. The country inhabited mainly by the Hindus is known as Hindusthān. Excluding this Hindusthān, more than half of the entire population of the rest of the globe profess

---

পুত্রের সহিত পিতার কর্ম্ম পিতার সহিত পুত্রের ধর্ম্ম আচরণ করিতে হইবেক যে:হতু এ সকল নিয়মের কর্ত্তা ব্রহ্ম হয়েন। মধ্যে মধ্যে কহিয়া থাকেন যে পৃথিবীর সকল লোকের যাহা মত হয় তাহা ত্যাগ করিয়া দুই এক ব্যক্তির কথা গ্রাহ্য কে করে আর পুর্ব্বে কেহো পণ্ডিত কি ছিলেন না এবং অন্য কেহ পণ্ডিত কি সংসারে নাই যে তাঁহারা এই মতকে জানিলেন না এবং উপদেশ করিলেন না। যদ্যপিও এমত সকল প্রশ্নের শ্রবণে কেবল মানস দুঃখ জন্মে তত্রাপি কর্ম্মানুরোধে উত্তর দিয়া যাইতেছি প্রথমত এ পর্য্যন্ত পৃথিবীর যে সীমা আমরা নির্দ্ধারণ করিয়াছি এবং যাতায়াত করিতেছি তাহার বিংশতি অংশের এক অংশ এই হিন্দোস্থান না হয়। হিন্দুরা যে দেশেতে প্রচুর রূপে বাস করেন তাহাকে হিন্দোস্থান কহা যায়। এই

faith in an invisible Supreme Being. In Hindusthān itself, the Nirvānists, the Nānaka Panthis, the followers of Dādu, the disciples of Çiva Nārayaṅa—ascetics and householders alike—worship one Supreme God. How is the view then tenable that the worship of one Supreme God is against the established ways of all the world? If the next contention,—that scholars before me have not joined such mode of prayer were true—how could we then possess the works of Vyāsa, Vaçistha and other sages who promulgated the pure doctrine of theism! The divine Çankaracharyya and other commentators of the Vedās have all tried to establish monotheistic principles, and Nānaka who lived only a few centuries ago, enjoined the worship of one Supreme Being as an imperative duty on the part of both the Sannyāsins and householders belonging to the sect founded by him. In modern

---

হিন্দোস্থান ভিন্ন অর্দ্ধেক হইতে অধিক প্রথিবীতে এক নিরঞ্জন পরব্রহ্মের উপাসনা লোকে করিয়া থাকেন এই হিন্দোস্থানেতেও শাস্ত্রোক্ত নির্ব্বাণ সম্প্রদা এবং নানক সম্প্রদা আর দাদূ সম্প্রদা এবং শিবনারায়ণী প্রভৃতি অনেকে কি গৃহস্থ কি বিরক্ত কেবল নিরাকার পরমেশ্বরের উপাসনা করেন তবে কিরূপে কহেন যে তাবৎ পৃথিবীর মতের বহির্ভূত এই বহ্মোপসনার মত হয় আর পুর্ব্বেও পণ্ডিতেরা যদি এই মতকে কেহ না জানিতেন এবং উপদেশ না করিতেন তবে ভগবান বেদব্যাস এই সকল সূত্র কিরূপ করিয়া লোকের উপকারের নিমিত্ত প্রকাশ করিলেন এবং বাদরী বশিষ্ঠাদি আচার্য্যেরা কি প্রকারে এইরূপ ব্রহ্মোপদেশের প্রচুর গ্রন্থ প্রকাশ করিয়াছেন। ভগবান শঙ্করাচার্য্য এবং ভাষ্যের টীকাকার সকলেই কেবল ব্রহ্ম স্থাপন এবং ব্রহ্মোপাসনার

times there are thousands of men, from Bengal to the Punjab, who uphold and preach the noble theistic principle."

The above shows that he had a rational answer for every argument of his antagonist, however petty or foolish; and the great patience with which he would try to convince them, knowing fully well that they were simply maligning him, is to be explained by his great love and his eagerness to lead others from error to truth. To know the superior merits of his composition, readers are referred to his Vedānta Sāra in Bengali and to his English works. As the field traversed by him in his original works comprehends a wide range of theological matter containing technicalities, we do not find it convenient to give further extracts or translations from them.

The Bengali grammar.

The Bengali grammar written by the Rājā, though a short treatise, bears the impress of his great genius. Some of the Europeans had already been in the field with treatises on this subject. Mr. Halhed's Bengali grammar, which is one of the earliest attempts in the direction, is more interesting as a vocabulary, since it gives on a somewhat elaborate scale the meanings of words and translations of short sentences. It also gives

---

উপদেশ করিয়াছেন নব্য আচার্য্য গুরু নানক প্রভৃতি এই ব্রহ্মোপাসনাকে গৃহস্থ এবং বিরক্তের প্রতি উপদেশ করেন এবং আধুনিকের মধ্যে এই দেশ অবধি পঞ্জাব পর্য্যন্ত সহস্র সহস্র লোক ব্রহ্মোপাসক এবং ব্রহ্মবিদ্যার উপদেশকর্ত্তা আছেন?"

Vedānta Sāra.

selections from some of our old poems. The purely grammatical element is not very prominent among the various subjects comprised in the book. The Bengali writers who wrote grammar before Rājā Rāma Mohana Roy had in their heads the rules of Sanskrit grammar, and thonght that the Bengali language as a matter of course was bound to conform to them. But Rājā Rāma Mohana Roy discarded Sanskrit grammar in so far as its rules could not be philologically applied to Bengali. We refer our readers to pages 727 and 738 of his Bengali works. He observed the genius of our language, and in what respects it differed from Sanskrit; he formulated principles based on the natural laws which govern Bengali, and treated the subject scientifically. He also indicated the broad lines on which a comprehensive Bengali grammar might be compiled. Unfortunately, however, no other writer on the subject after Rājā Rāma Mohana Roy was possessed of his great insight to continue the work that he had commenced; and the Bengali grammar has since fallen hopelessly into the hands of Sanskrit-knowing pandits. These with their erudite enunciation of rules about Sanskrit compound-words and its prosody have dominated the situation. Following too closely the steps of Mugdhavodha they are applauded by critics who belong to the same school. The Gauḍiya Bhāsār Vyākaraṅa by the Rājā is a highly original publication and contains many important rules. On page 724 he deals with the pronunciation of words. He says that in Bengali the difference of pronunciation between শ, ষ, স, is not observed; but there are certain exceptions to this rule. When শ is joined with র, ঋ, ন it is pronounced as স, as in শ্রদ্ধা, শৃগাল and প্রশ্ন; Similarly when স is joined with ত, থ, ন, র, ঋ it retains its Sanskritic sound of স as in স্তব, স্থান, স্রক্, সৃষ্টি. In all other places it is pronounced as শ. The chapter on Case is full of original observations. In the dative case, says the Rājā, those words which bear the long vowel আ in the last letter adopt তে or য় as suffix. But those words which have ই, ঈ, উ, ঊ, এ, ঐ, ও, ঔ in their last letters adopt only তে to denote the locative form. Instances of the former are to be found in the forms মৃত্তিকাতে and মৃত্তিকায়, থালাতে and থালায়, শয্যাতে and শয্যায় etc., and of the latter in ছুরিতে, হাতীতে, রজনীতে etc. Regarding the forms of Bengali words in singular and plural numbers, the learned author gives curious rules which are nevertheless correct and testify to his accurate observation. The suffixes গুলি, সকল etc., are generally adopted to indicate the plural number; in the case of men and higher beings the suffix রা is often used, and it is generally speaking restricted to them only; when however the suffix রা is used in the case of lower animals it is implied that such words do no longer signify them; for instance গরু সকল means cows, but গরুরা is used to imply those men who are stupid as cows.*

Before we close the account of Rājā Rāma Mohan Roy we have to say a few words regarding the movement led by him for the abolition of Suttee. His Bengali pamphlets against Suttee were translated by him into English; and they aim chiefly at establishing the superiority of an **The Suttee.**

* Bengali works of Raja Rama Mohana Roy. Page 733.

unimpeachable and pure widowhood of woman in accordance with the rules of Brahmachāryya after the death of her husband, over the practice that largely prevailed in his time of self immolation, against which he fought, in conjunction with European clergymen and officials.

Like other reforms this was also proposed and carried out at the teeth of great opposition. While alluding to the controversal literature that sprang up in connection with this movement, we propose to take a dispassionate view of the history of Suttee in Bengal. It is an usage which was prevalent amongst the ancients. The rite was practised in early times amongst the Thracians, the Getæ, and the Scythians. Diodorus wrote in B. C. 44 and he describes it to have occurred in the army of Eumenes, upwards of 300 years before the Christian era (Diodorus Siculus lib XIX, Chapter II.) The Danish Northmen of Europe retained the recollections of Suttee in the story of Balder, one of the sons of Odin.*

The custom grew in India as a natural result of the peculiarly organised social institutions of the Hindus. It has been more than once observed in the foregoing chapters that the Hindus aspire to a realisation of God through the various domestic ties which bind them to their homes. Without this value given to domestic virtues which was the main basis of the Indo-Aryan civilisation, their joint-family system could not have stood. It is the call of home that has always made Hindus

* The Cyclopædia of India by Balfour, P. 781.

endure the greatest sacrifices. Their immortal epics bear striking evidences of this ideal as governing society. But no sacrifice within the precincts of one's home is raised to so high a point of merit as that prompted by sacred nuptial devotion. There are a thousand fables, stories and poems illustrating these noble sacrifices of devoted wives for their husbands. The Hindu woman lives in the atmosphere of this ideal. From her tenderest years she is trained up to it. The stories of Sāvitrī, of Sītā, of Damayanti, of Behulā—these are what a Hindu girl is accustomed to hear every evening in Bengal and even when she is a mere child she willingly fasts on the day of Sāvitri Brata. The Hindu woman grew, as Spartan boys did in ancient Greece,—under great hardships imposed on them by society, but they were meant for a great purpose. Even now the stories and poems that she reads are full of high ideas illustrative of the noblest virtues attendant upon faithful wifehood. The ideal embodied in them would fascinate and attract any tender soul; for the tales of supreme sacrifice undergone for love, never pass in vain with those young audiences who are most susceptible to nobility of spirit.

The love of a Hindu wife is scarcely expressed in passionate utterances. It pervades her whole life. The sacrifices she runs, the spirit of resignation and of entirely losing herself in the thought of doing good to her husband, raise her love beyond all sorts of mundane considerations, not to speak of any for her own comforts. It is this spirit which made women court death willingly on the funeral pyre of the husband. They often died there like mute images without uttering a word,—without heeding the sensations of pain caused to the body. While their husbands lived, such women were not known to display their great love outwardly. They ministered to the wants of numerous members living together in the family, and gave the minutest attention to each of them and to the servants; but they really lived and moved, without ever saying so, in the thought of their husbands; they kept the vermillion mark on their forehead and the shell-bracelets on their wrists; and prized these sacred signs of wifehood more dearly than their lives. A Hindu wife would sooner agree to be killed than allow them to be removed. This patient all-engrossing sentiment, this love without a thought of return, constant and unchangeable through all vicissitudes of life, in spite of many ills,—its object only the offering of life-long devotion and humble service to the husband,—is expressed in many of the old poems of Bengal,—in our folk-lore and in those rustic songs which I have mentioned in previous chapters.

The peculiar position of the Hindu wife trained her silently to sacrifices of all sorts for domestic feeling. She is not the joy or inspiration of social gatherings as a western woman is. Outside her home there is absolutely no scope for the appreciation of her qualities. Praise from outside world would be as assuredly spurned by her as abuse. Even in one's own family, it would not be good taste to allude to the beauty of a woman who has once borne a child. Her environment develops her domestic instincts more than anything else. Cut off from the rest of the world—in her own little home she is trained to an idealism of the highest sort, without the facts being observed by any. She would only be seen in public when she was to ascend the funeral pyre of her husband. Foreign people are apt to suppose that her martyrdom was the result of compulsion, oppression or superstition. But those, who possess a more intimate knowledge on the point, will see in *Suttee* only an excess of that idealism that made Sāvitṛī, in our earliest times, shudder at the thought of her coming widowhood and Tārā express a wish to burn herself with her deceased husband in the Rāmāyaṇa. Suttee is the highest realisition of that dream of womanhood, the perfection of which was imagined by the ancients to lie in an all absorbed thought of the husband. Each country has a peculiar idea of its own to inspire its people with a spirit of self-sacrifice, the growth of which has depended upon a succession of causes and circumstances peculiar to itself. Some people in the world's history have staked their fortune and life for what they called "a national cause," others for what they believed to be the "word of God,"—as the iconoclasts once made it the mission of their lives to destroy temples and images at any cost or sacrifice. Hindu women similarly elected to die out of the devotion they bore to their husbands. Of various reports left of the Suttee by European observers, who were drawn to involuntary admiration on witnessing such scenes, I quote two below. This will be helpful in rightly understanding the controversy held by the pro-Suttee champions against the attempts of the Rājā.

"The widow was a remarkably handsome woman, apparently about thirty, and most superbly attired. Her manner was marked by great apathy to all around her, and by complete indifference to the preparations which for the first time met her eye. From this circumstance an impression was given that she might be under the influence of opium ; and in conformity with the declared intention of the European officers present to interfere, should any coercive measure be adopted by the Brahmins or relations, two medical officers were requested to give their opinions on the subject. They both agreed that she was quite free from any influence calculated to induce torpor or intoxication."

"Captain Burnes then addressed the woman, desiring to know whether the act she was about to perform was voluntary or enforced, and assuring her that, should she entertain the slightest reluctance to the fulfilment of her vow, on the part of the British Government he would guarantee the protection of her life and property. Her answer was calm, heroic and constant to her purpose. "I die of my own free will ; give me back my husband, and I will consent to live."

"Ere the renewal of the horrid ceremonies of death was permitted, again the voice of mercy, of expostulation and even of entreaty was heard; but the trial was vain, and the cool and collected manner with which the woman still declared her determination unalterable chilled and startled the most courageous. Physical pangs evidently excited no fears in her; her singular creed, the customs of her country, and her sense of conjugal duty, excluded from her mind the natural emotions of personal dread; and never did a martyr. to a true cause, go to the stake with more constancy and firmness than did this delicate and gentle woman prepare to become the victim of a deliberate sacrifice to the tenets of her heathen creed. Accompanied by the officiating Brahmin, the widow walked seven times round the pyre, repeating the usual mantras or prayers, strewing rice and cowries on the ground, and sprinkling water from her hand over the bystanders, who believed this to be efficacious in preventing disease and expiating committed sins. She then removed her jewels, and presented them to her relations, saying a few words to each with calm soft smile of encouragement and hope. The Brahmins then presented her with a lighted torch, bearing which——

"Fresh as a flower just blown,
And warm with life, her youthful
pulses playing,"

she stepped through the fatal door, and sat within the pile. The body of her husband wrapped in rich *kinkaubs*, was then carried seven times round the pile and finally laid across her knees. Thorns and grass were piled over the door; and again it was insisted that free space should be left, as it was hoped that the poor victim might yet relent, and rush from her fiery prison for the protection so freely offered. The command was readily obeyed; the strength of a child would have sufficed to burst the frail barrier which confined her, and a breathless pause succeeded; but the woman's constancy was faithful to the last. Not a sigh broke the death-like silence of the crowd, until a slight smoke, curling from the summit of the pyre, and then a tongue of flame, darting with bright and lightning-like rapidity into the clear blue sky, told us that the sacrifice was completed. Fearlessly had this courageous woman fired the pile, and not a groan had betrayed to us the moment when her spirit fled." *

The following is quoted from Bengal Under The Lieutenant Governors by C. E. Buckland, Vol. I, pages 160-161.

"Although it does not fall within his Lieutenant Governorship, I think the following account of a Suttee, as narrated by Sir F. Halliday, 70 years later, will be considered interesting, and it has never been printed elsewhere :—

"Suttee was prohibited by law in 1829. At and before that time I was acting as Magistrate of the district of Hoogly. Before the new law came into operation, notice was one day brought to me that a Suttee was about to occur a few miles from my residence. Such things were frequent in Hooghly as the banks of that side of the river were considered particularly propitious for such sacrifices. When the message reached me, Dr. Wise of the Medical Service and a clergyman (whose name I forget), who was Chaplain to the Governor General, were visiting me and expressed a wish to witness the ceremony. Accordingly we drove to the appointed place where a large crowd of natives was assembled on the river bank and the funeral pile

* Mrs. Porstan's Random Sketches during her residence in one of the northern provinces of Western India in 1839.

already prepared, the intended victim seated on the ground in front of it. Chairs were brought for us, and we sat down near the woman. My two companions, who did not speak the language, then began to press the widow with all the reasons they could urge to dissuade her from her purpose, all of which at their request I made the woman understand in her own language. To this she listened with grave and respectful attention but without being at all moved by it; the priests and many of the spectators also listening to what was said.

At length she showed some impatience and asked to be allowed to proceed to the pile. Seeing that nothing further could be done, I gave her the permission, but before she had moved, the clergyman begged me to put to her one more question,—"Did she know what pain she was about to suffer?" She seated on the ground close to my feet, looked up at me with a scornful expression in her intelligent face and said for answer, "Bring a lamp": the lamp was brought, of the small sauce-boat fashion used by peasants, and also some *ghi* or melted butter and a large cotton wick. These she herself arranged in the most effective form and then said, "Light it;" which was done and the lamp placed on the ground before her. Then steadfastly looking at me with an air of grave defiance she rested her right elbow on the ground and put her finger into the flame of the lamp. The finger scorched, blistered and blackened and finally twisted up in a way which I can only compare to what I have seen happen to a quill pen in the flame of a candle. This lasted for some time, during which she never moved her hand, uttered a sound or altered the expression of her countenance. She then said:—"Are you satisfied?" to which I answered hastily, "satisfied," upon which with great deliberation she removed her finger from the flame, saying: "Now may I go?" To this I assented and she moved down the slope to the pile. This was placed on the edge of the stream. It was about 4½ ft. high, about the same length, and perhaps 3 ft. broad, composed of alternate layers of small billets of wood and light dry brushwood between four upright stakes. Round this she was marched in a noisy procession 2 or 3 times and ascended it, laying herself down on her side with her face in her hands like one composing herself to sleep, after which she was covered up with light brushwood for several inches, but not so as to prevent her rising had she been so minded. The attendants then began to fasten her down with long bamboos. This I immediately prohibited and they desisted unwillingly but without any show of anger. Her son, a man of about 30, was now called upon to light the pile.

It was one of those frequent cases in which the husband's death had occurred too far off for the body to be brought to the pile, and instead of it a part of his clothing had been laid thereon by the widow's side. A great deal of powdered resin and, I think, some *ghi* had been thrown upon the wood which first gave a dense smoke and then burst into flame. Until the flames drove me back I stood near enough to touch the pile, but I heard no sound and saw no motion, except one gentle upheaving of the brushwood over the body, after which all was still. The son who had lighted the pile remained near it until it was in full combustion, and then rushing up the bank threw himself on the ground in a paroxysm of grief. So ended the last Suttee that was lawfully celebrated in the district of Hooghly and perhaps in Bengal."

But sacrifices made by a few, under promptings of extraordinary sentiments, are not such as may be enforced in the case of every widow in a society. The Suttees in later times increased in number from very many causes besides that of affection. Within six or seven centuries before the abolition of the rite, the Hindu widows found their position insecure, as the country was overrun by the Mahomedan conquerers and by the Burmese and Portuguese marauders who seized helpless young widows and carried them away or which was worse, put them to indelible infamy. Even Nawabs and noblemen would sometimes not let go the opportunity to do the same as the robbers did, regarding beautiful Hindu widows. The genealogical works referred to by us in pp. 73—91 contain many instances of such atrocities. The number of Suttees must have grown largely in proportion owing to these causes. Besides when one family boasted of its Suttees, the other families wanted, for the sake of increasing their prestige, to possess similar records of sacrifice from among their own members, so what had been in early ages a practice of but rare occurrence became frequent, often under compulsion. The following incident will show to what a heinous extent of barbarity the practice of Suttee might be carried.

*"About the year 1796, the following most shocking and atrocious murder, under the name of *Sahamarana*, was perpetrated at Mājilpur, about a day's journey south from Calcutta. Banchharāma, a Brahman of the above place, dying, his wife at a late hour went to be burnt with the body: all the previous ceremonies were performed; she was fastened on the pile, and the fire was kindled; but the night was dark and rainy. When the fire began to scorch this poor woman, she contrived to disentangle herself from the dead body, and creeping from under the file, hid herself among some brushwood. In a little time it was discovered that there was only one body on the pile. The relations immediately took the alarm and searched for the wretch; the son soon dragged her forth, and insisted that she should throw herself on the pile, or drown or hang herself; she pleaded for her life at the hands of her own son, and declared that she could not embrace so horrid a death—but she pleaded in vain: the son urged, that he should lose his caste, and that therefore he would die or she should. Unable to persuade her to hang or drown herself, the son and the others present then tied her hands and feet, and threw her on the funeral pile, where she quickly perished."

We ask our readers to read the vernacular treatises of the Rājā on Suttee-rites, which are master-pieces of close argumentative writings disclosing his great humane feelings and profound scholarship.†

* Ward's on the Hindus, Vol. II, Part III, Page 304.

† Raja Rama Mohana Roy's Bengali works, Pages 167-223.

Rājā Rama Mohana was born in Bengal when all the brightness had faded from the illuminated pages of our history, when the glorious had grown ignominous in many places, when faith and devotion had been reduced to superstition, "sweet religion become a mere rhapsody of words," and the scarcely audible beatings of the heart indicated the loss of all social vitality. He led us from superstition to faith, from darkness to light; and though he may seem to have found nothing good in the Hindu religion of his own day,—not even in the self-sacrificing devotion of true hearts which, though few, still weilded the greatest influence in the country, yet we must remember that, generally speaking, it was not the season for extolling a deteriorated virtue, for admiring the atrocious slaughter of women—too heinous an offence to be condoned by idle panegyric. The movements in various fields of enlightenment started by the Rājā have borne ample fruit. The educated community have followed his lead in the general awakening of the intellect observed thoroughout the country after his advent. The Rājā was a great admirer of the English people and, with a sincere heart, approached them with prayers to aid him in his beneficient attempt at reform, and he found a ready response and sympathetic hearing from the rulers of the land. Though a scholar of world-wide renown and a perfect master of the most important classical and many modern languages, he did not despise his mother tongue. He wrote master-pieces in Bengali. "It is a remarkable fact that the address he presented to Lord William Bentinck was in Bengali, a circumstance

The fruit of the Rājā's labours.

which showed how deep was his love for his mother tongue."* His works in Bengali struck the keynote of a new style, for though the Raja was full of admiration for the English, yet he would not accept any matter second-hand; with him began an attempt at free enquiry after truth. The works by the missionaries and those that wrote under their instructions consisted, as already said, mainly of compilations and translations: but in the Bengali works of the Rājā begins a new epoch and a movement for the right understanding of the truths of our own religion. Rāma Mohana Roy began with the Vedānta; and taking the cue of rational explanation from him we have come down to the Purañas. From the time of Rāma Mohana Roy, Bengali literature in its poems, romances and theologial works, has striven to restate the truths contained in our classics in the light of western rationalism of thought; it has tried to combine the realistic mode of thinking peculiar to the west with oriental idealism; sometimes the occidental element has been too prominent in Bengali writings almost alienating itself from our national ideal in the views propounded, at others verging on extreme conservativeness, and blind orthodoxy. The conflict is going on without intermission up to the present, and a harmony has not yet, I am afraid, crowned the attempts of the opposing forces in this field. But all the same, we are conscious of a great activity in our literature and we owe it preeminently to the devoted labours of Rājā Rāma Mohana Roy,

---

* The English works of Raja Rama Mohana Roy. Vol. I., Introduction, page XIX.

who advanced its cause, not only by writing monumental works in Bengali himself, but by raising a controversy which has contributed a great deal to the rapid development of prose. Taking this view of matters, it cannot be considered unjust to call him the father of modern Bengali prose.

(c) The writers that followed Rājā Rāma Mohana Roy—Devendra Nātha Tagore—Akṣaya Kumara Datta and others.

After the death of Rājā Rāma Mohana Roy the spirit of reform lay dormant for a while. Even the Brāhma-Sabhā that he had established, succumbed to those othodox forms against which the great leader had fought all his life. In the year 1862 it was found that the Brahmins only were admitted to it, and that they held meetings with closed doors against all of other castes. Içvara Chandra Nyayaratna used to lecture before a select body of Brahmins in the Theistic Hall; and in one of the subjects that he chose, he argued that Rāma had been an incarnation of God. The missionaries knew Rāma Mohana Roy to be their great foe inspite of all professions of amity and peace on both sides; for under the outward form of Unitarian Christianity which the Rājā seemed to profess, he was founding a new Theistic Church based on the Vedanta Philosophy and on Christian Morals. This would inevitably draw to itself those educated Hindus who, if such a society had not been organised by the Rājā, would have gravitated towards the Christian Churches, and proved willing

Renewed activities of the missionaries.

converts. The death of the Rājā, and a total absence in the field of any suitable personage on whom his mantle could fall, gave an opportunity for a time to the Christian Missionaries to renew their attempts at proselytising with redoubled zeal. Stray cases come to our notice which show the vigorous procedure of these gentlemen. In 1845, Umeça Chandra Sarkār and his wife were converted by Dr. Duff in a manner which created a great sensation amongst the whole native population of Calcutta. In fact on the very day of their conversion, the Hindus raised Rs. 40,000 to found a Hindu School in order to counteract the influence of Christian teaching in the schools established by the Missionaries.

Devendra Nātha Tagore.

At this juncture another great man appeared to take up the work of the great reformer. His intellectual powers were not so great as those of Rāma Mohana Roy, but his strength of character, faith in religious views, power of sacrifice for the cause of what he considered right, high-mindedness and unflinching advocacy of theism have deservedly lifted him to the rank of a Riṣi in popular estimation. Devendra Nātha Tagore has, moreover, furthered the cause of Bengali literature in no inconsiderable degree. He was the son of the distinguished Dwarka Natha Tagore who was called Prince Dwarkā Natha in England, and who enjoyed the great confidence of our revered and beloved Queen Victoria during his stay in that country. Devendra Nātha, heir to a princely fortune, and a man of remarkably handsome features and rare accomplishments, in his early youth realised the truth that life was short, fortune was transitory and religion the only solace of life. Impelled by a sense of moral duty,—for there was no legal obligation,—he handed over his immense inheritance to his father's creditors, who could have claimed no hold upon it. And the effect which this noble act of sacrifice produced on the minds of the people was evidenced by the bestowal of the title of Maharṣi or great Riṣi on him by his countrymen. His creditors, fortunately, were no Shylocks. They arranged for the liquidation of debts in a way convenient to the youthful owner of the property; but all the same a considerable portion of it had to be sold. But Devendra Natha was indifferent to worldly considerations. I quote an extract from his auto-biography which is written in a simple and attractive style.

An extract from his autobiography.

*"My grand-mother loved me very much. In childhood I cared not for any one else but her. I used to take my meals with her, sit by her the whole live-long day and sleep on the same bed with her. When she went to Kālighata to visit the shrine I used to accompany her thither. At one time she went to Vrindāvana and Puri leaving me at home. I recollect how bitterly I wept owing to my separation from her. She was intensely devoted to religion. Every day at early dawn she used to

---

*"দিদিমা আমাকে বড় ভাল বাসিতেন। শৈশবে তাঁহাকে ব্যতীত আমিও আর কাহাকে জানিতাম না। আমার শয়ন, উপবেশন, ভোজন, সকলই তাঁহার নিকট হইত। তিনি কালী-ঘাটে যাইতেন, আমি তাঁহার সহিত যাইতাম। তিনি যখন আমাকে ফেলে জগন্নাথক্ষেত্রে ও বৃন্দাবনে গিয়াছিলেন, তখন আমি বড়ই কাঁদিতাম। ধর্ম্মে তাঁহার অত্যন্ত নিষ্ঠা ছিল। তিনি প্রতিদিন অতি প্রত্যূষে গঙ্গাস্নান করিতেন। এবং প্রতিদিন

bathe in the Ganges and weave garlands for the tutelary god Sālagrāma. Sometimes she fasted from sunrise to sun-set and offered '*argha*' to the sun. I stayed with her on the roof and got by heart the hymn addressed to the sun, hearing it uttered so often. "O Thou of the colour of the *Java*, offspring of Kāçyapa, radiant with rays, the dispeller of darkness and destroyer of sin, O Sun. I salute thee."

My grand-mother sometimes fasted the whole day and night, and during the whole of such nights Kathakatās and Kirtana songs went on in the house; We could not sleep owing to the noise. She used to supervise the household work and herself assisted the domestics in their service. Owing to her efficient management and firm control, all the work of our house was conducted with strict regularity. When the inmates of the house had all taken their meal she would cook her own food herself. I

শালগ্রামের জন্য স্বহস্তে পুষ্পের মালা গাঁথিয়া দিতেন। কখনো কখনো তিনি সংকল্প করিয়া উদয়াস্ত সাধন করিতেন—সূর্য্যোদয় হইতে সূর্য্যের অস্তকাল পর্য্যন্ত সূর্য্যকে অর্ঘ্য দিতেন। আমিও সে সময়ে ছাতের উপরে রৌদ্রেতে তাঁহার সঙ্গে সঙ্গে থাকিতাম, এবং সেই সূর্য্য অর্ঘ্যের মন্ত্র শুনিয়া শুনিয়া আমার অভ্যাস হইয়া গেল। "জবাকুসুম সঙ্কাশং কাশ্যপেয়ং মহাদ্যুতিং। ধ্বান্তারিং সর্ব্বপাপঘ্নং প্রণতোঽস্মি দিবাকরং।" দিদিমা এক এক দিন হরিবাসর করিতেন, সমস্ত রাত্রি কথা হইত এবং কীর্ত্তন হইত; তাহার শব্দে আমরা রাত্রিতে ঘুমাইতে পারিতাম না। তিনি সংসারের সমস্ত তত্ত্বাবধারণ করিতেন। তাঁহার কার্য্যদক্ষতার জন্য তাঁহার শাসনে গৃহের সকল কার্য্য সুশৃঙ্খলরূপে চলিত। পরে সকলের আহারান্তে তিনি স্বপাকে আহার করিতেন।

used to share her plain meal composed of boiled rice and simple vegetables (হবিষ্যান্ন); this food I relished more than my own. The beauty of her person was as great as her accomplishments, and her faith in religion was equally great. But she could not bear the visit of Mā-gosāins (women who posed as teachers of the Vaiṣnava faith) to our house. Though her faith was mixed with superstition she also evinced a considerable freedom in her religious views. With her I often visited the image of Gopinātha in our family residence. I never wanted to come out of the temple without her. I used to sit on her lap and through the window quietly observe all that passed. My grand-mother is no more; but after how many days of weary search for the truth have I found One who is more than even my beloved grand-mother ever was

---

আমিও তাঁহার হবিষ্যান্নের ভাগী ছিলাম। তাঁহার সেই প্রসাদ আমার যেমন স্বাদু লাগিত তেমন আপনার খাওয়া ভাল লাগিত না। তাঁহার শরীর যেমন সুন্দর ছিল, কার্য্যেতে তেমনি তাঁহার পটুতা ছিল, এবং ধর্ম্মেতে ও তাঁহার তেমনি আস্থা ছিল। কিন্তু তিনি মা-গোঁসাইয়ের সতত যাতায়াত বড় সহিতে পারিতেন না। তাঁহার ধর্ম্মের অন্ধ বিশ্বাসের সহিত একটু স্বাধীনতাও ছিল। আমি তাঁহার সহিত আমাদের পুরাতন বাড়ীতে গোপীনাথ ঠাকুর দর্শনার্থে যাইতাম। কিন্তু আমি তাঁহাকে ছাড়িয়া বাহিরে আসিতে ভাল বাসিতাম না তাঁহার ক্রোড়ে বসিয়া গবাক্ষ দিয়া শান্ত ভাবে সমস্ত দেখিতাম। এখন আমার দিদিমা আর নাই। কিন্তু কতদিন পরে, কত অন্বেষণের পরে, আমি এখন আমার দিদিমার দিদিমাকে পাইয়াছি ও তাঁহার ক্রোড়ে বসিয়া জগতের লীলা দেখিতেছি। দিদিমার মৃত্যুর

to me! Seated on the lap of the divine Mother I quietly observe all that transpires through Her wishes.

Shortly before her death my grand mother one day told me 'I have decided to bequeath to you all that I have in the world, I won't give it to any one else.' Thereupon she gave me the key to her box; I opened it and found some gold and silver coins in it. I told people that I had found parched rice in my grand mother's box. In the year 1835 her end drew near. My father had at that time gone on a trip to the neighbourhood of Allahabad. The physician said that the patient should no longer be kept at home. Whereupon our relations came and brought my grand mother down to the ground-floor and made preparations to take her to the Ganges.* But she was still

---

কিছুদিন পূর্ব্বে আমাকে বলেন আমার যা কিছু আছে আমি তাহা আর কাহাকেও দিব না, তোমাকেই দিব। পরে তিনি তাঁহার বাক্সের চাবিটা আমাকে দেন। আমি তাঁহার বাক্স খুলিয়া কতকগুলিন টাকা ও মোহর পাইলাম, লোককে বলিলাম যে আমি মুড়ি মুড়কি পাইয়াছি। ১৭৫৭ শকে দিদিমার যখন মৃত্যুকাল উপস্থিত, তখন আমার পিতা এলাহাবাদ অঞ্চলে পর্য্যটন করিতে গিয়াছিলেন, বৈদ্য আসিয়া কহিল রোগীকে আর ঘরে রাখা হইবে না। অতএব সকলে আমার পিতামহীকে গঙ্গাতীরে লইয়া যাইবার জন্য বাড়ীর বাহিরে

* The usual custom of the Hindus is to take the dying people to the bank of the Ganges or to any other river that may be near, when the case is declared as hopeless and death is expected at every moment.

hoping to live and did not like to be carried to the Ganges. She said "If Dwarka Natha (her son) were here, he would never allow you to remove me from home as you are doing." The men did not pay any heed to her words, but went on carrying her towards the Ganges; upon which she said, "As you have not obeyed my wishes I shall cause you great trouble. I shall not die soon."* On reaching the Ganges they placed her in a hut of tiles. She lived three nights in that situation. I was with her all this time. On the night previous to the day when she would expire, I was seated on a mat spread near the tiled hut, the full moon had risen on the horizon and close by me was the funeral ground. At that time they were singing

---

আসিল। কিন্তু দিদিমা আরও বাঁচিতে চান, গঙ্গায় যাইতে তাঁহার মত নাই, তিনি বলিলেন যে "যদি দ্বারকানাথ বাড়ীতে থাকিত তবে তোরা কখনই আমাকে লইয়া যাইতে পারিতিস্ না।" কিন্তু লোকে তাহা শুনিল না। তাঁহাকে লইয়া গঙ্গা-তীর চলিল তখন তিনি কহিলেন, "তোরা যখন আমার কথা না শুনে আমাকে গঙ্গায় নিয়ে গেলি, তেমনি আমি তোদের সকলকে খুব কষ্ট দিব, আমি শীঘ্র মরিব না।" গঙ্গাতীরে লইয়া একটী খোলার চালাতে তাহাকে রাখা হইল। সেখানে তিনি তিন রাত্রি জীবিত ছিলেন্। আমি সেই সময়ে গঙ্গাতীরে তাহার সঙ্গে নিয়ত থাকিতাম। দিদিমার মৃত্যুর পূর্ব্বদিন রাত্রিতে আমি ঐ চালার নিকটবর্ত্তী নিমতলার ঘাটে একখানা চাঁচের উপর বসিয়া আছি, ঐ দিন পূর্ণিমার রাত্রি—চন্দ্রোদয় হইয়াছে, নিকটে শ্মশান। তখন দিদিমার নিকট নাম সঙ্কীর্ত্তন

* If a person does not die soon on reaching the Ganges, the carriers are required to wait there till her death and undergo great hardships.

kirtana songs around my grand-mother. One ran thus :—

"When will that blessed day come, when I shall leave this mortal body reciting thy name, O Hari?"

A gentle breeze was carrying the sound to my ear; suddenly at that moment a strange emotion passed over my mind. For the time being I became an entirely different man from what I was,—I felt a total abhorrence for wealth. The mat on which I sat appeared to me to be my proper and fit place. The rich carpets and all seemed worthless and of no value to me; I felt a complacency and joy which I had never experienced before. I was only 18 years old at the time.

(2)

So long I had lain deep-plunged in the pleasures of luxury. I had never for one moment felt any longing for truth. I never cared to know

---

হইতেছিল, "এমন দিন কি হবে হরি নাম বলিয়া প্রাণ যাবে।" বায়ুর সঙ্গে তাহা অল্প অল্প আমার কাণে আসিতেছিল। এই অবসরে হঠাৎ আমার মনে এক আশ্চর্য্য উদাস ভাব উপস্থিত হইল। আমি যেন আর পূর্ব্বের মানুষ নই। ঐশ্বর্য্যের উপর একেবারে বিরাগ জন্মিল। যে চাচের উপর বসিয়া আছি, তাহাই আমার পক্ষে ঠিক বোধ হইল, মনের মধ্যে এক অভূতপূর্ব্ব আনন্দ উপস্থিত হইল। তখন আমার বয়স ১৮ বৎসর।

দ্বিতীয় পরিচ্ছেদ।

এতদিন আমি বিলাসের আমোদে ডুবিয়া ছিলাম। তত্ত্বজ্ঞানের কিছুমাত্র আলোচনা করি নাই। ধর্ম্ম কি, ঈশ্বর কি,

what religion or God was; nobody gave me any instruction on the subject. The joy I felt on the funeral ground that day overflowed my soul. Language is feeble; how can I express it or convey what I felt to others? No one can experience this joy by filling his head with logical discussions. Who says there is no God? Here is the evidence of his existence: I was not prepared for it; how could I then have felt such joy! With this spirit of asceticism and joy I came home at midnight. I could not sleep that night. The reason of my sleeplessness was this ecstasy of soul; as if moonlight had spread itself over my mind for the whole of that night. At dawn I went to the bank of the Ganges to see my grand-mother. I found her drawing her last breath 'They had brought her

---

কিছুই জানি নাই, কিছুই শিখি নাই। শ্মশানের সেই উদাস আনন্দ, তৎকালের সে স্বাভাবিক সহজ আনন্দ মনে আর ধরে না। ভাষা সর্ব্বথা দুর্ব্বল, আমি সে আনন্দ কিরূপে লোককে বুঝাইব? তাহা স্বাভাবিক আনন্দ। তর্ক করিয়া যুক্তি করিয়া সে আনন্দ কেহ পাইতে পারে না। সেই আনন্দ ঢালিবার জন্য ঈশ্বর অবসর খোঁজেন। সময় বুঝিয়াই তিনি আমাকে এ আনন্দ দিয়াছিলেন। কে বলে ঈশ্বর নাই? এই তো তাঁর অস্তিত্বে প্রমাণ। আমি তো প্রস্তুত ছিলাম না, তবে কোথা হইতে এ আনন্দ পাইলাম? এই ঔদাস্য ও আনন্দ লইয়া রাত্রি দুই প্রহরের সময় আমি বাড়ীতে আসিলাম। সে রাত্রিতে আমার নিদ্রা হইল না। এ অনিদ্রার কারণ আনন্দ সারা রাত্রি যেন একটা আনন্দ-জ্যোৎস্না আমার হৃদয়ে জাগিয়া রহিল। রাত্রি প্রভাত হইলে দিদিমাকে দেখিবার জন্য আবার গঙ্গাতীরে যাই, তখন তাঁহার শ্বাস হইয়াছে। সকলে

down to the Ganges and were enthusiastically reciting in a loud voice "Gangā-Nārāyaṇa Brahma." She died immediately. I approached her and saw that one of her hands lay on her breast, the middle finger pointed towards heaven. 'Recite the name of Hari' she said at the last moment pointing with her finger, which remained fixed towards heaven. As I saw it I surmised that while leaving this world it was God and hereafter that she pointed to me, beloved as I was. My grand-mother was not only my greatest friend in this life, but also my friend in the hereafter."

The Early Brahma Samaja.

In the year 1845, Devendra Nātha organised a band of workers who accepted the Brahma Dharma and gave up "idolatrous practices." The number swelled to five hundred in 1849. We find the name of Akṣaya Kumāra Dutta, the great Bengali writer of this period, in the list of the first batch of Brāhmas.

Akhṣaya Kumāra Dutta.

In the year 1843, the Tatta Bodhini Patrikā was started by Devendra Nātha Tagore and Babu Akṣaya Kumāra Datta was appointed as editor.

ধরাধরি করিয়া দিদিমাকে গঙ্গার গর্ব্ভে নামাইয়াছে এবং উৎসাহের সহিত উচ্চৈঃস্বরে "গঙ্গা নারায়ণ ব্রহ্ম" বলিতেছে। দিদিমার মৃত্যু হইল। আমি নিকটস্থ হইয়া দেখিলাম, তাঁহার হস্ত বক্ষঃস্থলে, এবং অনামিকা অঙ্গুলীটী উর্দ্ধমুখে আছে। তিনি "হরিবোল" বলিয়া অঙ্গুলী ঘুরাইতে ঘুরাইতে পরলোকে চলিয়া গেলেন। তাহা দেখিয়া আমার বোধ হইল, মরিবার সময় উর্দ্ধে অঙ্গুলি নির্দ্দেশ করিয়া আমাকে দেখাইয়া গেলেন "ঐ ঈশ্বর ও পরকাল।" দিদিমা যেমন আমার ইহকালের বন্ধু ছিলেন, তেমনি পরলোকেরও বন্ধু।"

Devendra Nātha Tagore compiled a code for the guidance of Brāhma-life from the Upaniṣada in 1848, to which he also appended a Bengali translation. This serves as the hand-book and guide to the modern Brahmas,—specially to the members of the Ādi Samāja The Bengali translation does great credit to the compiler owing to its simplicity and elegance, and it is a interesting point to note that Devendra Nātha dictated the treatise to Akṣaya Kumāra Datta who took it down, the whole thing occupying only three hours.

The great activity and the religious earnestness displayed by the band of noble workers has borne great fruit in various spheres of Bengali life. Bengali literature particularly has been immensely profited by them. The Tattta Bodhini Patrikā under the editorship of Babu Akṣaya Kumāra Datta weilded an influence which it is difficult to conceive now-a-days. "It is scarcely possible" writes Mr. R. C. Dutt "in the present day when journals have multiplied all over the country to describe adequately how eagerly the moral instructions and earnest teachings of Akṣaya Kumāra conveyed in that famous paper, were perused by a large circle of thinking and enlightened readers. People all over Bengal awaited every issue of the paper with eagerness; and the silent and sickly, but indefatigueable, worker at his desk swayed for a number of years the thoughts and opinions of the thinking portion of Bengal."*

* Literature of Bengal by R. C. Dutt, Page 87.

Içwara Chandra Vidyā-Sāgara.

It was at this time also that the young Içwara Chandra Vidyasāgara, who had already passed through his novitiate in the art of Bengali composition as a pandit in Fort William College, was first winning his laurels in the literary field. He had already written his Vatriça Simhasana which showed unmistakable traces of that elegant and correct style which later on developed so splendidly in his Sitar Vanabasa, Çakuntala and other works. It was at this time also that Peary Chand Mitra (*nom de plume*) Tek Chand Thakur—whose 'Alaler Gharer Dulal' or 'The Spoilt Child' many European writers have so freely eulogised, some comparing it with the best productions of Moliere or Fielding,—was trying to master the simple and colloquial style spoken by the gentle and rustic folk of Bengal. We can not however review the works of these master-minds, as our scope is limited to a treatment of the subject up to 1850, and most of their works were written in the decade that followed that year. Babu Aksaya Kumara Dutta, however, whose life like Pope's was "a long disease" had already written a considerable portion of those valuable contributions to the Tatta Bodhini Patrika by 1850,—which were subsequently compiled by him and published in the form of separate books such as, 'Charu Patha,' 'Vahya Bastur Sahita Manava Prakritir Sāmvanda Vichara' &c. and we trust it will not be going beyond the limit to give a few extracts from his contributions to the Tattva Bodhini Patrika. The following is taken from one of the issues of the paper published in 1850.

Tek Chand Thakur.

Extracts from Aksaya Babu's works.

* "A heart void of love may be compared to a desert through which no current of water flows. Both are barren and fruitless. It is a highly fortunate circumstance for us that our Almighty Father has endowed the beings of the earth with abundance of love and devotion. There are persons who love wealth, some seek after reputation, some knowledge, but those that are particularly blessed love God. There is no object higher than love. If there were no love in this earth, where then would have been the heart to enjoy the beauty of a delightful garden, diffusing pleasant fragrance in the breeze, the glad-some beauty of a night clothed in the charming white light of the full moon! Where then would have been the pleasures of conversation with one's devoted, chaste and accomplished wife, whose face radiant with love's glow, beams forth the light of the full moon! Where would have been without love the sweet smiling faces of children, beautiful as painted cherubs and innocent, pure and gay as flowers,—the wonderful harmony that pervades a family

---

*" জলশূন্য মরুভূমি ও প্রীতিবিহীন অন্তঃকরণ উভয়ই তুল্য। উভয়ই নীরস ও নিষ্ফল। কিন্তু ইহা আমাদিগের পরম সৌভাগ্যের বিষয় এই যে প্রীতিপূর্ণ পরমেশ্বর মর্ত্ত্যলোকে অপর্য্যাপ্ত প্রেম বিতরণ করিয়াছেন। কেহ বা ধনের, কেহ বা মানের, কেহ বা জ্ঞানের, কেহ বা যশের এবং কোন কোন ভাগ্যবান ব্যক্তি পরমেশ্বরের প্রেমে মগ্ন হইয়া রহিয়াছেন। প্রীতির পর আর পদার্থ নাই। প্রীতি না থাকিলে কোথায় বা সুগন্ধময় পুষ্পো-দ্যানের মনোহর শোভা, কোথায় বা শুভ্রবর্ণা সুধাময়ী পূর্ণিমা নিশির সুশীতল নির্ম্মল সুখকর জ্যোতি, কোথায় বা গুণবতী

of spotless reputation, the members bound by ties of love and full of reverence for religion! Where would have been that vivifying and heavenly intercourse with friends of high character, dearer to us than our own selves, and in whose hearts dwell self-sacrificing love and all high qualities! Where would have been those soul-stirring poems, store-houses of high and lofty emotions, which over-whelm us with the never-failing effect of their sweet and matchless melody!

Imitation of English style.

This appears like a Bengali version of one of the familiar essays of the Rambler with Seneca's sayings as head-lines, the difference being that the oriental imitation is even more over-coloured and high flown than the style of Dr. Johnson himself. The writings of Addison and Steele in the Spectator and those of Dr. Johnson in the Rambler supplied models for the Bengali writer, who combined with his Moral and Theological discourses dissertations on Etiolgy and Science much after Paley.

পুণ্যবতী পতিপিয়া প্রিয়তমার পৌর্ণমাসী তুল্য প্রেমোৎফুল্ল মনোহর আনন সন্দর্শন ও তাগার সহিত সুধাময় মধুর আলাপ কোথায় বা চিত্রিতপুত্তলিকা তুল্য প্রফুল্ল কুসুম সদৃশ সহাস্য শিশুগুলির নিষ্কলঙ্ক মুখশ্রী, কোথায় বা পরস্পর প্রীতিযুক্ত নিষ্পাপ পুণ্যশীল পরিবারের আশ্চর্য্য সুদৃশ্যতা, কোথায় বা হৃদয়াধিক প্রণয় পবিত্র সুচরিত্র মিত্রের স্বর্গোপম নিরুপম সুখদায়ক সহবাস, কোথায় বা রসার্দ্রচিত্ত পদাবলীর সরস লালিত্য ও অনুপম মাধুর্য্য থাকিত?"

Supplementary Notes to Chapter VII.

(i) Three early centres of Vernacular writings.

(ii) The patronage accorded to Vernacular writers

(iii) Peace and her boon.

(i) Three early centres of Vernacular writings :—

Before the advent of Chaitanya Deva we find three recognized centres of Vernacular composition. The songs of the Vaiṣṇavas had for their principal seat the historic land of Birbhum and its contiguous districts. Jaya Deva hailed from Kenduli in Birbhum; and a few centuries after him, Chandi-Das sang his celestial lay from the village Nannur in the same district. When Vaiṣṇavism was at its zenith in Bengal, its chief exponents and song-masters flourished in this part of the country. This Vaiṣṇava movement belonged to the people and required no aristocratic patronage to push it in its forward course; it drew its nutrition straight from the soil and soon, by its own power, attained a most luxuriant growth.

Birbhum, the early Vaiṣṇava centre.

In Eastern Bengal where Vaiṣṇavism was yet unknown, the traditions of the Buddhistic age were the inspiration of the songs of the Manasā and Chandi cults. The traditions of Behulā's wonderful devotion and Chānd-Sadagar's stern defiance to Manasā Devi,—the story of Dhanapati Sadāgara and his adherence to the Çaiva faith in the face of great dangers—belong to a period when Brahmanic influence had not yet commenced.

Eastern Bengal, the centre of Renaissance.

As I have already said, the chief actors in the drama of these stories belong to the mercantile classes and some of them are of even humbler origin. The Brahmin has hardly any function to discharge in them. Though after the Hindu Renaissance, these stories were recast by the Brahmins and worked out from mere popular fables into poems of great beauty, their original ground-work, with its traditions of a society which is anterior to that built up by Brahmanical influence, remains unchanged. The earliest writer of Manasā-mañgala, that we have yet been able to trace, was one Hari Dutta. He lived in Mymensing, or somewhere in its vicinity, more than six hundred years ago. Narāyaṅa Deva and Bijaya Gupta came after him in the 15th century and latterly Ṣaṣthibara and Gangā Das, father and son, wrote Manasā-mañgalas, which the subsequent poets of the Manasā cult of east and west alike imitated. These early poets were all of Eastern Bengal. We must remember that the tale of Manasā Devi is of much older date than even six hundred years. In this country earlier efforts are always lost when a gifted successor assimilates and embodies the best features of his predecessors' works in his new poem. Thus nearly a dozen early poems of the Mahābhārata, written before Kaçi Dās, were all forgotten by the people, until quite lately, these works were again brought to the notice of the public by scholarly research. The earlier poets of the Manasā-cult all wrote their poems in Eastern Bengal; and these supplied inspiration to the poets of the western districts in a subsequent age. Ketakādas

Kshemānanda and other poets of the Rāḍa Deça abridged the story described by East Bengal poets, adding some poetical features which the improved resources of our tongue had placed at their command. The Chandi-cult had also its earliest exponents in the poets of Eastern Bengal. Mādhavāchāryya was a native of Mymensing and Dvija Janārdana, probably of Tipara. Owing to to the great beauty of Mukundarāma's poem written in later times, preceding attempts in the same field which had belonged to Eastern Bengal, were cast into the shade. Manuscripts of these early works, from two to three centures old, have been recovered not only from Eastern Bengal but also from the Raḍa-Deça, showing that they were at one time read by the people of the whole of Bengal. We thus see that poems belonging to the various Çākta-cults had for their earliest home the much despised east of the country, which remained politically free for more than a century, after western Bengal had been conquered by the Mahamadans. The Sen-kings at Vikrampur patronised Brahmins; and it was natural that in the 13th century Vikrampur should be turned into an important seat of classical learning. The first translation of the Mahābhārata was undertaken by Sanjaya, probably a Brahmin of Vikrampur. He belonged to the Varatdwāja Gotra. and compiled the translation in an abridged form. The next translation of the great epic by Kabīndra Parameçvara, an inhabitant of Chittagong rose to the highest point of popularity; it was written in the latter part of the 15th century, and was read by the people of east and west alike. Manuscripts of this recension of the

Mahabhārata, written about three centuries ago, have been received not only from Chittagong, Noakhali, Dacca, Mymensing, Tippara, and Sylhet, but also from various parts of Western Bengal. We have with us an old manuscript of the poem recovered from the village of Khalisani, near French Chandarnagar, and several others are to be found in the library of Babu Nagendra Nath Vaṣu, obtained by him from Pātrasâyer and other villages of Birbhum. A manuscript of this poem about 200 years old was collected by the late Mr. Umesh Chandra Batabyal from a village in the district of Rangpur. We may conceive from all this how extensively popular Kabīndra's Mahābhārata was in those days. Amongst the older recensionists of the Mahābhārata, the influence of Kabīndra Parameçvara was the greatest on Nityānanda and Kaçi Das—the two great luminaries who have enlightened our masses on the beauties of the classical epic in comparatively recent times. There is a host of other early Eastern Bengal poets on the subject of the Mahābhārata whose works will be found mentioned in the body of this book.

Krittibāsa, the earliest writer of the Rāmāyaṅa, got his education in Eastern Bengal, somewhere on the banks of the Padma, as he has himself informed us, in his auto-biography. His ancestors had belonged to Vikramapur, and the family were driven to Phuliā by the oppression of Tugral Khan in the year 1348. Ṣaṣthibar and Gangādās, whose poems have been already mentioned here in connecttion with Manasā-literature, wrote elaborate works on the Ramayaṅa and the Mahābhārata, about 350 year ago. These poets were inhabitants of Jhinārdi in Vikrampore; manuscripts of their poems have been found in large numbers, in various districts of Western Bengal, as they have been in the native districts of the poets themselves. It will thus appear that Eastern Bengal, having been one of the great seats of Sanskrit learning, produced a number of translations that helped to disseminate Pouranik ideas amongst the masses. Before the advent of Chaitanya, Eastern Bengal thus formed the chief nucleus of Vernacular composition. Çakta-cult had strong adherents in that part of the country and classical learning was encouraged by Hindu Kings and noble men. These helped powerfully in the importation of Sanskrit words into our tongue—a process which is especially conspicuous in the translations that were compiled in that province.

Eastern Bengal falls to the back ground.

This wave was retarded by the democratic movement in letters that was inspired by Chaitanya. The Vaiṣṅavas adopted Bengali as the chief vehicle for the teaching of their religion and at once monopolised the right of producing literature in it. This accounts for the flourishing growth of vernacular literature in the Raḍa Deça from the 16th century onwards. The light that came from the East gradually subsided below the horizon of our letters, and under Vaiṣṅava influence, even the Çākta writers of Western Bengal profited by the general intellectual awakening there, and wrote poems of considerable beauty, which gradually over-shadowed the works written by the poets of Eastern Bengal, till the latter lost all the lustre that she had once possessed. She had once occupied the place of pioneer in Vernacular composition, but this has now passed completely out of our memory. The Battala-publishers have confined their attention to manuscripts of Bengali poems of comparatively later date, such as were available in the vicinity of Calcutta, and this fact has further helped to obliterate the memory of the early poems of Eastern Bengal until recent discoveries brought to light heaps of long forgotten manuscripts mainly from the houses of the rustics of that country.

The Songs of Pāl Kings and Dharma-maṅgala poems, came from North Bengal.

The third seat of Vernacular composition, which was perhaps one of the oldest, was North Bengal. The songs of the Pāl Kings were first sung in the old capital of Gauḍa and its vicinity. Rāmāi Pandit composed his Manual of Dharma worship in Bengali towards the end of the 10th century. He was born in the district of Bankura but Gauḍa was his chief of field of work. The story of Lāusen, to be found in the Dharma-Maṅgala, relates to the adventures and successes of the hero who was a nephew of the King, Darmapāl II, and the incidents of the poem gather round the old capital of Bengal. The Darma-cult flourished under the patronage of the Pāl Kings, and the Vernacular literature of this cult had, for its original home, the historic land where these Kings reigned.

Summary.

We thus arrive at the following conclusions:—

(1) Rāḍa Deça in olden times was the favoured seat of the growth of Vaisṅava ideas. Long before Chaitanya, she delighted in Vaiṣṅava songs and in the study of the Bhāgabata which

was first translated into Bengali metrical verse, about 425 years ago, by Mālādhara Basu, one of her illustrious poets.

(2) Eastern Bengal produced the earliest works of the Chandi and Manasā-cults, and her learned writers compiled most of the earliest recensions of the Sanskrit epics. Eastern Bengal thus gave the earliest impetus towards the dissemination of Pourānik ideas amongst the masses.

(3) From North Bengal we received our songs of the Pâl Kings and our earliest Dharma-mañgāls. These, as we have said, deal with the exploits and adventures of Lâu-sen, a nephew of the King Darmapála II of Gauḍa.

These were the three centres,—the early fields of the activities of our poets in vernacular composition. Rāḍa Deça in the 16th century came to the fore and dominated the great intellectual awakening brought about by Chaitanya.

II.—The patronage accorded to Vernacular writers.

In the first chapter of this book, we indicated how the Hindu Courts, following the examples of Moslem chiefs and noblemen, extended their patronage to the Vernacular poets. Bengali gradually became a favourite vehicle for the expression of thought with scholarly people; and we scarcely find a poet of any renown who was not rewarded and patronised by some noble man. The Vaiṣṅava poets alone did not care for such patronage, but all others considered it a great privilege and honour to dedicate their poems to their rich patrons, extolling their qualities in terms of high sounding panegyric and poetry.

We find Kavi Kañkaṅa patronised by Bānkura Roy, Rājā of Arrah Brahman Bhumi at a very critical moment of his life, when 8 maunds of rice offered by the Rājā to the famished members of the poet's family elicited his grateful acknowledgements which have found a place in the immortal poem of Chandi. But gradually the Rājās became more bountiful to the vernacular poets and towards the end of the 17th and the beginning of the 18th century, we find vernacular writings of merit very considerably rewarded. We have seen that Rājā Jaya Nārāyaṅa of Bhu-kailāsa made considerable sacrifices of time and money to bring his translation of the Kaçi Khanda to a satisfactory completion. He travelled in different parts of the country for a period of six months in quest of Mss. of the Sanskrit poem. This journey in those days, made in a style befitting the rank of a Rājā of his high status, meant a very considerable expenditure. Besides this, he had to maintain a long time nearly a dozen Pundits for the purpose. Rājā Krisṅa Chandra's bounty towards classical learning was well-known. His liberal gifts to Bhārata Chandra and Rāma Prasāda, two gifted Vernacular poets of his time, is also not less worthy of note. Bhārata Chandra was appointed his Court-poet on Rs. 40 a month. This amount about the time of the battle of Plassey was not at all insignificant or small, when we see that Warren Hastings at a

Remuneration to the poets and copyists.

much later period drew a pay of Rs. 300 a month, as member of the Council. Major Rennell as Survey General of India was in 1767 granted a pay of Rs. 300 a month, and this amount was considered to be unusally high requiring an elaborate explanation from the authorities! We find Jaya Chandra a Rājā of the Chittagong district, granting an allowance of Rs. 10 per day to the poet Bhavāni Nātha for translating a poem called the Lakṣmaṅa Digvijaya into Bengali verse. This book was compiled about the middle of the eighteenth century and must have occupied the poet for at least six months. Rs. 300 a month in those days must have been equal to at least 10 times its present value.

Not only poets but even copyists of vernacular poems received a high remuneration for their labour. A copyist of the 18 Parvas of the Mahabharata by Kavīndra Parameçwara wrote the following concluding paragraph at the close of his Ms. in 1714 A.D.

"This Mahabhrata, containing 18 Parvas (copied by me) belongs to Çri Govinda Rāma Roy. The total number of pages is 789. My name is Ananta Rama Çarmā—copyist. The remuneration promised is the maintenance of my family for life in a becoming style. On this condition I have copied the work with great care. Besides this, I have received rewards in cash; and orders for daily allowance and annual gifts have also been obtained. Good luck attend the donor, Çaka 1636–1124 B.S. This the 25th day of Kartic. Finished on Thursday at noon, at Solagram—the native

* Major Reunell's life in Asiatic Society's Journal No. 3 Vol. III p. 2.

village of the copyist." This Solagram is in the District of Tippera and the Ms. from which the above is quoted now belongs to the Asiatic Society of Bengal.

III.—Peace and her boon.

The rapid growth of Bengali prose.

A peaceful administration stimulates and nourishes intellectual activities ; and under British rule we are in enjoyment of the manifold benefits of peace. This has caused the rapid and astonishing growth of our prose within the past century. Bengali now heads the list of the Vernaculars of India in point of its many-sided literary activities and general excellence. Many books written in our tongue have been translated into the Vernaculars of other provinces of India ; and the number of our readers is fast increasing, as the field and scope of our language are widening. This excellent result is in a large measure due to Bengal being the chief seat of Government. We have been in touch with the civilisation of the West earlier than other Provinces. By the introduction of Bengali into our University, a healthy impetus has been given to the cause of Vernacular literature, and we may confidently hope that this will be productive of strikingly good results. May my country steadily advance in her onward course under the benign administration of our present Rulers. Our review of the Bengali Literature, however, ends with 1850. The historian of a later epoch of this literature will have to acknowldge with gratitude the deep debt which our tongue has owed to England and her people in comparatively recent times.

THE END.

*INDEX.

* Read c as ç=শ, sh as ṣ=ষ, s as স, d as ḍ=ড়.